MW01200119

SPIES AND SCHOLARS

SPIES AND SCHOLARS

Chinese Secrets and Imperial Russia's Quest for World Power

GREGORY AFINOGENOV

THE BELKNAP PRESS OF HARVARD UNIVERSITY PRESS

Cambridge, Massachusetts & London, England

2020

Library of Congress Cataloging-in-Publication Data
Names: Afinogenov, Gregory, author.
Title: Spies and scholars : Chinese secrets and Imperial
Russia's quest for world power / Gregory Afinogenov.
Description: Cambridge, Massachusetts : The Belknap Press of Harvard
University Press, 2020. | Includes bibliographical references and index.
Identifiers: LCCN 2019045276 | ISBN 9780674241855 (cloth)
Subjects: LCSH: Espionage, Russian—China—History. |
Intellectuals—Russia—Attitudes. | East and West. |
China—Study and teaching—Russia—History.
Classification: LCC DS734.97.R8 A35 2020 | DDC 327.124705109 / 032—dc23
LC record available at https://lccn.loc.gov/2019045276

For my parents

Contents

Maps and Illustrations   *ix*

Note on Calendar and Transliteration   *xi*

Introduction   1

I. MUSCOVITE STATECRAFT AND HYBRID KNOWLEDGE

  1. Muscovy on the Knowledge Frontier   25

  2. Seeing China through Russian Eyes   45

II. BUREAUCRATS AND THEIR SECRETS

  3. Secret Missions, Troublesome Missionaries   67

  4. Scholarship and Expertise at Home and Abroad   89

  5. The Caravan as a Knowledge Bureaucracy   104

  6. The Commerce of Long-Distance Letters   120

III. REMAKING KNOWLEDGE ON THE FRONTIER

  7. Frontier Intelligence and the Struggle for Inner Asia   139

  8. Spies and Subversion in Eastern Siberia   159

IV. INTELLIGENCE AND SINOLOGY IN SEARCH OF WORLD POWER

  9. Imperial Encounters in the North Pacific   185

 10. Making Russian Sinology in the Age of Napoleon   210

 11. Conspiracy and Conquest on the Amur   234

     Conclusion   257

Appendix: Reign Dates   267

Abbreviations   269

Notes   271

Bibliography   323

Acknowledgments   357

Index   359

Maps and Illustrations

1.1 Eurasia in the 1690s   31

1.2 The Godunov map, 1667   37

3.1 A Russian caravan map of Beijing, 1736   78

3.2 Andrei Kaniaev's headstone in Beijing, 1755   83

5.1 Qing soldiers, from a caravan journal, 1736   110

5.2 The fortifications at Xuanfu, from a caravan journal, 1736   111

7.1 The Siberian Line frontier in the 1750s   142

8.1 The Mongolian and Manchurian frontier in the 1750s–1760s   161

8.2 Qing Aigun, around 1700   164

8.3 Kiakhta in the 1790s   175

8.4 Eurasia in 1800   181

9.1 The North Pacific, around 1800   188

11.1 The Amur frontier in the 1850s   236

Note on Calendar and Transliteration

Historical dates are given as they appear in sources: Russian ones in the Julian calendar, which in the eighteenth century was eleven days behind the Gregorian; Jesuit, French, and British in the Gregorian. Russian words, including names of foreign origin, are transliterated according to the modified Library of Congress system (diacritics omitted). Chinese is rendered in Pinyin, including, where possible, within Russian translations. Manchu is transliterated using the Möllendorf system. The Mongolian capital now known as Ulaanbaatar is referred to by its Russian name, Urga, from the Mongol Örgöö; contemporaries sometimes referred to it by its Manchu name, Kuren, or the Mongol Khüree. Translations are mine except where noted.

SPIES AND SCHOLARS

Spies, you are lights in state, but of base stuffe
Who, when you have burnt your selves down to the snuffe,
Stinke, and are throwne away. End faire enough.

—BEN JONSON, 1616

Introduction

ON SEPTEMBER 17, 1807, a group of Russian missionaries led by a monk named Iakinf prepared to cross the longest land border in the world: the one separating the Russian Empire from the Qing realm, the vast territory ruled by Manchu emperors in Beijing. From the wooded cliffs of the Pacific coast in the east to the arid Mongol steppes and the grassy foothills of the Altai in the west, only parts of this border existed as enforceable realities on the ground; pastoralist populations often crossed freely from side to side. And yet, if an official traveler like Iakinf wanted to enter Qing territory from Russia, there was only one place he could go: the town of Kiakhta southeast of Lake Baikal. Here, in a valley between two hills, the empires faced each other as two small stockaded settlements divided by an unassuming wooden fence. The fence was a real, physical border. The town's main ceremonial occasion was the opening of the gate that marked the start of the annual trading season; when the gate remained closed, it was an ominous sign of rising international tensions. For now, however, the two empires were at peace—a stark contrast to the apocalyptic conflict in Europe, where Napoleon had just defeated Russia and forced it to enter an alliance against Great Britain.

In subsequent decades, Iakinf—best known by his secular surname, Bichurin—would become the Russian Empire's most famous academic expert on Chinese and Inner Asian history and culture. Surrounded by scandals that had almost led to his expulsion from the Church, close friends with the poet Aleksandr Pushkin and his circle of literary luminaries, Bichurin seemed to represent the epitome of a new breed of independent-minded intellectual dedicated to promoting the generative scholarly encounter between East and West. But on that autumn day in Kiakhta, he had been charged with a different kind of task. In a secret package of instructions issued to him and the other members of his mission as they crossed the border, he was ordered to "collect various pieces of intelligence" and "investigate in a subtle manner, unnoticeable to the local population" questions relating to "commercial . . . political and other matters." This meant not only probing the loyalties of Mongols and other non-Manchu populations, tracking the spread of diseases, and analyzing military preparations. It also involved testing the Qing court's ties with the British, investigating rumored French attempts to forge an anti-Russian alliance, and strengthening long-running ties with the Jesuits. His companions, meanwhile, would "covertly" paint views of key buildings in the capital and gather items of technological, scientific, and geographical interest. Before he was a scholar, Bichurin was a spy.[1]

This book is about how spies and scholars were part of the same project: the drive to integrate knowledge with state power in an effort to project Russian influence beyond the Qing frontier. The distinct but interwoven paradigms of scholarship and espionage were related to one another in radically different institutional forms that changed over time, just as Russia and China's relationship changed in response to global and regional transformations. At first, in the seventeenth and eighteenth centuries, Russian bureaucratic institutions were called on to gather intelligence in order to counter the terrifying specter of Qing power in East Asia; academic scholarship acted as an adjunct to a drive for regional supremacy. By the time Bichurin returned to St. Petersburg in the 1820s, haunted by accusations of sexual depravity committed in the Qing capital, the weight of what counted as legitimate and prestigious knowledge had begun to shift to the Academy of Sciences; Russia came to see itself as a global empire that needed to develop world-class Oriental scholars and to see China as a target of opportunity rather than a dangerous competitor.

Did knowledge help the Russian Empire dominate its southeastern rival? As it turned out, not nearly to the extent that Russian leaders anticipated. Again and again the Russian state's reliance on intelligence gathering failed to deliver sought-for geopolitical advantages like the defection of the Mongols or the formation of an alliance against the British. By 1860, Russian influence in the Qing Empire had reached an unprecedented peak—but only because of the devastating Taiping Rebellion and Second Opium War, which prevented Qing officials from resisting the annexation of the vast territory now known as the Russian Far East. Russian frontier administrators turned the crisis to their advantage, but their understanding of how information could be used to manipulate their superiors in St. Petersburg far outstripped their knowledge of conditions across the border. Instead of holding the secret key to Russian power in East Asia, the Russian Empire's effort to understand its most powerful neighbor tells us about how knowledge worked within the empire itself.

The intellectual encounter with China offers a privileged perspective on imperial knowledge because it seemed to promise such incalculable rewards, whether in the quest for influence in Inner Asia or the nineteenth-century struggle with Britain, while demanding uniquely specialized forms of expertise. The idea that the Russian imperial state relied on surveillance and information gathering has become increasingly mainstream, but *Spies and Scholars* moves beyond this narrative to focus both on individual lives and global contexts.[2] Russian intelligence institutions and scholarly bodies incubated entire careers, taking the children of frontier servitors or the graduates of schools like the Slavic-Latin-Greek Academy and turning them permanently into experienced spies or sophisticated translators. Their participation determined the effectiveness of Russian policies, but as different approaches to knowledge grew more or less valued, these careers could terminate in celebrity or obscurity, be recognized as successful or consigned to forgotten archives. Institutional power, in turn, depended on the narratives and structures that linked Russia to the outside world; for instance, when Catherine II ceased to view China primarily as a source of luxury goods and began to see it as a fulcrum for a new Pacific empire, ambitious projects of industrial espionage were replaced with conspiracies focused on maritime trade. At such moments, the web of international diplomacy centered on St. Petersburg seemed more important than a network of spies and informants on the Mongol frontier, a network that had been laboriously developed in previous decades. Knowledge did not lead to power, but studying knowledge is a way to understand what power was supposed to mean—both its ends and the means that they entailed.

Historians of European, including Russian, empire have typically understood knowledge as a source of power in itself. Even if Michel Foucault's view that the two are mutually constitutive has not been comprehensively assimilated into the scholarly tradition, the general notion that one *is* the other has become a cliché. The influence of Edward Said and other ground-breaking theorists has helped to frame the debate in terms of the degree to which intellectuals are complicit in the Western colonial project. In one widely held view, the various "investigative modalities" of imperial scholarship, from history to linguistics, directly shaped the ability of empire to exert power over non-Western subalterns. When British scholars reconstructed what they thought was the legal history of India, for instance, it was in order to govern it more effectively.[3] Even in China, where there was no direct European rule, British control over the way information was organized and understood was essential for facilitating the process of colonial domination.[4] On the other hand, an equally influential critique holds that colonial knowledge should not be reduced to its complicity with power relations. Relationships between states and their scholars were often tense, and in some cases the latter even saw their work in anticolonial terms or were more sympathetic to the societies they studied than to their own.[5] Yet, whether or not particular intellectuals were individually complicit, the idea that European power rested both on brute force and on subtler, more discursive ways of rearranging the world in its favor has become axiomatic—and for good reasons.[6]

Yet these approaches to understanding the relationship between knowledge and power, despite their diversity, generally share some fundamental and often unspoken expectations. They expect intellectual work to be driven by an ideal of autonomy from immediate political ends, variously upheld or betrayed in practice; it is this expectation that lends the hermeneutics of suspicion their debunking, critical bite. They see imperial intellectual engagement with "the Orient" as being inherently a different type of project from apparently similar activities elsewhere. And most importantly, they take for granted that European empires were more powerful than the targets of their global ambitions, no matter what the place of knowledge in their arsenal might have been.

Whatever the validity of these assumptions for other times and places, almost no one in the Russian Empire prior to the mid-nineteenth century would have recognized them as applicable in their case. Russian intelligence gathering and scholarly enterprises were explicitly oriented toward the glory of the sovereign, whether in her guise as conquering empress or patron of the arts; from programmatic essays to routine requests for raises and promotions, documents pertaining to knowledge production were framed in terms of their "usefulness" (*pol'za*) to the prestige, power, or commercial advantage of the state.[7] Though Russians did sometimes deploy racialized and civilizational tropes familiar from Orientalist writing elsewhere, until they were paired with material dominance they lacked the weight they would later obtain. China was still a dangerous neighbor, like Sweden or the Ottoman Empire, not a colony where Russia possessed the kind of paramount or hegemonic control Britain had in India. Far from it: after its defeat by Qing forces in the late seventeenth century and until its reoccupation of the Russian Far East in the mid-nineteenth, the Russian Empire was much weaker than the Qing where it counted. It was unable to use the logistical and technological advantages of the modernized army it developed in the reign of Peter the Great to overcome the limitations of Siberia's infrastructure; nor was it capable of consistently competing with British trade after that trade began ramping up in earnest in the late eighteenth century. The Russian Empire tried to use knowledge to bridge the gap between its conquering aspirations and its limited coercive power. Its institutional web spread out to embrace merchants, frontier nomads, and missionary students, but not in a unified or monolithic structure. Instead, its institutions competed with one another and pursued diverging, sometimes clashing priorities. From below, imperial knowledge production was as unruly as the bureaucracy itself.

For Russians seeking to exert power in East Asia, the connection between knowledge and power was thus an aspiration rather than a reality, but it is an aspiration that reveals a key feature of imperial rule long neglected by historians. Most studies of Russo-Chinese relations, a story historians have studied closely for over two centuries, focus either on trade negotiations and high-level diplomacy or on academic scholarship and elite Orientalist tropes.[8] But the quest for knowledge and the effort to restrict or promote its circulation underlay all of these relationships. Scholarly enterprises like the Academy of Sciences were merely special nodes in a much larger web of institutions, in which anonymous or nearly anonymous officials toiled to produce knowledge in the pursuit of imperial goals. To pull on the thread of Russian espionage in China is to unravel a skein of relationships that historians have up until now understood in sketchy, fragmentary ways.

Intelligence and Knowledge Regimes

Creating knowledge—forming coherent beliefs about the world by deriving conclusions from impressions, memories, and observations—is basic to the lives of both human beings and organizations. In this book, I take knowledge to be a kind of commodity, though there are as many alternate ways of understanding it as there are of describing society itself. As a commodity, knowledge is produced by people, whether professors in St. Petersburg or secret agents in Mongolia, who draw conclusions from what they read, hear, and observe, then package these conclusions, usually as a written document. In addition to a producer, knowledge also needs a consumer: someone who can read the text and make use of it by taking some kind of action or by reprocessing it and passing it on to somebody else (or by putting it in a drawer and forgetting about it).

In the long eighteenth century, knowledge in Russia was not distributed by means of a market mechanism; unlike in Western Europe, most of the texts produced by Russian specialists on China never became publicly available books. But the officials who consumed the never-ending stream of reports that flowed to them still had a choice between different interpretations and institutional sources, creating competition. Institutions that no longer produced the kind of knowledge officials considered useful quickly found themselves sidelined. With their outsized role in choosing winners and losers, the sovereign and the officials around the throne could shape the structure of knowledge production without micromanaging it, but they were also constrained by the personnel and institutions they had available to them.

Spies and Scholars shows how a familiar form of knowledge, scholarship, emerged out of a bureaucratic setting defined by very different assumptions. In general terms, scholarly knowledge is concerned not with immediate action but with broader claims, such as those about culture or language; it is associated with named, often high-status intellectuals and authors; and it may be read both by policy makers and by other people who access it through a market or through learned correspondence networks. Because we are used to intellectual cultures in which books and articles are the principal vehicles for information, scholarship is recognizable as knowledge far more readily than its counterpart, which is often produced in bureaucracies: intelligence. For my purposes, intelligence is a form of knowledge, typically access restricted, generated within state institutions by bureaucrats concerned with the immediate goals of promoting imperial power in an evolving geopolitical situation.[9] It is typically found in the form of manuscript reports, not articles. The typical Russian term for intelligence generally was *svedeniia*; to gather it was *razvedyvat'* (both words share a distant origin with the English "wisdom" and "vision," the Proto-Indo-European root **weyd-*). In pre-nineteenth-century Russia, intelligence was far more influential than scholarship: printing presses, literate readers, and professors were scarce, while bureaucrats and offices were comparatively plentiful. For every institution that had any contact with China at all, from the Siberian Bureau to the College of Foreign Affairs, producing intelligence was one of its central functions. Only in the nineteenth century did academic scholarship begin to be the dominant mode of making knowledge about China in the Russian Empire.

I speak of institutions and not of a unified Russian state because there was no such thing. For instance, although in theory the College of Foreign Affairs was responsible for diplomacy, most day-to-day Russo-Chinese encounters took place at the Russian Ecclesiastical Mission in Beijing and at Kiakhta on the Mongolian border, both of which were in the purview of other government bodies, which sometimes acted at cross-purposes. To make sense of how these institutions were related to one another and to state policy, I draw on the concept of "knowledge regimes" as articulated by the sociologist John L. Campbell and the political scientist Ove Kaj Pedersen:

> Knowledge regimes are the organizational and institutional machinery that generates data, research, policy recommendations, and other ideas that influence public debate and policymaking. Policymakers need the information produced by knowledge regimes insofar as the policy problems they confront often involve ambiguity and uncertainty. They need it to make sense of these problems. Sense making is often a contested process involving varying degrees of competition, negotiation, and compromise—often involving power struggles—over the interpretation of problems and solutions for them. A knowledge regime, then, is a sense-making apparatus.[10]

Though their work was developed for a very different era and set of questions, certain key insights apply just as usefully to eighteenth-century Russia's China policy as to twentieth-century political economy. First, institutions are not direct instruments of the monarch's will, but neither are they fully autonomous. Policy makers need institutions' input to make sense of their world, but their decisions also restructure institutions in accordance with changing goals and values. Second, changing relationships between different types of knowledge and knowledge-producing institutions (in Campbell and Pedersen's case, such organizations as universities and think tanks, with one generating scholarship and the other advocacy) can be just as significant as changing ties between those organizations and policy makers. Finally, knowledge regimes do not develop in any predictable way in response to actors' intentions. As Campbell and Pedersen put it, "Even when people try to improve their knowledge regimes . . . there is no guarantee that they will succeed. There is simply too much trial-and-error experimentation, puzzling, haphazard casting about, muddling through, and struggle for it to be otherwise."[11]

The knowledge regime model differs from two other influential perspectives that have shaped how we understand the history of knowledge. One view, drawing on the work of the anthropologist James Scott, depicts the state as a monolithic entity that sees the world as a canvas for the imposition of ideologically "high modernist" rationalizing transformation—turning a wild forest into a tree-farm monoculture, for instance. When it gathers information, it tries to make the unruly world ordered and "legible" to state apparatuses so that it can more easily be reshaped from above.[12] On the other hand, the network model that has gained more popularity in recent years understands the relationship between knowledge producers and objects of study as distributed rather than top down. A network might consist of intellectuals corresponding with one another or a more layered system of administrators, scholars, and local informants, but in general it is defined by horizontal and not hierarchical relationships.[13] Unlike the Scott model, a knowledge regime is defined by its internal mutability and heterogeneity, indeed competition; unlike the networked view, it relies on an overall hierarchy of state power to regulate the general structure within which connections are made. A knowledge regime also bears some similarities to Michel Foucault's concept of a "regime of truth"—the system of institutions and practices that enables statements to be true or false—although it focuses on the contingent and local aspects of institutions rather than their place in a single governing episteme.[14]

This approach helps explain how knowledge making about China in Impe-rial Russia changed so profoundly between the mid-seventeenth and the mid-nineteenth centuries without showing much evidence either of "progress" or of successfully guided development. Peter the Great may have wanted to Westernize Russia—whatever that entailed in any particular case—but Russian intelligence institutions evolved out of an unpredictable encounter between the demands of eighteenth-century statecraft and the realities they found on the ground. Likewise, imperial approval helped academic scholars to become the default bearers of intellectual credibility in the early nineteenth century, but the overall institutional landscape remained diverse and complex, with older forms persisting alongside newer ones and re-sponding very differently to the growing challenge of rivalry with Western European powers.

Knowledge regimes, then, don't change at random: they are shaped by the rise and fall of overarching paradigmatic ideas.[15] In Imperial Russia, these paradigms reflected how Russian rulers and officials envisioned their place in the world and in Inner Asia. Trade-oriented Muscovites in the seventeenth century valued commercial gains over stretches of barren land in Eastern Siberia, and in the 1689 Treaty of Nerchinsk, they traded the former for the latter (if not entirely without duress). For eighteenth-century Russians, how-ever, the goal had become regional political hegemony, and they plotted to regain their lost territory and seize even more—even at the risk of threatening trade. As Russian elites turned to different paradigms, the structure and sources of their knowledge regime changed to accommodate their priorities, moving from an emphasis on commercial and industrial espionage to a fas-cination with globe-spanning connections between Russia's imperial rivals. Through changes like these, the knowledge-regime framework models how ideas and tactics were linked to serve particular ends.

Although wide-ranging ideas shaped institutional contexts, specific texts and flows of information were more important than broad, generalized dis-courses. Scholars often speak of "images of China," eliding the boundaries between stylized literary forms, academic discourse, and claims founded on the reason of state.[16] But a foreign-service official did not use "Chinese-style" poetry to understand military deployments in Mongolia; nor did an academician normally have access to intelligence reports. By following concrete trails of documentation, historians of other regions and political environments, such as Ottoman Constantinople, have been able to reconstruct a much more fine-grained picture of their information ecologies.[17] The importance of intelligence as opposed to academic knowledge in the eighteenth century makes specific textual connections even more important, because most of the people working in the Imperial Russian knowledge regime had little formal education and were operating in hierarchical bureaucracies rather than a scholarly marketplace of print.

Specific intelligence flows also show how Russia shaped the world around it instead of simply gathering influences from abroad. In seventeenth-century Western countries, its Siberian intelligence apparatus made it one of the favored sources for information about China and Northeast Asia. In the eighteenth century, the Russian Empire was taken seriously in Paris and London as a rival with privileged access to the closed world of Beijing and the Forbidden City. The Jesuits, Europe's most influential producers of knowledge about China, came to depend on Russia in the 1770s, for everywhere else they had been dissolved by papal decree. (Catherine protected them because of their role in the Polish-Lithuanian territories she had recently annexed.) As a result, they were drawn deeply into the Russian intelligence agenda, because Catherine's state offered them its patronage in hopes of using them for political ends. When European forces on the ground were as limited as they were in this region, intelligence policy in particular was a leading edge of Russian global power, and Russia itself must be considered a shaper of European global empire and not merely a reactive Johnny-come-lately.

The Imperial Russian knowledge regime was linked to the rest of the world both through broad paradigms and specific flows of information, but the day-to-day life of the Russian knowledge regime took place on the institutional and organizational level. To collect and make use of intelligence, officials appropriated money to institutions and redirected personnel to staff them. Historians have offered a number of different accounts of how institutions in Imperial Russia developed; in the most currently accepted one, Peter the Great and his successors designed the state in accordance with the German ideology of cameralism. Cameralism prescribed that the ruler should implement a centralized apparatus to inventory and efficiently exploit their possessions—in other words, that top-down knowledge was integral to administration.[18] But while this model has much to recommend it, in practice the Russian state was not nearly as coherent or vertical as this implied—and indeed much of what we think of as cameralist ideology was promoted by experts competing for state patronage.[19]

Instead, different logics could drive different institutions, leading to deep-seated conflicts alongside more prosaic clashes between patronage networks or ruling cliques.[20] In other words, different institutions had different ideas about which knowledge was valuable and what needed to be done with it; changes in the organizational game marked changes in the orientation of the Russian Empire to the world. The Synod, the supreme body of the Russian Orthodox Church, dealt with the mission in Beijing and prioritized doctrinal and ecclesiastical matters; the Senate and its Siberian Bureau (*prikaz*) had authority over trade caravans and finance, which made it weigh commercial considerations more heavily; the Academy of Sciences engaged with China capriciously, driven by the interests of its professoriate; and the College of Foreign Affairs served as Russia's foreign ministry and supervised many intelligence matters, sometimes leading it into conflict with the first three. But the institutional confusion could also be productive, not just disruptive. In the 1730s Russian academicians built an entire scholarly correspondence with Jesuits in Beijing on top of the infrastructure of a trade caravan organized by Russian officials who cared much less about Ming astronomy than about the layout of Great Wall fortifications. Institutions, in other words, channeled an array of wider priorities and created pathways through which information could travel.

Ultimately, looking at intelligence gathering helps us understand how the knowledge-making apparatus of the Russian Empire rested on people: missionary students, administrators, Bukharan merchants.[21] This could sometimes be an astonishingly small number of individuals; at no one time during the eighteenth century were there more than about a half dozen Chinese speakers employed by the Russian state (although more Russian subjects knew Mongol and Manchu, especially the former). In 1781 the College of Foreign Affairs had fifteen French-language experts, five Turkish-language ones, and just one who spoke Manchu and Chinese.[22] This meant that a single specialist could fit into several institutions, each of which would conceptualize his role in different ways. If one of them turned out to be a drunk, a tyrant, an incompetent, or a victim of disease, he could transform the fate of an entire institution. On the other hand, individuals often had broader goals than their institutional roles permitted; more than one missionary student left evidence that he would have liked his work to be read more widely and more usefully.

Elsewhere in the early modern world, scholars have come to recognize the importance of "go-betweens"—"brokers and spies, messengers and translators"—who crossed cultural and political borders and mediated between different contexts.[23] But for most of their equivalents who emerged in the Russian context, like frontier intelligence agents or Russian student-missionaries in Beijing, the fundamental reality of their lives was the structure of social identity implemented in Imperial Russia during the reign of Peter the Great. Some of them lived out their careers on the lower bureaucratic rungs of the Table of Ranks, while others navigated the system of aristocratic patronage or the treacherous balancing act of frontier officialdom. While none of them were enserfed, neither were any of them true social elites possessing landed estates or the dignity of full academicians.[24] They had no choice but to adapt to the ideological context that dictated institution building in the empire, but they could also creatively exploit it for their own ends.[25] Some failed to do so: as priorities changed, the apparatus was left with remaindered people whose skills and contacts no longer matched what was in demand. This too was an integral consequence of the structure of the imperial knowledge regime.

As the changing logic of Russian concerns about the Qing drove continual institutional change, it pulled in numerous Qing subjects—Mongols, Manchus, and, to a much lesser extent, Chinese—who participated in Russian intelligence as informants, counterintelligence operatives, or spies for their own side.[26] Both Russia and the Qing were multiethnic states, and in Inner Asia they often incorporated the same ethnicities. Buriats and Mongols shared a common faith and language despite being subjects of different empires; Evenki hunters crossed freely over the undemarcated border in Manchuria. These connections enabled Russian officials to gather intelligence on the frontier.[27]

Russia and China often competed over territory and the loyalties of subject peoples, sometimes to the point of military conflict, but in terms of intelligence the rivalry between Russia and China remained mostly one-sided. Qing frontier intelligence gathering was wide ranging and sophisticated, but the Qing were far less interested in seeking information about Russia on a deliberate, institutionalized basis than the other way around. To Qing officials, Russia was an unruly border state to be pacified, not dominated; not until the nineteenth century did Qing officials begin to conceive of Russia as a predatory rival as powerful and virulent as the British.[28] For Russians, China played a much more diverse set of roles: on the one hand, it constantly loomed large as a potential foe, an obstacle to imperial ambitions, or an opportunity to gain global ascendancy—but on the other, it was a source of alluring luxury commodities, technologies, and literary texts.

Along with Mongols and other Qing subjects, Russian intelligence also relied on collaboration with other Europeans who found themselves in the Chinese world. For decades or even centuries, studies of the "great encounter of China and the West" have focused on the Jesuit missionaries in Beijing.[29] With the dozens of volumes of reports and essays they sent back to Europe, the Jesuits unquestionably played the leading role in shaping eighteenth-century European—and, indeed, Russian—views of Chinese culture. At the same time, the Jesuits were constrained by their dependence on the Qing emperors in Beijing, working within the confines of a court culture that by the middle of the century presented them with steadily shrinking opportunities. Russian actors in China were more independent, but they sought to serve their global ambitions by forging alliances with Jesuits and other Catholic missionaries in Beijing and elsewhere.[30] At times, the Jesuits also served as the ultimate aspiration for Russian policy makers: their supposed influence on the emperor stood in for the kind of bloodless victory only covert action could deliver. This was because Russian rulers and high officials saw Jesuits through a European lens, as consummate global movers and shakers. The Jesuits' familiar presence in an unfamiliar political landscape helped Russian officials to construct narratives about grand intercontinental connections and conspiracies.

Fragile threads of intelligence thus linked individual people in Beijing to courts in Europe and fleets in the Pacific. By gathering these threads, institutions like the College of Foreign Affairs could create an image of the world in which what happened in China could have enormous consequences for what happened in Europe, and vice-versa. By the late eighteenth century, Russian agents on the Qing border (like Bichurin himself) were being charged with missions that originated in rumors picked up by diplomatic residents in London. We need to understand the Imperial Russian knowledge regime on all three levels of analysis—ideas, institutions, and people—to see how it developed and shaped policy in such far-reaching and unexpected ways. Knowledge was so important to Russia's encounter with the world, so interwoven into the infrastructure of empire, that it created vast and conflicting expectations about the power it could deliver.

Ideas and Archives

By focusing on China expertise as a diverse set of institutions within an overall field bounded by state power, this book helps us to see the history of ideas and information in eighteenth-century Europe and Russia in a new light. In recent decades, European intellectual historians and especially historians of science have shifted away from studying the traditional scientific or Enlightenment canon and toward investigating how ideas and knowledge move from place to place.[31] Yet this approach has left bureaucracies relatively neglected, because European intellectuals tended to be social elites or market actors; as a result, scholars have focused on the Republic of Letters and the marketplace of print as the basic sites for knowledge transmission and exchange.[32] The case of European views of China, however, shows that state-based knowledge making was essential. China was a perennial focus for the eighteenth-century European learned world, whether as a point of reference for theories of political economy or as a wellspring of new geographical and technological data.[33] Russia provided material for these discussions, but its learned world was shaped by pragmatic state institutions without much of a corresponding sphere of autonomous intellectuals or elite authors. Looking toward Russia helps us see the key role bureaucratic knowledge production played in eighteenth-century Europe.

The Russian Enlightenment has been a major focus of scholarly efforts in recent years, but here too the knowledge-regime perspective offers new interpretive possibilities. While some historians still depict the many European Enlightenments as having been incompletely digested by conservative Muscovite culture and thus not widely influential in Russia, historians have generally come to recognize the ways in which it was creatively adapted to the Russian context.[34] What that adaptation entailed remains up for debate, however. As consumers of European texts in the enlightened tradition, certain Russian elites took part in the French, German, and Scottish Enlightenment, but not in a way that filtered down to the population as a whole. Cultural and ideological institutions molded by Enlightenment frameworks (like the

Academy of Sciences itself) were more universal, but often the connection was in the form of a nebulous orientation toward classification or moral improvement than any particular doctrine or debate.[35] By focusing on specific bureaucracies, their goals and personnel, and the texts that they generated, this book explores the limits of approaching the Russian Enlightenment using concept-oriented frameworks inherited from studies of the Enlightenments in the West. It is more interested in how knowledge making functioned than in whether it fit a preexisting set of conceptual definitions.

Until the early nineteenth century, the pragmatic orientation of Russian bureaucrats resisted the kind of theoretical and conceptual thinking that characterized Enlightenment attitudes to China. For instance, in 1757 the diplomat Vasilii Bratishchev was asked to comment on Voltaire's observations on China based on his experiences in Beijing. Though this was one of the few direct encounters between Russian intelligence institutions and Enlightenment thinkers, Bratishchev treated Voltaire's work as a repository of factual claims, showing no interest in what it meant for the philosophe to treat Confucianism as "natural law" or China itself as a well-governed state.[36] Only in the nineteenth century, as the academic approach gained influence, did Russians begin to confront such questions in earnest: the new disciplinary paradigm stressed the importance of taking part in the Western conversation about China and began to draw sharp, critical lines between Chinese and European (including Russian) civilization.

If participants in Russia's knowledge regime valued ideas less than institutional goals, that does not mean that they were bureaucrats in the way that many scholars understand bureaucracy—as defined by Max Weber, who distinguished it from more personalistic ways of organizing power. Certain aspects of Weber's model are deeply relevant for understanding Russian officials: the formation of Russian administrative institutions was closely linked to knowledge, the people wielding that knowledge were subject-matter experts and "cogs" more than elite intellectuals, and the entire apparatus was supposed to be driven by a norm of administrative secrecy.[37] Yet to the extent that an ideal-type bureaucracy was defined by the goals of "precision, speed, unambiguity, knowledge of the files, continuity, discretion, unity, strict subordination, reduction of friction and of material and personal costs," this concept had little relevance to China policy as practiced or understood.[38] Unlike other early modern information projects, such as those of Louis XIV's minister Jean-Baptiste Colbert, the Russian bureaucracy that faced China was fragmented rather than centralized, opportunistic rather than methodical, and chaotic rather than panoptic.[39] In its heterogeneity, it resembled the complex, interlocking machinery of information gathering and circulation found and partially appropriated by the British as they began to take possession of India in the eighteenth century.[40]

It would be tempting to turn instead to the extensive scholarship on Russia as an "empire of difference" that has developed in recent decades. Known generally as the "imperial turn," this approach places the Russian Empire alongside other early modern empires, defining it by its internal heterogeneity and "alienness" to itself.[41] The ways that Romanov Russia understood and managed this diversity implicated intellectuals and especially Orientalists (whether that term is seen negatively or neutrally) in imperial rule but also gave them opportunities to struggle against its implementation on the ground.[42] Russian Orientalists participated in a more general European literary and artistic culture of *turquerie* and *chinoiserie* but, perhaps unlike their British or French colleagues, were both interpreters and products of their empire's diversity. They both counterposed "the East" to Russia's Westernized Europeanness and defined themselves in "Oriental" terms to distinguish themselves from other Europeans.[43] The Buriats, Kazakhs, and other colonized peoples who became Orientalist experts in the nineteenth century used this framework to stake their own claims to legitimate knowledge.[44] In this view, the origins of Russian Orientalism in an empire of difference made it a distinctive intellectual approach that brought it closer to other Asian countries and distinguished it from the mainstream of Orientalist scholarship.

Spies and Scholars, in contrast, argues that in the Chinese context the starkness of Russia's geopolitical priorities overrode the pluralism of making knowledge in an empire of difference; the distinctive Russian approach to Orientalism instead originated in the race to compete with European rivals in the early nineteenth century. The eighteenth-century Russian knowledge regime encountered China not as a territory to be governed or a culturally adjacent community but as a foreign-policy problem to be managed. In this pragmatic framework, granular understandings of the loyalties of particular peoples or the state of specific aspects of the Qing economy displaced any effort to generalize about the civilizational underpinnings of the imperial competition. Border-crossing experts and informants like the Chinese and Manchu translator Anton Vladykin, born into a Torghut (Kalmyk) community on the lower Volga, played a key role in this apparatus, but not in ways that significantly altered its contours. Only when Russia came to see itself as a global power, reenvisioned its relationship with China as a facet of its competition with Britain and other Western powers, and began to view academic prestige as a key site for competitive advantage did the characteristic discourse of Orientalism—with its emphasis on fundamental racial, civilizational, and cultural difference—come to play a dominant role in Russian knowledge making. In this sense, Russian Orientalism was a product of the global transformations of the Napoleonic era.

One reason that scholars have tended to lump together the peculiar modes of thought that characterized Russian intelligence institutions with more general cultural trends like chinoiserie is that, since the early twentieth century, no Western historian of Russia has had access to the kinds of archival sources that would have made it possible to reconstruct the making of Russian intelligence on the ground.[45] By contrast, careful attention to the varieties of available sources was the great achievement of Soviet-era scholarship, especially the pathbreaking work of P. E. Skachkov. For these historians, the forgotten manuscripts of students or caravan agents were just as key to the formation of *kitaevedenie* (the study of China) as any treatise written in the Academy of Sciences; the immensity of the work they did to reconstruct its manuscript legacy is hard to overstate.[46] Yet among the central defects of this approach was its teleology, its assumption that the fate of all of this preparatory miscellanea was to evolve into something dignified and professorial—as if academic knowledge defined knowledge itself instead of forming one subcategory of it. Soviet scholars often failed to appreciate the distinctiveness of an intellectual world not yet defined by university faculties.

The more serious liability of the Soviet tradition of work on Russo-Qing relations—and to some extent its contemporary Russian descendants—was its intimate connection to the international political context of the Sino-Soviet split, which caused Soviet historians to downplay and eventually deny the role of imperialism in Russian policy.[47] This attitude of denial had not always characterized Soviet-era research; the 1920s scholarship of B. G. Kurts creatively built on the prerevolutionary legacy in ways that acknowledged Russian imperialism.[48] But by the time the split began in earnest in the late 1950s, the imperative of work on the period became defending Imperial

Russian claims to the territory that would become the Russian Far East. In the Chinese view, the region had been annexed through an unequal treaty that capped off centuries of Russian aggression. Soviet scholars retorted that Qing control of the region had also been imposed by force and that the ambitions of the Russian Empire were by contrast modest and humane. Though both Russia and the Qing clearly maintained their power over smaller communities in the region through a mixture of ideology and violence, Soviet scholars downplayed aspects of the Russo-Qing relationship that did not necessarily redound to Russia's credit and ignored a long legacy of plans for aggressive conquest. (A more positive effect of the Sino-Soviet split was the beginning of a still-ongoing effort to publish vast numbers of archival sources.[49]) Studying the origins of Russian sinology became a useful way to segregate the intellectual and the political aspects of Russo-Qing relations: knowledge seemed to be a separate matter from the Russian Empire's foreign-policy goals in the region, even when it was collected explicitly in the context of improving Russia's strategic position.

The politicized legacy of this topic has also shaped the availability of sources. While archival access to imperial-era materials before 1991 was looser than for more recent documents, manuscript materials dealing with the Qing border were sometimes listed under "special" classifications, meaning access to them was more restricted. A large amount of material was published in the nineteenth century, generally to buttress a narrative of inevitability surrounding the annexation of the Russian Far East, but this remained fragmentary and selective; likewise, massive Soviet-era projects for publishing primary documents have only scratched the surface of the material available in Russian archives.[50] In particular, an aspect that has only become visible with the advent of comprehensive archival access is the importance of trails that lead between two or more archival collections—like those of the Synod, the Senate, and the College of Foreign Affairs. Archives in Western Europe have also sometimes proven illuminating: for well-known figures like the British ambassador Lord Macartney, the Russian precedent turned out to have been unexpectedly significant. The emphasis on Russian sources and their Western connections has led *Spies and Scholars* away from Chinese sources, though Manchu works about the frontier have provided key local context.

This work stresses particular texts over general discourses, bureaucrats over academics, and archives over printed sources. Yet the overarching paradox of the eighteenth-century Russian knowledge regime is its failure to create an archive. In the Petrine era, Russian state agencies began to differentiate between working and historical archives, and many regularly referenced old files or created archival overviews for internal use.[51] There never was a single place where documents relating to China ended up. Asking for reference information between institutions was a difficult and cumbersome process, and in many cases, different bureaucracies did not even know what their parallel counterparts possessed. The early sinologist Larion Rossokhin's large collection of manuscript translations at the library of the Academy of Sciences was apparently not consulted in the preparation of memoranda at the College of Foreign Affairs, even when these explicitly concerned questions of diplomacy or security. In the nineteenth century, the institutional chasm between the Asiatic Department of the Ministry of Foreign Affairs and the frontier administration in Eastern Siberia evolved into a full-scale bureaucratic turf war, which formed the background to the annexation of the Far East. The continual process of forgetting, both accidental and deliberate, eroded the institutional memory of figures like Rossokhin. Indeed, in some ways, the interrelations between intelligence-gathering institutions that dealt with China are more accessible from a contemporary vantage point than they were to their contemporaries. We can often follow these interrelations from archive to archive in the literal form of borrowed, patchwork, and misattributed texts whose movements between countries and institutions testify to the social world that produced them.

In the seventeenth century, connections between institutions were also connections between states, in part because the institutions depended so heavily on border-crossing intelligence go-betweens. *Spies and Scholars* begins by sketching out the Muscovite view of the Inner Asian frontier, a region linked from the very beginning to the wider commercial aspirations of both Russian and foreign actors. Chapter 1 shows how Russia's attempt to understand the contours of the newly ascendant Qing Dynasty in China took shape through the production of hybrid texts: documents that incorporated a variety of European, Jesuit, Russian, and Inner Asian sources, which, in some cases, had legacies extending deep into the following century. As Chapter 2 shows, they also had a surprisingly wide geographical reach: a diverse community of Westerners began to steal, adapt, and publicize privileged Muscovite geographical knowledge for audiences in Western Europe.

There, these texts entered an entirely different economy of readership and plagiarism. As a whole, Muscovite intelligence gathering in China fits few established stereotypes about the pre-Petrine era: far from being hermetic or
isolationist, Muscovites were as avid about gathering intelligence abroad as
they were vulnerable to foreign espionage at home.

The Petrine era transformed the institutional landscape of intelligence
gathering along with the other structures of the Russian state. Among its most
consequential innovations was the way it created an explicit division between
public and secret knowledge, funneling different types of intellectual production into different bureaucratic structures—public knowledge through the
Imperial Academy of Sciences, secret knowledge into the College of Foreign
Affairs, among others. Chapter 3 explores how the post-Petrine state tried to
train a new breed of China experts under the auspices of the Russian Ecclesiastical Mission in Beijing. The unruly realities of Beijing life modified these
ambitions and led to the emergence of a small class of specialists, such as Rossokhin, whose unique specialization nevertheless gave them little access to
high-level policy making. Chapter 4 shows how a similar dynamic played out
at the Imperial Academy of Sciences, where these same individuals tried to
make claims on a broader scholarly world. Here, too, their subordinate
position—effectively as technicians of the imperial knowledge regime—
prevented them from making the kinds of careers associated with intellectual prestige in Western Europe.

At the same time, institutional change opened up new kinds of opportunities for intelligence. Among the most important institutions in this regard
was the state-run trade caravan that circulated between Moscow and Beijing
in the middle of the eighteenth century, tying the capitals to the Siberian periphery and the Siberian periphery to China. It was a bureaucratic institution that combined commercial significance with a diverse array of intelligence functions supplied to it by various state agencies. Chapter 5 shows how
caravan directors, doctors, clerks, and merchants frequently doubled as spies,
especially in the pursuit of industrial espionage. Though Russians never succeeded in adapting porcelain manufacturing or other stolen trade secrets
from the Qing, the caravan's employees spent a considerable amount of time
and resources attempting to do so. Chapter 6 reveals another facet of the
caravan: its role as a carrier of correspondence, "that noblest commerce,"
between the Academy of Sciences and the Jesuit community in Beijing. The

intellectual function of this correspondence was not separate from but intertwined with the caravan's other responsibilities; the acquisition of material goods underpinned both the caravan's correspondence-carrying function and its commercial role. Within the mobile intelligence platform of the caravan, commerce and scholarly knowledge were both interdependent and shaped by an underlying institutional logic.

The crisis that led to the end of the caravan as an institution was the Qing conquest of the formerly independent Junghar Confederation in 1755–1757. Chapter 7 explores the rise of intelligence as a tool of choice for the Russian Empire in this watershed period. On the former Russo-Junghar frontier, intelligence and covert action substituted both for direct military conflict and for defensive retrenchment, leading to an unprecedented concentration of focus on this changing periphery. Here, merchants and military officers circulated widely and secretly in an effort to advance Russian claims on the region. Chapter 8 shifts to Eastern Siberia, where the same geopolitical escalation created an intelligence establishment focused on the subversion of Khalkha (Outer) Mongolia. Despite the extent and sophistication of this establishment, its long-term consequences were meager, as significant investments in intelligence failed to translate into diplomatic leverage against the Qing. Frontier intelligence defined a new era of regional competition between Russia and its neighbor, but it could not resolve the conflict; instead, it tantalized Russian authorities with the prospect of easy, low-cost advances.

The final arc of *Spies and Scholars* shows how a sense of rivalry with Britain and other European powers supplanted the regional power struggle with the Qing in the Russian imperial mind. At the end of the eighteenth century, Russia found itself apparently under siege by pinpricks of British encroachment, from spies to naval raiders. Chapter 9 takes a global view of the emergence of the North Pacific as a new theater for imperial conflict, drawing on French and British as well as Russian archives to reconstruct how discourses of threat drew on intelligence to shape geopolitics in the region—and thus how conflict in the North Pacific predated the ability of any major power to deploy significant military forces there. The failure both of the 1792 British Macartney embassy to China and its Russian successor, Golovkin's embassy of 1805, seemed to demonstrate the limits of imperial reach, but the global vantage point that these developments brought to the Russian understanding of China would become permanent.

This new perspective, as Chapter 10 shows, reshaped the imperial knowledge regime, making the discipline of sinology and academic authorship a cornerstone of an intellectual world now oriented toward European rivals. The legacy of the past century's frontier intelligence gathering was now consigned to oblivion as insufficiently scholarly and irrelevant to the questions that drove Western Orientalism. On the other side of the empire, a different information politics materially reshaped the reality of the Russo-Qing relationship. Chapter 11 shows how in the 1850s a new generation of Russian administrators on the Mongolian frontier deftly manipulated anxieties about foreign rivals and realized the conquering aspirations of their eighteenth-century predecessors through an intelligence coup directed at rival institutions in St. Petersburg itself. Though the empire's knowledge regime would remain as heterogeneous and driven by institutional amnesia as ever, it could now serve as an adjunct to power instead of a substitute for it. In the minds of the people who governed Russia, the subjugation of the southeast frontier was now just a matter of time.

This book is about the prehistory of that moment of apparently inevitable Russian triumph, two centuries in which the problem of China seemed to imperial officials to be so insoluble that no single office or administrator could be trusted with it. The way the empire dealt with this challenge drew on the entire infrastructure of knowledge production that underpinned its institutions, especially the small company of low-ranking people who gathered intelligence on the ground in Beijing and beyond. For historians, scholarly and literary tropes have defined both Russia's and Europe's intellectual relationship to China—but in Russian practice, the day-to-day circulation of official intelligence meant far more than any landmark text a given poet or academic could write. This system was not static or devoid of ideas, however. It was shaped by the grand narratives of Russian decision making, which constantly remade and reoriented Russia's institutions. In allowing officials to make sense of an enormous and confusing frontier that sometimes seemed to stretch from Manchuria to the Kazakh steppe and sometimes from London to Alaska, it also helped to define what that frontier meant for Russia itself.

PART I

MUSCOVITE STATECRAFT
and HYBRID KNOWLEDGE

Chapter 1

Muscovy on the Knowledge Frontier

R ussia's vastness, extending today to one-ninth of the Earth's land surface, is its defining geographical feature. Most of it was occupied in a single sustained burst of colonial expansion: Russian borders reached the lower Volga in the 1550s and the Pacific, almost four thousand miles away, less than a century later. Watching the red blot stain the early modern map, it would be easy to imagine the Muscovites' arrival as an earthshaking event for the people of northern Eurasia. Mostly, it was not. Like England, Portugal, and the Netherlands—European states that were also beginning to seek an imperial fortune in Asia—Russia entered the Asian world as one player among many, pulled in by local conflicts and struggling to take advantage of local opportunities. To orient itself in this unfamiliar landscape, Russia needed knowledge and not just the technological advantages of firearms or fortifications. Other European empires had a vanguard of missionaries and traveling writers to sketch the outlines of the densely populated world they sought to dominate; Russia used Bukharan traders, Cossack diplomats, and Jesuit informants.[1] In the absence of a book market or a Republic of Letters, Russia relied on state institutions to make this knowledge accessible and useful to the prying bureaucrats and rapacious governors that managed Siberian affairs, and in Muscovy those institutions came to produce a distinctively hybrid, synthetic genre of frontier texts.

Seeking out local knowledge was vital, because the Russian conquerors now found themselves in a political environment far more complex and diverse than the single-paragraph caricatures of "Tartary" in their translations of sixteenth-century European geographies.[2] At the dawn of the seventeenth century, Inner Asia was not yet the Russo-Qing borderland it would eventually become. Instead it retained the faint outlines of the Mongol Empire, which had begun to fracture three hundred years earlier and whose shards were now fully independent entities. In the oasis states of Bukhara and Khiva in modern-day Uzbekistan, puppet Chinggisid khans retained nominal authority even as military rulers called emirs wielded actual power. In the 1380s, the emir Timur (or Tamerlane) had begun a project of Mongol revival there that briefly reconstituted almost the entire western part of the old empire, but it was short-lived. By the sixteenth century the Safavids and Ottomans had fully extirpated Timurid rule outside Inner Asia proper, in Persia and the Middle East, leaving only institutional and cultural remnants; in South Asia, however, the Mughal rulers continued to trace their descent to the Timurids.[3] In China, the Chinese-nativist Ming destroyed the Mongol Yuan Dynasty in 1368, pushing the remaining Mongols north beyond a strengthened Great Wall and giving rise to a shatter zone of claimants to the throne of the Great Khan. In each of these places, the Mongol heritage was reinterpreted in different ways, recombining with local, Buddhist, and Islamic traditions instead of displacing them. The ideological and cultural legacy of Chinggis Khan continued to give his heirs a common lingua franca, and Muscovy at first shared it too.

It is the broad swath of relatively sparsely populated territory between the Caspian Sea and the Pacific that became most significant for the Qing relationship and, in particular, three contested sites in it. The first is the Kazakh steppe and Jungharia, around the area where the borders of Russia, China, Kazakhstan, and Mongolia meet each other today. The Muslim, Turkic-speaking Kazakhs established themselves here in the late fifteenth century, as the last remnants of the Qipchaq Khanate (commonly known as the Golden Horde, the northwest quadrant of the Mongol Empire) collapsed into a patchwork of rump states. This nomadic pastoralist community was numerous but politically decentralized, dominated by a Chinggisid elite that typically did not see a need for a single khan. Next door, in the steppes and mountains of modern Xinjiang and western Mongolia, they met a confederation of four western Mongol tribes known as the Oirats, who would soon begin to convert to Buddhism. The Oirats gave rise to the Junghars, who would dominate Inner Asian politics in the seventeenth century; one of their constituent tribes, the Torghuts (Kalmyks), migrated westward to the lower Volga region in the late sixteenth century and eventually became autonomous subjects of the Russian Empire. United by their shared post-Mongol political culture, the Kazakhs, Junghars, and Torghuts became vital and independent players in regional politics. Until the eighteenth century, Russia's most important relationships in Inner Asia were with these peoples rather than with any ruler in Beijing.[4]

To the east of the Oirats, in the heart of modern Mongolia, lived the Khalkha Mongols. A century after their expulsion from southern China, the Chinggisid Dayan Khan had reforged the eastern Mongol tribes around the nucleus of Chinggis Khan's empire, the old capital of Karakorum. His grandson Altan Khan, whose patronage of Buddhism helped make it the dominant religion among the Mongols, remained the most powerful ruler in Inner Asia until his death in 1582; his descendants would be known as Altan Khans ("Golden Khans") as well. But Khalkha unity was already fracturing. By the end of his reign, the peoples of what would become Inner Mongolia had splintered away from the Khalkha community. During the seventeenth century the component societies of the renewed Mongol state fragmented further as they were pulled between the Russians in the north, the Junghars in the west, and the Manchus in the east and south. At the Dolon Nor Council in 1691, after defeating the Junghar bid to control the Khalkha, the Manchu Qing Empire incorporated the remains of Altan Khan's realm, though the Mongols retained a distinct system of government and social organization and were not yet fully loyal to the Qing.[5] The common heritage the Khalkha shared with Russian-subject Buriats in the north remained a potent source of mutual influence and a reminder that another destiny was possible outside of the framework of Qing rule.

Finally, the humid forests and river valleys of Manchuria in the east were home to Evenki (Tungus) hunters and reindeer herders, the Solons, the Daurs, and other smaller communities. They were also the homeland of the Manchus, who would soon found one of the most successful dynasties in Chinese history. Just a few decades earlier, they had been known as Jurchens—a group of mainly seminomadic clans who lived by hunting, fishing, and herding. Between 1582 and 1626, the leader of the Aisin Gioro clan, Nurhaci, united the Jurchens into a powerful military force, renamed them Manchus, and drove the Ming Dynasty out of China's northeast. His son Hong Taiji proclaimed the establishment of the Qing Dynasty in 1636 and made clear to all of the successor states of the Mongol Empire that henceforth the Manchu emperors would claim the mantle of Great Khan. By the time the Qianlong emperor completed the conquest of the Junghars in 1757, all the remaining peoples of the Mongol Empire had been incorporated into the Qing realm—with the exception of those who were conquered by the Russian Empire.[6]

Muscovy had emerged from the disintegration of the Qipchaq Khanate as the strongest of the Russian principalities, making full use of the institutions and trade routes it was able to borrow from its former overlords. Once it subdued the other princely states, it began to make claims on the Mongol legacy in the east, especially after Ivan the Terrible crowned himself tsar in 1547. Although the precise relationship between the terms "khan" and "tsar" is complex, within Muscovite political discourse the equivalence of the two terms and the legitimating function of Ivan's descent from Chinggis Khan was a recognized fact.[7] Just as Russia itself sat at the hinge of the post-Roman and post-Mongol worlds, so did its sovereign claim legitimacy through descent from both Augustus (hence *tsar*, i.e., "Caesar") and Chinggis. In the 1550s this latter claim was made concrete when Muscovite troops conquered the post-Qipchaq Tatar khanates (*tsarstva* in Russian) of Kazan and Astrakhan. These conquests helped to make Muscovy a multiethnic and multiconfessional empire that not only ruled over but also employed and elevated Muslim and Tatar subjects.[8] Inner Asians understood the Muscovites they met to be part of the Mongol *oikoumene*, even if an unusual one. Writing in Manchu at the end of the eighteenth century, one Qing Mongol official carefully distinguished between Russians and other Europeans: "In their clothes and headgear they resemble Westerners [*si yang ba-i niyalma*]. There are Westerners in their territory and they revere the Westerners' teaching [Christianity]. As for their khan, when it is a man he is called the Chagan Khan, and when it is a woman she is called the Katun Khan." These were the titles used in official Russo-Qing correspondence and elsewhere in Inner Asia.[9]

The conquest of Kazan and Astrakhan by itself did not bring Russia into diplomatic contact with China or even, in any sustained way, with the peoples of Inner Asia. A quasi-freelance band of Cossacks under Ermak Timofeevich conquered the khanate of Sibir in Western Siberia in the 1580s, but all this immediately entailed was the capture of the khanate's court, near which the Siberian capital Tobolsk was founded in 1585. It also meant the replacement of fur tribute gatherers loyal to the khan with ones loyal to the tsar (often, in fact, the same individuals); the Russian state continued to use steppe terms like *iasak* ("tribute") and *amanat* ("hostage") until the nineteenth century.[10] Muscovite power in early modern Siberia was brutal but weakly institutionalized: it largely took the form of a string of forts and towns that concentrated small administrative staffs, warehouses for fur tribute, markets, garrisons, and religious communities within a walled enclosure, with little effort to project day-to-day political power into their vast hinterlands. Nonetheless, this attenuated state provided ample opportunities for long-distance commerce in furs and other products, whose profits enabled the accumulation of huge mercantile fortunes and the tariffs from which helped recoup the costs of the Siberian colonial enterprise.[11]

The Bukharans did the most to bring Russia into the Inner Asian world. A large, diasporic mercantile community like the Greeks and Armenians in the Black Sea region or the Jews in Europe, these Muslim expatriates largely from the Central Asian khanate of Bukhara traded in a zone stretching from Beijing to the Ottoman Empire. In Russia, their control of the caravan trade from Tobolsk and Astrakhan to Central Asia made them especially influential merchants; in Siberia, where they long preceded the Muscovites, they enjoyed a substantial tariff privilege compared to their Russian competitors. Their role was not strictly commercial, however. Their transnational connections also made them indispensable to the Russian state in its dealings with other Eurasian polities. In particular, beginning in 1653 the caravans of the Bukharan Seitkul Ablin, in a highly profitable form of shuttle diplomacy, midwifed the emergence of Russo-Qing relations.[12]

Before that point, Russia's relationship with China and Inner Asia consisted of a series of false starts motivated more by immediate external pressures than by a macroscopic view of its potential role in the Eurasian world. Though local commercial agreements with Inner Asian elites developed as Russian occupiers moved eastward through Siberia, more wide-ranging alliances were elusive. In 1604 the English ambassador Thomas Smith inquired in Moscow about passage to China. As if in direct response, an informal Muscovite embassy intended for China and the court of the Altan Khan departed from Tomsk in 1608, although it was foiled by the refusal of a Kazakh prince to permit them to pass. In 1615 the new English ambassador John Merrick inquired about China again, and the governor of Tobolsk sent out another embassy, this time successfully reaching the Altan Khan's court.[13] A potential Muscovite alliance with the khan never came to fruition. Though the newly-elected Romanov tsar Mikhail Fëdorovich made clear that further embassies to China would not be driven by English requests, he nevertheless promised that he would investigate the China question thoroughly and make the resulting intelligence available.[14] The governor (*voevoda*) of the Siberian town of Tomsk sent a clerk named Ivashko Petlin to Beijing in 1618, but the only concrete result of this was a rescript from the Wanli emperor authorizing Russia to trade with the Ming court.

This might have been the beginning of a fruitful commercial relationship, except that nobody in Russia could read Chinese or otherwise figure out how to make use of the rescript—and that they never had the chance. As Petlin was arriving in the Ming capital, multiethnic Qing armies were already beginning to make inroads against the dynasty in the north. Meanwhile, famine, banditry, natural disasters, and fiscal mismanagement were eroding the realm from within. In 1644 Beijing itself was captured by the bandit leader Li Zicheng, and in a desperate attempt to salvage the remains of the dynasty, the loyalist general Wu Sangui invited the Qing army in to remove him. Instead of dutifully returning north as Wu had hoped, the Qing stayed in power for almost three centuries.[15] Russian contacts with China were resumed only thanks to Seitkul Ablin's arrival in Moscow as part of a Kalmyk embassy eight years after the Ming-Qing transition. On November 23, 1652, he and his fellow Bukharan companion Ezhbab Seitov were taken to the Treasury Bureau (Prikaz Bol'shoi kazny) for questioning; exactly one week later, the Bureau issued orders for a merchant named Fëdor Baikov to take Ablin and Seitov with him to Tobolsk and then onward as ambassador to China.[16]

Despite the work Ablin did in laying the groundwork for his embassy in Beijing, Baikov did not succeed in forging an agreement with the Shunzhi emperor, mostly because he was unwilling to observe the unequal ceremonies of tribute-mission protocol. As a formal Russian ambassador surrounded by a staff that reported his every move to his superiors, he could not risk performing the rituals of obeisance expected of a foreign envoy at the Qing court without risking prosecution in Moscow. His superiors learned from this mistake. Two more caravans from Russia, now again headed by Ablin instead of Baikov, arrived in Beijing in the subsequent two decades, and indications are that the Bukharan was far less punctilious about the tsar's honor than the Russian had been (which his instructions tacitly condoned). His profit was accordingly quite substantial.[17] From the beginning of the seventeenth

1.1 Eurasia in the 1690s (boundaries approximate).

century until the Treaty of Nerchinsk finally regularized trade relations between Russia and China in 1689, only the help of Inner Asian intermediaries
like the Bukharans enabled Russia to establish regional commercial links.
These were manifested not just in the form of direct Beijing caravan profits,
which were only a small percentage of Siberian commerce, but also in indirect trade conducted throughout Siberia, from border marts like Lake Iamysh
near the Altai Mountains to the main emporium at Tobolsk. By the time Russian traders began to displace the Bukharans on their side of the border in
the 1690s, those intermediaries had already made Muscovy the dominant
route for overland commerce between China and the West.[18]

Assembling Siberian Knowledge

If the Muscovite state entrusted much of its Inner Asian diplomacy to non-
Russians, it created its intelligence apparatus much more deliberately, though
local intermediaries remained essential. The importance of intelligence, in
fact, partially explains the halting nature of Russia's early diplomatic efforts. In
1616 the Boyar Duma in Moscow ordered that "there be no [further] relations

with the Altan Khan or the Chinese state until intelligence is collected beforehand."[19] The implications of this were spelled out by the Ambassadorial Bureau (Posol'skii prikaz) in its instructions to the Tobolsk governor Ivan Kurakin in 1617 (summarized here in 1620):

> We ordered that all sorts of intelligence be collected about them [rozvedyvat'. . . vsiakikh vestei], how populous their lands are, which towns they possess and how large they are, and which towns they are in communication with, and which faith they have, and whether they respect our great state more than others and more than their own, and whether they are at war with any state and which, and what military they have, and how strong it is, and what trade goods they have, and which lands border theirs aside from our own and the Kalmyks? And if possible, [the governor] should send his own people to Altan Khan and to the Chinese state, not as ambassadors or envoys from himself, but rather various Cossacks and assorted people, as if they ended up there by accident.[20]

In response to this assignment, Kurakin conceived and dispatched the Petlin embassy, evidently without consulting with Moscow—after all, he was not supposed to send "ambassadors or envoys" of his own accord, and this Cossack would be properly unofficial. Upon his return to Tobolsk in 1619 Petlin submitted a report (rospis') about China that answered the questions asked by the Bureau, while deemphasizing his own role as an envoy. The information Petlin provided was also what the English ambassador had wanted to know.[21]

Where Petlin's intelligence assignment was tentative and exploratory in nature, the one Baikov received three decades later was more substantial, and its espionage component, more explicit. The new ambassador was instructed to "investigate by means of all measures, secretly, using bribes and liquor to recruit the [Qing] escorting officer or some other person" such questions as the Qing emperor's attitude to the tsar and the prospects of Russo-Qing trade. More generally, he was to inquire widely into Qing commodities, geography, foreign relations, and economics, as well as describe the peoples living between Siberia and the Qing border. Although in contemporary terms such forms of knowledge gathering would belong to very different categories of activity—espionage and geography, human intelligence and open-source intelligence—there is no evidence the Muscovites saw it that way. Whatever public or private source his information came from, Baikov was to observe official secrecy, ensuring that "no person or anyone would know about these instructions in any way, and not to speak to anyone either in China or on the way there about his mission." The 1657 document that resulted from Baikov's assignment was considerably longer than Petlin's report and reflected Baikov's greater prestige in the Qing capital but was not otherwise much different.[22]

Intelligence gathering, then, could be said to have come more naturally to the Russians in the Inner Asian context than either diplomacy or trade. This would have surprised an early modern European observer. Russians in the seventeenth century were widely regarded by ethnographers not only as slavish but as fundamentally uncurious, people who saw spies in innocent foreigners in search even of basic information.[23] "Indeed, hitherto no man of parts or abilities has been suffered to travel the Country," wrote the English doctor Samuel Collins in 1671, "for the people are very jealous, and suspect those who ask them any questions concerning their Policy, or Religion, they being wholly devoted to their own Ignorance . . . and thus they verifie the old Saying, *Ars nullum habet inimicum prater ignorantem* [Knowledge has no enemy but the ignorant]."[24] Neither did Muscovites appear inclined to learn from their neighbors. Grigorii Kotoshikhin, a longtime bureaucrat in the diplomatic service, said as much in 1666—after escaping to Sweden. "Men of the Russian state are in their nature boastful and unsuited to any affairs, because they have no good learning in their state and accept none besides boastfulness and shamelessness and hate and injustice." Accordingly, anyone who travels abroad is "tortured in the same fashion as one who has taken up arms against the tsar."[25]

Despite this stereotype, officials within Russia's administrative apparatus were avid for information. Russia's institutions and the clerks who staffed them had a strongly professionalized, albeit hereditary, ethos and system of practices.[26] This applied especially to the Ambassadorial Bureau, which in the later seventeenth century became one of the centers of Muscovite state power. In early modern Western Europe, diplomacy was a clearinghouse for intelligence of all kinds.[27] Russia did not yet send resident ambassadors, whose main function in Europe was intelligence gathering; nor did its elites form a receptive audience for the in-depth policy analysis common in places like the Venetian court. Still, Muscovite embassies did consistently accumulate knowledge of both court ritual and ethnographic detail through the system of diplomatic reports (*stateinye spiski*). Both Petlin and Baikov's reports belonged to this genre. Muscovite ambassadors returning from embassies abroad submitted these documents as a required duty, though they were generally composed by the embassy's clerical staff (since many ambassadors were illiterate).[28] Reports served multiple functions, including making sure that the ambassador did not allow the tsar's honor to be insulted in any way, but among their goals was to record information about foreign lands. Such documents are attested starting from the sixteenth century and deal with destinations as far apart as England, Georgia, and Florence.[29]

Learning about Chinese and Inner Asian affairs had meanwhile become a matter of more than commercial significance, as territorial friction between Russia and the Qing spilled out into open warfare. Over the course of the early seventeenth century, parties of Russian Cossacks had steadily made their way eastward; Okhotsk, mainland Russia's first (and for two hundred years almost its only) Pacific port, was founded in 1647. As Chukchi resistance prevented further conquest northeast, and powerful Mongol and Turkic-speaking nomadic confederacies blocked the way southward, the drive of Russian colonialism in the 1640s and 1650s was redirected southeast, into the more vulnerable Amur valley. There, groups of Cossacks led by such violent entrepreneurs as Ivan Khabarov and Vasilii Poiarkov encountered Daur, Solon, and other indigenous residents of northern Manchuria (then called Dauria), who paid tribute to the Qing but whose settlements were not actively garrisoned by Manchu troops. Qing efforts to defend their subjects from Russian aggression (or, from a different perspective, their attempt to violently reassert control over defecting tributaries) led to two military conflicts, one in the 1650s and another in the 1680s, with a sustained stalemate in between.[30] This border war was not finally concluded until 1689, when the Russian boyar Fëdor Golovin and the Qing amban Songgotu signed China's first treaty with a Western power—the Treaty of Nerchinsk. The agreement forced Muscovy to withdraw from the Amur valley almost entirely, a defeat that haunted the dreams of Russian imperialists until the region was annexed again in the 1850s; at the same time, Qing negotiators formally allowed Russia to send regular trade caravans to Beijing, as well as to regularize border commerce. Various writers have credited the Jesuit interpreters Tomás Pereira and Jean-François Gerbillon with a decisive role in the negotiations or even with contributing to the creation of an unequal agreement in which Russia was vic-timized.[31] It would be more accurate to say that the agreement reflected the overall balance of power in the region, as well as the Muscovite crown's pref-erence for commercial rather than territorial advantages.[32]

Golovin came to Nerchinsk bearing maps, ready to cultivate intelligence connections, and equipped with a relatively detailed knowledge of Qing and Mongol affairs. For instance, a subsidiary envoy whom Golovin sent to a Khalkha Mongol religious leader met secretly with an enslaved Russian in-formant who provided information on Qing-Khalkha diplomacy.[33] These practices built on skills developed during the preceding decades, as Russian troops along the Amur interviewed Qing fugitives about their knowledge of military affairs and local conditions. Once Russian administration had be-come established in a region, in short, its intelligence-gathering abilities al-lowed it to develop a high-resolution view of the surrounding strategic land-scape.[34] Yet none of this would have been possible even just a few decades earlier: as late as 1670 the Nerchinsk governor Danila Arshinskii knew so little about China that he sent an envoy to the Qing court with instructions to de-mand an oath of fealty from the emperor to the tsar.[35]

The Muscovite Frontier Text

Baikov's report had only broken the ground for the creation of intelligence about China. In the second half of the seventeenth century, writers of both foreign and Russian works about Siberia began to create a new and distinc-tive frontier literature, which enabled Muscovite officials gradually to con-struct a coherent spatial, economic, and political picture of Inner Asia that incorporated Russo-Qing relations.[36] Its first major effort commenced in To-bolsk in 1667, when the governor Pëtr Godunov commissioned a map and supporting documents that would begin to make sense of Russia's position in relation to its southern neighbors. This was the first map (*chertëzh*) that included Eastern Siberian lands. In later years the preeminent Siberian car-tographer would be a Tobolsk clerk named Semën Remezov, whose produc-tivity was astonishing.[37] In terms of Russian geographical practice, however, the supporting materials were just as significant. Maps in Muscovy were linked to a range of textual works similar to gazetteers or chorographies.

Unlike maps, which offered a bird's-eye view, these descriptions mapped out routes from place to place from the perspective of a traveler, often including the length of time it took to move from one town to another along roads or riverine routes.[38] Along the way, they incorporated accounts of local peoples, trading opportunities, and foreign countries beyond the border—often drawing on existing texts for material. In the Western parts of the empire, geography and cartography were more developed, with European Russia having been largely mapped by the 1510s; by contrast, in Siberia the sparse state presence and linguistic diversity meant that textual fragments and non-Russian informants were much more significant.[39]

The surviving manuscripts of Godunov's project represent a closely interrelated but imperfectly preserved patchwork of documents. His 1667 map was composed in Tobolsk in conjunction with two other texts: a "Memorandum concerning the Qing Land" ("Vedomost' o Kitaiskoi zemle") and a prose chorography that traced Siberian routes and contained repeated mentions of the Qing. (Though the Russian word *Kitai* is usually translated "China," in the seventeenth century its meaning was more capacious and multiethnic and is thus better rendered as "Qing.") Together, the three documents illustrate the complex web of sources and interactions that governed the production of knowledge about the Qing state in Muscovy. The map itself, seen here in one of its handful of surviving versions, reveals the layers of information gathering that went into it. Despite its seemingly primitive features—like the placing of north at the bottom rather than the top of the sheet—this map built on a well-developed Muscovite tradition of administrative cartography.[40] The place-names it identifies come not from any Western source but from the textual reports on China, like Baikov's, that had trickled into Tobolsk in the previous decades. It wasn't always easy for the cartographer to figure out where to locate these, leading to oddities like the Great Wall gate city of Zhangjiakou being placed well outside of the wall itself. The Godunov map was an effort to reconcile a variety of sources and thus to make sense of Russia's Siberian neighborhood.[41]

The "Description of the Qing Land," which formed the second of Godunov's documents, contains the same diversity of testimony. This document is an abstract of information largely based on Baikov's and Petlin's reports and dealing with customs, religion, trade, and so forth. It also incorporates information from "foreigners and visiting Bukharans and Tatar servitors"—most

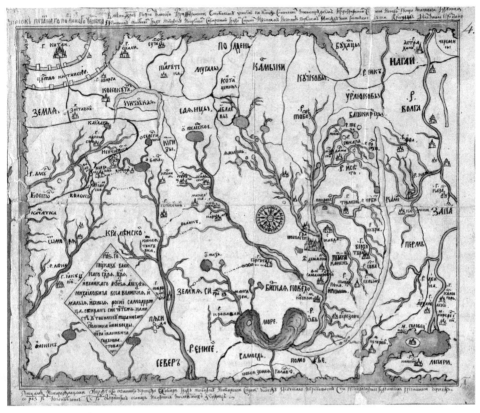

1.2 The Godunov map, 1667. South is up. Leo Bagrow collection, Houghton Library, Harvard University.

certainly including Ablin, who was in Tobolsk in mid-1666—as a result of which certain sections are far better developed than others. For instance, the text includes a detailed account of Tibetan Buddhism, while persisting (like Baikov) in calling Beijing "Khanbalyk"—a name it had not held for three centuries.[42] In the same chronicle (*khronograf*), which contains the surviving version of the description, Godunov's text is followed by another that is marked as "from a different report of the same year, written by a native-born Qing citizen through the Kalmyk [i.e., Western Mongol] language." This account, likely also collected by Godunov, tells the story of the origins of the *kitaiskii* (in this case, Manchu rather than Chinese) people. It depicts them as having migrated from the region of Tobolsk around 1100, under pressure from

Muslims and growing forestation of the steppe. This "native Qing" report is a mixture of origin myth and historical testimony about Chinggis Khan and his descendants—but parts of it also strongly resemble the *Manzhou shilu*, the official Manchu origin story promoted by the Qing government.[43]

In other words, Godunov in Tobolsk had access to both manuscript Russian sources and miscellaneous informants from different parts of Inner Asia, which he strove to reconcile into a coherent intelligence compendium. The written transcription that accompanied his map demonstrates how this kind of information was woven into the general texture of Siberian geography by indicating places where knowledge was uncertain due to the lack of eyewitnesses. Like the map, its use of place-names reflects a heterogeneous collection of sources: for instance, between the three documents, the Inner Mongolian city of Hohhot is referred to variously by the Chinese name of Qingcheng and the Manchu or Mongol name of Huhu hoton. Although this is only one example of a geographical description from the second half of the seventeenth century, it is far from the only one to display a preoccupation with Russo-Qing relations. Nor is it the only one in which frontier sources reflect a miscellaneous approach to research. These two features defined Siberian geographic writing through the end of the Muscovite period.[44]

In Moscow, meanwhile, the Ambassadorial Bureau was also evolving into a center for the production of knowledge about China. It reached the apex of its influence in the 1680s, under the leadership of the Westernizing boyar Vasilii Golitsyn—the favorite of Muscovy's regent in that decade, Princess Sofiia. In this period, the Bureau's clerk A. A. Vinius, a Muscovite of Dutch origin who would later serve as a crucial transmission belt to Western information seekers, created a new map by integrating novel European techniques with Godunov-era traditions. He rendered the Qing frontier far more accurately, for instance, by removing the superfluous second Great Wall and omitting the "gate city" so misleadingly borrowed from Baikov. Although it also includes a putative cartographic grid, in fact this seems more impressionistic than accurate: the lines do not correspond to known latitudes, and the distances between them are unequal. Vinius's map would later serve as a major influence on the Siberian maps composed by Remezov and his sons between 1698 and 1702. Although Remezov never flirted with grids or other appurtenances of European scientific mapping, his maps paid close attention to detail, avoided the Godunov map's errors, and carefully noted nomadic lands.[45]

This evolving cartographic tradition built on the experiences of the previous decades: retaining the pluralism of its sources, it was beginning to incorporate Western influences more overtly.

This did not mean that Siberian geographic writing was necessarily becoming more accurate or empirically grounded; Remezov himself added a spurious "Nikan tsardom" (using the Manchu word for "Chinese") to his 1699 map.[46] A 1686 text almost certainly composed by the Ambassadorial Bureau subclerk Nikifor Veniukov reveals the deep confusion its congeries of sources could sow. When Godunov was compiling his texts, he could consult informants in person to resolve any discrepancies among the testimonies at his disposal. Veniukov, it seems, was not so lucky. He had the Bureau's entire library at his disposal and had even traveled to Beijing twice (in 1675 and again in 1685–1686). Yet the account he wrote was far less coherent than its predecessors. His "Description of the New Territory of the Siberian State" ("Opisanie novyia zemli sibirskogo tsarstva") is on solid ground when it draws on standard chronicles and chorographies to describe Siberia but gets into trouble as soon as he crosses the border. Like Remezov, he thinks China and the "Nikan tsardom" are separate. He also manages to misdate the Qing conquest by a decade, confuse different stages of the dynastic transition, and incorrectly name and describe every participating actor. Certain word choices suggest a Bukharan informant, while a passage describing imperial patronage of the Jesuits and the remarkable success of the Society of Jesus in building churches and converting a full quarter of the Qing population (these Jesuits are said incorrectly to have reached Beijing through the Siberian overland route from Poland) seems to come from a Jesuit source. Unexplained linguistic borrowings like "burkhanniger" (probably Mongol *burqan-u ger,* "the god's yurt," a Buddhist shrine) highlight the internal heterogeneity of the text. Muscovite textual hybridity did not necessarily create robust texts, but it did encourage the synthesis of a wide-ranging selection of testimonies.[47]

Spafarii and the Art of Hybridity

Veniukov's awkward grappling with his sources looks even stranger in light of the fact that a detailed and factually reliable account of the Qing conquest and empire had been available at the Ambassadorial Bureau for a decade by the time he began to write. Its author was a Moldavian aristocrat named Nikolai Spafarii (a.k.a. Nicolae Milescu). Born to a Greek family in 1636, he was educated both in Orthodox Constantinople and in Catholic Padua and was comfortable in Latin and in Greek, spoken as well as written. By the time he was thirty years old, he had traveled all over Europe, including France, Prussia, and Sweden, on a variety of official and unofficial diplomatic missions. But in 1668 he became involved in a plot against the sitting hospodar of Moldavia, hoping to replace him on the throne after accusing him of treason against the Ottoman Empire. The plot fell through. Milescu was arrested, his nose was slit through the middle as a visible and disqualifying mutilation, and he was exiled from Ottoman lands. Spafarii (this was actually a title, but he used it as a surname) arrived in Russia in 1671 as part of the entourage of Patriarch Dositheos II of Jerusalem, then conducting a high-profile visit to Moscow. Spafarii soon found a job as a translator at the Ambassadorial Bureau, which made him a protégé of the powerful, Western-aligned boyar Artamon Matveev. Spafarii's roots in the Orthodox-Catholic contact zone of the Balkans, which he shared with other leading seventeenth-century Muscovite intellectuals, made him a useful asset for a state that was deeply dependent on foreign expertise.[48] During the next few years, Spafarii's star rose steadily at court, and in 1674 it was decided that he would lead a grand embassy to the Kangxi emperor in Beijing.[49]

In Beijing, Spafarii met Ferdinand Verbiest, the leader of the Jesuit mission in China, who had been sent over to his residence by the Qing emperor to serve as a Latin-Manchu translator for the embassy. Verbiest hoped that currying the favor of the Russian tsar would help Jesuit missionaries obtain permission to travel to China by an overland route through Siberia, which he regarded as safer than sailing to Macao around the Cape of Good Hope. Although the sources do not give us any reason to think that Verbiest actually gave Spafarii any secret information, he certainly cultivated the impression of being a trusted contact in the Qing capital. Spafarii went home with a letter from Verbiest to the tsar and a number of books, including Martino Martini's 1655 *Novus Atlas Sinensis* and 1654 *De Bello Tartarico*.[50] These two texts would form the foundation of Spafarii's greatest work, the misleadingly named *Description of the First Part of the Universe . . . (Opisanie per-*

vyia chasti vselennyiia . . .). In essence it is a translation of the *Novus Atlas Sinensis*, with original portions or extracts from external materials in the beginning and at the end, bound together with a description of the Amur River that Spafarii acquired from a third party before or during his journey and with the translated *De Bello Tartarico* added at the end.[51] The *Opisanie* exists in dozens of manuscript copies, dating from its date of composition (1677–1678) to the early nineteenth century.[52] This suggests that in its time it was the most popular description of China available in Muscovy or in the Russian Empire. Although it was not printed until 1910, not a single Russian-language published work of comparable length or depth existed until 1774, when Du Halde's *Description . . . de la Chine* was translated and issued in Russian.

No other Russian manuscript work dealing with China has survived in such a diverse array of forms. Ex-libris inscriptions and other paratextual material reveal a wide range of readers, from clerics to nobles and merchants. They also hint at the breadth of the uses to which the book's readers put it. A 1735 copy contains a long and turgid acrostic dedication to a cousin of Catherine I, spelling out "WITH THE INDUSTRIOUSNESS AND EAGER STRIVING OF HER GRACE THE LADY-IN-WAITING MARFA KARLOVNA SKOVRONSKAIA."[53] Another copy, from fifty years later, says "this book was given to me in Kazan in the year 1778 by Lieutenant General and Cavalier Count Pëtr Fëdorovich Apraksin, which he received in Dalmatov Monastery [in the southern Urals], where he was imprisoned for eloping with the lady-in-waiting Countess Razumovskaia and for marrying her while having a living wife."[54] A third came from the personal library of the favorite Vasilii Golitsyn; a fourth belonged to a Moscow merchant.[55] Although secular manuscript books, even those with such an evidently wide circulation, are typically sidelined in both Russian and Western studies of readership and book culture, indications are that Spafarii's text is highly unusual in the geographical and social breadth of its circulation.[56]

What made its success possible was a convergence between Spafarii's Latin learning and the Muscovite tradition of frontier texts. Leafing through his 1910 published version of Spafarii's *Opisanie,* the early twentieth-century scholar John Baddeley reluctantly accused Spafarii of deliberate plagiarism.[57] In part, he had good reason to: nearly the entire text is borrowed

from Martini, and certain passages are altered to conceal Jesuit authorship. But what Baddeley failed to appreciate was the extent to which the
Opisanie is a hybrid text in the Muscovite tradition, one never intended
to be seen as original work. Spafarii's authorial manuscript has survived
unrecognized among any number of derivative versions since 1678, because
it lacks a title page, attribution, signature, or any indication of authorship; an apparently eighteenth-century scrawl on the end flyleaf pro-
claims, "This book was written nobody knows by whom."[58] Few of the
surviving versions mention Spafarii's name, and many are misclassified
in library catalogs as cosmographies or the like. (By contrast, even plagiarized books published in Western Europe in this period generally came
with authorial attributions to the plagiarist.) In the context of an essentially medieval authorship regime like Muscovy's, plagiarism as such did
not exist.

Instead of claiming the entire work for himself, Spafarii hybridized it
with other sources in his possession. Because (as his readers well knew) he
had never gone south of Beijing, he had nothing to tweak in most of Martini's original Latin text, which gives the work its basic structure. In the north,
however, Spafarii found the work lacking and incorporated a description of
the Amur composed by a Cossack who had traveled in that region.[59] He also
deployed the same kinds of geographical sources previously used by Veniukov and Godunov to reconstruct the northern routes into China by land
and sea. The Amur description itself incorporated the testimony of native
informants, to which Spafarii added his own contribution: "the askaniama
[*ashan i amban*, i.e., Spafarii's escorting Manchu official Mala] said that
you can sail from the mouth of the Amur to China but it is far, because you
need to circle the great Korean peninsula which extends far into the sea."[60]
Finally, Spafarii littered the text with marginal notes dealing with everything from Mongol saddles to the deliciousness of lychees, talking back to
all of these diverse informants and bringing the text together as the work
of a single compiler.[61] He also composed a map that built on the legacy of
Godunov and contained an unparalleled level of detail.[62] The purpose of
Muscovite intelligence gathering was not to produce original documents
but to assemble individual testimonies into a collective whole, if not always
a coherent one.

As he negotiated the Treaty of Nerchinsk in 1689, the boyar Fëdor Golovin drew directly and indirectly on the entire body of knowledge the Muscovites had been able to build up over the preceding half century. He relied on the tradition of composite maps and chorographies from Godunov to Veniukov as he tried to determine territorial boundaries. Ethnographic observations collected by state envoys from Petlin onward helped Russians decode the interethnic relationships of the Inner Asian world. Commercial and diplomatic intelligence from Bukharans and other foreign informants defined the stakes for Russia's immersion in that world. The Muscovite corpus of hybrid texts about Siberia and the Qing Empire, then, was not the product of an intellectual establishment hidebound by illiteracy, xenophobia, and superstition. Rather, it reveals an official bureaucracy scrambling to collate and reconcile a growing pile of diverse and global sources about a topic of unusually pressing strategic interest, with greater or lesser success.

Muscovy was by no means alone in this process: as we will see, Jesuits and other Western experts were also trying to synthesize information about China and other "Oriental" lands from different sources. Where Muscovite efforts were shaped by institutions that deemphasized authorship and were preoccupied with pragmatic questions, Western investigations were framed by the twin pillars of the Republic of Letters and the early modern book market. French and English book collectors began to assemble libraries of Persian, Arabic, and Chinese books in the middle of the seventeenth century. Translations, glossaries, and compiled histories were the mainstay of this enterprise, one that took shape largely in private studies across Europe rather than bureaucratic offices.[63] For European intellectuals, China was most interesting as a source of luxury goods and as an ethnographic case study, particularly insofar as it reflected competing ideas about the origins and nature of "politeness," civilization, and enlightenment. Synthetic works by writers who never went to China, such as Jean-Baptiste Du Halde, Nicolaas Witsen, and, at an even greater remove, philosophers like Voltaire, were far more influential in Europe than any work by a merchant or diplomat who had physically gone there.[64]

While individual Muscovites and most foreigners in Russian service showed no willingness to participate in the Republic of Letters, this foreign book market created an unforeseen second audience for their work. As Russians continued to develop their intelligence apparatus in Siberia, the knowledge they produced—which in theory was supposed to remain locked in the kremlins of Moscow and Tobolsk—was eagerly harvested and redistributed by Westerners who spent time, energy, and cash to obtain access to the maps and documents emanating from the Chinese frontier. By the Petrine era, Russia's Siberian venture had come to shape the European encounter with Northeast Asia.

Chapter 2

Seeing China through Russian Eyes

T HE MUSCOVITE CONQUEST of Siberia placed Russia alongside other European empires in the global colonial venture that defined the early modern era, yet both Muscovites and Europeans were uneasy about their relationship. Russian elites held the state together with an ideology of religious and cultural self-reliance, even as that framework was undermined by their dependence on servitors and technologies from abroad.[1] The absence of Russians in the Western European scholarly world made it difficult to take them seriously as equals, and Westerners relentlessly portrayed Muscovy as "rude and barbarous" despite the diplomatic common ground they shared.[2] But Muscovy's arrival in Inner Asia meant that at least in one area, Russian observers—no matter how unscholarly or semiliterate—were on an equal footing with their counterparts in other empires. Seventeenth-century Europeans were just as interested in China as seventeenth-century Russians, and neither party held a monopoly on information. By the time Peter the Great died in 1725, Russian texts about the region had been circulating in Europe for over a century, both through licit authorship and illicit espionage. The Muscovite state's effort to understand Inner Asia left an enduring mark on early European writing about Siberia and China, an intellectual exchange interrupted rather than accelerated by later Westernization.

Two centuries earlier, as Muscovy was breaking free of its Chinggisid connections, Europeans had known about the fabulously wealthy Chinese state mostly through books like Marco Polo's *Travels*. But in the 1500s, fragmentary reports gave way to direct contact as European ships plied the waters between the Indian Ocean and the Pacific in search of lucrative commercial opportunities. Soon there were other forms of contact as well. In 1552 the Jesuit

St. Francis Xavier died off the south China coast in a failed effort to start a Catholic mission there; by 1601 Jesuits were being invited to audiences in the Forbidden City. A flourishing Portuguese trading post developed at Macao, near the major port of Guangzhou (which soon came to be known everywhere in Europe as Canton). Despite these successes, however, Europeans faced enormous difficulties in China. Finding a toehold in the capital proved impossible for anyone except missionaries; opportunities to travel beyond Canton were few. Even to reach China required a lengthy, dangerous sea voyage around the Cape of Good Hope or a treacherous journey through the non-Christian states of Southwest and Central Asia.[3]

Muscovites, on the other hand, had few problems getting to China. Once diplomatic contact with the Qing was established, there was always a relatively safe, albeit lengthy, northern route to Beijing via Siberia, Mongolia, and the Great Wall. A route controlled in almost its entire span by a Christian power was powerfully attractive to commercial as well religious interests in Europe.[4] For all their efforts, Western powers never were able to use the Siberian road as a means for travel to China. Instead, it became a channel for something else: texts, maps, and images, eagerly consumed by European governments and book buyers. By the end of the seventeenth century, these readers ensured that almost nothing related to military, diplomatic, and commercial relationships between the two empires remained a secret in Europe. But tracing the precise chain of transmission can be difficult. In 1698, a London physician named Jodocus Crull wrote confidently that "the Muscovites having once been made sensible of . . . the vast Profit that must needs arise to their own Country . . . have left no stone unturn'd, not only to make the best Discovery they could of those *Tartarian* Nations, but also by settling a fair Correspondence with them, to open to themselves a free passage into China."[5] Crull was a hack who composed translations and compiled books on hot topics of the day, often with almost no original content of his own. He was certainly no expert on Russia, any more than he was a specialist on Spain.[6] So how could he make such an assertive claim and then describe, in detail, a portion of Inner Asia where no English speaker had ever set foot?

An invaluable tool for tracing such connections in the early modern era is textual borrowing, though it requires us to step away from our familiar vocabulary of "facts," "data," and "information."[7] When an early modern writer wanted to fill their text with data about a remote and inaccessible country, their instinct was typically not to survey the range of available testimonies and present an overall analysis in their own words. Instead, they generally turned to the closest and, in their view, the best source they had and copied it as needed directly into their text.[8] This was doubly true in the case of a writer like Crull, who was on a tight schedule (the afterglow of Peter the Great's Grand Embassy to Europe in 1697–1698, which made the incognito tsar a celebrity everywhere he went) and thus borrowed liberally from such predecessors as John Milton.[9] Crull took his account of Russo-Qing relations directly from a 1693 English translation of the Jesuit Philippe Avril's *Voyage en divers états d'Europe*.[10] Avril's own account was plagiarized from a book by Nikolai Spafarii, which, as we have seen, was itself a hybrid text borrowed from Western and non-Western sources, including a 1655 publication by the Jesuit Martino Martini. What Crull's well-timed plagiarism (a word first popularized early in this period) shows us is that early modern "facts" existed not in the form of decontextualized bits of abstract data but more often as concrete passages of text passed freely from one book to another.[11]

The best image of this process the era produced was Laurence Sterne's Slawkenbergius (from *Tristram Shandy,* published in 1759–1767), the writer of a treatise on noses, who goes "begging, borrowing, and stealing . . . all that had been wrote or wrangled thereupon in the schools and porticoes of the learned" and produces a "thorough stitched DIGEST" as a result.[12] Undoing the stitches of early modern European writing about China and Siberia reveals how European avidity, Muscovite dependence on foreigners, and the relative imperviousness of Northeast Asia to European explorers came together to produce a transnational intellectual commerce. Muscovy was a central rather than peripheral part of the early European encounter with China, above all because it was a source and a conduit for privileged information.[13]

The English (after 1707, British) were especially significant customers for Russian knowledge. Russian sources were so important to them because they had begun to be aware not only of the growing scale of Spanish, Portuguese, and Dutch entanglement with Ming trade but also the place of the Ming in a broader East Asian world—as powerfully suggested by a series of Ming maps brought back to London starting in the 1580s.[14] Muscovy became a keystone of the English effort to circumvent their rivals' dominance. From the middle of the sixteenth century, English (as well as Dutch) navigators began actively looking for a northeastern sea route around the Arctic Circle north of

Siberia.[15] But going *through* Russia was even more promising. In addition to the safety offered by the overland route, the English merchants of the Muscovy Company would be able to capitalize on their long-established and sometimes even monopolistic relationship with Russian and (indirectly) Inner Asian merchants.

The expansion of European commercial contacts and small-scale imperial ventures in the Indian and Pacific Oceans fueled the development of a whole genre of the Republic of Letters. Intellectuals, of course, had long corresponded with one another through letters both open and closed, and the number of surviving manuscripts of, say, Marco Polo testifies to the popularity of travel writing in the medieval era. Yet the sixteenth-century emergence of news networks and of a transnational print culture fundamentally redefined the genre. As the diversity and number of travelers abroad increased, so did the number of venues and the scope of audiences for their work; scholarly and nonscholarly readers alike participated in the compilation, distribution, and redistribution of testimonies about foreign lands. By the end of the seventeenth century, no field of intellectual endeavor remained untouched by the translations and travelogues pouring into Europe from abroad.[16]

European Intelligence Learns from Muscovy

Russian sources formed part of this transimperial intellectual enterprise from an early period. Between 1582 and 1625, Richard Hakluyt and his successor Samuel Purchas published the most influential English compilation of travel narratives. Hakluyt's *Principall Navigations . . . of the English Nation* (1589–1600) grew to sixteen volumes and covered testimonies from the entire known world. Purchas's compilation, the *Hakluytus Posthumus,* built on Hakluyt's and grew to twenty. Volume 14 of this latter work, devoted to Arctic exploration in general and Russia and Siberia in particular, contained a translation of Ivashko Petlin's report on his embassy to the Ming, obtained through the English ambassador and Muscovy Company agent Sir John Merrick.[17] Audiences in England had access to confidential Russian documents about relations with China a scant six years after they arrived in the Kremlin, and the fact that Muscovy in the 1620s had no secular printing presses or broad reading publics of any kind meant far more people probably read Petlin in English than in Russian—despite the fact that Petlin neither spoke any Western language nor had ever traveled west of Moscow. The intrigues of the intelligence world as it played out in Russia had thus spilled over into the European republic of letters.

In Europe, the lines between scholarly knowledge production and the world of spies and informants could be as vague then as they are now. Even if given compilers or historians were not themselves purveyors of privileged information to state officials, they were often recipients and publishers of such documents. Only a few degrees of separation sufficed to erase their origins, if indeed this was even necessary. Much of what academic Europeans knew about the Islamic world before the nineteenth century was the product of just this kind of intellectual knowledge laundering: books whose focus was historical or religious were based on materials gathered by diplomats and consuls, who themselves worked through agents on the ground.[18] In the Chinese context, the most important sources of information were the Jesuits, who provided a steady stream of reports on their activities in China. These reached a new level in 1685, when Louis XIV sent a team of mathematicians and other scientific experts to Beijing to establish their own independently funded French Jesuit mission and prioritize scholarly work alongside their missionary activities. It was essential that they be French subjects, because this mission was specifically linked to the ambitions of the French state in a complex diplomatic game involving Portugal, the Netherlands, and the Vatican.[19] These missionaries became the principal producers of knowledge on China in eighteenth-century Europe; eventually their Parisian correspondent Jean-Baptiste Du Halde authored the most influential work on the subject, the *Description . . . de la Chine,* in 1735.

Petlin's report, for Europeans, represented the earliest textual sketch of what it would be like to visit China by the northern route instead of the southern maritime one. But by the middle of the seventeenth century, the Russo-Chinese connection had become real for Englishmen and other Europeans in a far more concrete way: rhubarb, a medicinal root obtained from the Sichuan-Gansu region of China via Bukharan merchants, became a major Russian export to Europe by the 1650s, with thousands of pounds sold every year in London and elsewhere. As a purgative for digestive systems ruined by the rich diets of wealthy Europeans, Russian rhubarb was a daily reminder of the benefits of the overland route.[20] For the Dutch, who had consolidated control over Japanese trade with Europe through Nagasaki but had been driven out of Taiwan by the Qing in 1662, Russian Northeast Asia held the promise of unexploited commercial potential. Dutch trade everywhere in East Asia was linked to the collection of information, for which the Russian foreign-policy establishment was a crucial source.[21] Prospecting the Russian Ambassadorial Bureau for information soon became a general pastime, even for states whose practical interest in Northeast Asia was more remote.

Other states also became interested in Russo-Chinese contacts. In 1673, a Swedish military agent named Erik Palmqvist traveled to Moscow, where he obtained no fewer than sixteen different maps, including Godunov's 1667 map of Siberia and a later one from 1673. He "secretly observed and drew them, with risk to my own person, and also received information from Russian citizens in exchange for money." Palmqvist's album is one of the earliest surviving cartographic sources on Siberia.[22] After his return from Beijing, Spafarii, perhaps smarting from his lackluster post-China career, was the primary point of contact for foreigners in search of privileged information. In 1684–1687, the Swedish envoy J. G. Sparwenfeld was dispatched to Moscow, where he met Spafarii and "had a long talk with him about his Chinese journey." Though this brief encounter seems casual, Sparwenfeld returned to Stockholm with (among other things) a map of Siberia and a copy of Spafarii's magnum opus.[23] In 1689, the French traveler Foy de la Neuville, who served as a kind of unofficial agent for the French and Polish crowns, also met Spafarii, found him "very clever," and had numerous conversations with him. Neuville mentions Spafarii's reticence, because "telling me all I wanted to know could have earned him a beating on the tsars' orders." Yet the unpublished manuscript of his work (unlike the published version) says that Spafarii had been sent to Beijing "on the pretext of establishing a peace treaty with the Chinese, but actually solely to discover a means of establishing overland commerce through Muscovy." Neuville's geopolitics are garbled, but it is clear that Spafarii was not as discreet as the published version suggests.[24]

Religious and intellectual ideas, more abstract but no less important than commerce, linked Russo-Chinese relations with grand political projects. European visionaries were drawn to Russia's geographical location as a Christian state placed directly between Europe and China. In the 1670s, a Saxon envoy named Lorenz Rinhuber attempted to persuade the Muscovite court that Russia was unusually well placed to mediate between the two powers. This proposal may even have helped motivate the Russians to send Spafarii to Beijing.[25] The philosopher Gottfried Leibniz had even grander plans for Russia. In his 1697 work *Novissima Sinica,* he praised Providence for ordaining that Peter I, "the Monarch of the Muscovites, whose vast dominions connect China and Europe," had seen fit to emulate Western European civilization: Russia would serve as the nexus between two great civilizations. Leibniz did not restrict himself to idle musings. His correspondence with Russian and Western diplomats and statesmen reveals repeated efforts to bring into being a Siberian overland route for Westerners to travel to Beijing and back.[26]

Although Leibniz was not preoccupied with Christian missionary goals, the Jesuits were among his principal clients in the search for an overland route. Ferdinand Verbiest's concerns about the dangers of the naval voyage were widely shared by other Jesuit leaders. The first major problem with the sea route was mortality. In 1687, the Jesuit Philippe Couplet lamented that out of six hundred missionaries sent to China only one hundred had arrived, "the rest having consummated their sacrifice along the way by means of disease or shipwreck." This was an exaggeration, but around a quarter of China-bound Jesuits—the society's elite, who had often trained for years to obtain this highly desirable assignment—did die en route to Macao.[27] There was a further problem, however. The China mission relied on the Portuguese Padroado, the authority over the Eastern Hemisphere granted by the papacy to the Portuguese crown by the 1494 Treaty of Tordesillas. But by the middle of the seventeenth century, Portuguese power in the Indian and Pacific Oceans was at a nadir, displaced by Dutch—hence Protestant—competition. Moreover, French Jesuits were reluctant to rely on Portuguese ships owing both to interimperial and inter-Jesuit rivalry. The sea route thus posed a political as well as a practical problem.[28]

The Jesuits thus turned to Russia for eminently practical reasons. By 1687 (a year before his death), Verbiest was corresponding with Rome about the Russian route and reporting that he had already had productive meetings with the Muscovite envoy Veniukov about the issue.[29] From the Western end, Rome entrusted the project to the Czech Jesuit Jerzy David, then in Moscow as part of a small delegation.[30] David managed to procure a map of the route from Moscow to Beijing, possibly from Spafarii or another Ambassadorial

Bureau official—and at just the right time, because in 1689 the Jesuits were expelled from Muscovy after the fall of Princess Sofiia and her Jesuit-friendly favorite Vasilii Golitsyn. At the same time, Verbiest's close Beijing associate Antoine Thomas sent his own set of maps to Rome, which bear marked similarities to David's. According to the seventeenth-century Jesuit historian T. I. Dunyn-Szpot, who was writing a history of the China mission as these events unfolded, Verbiest had managed to persuade the Russian envoy to give the Jesuits a copy of the map that Russians used on their way to Beijing. This common parentage likely accounts for the similarities between the maps. In this key period, Jesuits halfway across the world from each other were simultaneously struggling to take advantage of Russian geographical sources.[31] At the same time, Jesuit and Russian agendas in China were also becoming more closely aligned: even as the Treaty of Nerchinsk opened the way for Russian caravans to travel directly to Beijing, it also radically improved the fortunes of the China Jesuits, whose participation in the negotiations contributed to the Kangxi emperor's 1692 decree of toleration for Christianity.[32]

Philippe Avril was the most influential Jesuit author to take up the Russian route as a project. Under the influence of Verbiest's earlier plans, Avril first traveled throughout the Middle East and the southern shore of the Caspian Sea in search of a route to China through Muslim-controlled territories.[33] In 1686, however, a peace treaty between Russia and the Polish-Lithuanian Commonwealth made provision for anyone with a passport from the Polish king to travel through Muscovite lands. (The Jesuits had pushed for a special provision for missionaries to be allowed through to China, but Muscovite negotiators declared this to be superfluous.) Avril met with King Jan III Sobieski and obtained his support for a Jesuit expedition, but ultimately all the assembled missionaries were expelled from Russia at the last minute on the pretext of a border conflict in Siberia.[34] The fall of Regent Sofiia put a definitive end to Avril's plans, like David's. He returned to Paris bitterly disappointed, but the narrative of his travels he produced turned out to be a massive literary success.[35]

Avril's book, the *Voyage to Various Countries in Europe and Asia,* reveals both the extreme suspicion with which Jesuits were treated in Russia and, ironically, the numerous ways in which they justified that suspicion. He describes a grueling four-hour session of questioning by paranoid Muscovite officials "just as if we had been actual criminals."[36] Yet ten pages later, he offers readers a look at "what the Relations kept in the Moscow Chancellery tell us" about the "many new routes which have taken them gradually towards China"—reflecting his success in obtaining privileged information. Avril's list of routes is in fact a free, adapted translation of the fifth chapter of Spafarii's *Opisanie pervyia chasti . . .* , entitled "Of what land routes there are to China, and where various Siberian peoples go." This chapter is one of Spafarii's original contributions to Martini's text; later, Crull would copy it from Avril.[37] Though the ease with which Avril was able to obtain a copy of Spafarii's text seems to suggest that it was not especially well hidden, the impression in Russia was unquestionably that Jesuit espionage had become brazen and unwelcome. An anonymous memoir written around 1699 (probably by the papal envoy Christoph Ignaz von Guarient) argued that it was "useless and dangerous to send missionaries to the Muscovite state" because "the Muscovites are convinced . . . that Roman missionaries . . . are studying the shortest routes [to China] . . . to acquire the goodwill and mercy of the Chinese, and that from this will come great ruin to the entire Muscovite state."[38] Evidently, even if Spafarii did not feel that it was totally safe to discuss privileged affairs with foreigners (as he indicated to Neuville), he felt no similar qualms about providing them with copies or extracts of his work. Yet Guarient's observation implies Muscovite authorities continued to regard the pursuit of such information as espionage.

The foreigner who had by far the greatest success in appropriating Russia's hybrid frontier texts was a Dutchman named Nicolaas Witsen, author of *Noord en oost Tartarye* (*North and East Tartary,* first published 1692, 2nd ed., 1705). He was born in 1641 in a wealthy Amsterdam family, received a law degree from Leiden University, and went on his only voyage to Russia in 1664–1665—before Spafarii had even arrived in Russia and before Pëtr Godunov had begun assembling information on China in Tobolsk.[39] In that brief sojourn, he managed to obtain a copy of Baikov's report, which he eventually published in Melchisédech Thévenot's *Recueil des voyages* (a Continental counterpart to Haklyut and Purchas).[40] In subsequent years, Witsen was elected burgomaster of Amsterdam thirteen times and numbered among the most influential Dutch statesmen of his generation. His approach to Russian intelligence was different from that of English or Swedish envoys. Instead of meeting Russia's Ambassadorial Bureau officials on their own turf, Witsen made contact with them as they conducted negotiations in Europe.

Eager for Witsen's support, powerful men like the Bureau head A. A. Vinius (who was a relative and whom the Dutchman eventually rescued when he fell into disfavor with the tsar) were happy to provide him with the geographical and ethnographic materials he craved. In addition to Vinius, who held the key to the Bureau's collections, after Peter's Grand Embassy of 1697, Witsen was also on good terms with Fëdor Golovin, the Russian negotiator at Nerchinsk, who became a key source. Finally, Witsen regularly corresponded with Peter the Great himself, whom he met during the embassy, and with A. A. Matveev, the powerful Russian ambassador in London, Paris, and The Hague.[41]

The result of this correspondence was one of the most compendious works on Eurasian history written before the nineteenth century. Its second edition consists of over a thousand pages of material covering roughly everything north and east of Constantinople (though not, for example, Japan, despite the extensive Dutch-Japanese contacts in that period). Starting from what is today called Manchuria, *Noord en oost Tartarye* winds its leisurely way counterclockwise, working westward toward the Crimea and then eastward through Siberia.[42] Beyond this loose structure, the book is a jumble of secondhand reports assembled and then jammed together without regard for conflict, repetition, or digression. The sheer diversity and originality of the sources Witsen was able to bring to bear on his chosen topic remains in some ways unmatched to this day. In his preface, he boasts of the scope of his work:

> I gave myself the goal of compiling a map and description of these little-known lands, because I had the opportunity to converse with many *Tartars, Greeks, Persians,* and with people who have experienced captivity in Asian lands. I have discoursed with Chinese who have visited *Tartary* and given me samples of Chinese and Tartar script; I have received communications from Dutchmen who have visited Beijing and Hocksieu [Fuzhou]. Besides this, I received intelligence from *Tartary* itself as well as *Muscovy, Astrakhan, Siberia, Persia, Georgia, Turkey.* Even from *India* I have received descriptions of life in East and Northeast Asia; from *Niuhe* [Manchuria], *Mongolia, Kalmuckia* [Jungharia], *Altyn* [Western Mongolia], *Siberia, Samoedia, Tungusia,* countries lying beyond the Chinese Wall.[43]

This passage, which appears to represent Witsen as the hub of a global intelligence network of monumental scope, in fact understates his reliance on Russia and its ethnographic collections. Of the seventeen places named in the second half of this passage, nine were covered almost entirely through Russian sources, and at least two more drew on them partially.[44]

Muscovite sources appear in Witsen's text in a number of forms. Sometimes they are direct translations of documents from Muscovite archives, reproduced with clear titles and a certain degree of fidelity—for instance, a direct copy of Baikov's report. But Witsen also had access to more obscure documents, such as "A report from a letter written from Selenginsk in 1687 about a voyage on Lake Baikal" (provided to him by Golovin).[45] In other cases, Russian sources include reports of conversations or correspondence, either with a named or an unnamed interlocutor. This can include Golovin himself or, say, "a Kalmyk prince with whom I conversed in Moscow."[46] Finally, certain passages that appear in text that seems to be Witsen's original work are in fact taken directly from Russian texts; for example, Witsen directly reproduces Spafarii's remark on the *askaniama*.[47] Indeed, Spafarii appears repeatedly unnamed in the text as "a Slavic writer whose works are still unpublished." Witsen quotes from him in describing Korea, apparently unaware that he is in fact quoting Spafarii's translation of Martini.[48]

With its overwhelming profusion of Russian materials, Witsen's *Noord en oost Tartarye* represents the convergence of late seventeenth-century European learned culture and the Muscovite practice of creating hybrid geographic texts about the Siberian borderlands. Much like Veniukov—part of whose *Opisanie novyia zemli . . .* appears in Witsen's book—the Dutch writer was less interested in creating a coherent, interpretive narrative than in the accumulation of available evidence. If this practice raised concerns among Muscovite elites for the secrecy of the information he published, they did not say so in writing. Instead Witsen seems to have deliberately restricted the circulation of his work (and his monumental map of Siberia) out of discretion.[49] In the 1730s, Philipp von Strahlenberg wrote that although "the Curious of our Times have flatter'd themselves with the Hopes of seeing a Treatise written by the late Mr. Nicholas Wittsen . . . the Copy of this Work, being bought by a great Prince and taken away from the Press, those Hopes were frustrated." The implication was that Peter the Great had deliberately bought and suppressed the book.[50] *Noord en oost Tartarye* was not widely available until the posthumous third edition, published in 1785—long after it had ceased to have any practical relevance in intelligence terms.[51] Still, Witsen played a major role in publishing other Russian texts about Siberia.

By the late seventeenth century, Muscovite documents had become so naturalized in the European Republic of Letters they no longer even appeared exotic. One reader who did attempt to reflect on the nature of his Russian sources was the renowned natural philosopher Robert Hooke. Between the 1680s and the 1700s, he acquired multiple translated, published versions of Petlin's and Baikov's travel accounts. But Hooke found these documents so unsatisfying that in December 1689 he decided to make them the occasion for a lecture at the Royal Society. "We are," he admitted, "obliged to all such travelers who give us an account of those things that they have remark'd in their travels . . . since they may give some usefull informations of another kind they deserve to be collected and adjoined to other informations concerning those places." But a narrative like Baikov's was almost worse than useless when compared with a Western map like Witsen's: "Neither the Latitude nor Longitude nor Distance noe nor what way or quarter one place lyes from the other all which are wanting in this Relation. Every one of which notwithstanding might with very little trouble have been observed and recorded." Hooke never asked under what circumstances these documents were produced or acquired or whether they had been intended for a learned scientific audience at all: in his mind, Petlin and Baikov were not native informants but participants in the European relationship with China, however poorly trained.[52]

Muscovite frontier intelligence had thus become entangled with Western intelligence in Moscow and from there with the European intellectual community. This entanglement was the result of some distinct features of the Muscovite knowledge regime—its remarkable and certainly unintentional porosity to outsiders, for instance—but also of aspects of the Russo-Qing encounter that would survive far into the nineteenth century. Though Muscovites did not intend or realize this, their production of knowledge about China was already becoming more relevant to Muscovy's connection to Europe than it was to promoting Russian power in China itself—perhaps inevitably, since it was concentrated some three thousand miles away from the Qing border. The two embassies that followed the 1689 Treaty of Nerchinsk, Isbrandt Ides's in 1693–1695 and Lev Izmailov's in 1719–1721, only reinforced this pattern: they led to influential publications that far outpaced their meager diplomatic results.

Russia's Foreign Diplomats and European Letters

Although European agents acquired Russian diplomatic documents on a wide scale, most Europeans who were interested in Russia's connections to China did not learn about them from such texts. Instead, the most popular genre was the published work of foreign-born employees of the Muscovite state who had traveled to Beijing on diplomatic missions. The Russians whose works traveled west before the 1690s were not authors in the conventional sense, because they did not publish. Nikolai Spafarii, as we have seen, was the principal contact for foreign visitors to Moscow who wanted to learn about his voyage to Beijing. Yet he himself never deliberately published a single line, and Witsen's publications of parts of his work never acknowledged his authorship by name. Despite his extensive connections and Western education, then, his audience in the West was ultimately considerably smaller than Petlin's or Baikov's unwitting one. (In addition to Thévenot's publication and the extract in Witsen, Baikov's report appeared in at least one edition by the Prussian sinologist Andreas Müller.[53]) In the 1690s, however, this calculus would change, as the Germans Isbrandt Ides and his secretary Adam Brand published widely read accounts of their embassy to Kangxi's court. The fact that they were not Russian proved to be decisive. In the next century and a half, Russia's relationship to the Qing would be narrated to Western Europe by people who maintained a certain distance from Muscovite political culture.

Ides was a merchant from then-Danish Schleswig-Holstein who probably moved to Russia around 1687, at the age of thirty, having already amassed a solid commercial fortune. His personal proximity to Peter the Great led to his being named head of an embassy to Beijing, which he regarded primarily as a lucrative commercial opportunity: instead of achieving any of his minor diplomatic goals, he realized nearly a 50 percent profit on the goods he brought with him and acquired a pile of commodities, which he immediately distributed to creditors and allies upon his return. Since neither he nor Brand spoke Latin, it is unlikely that any serious calculations about dialogue with the Jesuits influenced the decision to send them to Beijing: more likely, they were simply in the right place at the right time.[54]

Reflecting widespread interest in this account, an abbreviated initial version of Ides's voyage appeared in Berlin via a diplomatic source in Moscow only a year after his return, as part of a compilation by Christian Mentzel; later, Leibniz published a Latin translation of this version.[55] The full version, however, was only printed much later, in 1704, as part of a Witsen-supervised Dutch edition. In the ensuing two decades, this landmark text would go through a half dozen more editions in English, German, and French. (The English actually antedated the German by a year despite the fact that Ides had originally written in Hamburg dialect.) Later it would also be included in such composite works as the 1737 English edition of Cornelius de Bruyn's *Travels into Muscovy, Persia, and Parts of the East-Indies.* Meanwhile, Adam Brand's notes had appeared separately in Hamburg in 1698 and were then reissued in English and French. Ides and Brand, despite the fact that they were neither scholarly nor particularly curious, and despite the insignificance of their embassy, became by far the most widely distributed sources on Russo-Qing relations—far outpacing, for instance, Witsen's own.[56]

Neither publication was in any sense illicit. Peter the Great specifically authorized Ides to print maps and engravings of Siberia to illustrate his journey, and Ides obliged with gusto—the final version included twenty-nine images and a map.[57] Unlike *Noord en oost Tartarye,* neither Ides nor Brand included privileged materials or revealed confidential information. In comparison with the official diplomatic report Ides submitted on his return, the published travelogues are silent about the details of his instructions or the substance of Russo-Qing negotiations, secrecy in which was considered part of his responsibility; details of court ceremonies, on the other hand, appear to have been fair game for publication abroad. But such privileged details form a small minority of Ides and Brand's material: the report itself is less than thirty pages long, while the books are many times longer.[58] What attracted audiences to their work, in addition to the material on Beijing, were the numerous details about the towns, landscapes, and non-Russian peoples of Siberia, which the official report omitted. Ides satisfied their ethnographic curiosity in an exoticizing style designed for the benefit of ordinary readers rather than diplomatic experts, describing indigenous customs and practices like eating with chopsticks.[59] In effect, Ides and Brand gave readers a tour of two unknown lands for the price of one.

Unlike Ides and Brand, whose involvement with the southeastern frontier was accidental and fleeting, another foreigner named Lorents Lang (Lorenz Lange) spoke from a position of much greater authority. Like many of the other foreigners in Siberia, he was probably a prisoner of war captured at Poltava in 1709; unlike most of them, Lang ended up with a lifelong career in the imperial hierarchy, dying a vice-governor of Irkutsk in 1753. In the intervening years, Lang became a pivotal figure in the eighteenth-century history of Russo-Qing contact. He traveled to Beijing no fewer than six times between 1715 and 1737, sometimes spending years at a time there. Journals relating to four of these voyages were published in various European languages in the eighteenth century, although only two of these publications were contemporary.[60] The most well known of these was published in Friedrich Weber's 1721 work *Das Veränderte Rußland* (known in English as *The Present State of Russia*). Weber, whom Lang had met in 1718 on his return from Beijing, was among the first Westerners to provide a systematic assessment of the transformation that had taken place in Russia during the reign of Peter the Great; two editions in English and two in French appeared within four years. Although Lang's diary did not fit neatly with the rest of Weber's text, it certainly served to demonstrate Russia's widening ambitions in the new era.[61]

Within the pages of Weber's book, the 1715–1716 journal was followed by a more descriptive text by Lang, one that literally crossed borders. This brief but comprehensive "Description of China" illustrates some of the peculiar ways in which the Muscovite manuscript tradition intersected with the world of published work. It covers topics like science and history but also draws on manuscript materials Lang acquired from Jesuits in Beijing to send to the Holy Roman Empire.[62] Although it is unclear if he ever composed a version of his description in Russian, several contemporary manuscript copies, without any indication of source or authorship, exist in Russian translation; they must have been made before the text was sent to the German lands.[63] In other words, Lang's description was also able to circulate in Russia independently of Western mediation, though a separate Russian version is translated directly from Weber.[64] As a composite of Russian, Qing, and Jesuit sources, assembled by concatenation and circulated anonymously, Lang's

"Description" was just like a traditional Muscovite hybrid text. Unlike Pet-lin's and Baikov's reports and the extracts from Spafarii popularized in Eu-rope, however, Lang also disseminated his text deliberately through the Eu-ropean marketplace of print.

The most important eighteenth-century direct source about Russia and the Qing for the English-speaking world was in many ways an anomaly—not least because it was published long after the others. This was the Scot John Bell's *Travels from St. Petersburgh in Russia, to various parts of Asia,* first published in Glasgow in 1763 and widely circulated thereafter (including in Russia, where it was published in 1774). Despite the late date of its publication, it contains travel notes from Bell's youth as a doctor in the Izmailov embassy four decades earlier. Since Bell had no particular diplomatic role and was not entrusted with any privileged assignments, there is no official Russian version with which to compare it; his charms lay elsewhere, as a keen, detail-oriented, and often funny observer of Qing and Siberian life. He notes, for example, that "when a Chinese and a Tartar are angry at one another, the Tartar, in reproach, calls the Chinese louse-eater; and the latter, in return, calls the other fish-skin coat; because the Mantzur Tartars, who live near the river Amoor, subsist by fishing, and, in summer, wear coats made out of the skins of fishes."[65]

The success of Bell's work testifies not just to the enduring appeal of the Russo-Chinese frontier in Western Europe but also to the closure of that fron-tier to Western readers. This break was rooted, as we will see, in the Petrine reorganization of Russia's intelligence institutions, but it also had to do with the fact that Russian elites were increasingly more interested in European in-stead of domestic writing on China. After the Izmailov embassy's return, both British state archives (like the papers of the various British resident ambassadors in St. Petersburg) and publications fall almost completely silent on the topic of Russo-Qing relations. The most an eighteenth-century British reader would have been able to learn was that there was some trade between Russia and China at Kiakhta, though it was occasionally halted.[66] To fill the gap, in the 1760s books like John Bell's—drawing on long-outdated information—were marketed as providing accounts of "those Parts . . . which are like to be the Scene of Action in the War apprehended between the two potent Empires of Russia and China."[67] Though rising tensions in that era were real, Western European readers had none of the context needed to un-

derstand the background to the anticipated conflict. Only the work of William Coxe, a British scholar and clergyman who visited the region under
Catherine II's patronage in the 1770s, brought European readers up to date:
in 1780, he finally traced the history of the relationship from the conquest of
Siberia to the present and described the day-to-day workings of the Kiakhta
trade.[68]

In other fields the mid-eighteenth century also saw direct connections decline. In 1730, Strahlenberg's *Das nord- und ostliche Theil von Europa und Asia*
(*The Northern and Eastern Part of Europe and Asia*) became the first competitor to Witsen's restricted *Noord en oost Tartarye* to reach a wide audience.
Strahlenberg, who had lived in Tobolsk for a decade, had every opportunity
to produce a text superior to Witsen's in the scope and quality of its documentary research. Yet he makes almost no mention of the Qing, provides
details about Siberia that are much more rudimentary than Witsen's, and
substitutes speculation about linguistic origins for Witsen's primary-source
evidence.[69] The document pipeline that had worked so well for Witsen, funneling texts from Siberia to Moscow and thence to Amsterdam, was now essentially sealed, largely because the porous Muscovite intelligence apparatus
was no longer available as a source of information.

One reason might have been that the circulation of these texts in Russia
itself was also more restricted. Although Petrine Westernization created a
secular print market and a limited system of state schools, no substantial
printed descriptions of China appeared until the work of Du Halde was
translated in the 1770s. Nor did any manuscript supplant Spafarii. The only
remotely comparable document that survives in more than one copy is
Savva Vladislavich's *Secret Information about the Strength and Condition of
the Qing State* (*Sekretnaia informatsiia o sile i sostoianii Kitaiskago gosudarstva*), composed in 1731. In this intelligence report Vladislavich draws on
personal observations as well as Spafarii and a number of contemporary Jesuit and European writers to provide an up-to-date secret assessment of
Qing power, urging caution and farsightedness in planning for a military
confrontation. The handful of surviving copies of this text show no indications of sale, ownership, or use, like ex-libris inscriptions or marginalia. If it
circulated, its range was confined to a narrow set of institutions.[70] Instead,
all evidence points to the fact that for Russian manuscript (and presumably

print) consumers, Spafarii continued to fill the role more contemporary works might have played until new translated publications overtook him by the last quarter of the century. This meant, of course, that Russians were relying on a Jesuit work from 1655 for well over one hundred years.

For Western European—especially British—readers, too, the legacy of this period of Muscovite-European encounter was both durable and subsequently unmatched. References to publications about Russia and China appear in the unlikeliest of British sources. The papers of the dissenting minister Samuel Say contain some reflections on Ides, likely from the 1720s.[71] In 1742, the twelve-year-old future botanist Richard Pulteney copied a section of Ides's work into one of his notebooks, complete with an elaborate vignette.[72] These readers were probably looking through Ides to learn about Siberia, not China, but the information his book contained about Beijing and the northern parts of the Qing in general was uncommon in other English sources. These eager consumers of writing from Muscovy were not fully conscious of the informational infrastructures that underlay their reading nor of the role played by Muscovite bureaucracies in making the genre possible—but they were influenced by these infrastructures nonetheless, and their disappearance would leave a void.

Unexpectedly, traces of the infrastructure that linked Europe to China through Russia appear in eighteenth-century British literature instead. Daniel Defoe's sequel to *Robinson Crusoe,* 1719's *The Farther Adventures of Robinson Crusoe,* eventually takes its hero through China and into Siberia. This final portion takes its local color from publications like Ides's. Having traveled from Macao to Beijing with his friend, a Portuguese navigator, Robinson finds himself stranded until he learns some delightful news, that "there was a great Caravan of *Muscovite* and *Polish* Merchants in the City, and they were preparing to set out on their Journey by land to *Muscovy* within four or five Weeks. . . . I confess, I was surpris' d with his News, a secret Joy spread itself over my whole Soul, which I cannot describe, and never felt before or since."[73] The joy Crusoe feels, of course, is the sudden realization that China is in fact connected to Europe through Russia. The caravan on which Crusoe will rely for his journey home is the Russian one that European readers knew so well from reading accounts like those of Ides. (Indeed, Crusoe is now commemorated with a public monument in Tobolsk for his positive remarks on the city.)

This caravan also forms the backbone of Oliver Goldsmith's *The Citizen of the World,* first published in the *Public Ledger* in 1760–1761. This work takes the form of letters written "from Lien Chi Altangi to the care of Fipsihi, resident in Moscow; to be forwarded by the Russian caravan to Fum Hoam, first president of the ceremonial academy at Pekin in China." Altangi is a man who has known "all the rigours of Siberian skies," but in London finds himself in an alien and very distant world (which Goldsmith, in imitation of Montesquieu's *Lettres Persanes*, hopes to criticize). Only the slim thread of the Russian trade route connects him with Beijing; it is, as in Defoe, the final trace of Leibniz's imagined chain connecting the European and Chinese civilizations. Unbeknownst to Goldsmith, just three years before the *Citizen*'s publication the caravan had made its final journey.[74]

What Goldsmith and Defoe knew but we have forgotten is that the early European encounter with East Asia—which has buttressed countless narratives about the rise of the global and helped spark the "crisis of the European conscience" that, for some, led to the Enlightenment—was not just about merchants and missionaries and their perilous sea voyages.[75] It was also an overland Russo-Qing encounter to which Western Europeans were spectators, watching from a distance as Russians signed treaties with the Qing emperor, established permanent footholds in Beijing's Inner City, and sent caravan after caravan without fear of vanishing abruptly into the briny deep somewhere between Lisbon and Macao, all of them advantages thus far inaccessible to Western powers. Instead of being eternally at the periphery of an ever more triumphant European globalization, as historians have often assumed, Russia played an active part in it from the outset, intellectually no less than economically.

Europeans learned from Muscovy, above all, by procuring, translating, and copying Muscovite geographical compilations and diplomatic reports. Its intellectual contribution was not the result of the religious and cultural uniqueness its elites, then as now, constantly proclaimed. Instead, it was in the very hybridity of its texts, the way they incorporated the voices of texts and informants from all over the Eurasian world. This process of exchange, however, would soon come to an end. As the Petrine era wore on, the growing imperial bureaucracy fundamentally reshaped the structure of the knowledge regime that it relied on to make sense of its relationship to China. Less flexible but more skilled and specialized, the new breed of Russian experts would talk almost exclusively to each other and their superiors.

PART II

BUREAUCRATS
and THEIR SECRETS

Chapter 3

Secret Missions, Troublesome Missionaries

PETER THE GREAT IS OFTEN credited with bringing a form of modernity to Russia and, in particular, a new logic of governance. Unlike those of Muscovy, Peter's institutions were supposed to be relatively impartial, impersonal, well structured, and concerned with the optimal exploitation of the empire's human and natural resources.[1] The situation on the Qing frontier seems at first glance to confirm this impression, even if the full scope of the changes had yet to manifest by the time Peter died in 1725. Muscovite intelligence gathering functioned on an ad hoc basis, with little clear differentiation between different areas of responsibility and levels of secrecy; it relied on non-Russians like Seitkul Ablin, Nikolai Spafarii, and (indirectly) Martino Martini; and it remained accessible to European savants through both licit and illicit channels. By midcentury none of this would hold true. There was no China-specific manifesto laying out the new institutional structure, but its principles followed directly from the other innovations in Peter's government. In place of Muscovite informality, there would be a functionally organized knowledge regime made up of discrete bodies with different tasks. Instead of foreign-born servitors, the empire would rely on Russians it trained from childhood, whose careers it would control from beginning to end. Finally, the porosity and fluidity of Muscovy's knowledge regime would give way to an explicit and enforced division between public and secret knowledge.

But how did these structures work on the ground, especially in Beijing? This turned out to be a much more complicated question. Even in its German birthplace, the cameralist ideology that drove Peter's reforms was more of an idealized marketing pitch for a new breed of bureaucrat than an accurate account of how the state worked in practice.[2] Russia's new intellectual relationship with China was no less troublesome. At its core lay the new Russian Ecclesiastical Mission in the Qing capital, but the mission's unusual circumstances pulled it between the empire's foreign policy apparatus, its religious establishment, and its commercial interests. The missionaries and students who served in the rank and file of Russo-Qing relations as spies or translators were always an unruly crowd, and when they did become true specialists, they ceased to fit comfortably in their institutional boxes. The eighteenth-century knowledge regime was not a Weberian bureaucracy—though, as in Prussia, "bureaucratic knowledge production" had a distinctive epistemological framework—but a zone of conflict and negotiation between the top-down institutional imperatives of the post-Petrine state and the flawed but irreplaceable humans on which it depended.[3] In the compromise that emerged, a select few Russians became experts occupying a niche that made them neither academic sinologists nor shapers of policy.

Institutions in Theory and Practice

The reforms of Peter the Great affected every corner of Russian society, but they were especially visible at the top of the administrative hierarchy. In the last decade of his reign, a system of "colleges" (*kollegii*) replaced the old Muscovite "bureaus" (*prikazy*). The name was not accidental: their distinguishing feature was collegiality, that is, the principle that "members" (senior officials) as opposed to quasi-autocratic directors made decisions collectively. Peter had derived his system from the Swedish governmental structure, which a secret agent named Heinrich Fick extensively outlined for him in a series of reports from Stockholm starting in 1715.[4] But Peter adapted the Swedish system to Russian ends and, in particular, singled out the College of Foreign Affairs as an institution that needed to be under the direct control of the tsar at all times. Its chancellor, Andrei Osterman, sought to recruit an elite and well-compensated staff. The College soon became one of the most powerful and least collegial of the colleges.[5]

Peter saw knowledge as fundamental both to the Russian state and to the society he was transforming, and he was careful to distinguish between the secrecy that was proper to the former and the publicness that aided the latter. The public / secret division defined the absolutist information order that took shape in the German lands in the same period: there, the state actively addressed newspaper readers and brought them in as audiences while preserving a realm of privileged knowledge to itself.[6] This approach seems to have influenced Peter as well. Secrecy appeared in the 1720 *General Regulation*—the official document governing most of the colleges—in stipulating either death or eternal galley slavery for such crimes as "secretly carrying off College letters or documents for evil purposes, either temporarily or permanently," and "revealing College resolutions to inappropriate outside persons, announcing protocols prematurely, or disclosing the votes or opinions of members."[7] But the College of Foreign Affairs and the Academy were the central sites for the division between secret and public, for it was through institutions such as these that the appropriate forms of knowledge were to be disseminated outward to the still-hypothetical reading audience. Petrine Russia simultaneously opened a space for public knowledge and expanded the scope of secrecy. In 1725, for instance, an edict of Catherine I confirmed a Petrine norm that "all notable affairs belonging to the purview of the people [*prinadlezhashchikh k vedeniiu narodnomu*], those which are public, but excluding secret intelligence," be sent by all colleges and chancelleries for publication in a newspaper. Founded in 1704 by the tsar himself, this newspaper was called *Vedomosti* and was later added to the portfolio of the Academy of Sciences.[8]

Osterman ensured that knowledge was central to the College of Foreign Affairs, aiming to make the institution "a perpetual state archive and a permanent [source of] information about everything old and which has transpired in state affairs, behaviour, conduct, and the measures taken."[9] In 1720 the College was divided into public and secret "expeditions," a term for functional departments borrowed from the Swedes. In theory there was a clear distinction between the two: the former dealt with interior and personnel matters, while the latter occupied itself with the stuff of foreign diplomacy properly speaking. (In practice, the line was not always consistently drawn, since the non-Russian peripheries of the empire could fit into one or the other.) The Public Expedition remained neglected, lacking even a formal definition of its duties until the reign of Catherine II. By far the larger, the Secret

Expedition was divided into anywhere from four to eight bureaus that cultivated competencies in various geographical areas. On the whole, the College,
with the Secret Expedition at its heart, became an unusually potent nexus of
power; though the institutional structure at the top of the empire shifted
repeatedly in the eighteenth century, the College's authority rivaled that of
the Governing Senate, Petrine and post-Petrine Russia's supreme bureaucratic and judicial body.[10]

The structure of Russian foreign-policy governance incorporated explicit
secrecy rules. Peter took measures to prevent "leaks" (*dyriavost'*) at the College of Foreign Affairs, making it the laboratory for his general approach to
secrecy. Afterward he held it up as a model for the Senate and other colleges
for the care with which it entrusted "secret affairs specially to reliable people"
rather than spreading them around various departments. In 1724 an imperial decree banned speaking of secret matters in private correspondence, even
letters addressed to one's superiors, as opposed to official reports—likely an
anticorruption measure as well as a security one, for it prevented bypassing
the usual chain of command.[11] In subsequent decades, decrees reinforced the
importance of restricting the circulation of information, especially when reports from abroad were involved; the tendency was to cut the Senate out of
the loop entirely.[12] The College of Foreign Affairs thus emerged alongside the
Military and Naval Colleges as a uniquely autonomous and (at least in theory)
informationally sealed branch of the state.

The College of Foreign Affairs was responsible for the care and preparation of its personnel, who often came from the lower ranks; this created a kind
of "democratic intelligentsia," albeit one with a narrowly institutional outlook.[13] Regarding what might be called "Oriental studies" (though no such
term existed at the time), training was especially difficult. Linguistic com-
petency served in the College as a proxy for regional expertise. In the early
years of the Secret Expedition, Russian and Polish received their own departments, while "foreign [Western] languages" and "Oriental languages" were
each lumped into unified bureaus (the former with five translators, the latter
with three).[14] But whereas specialists in European languages could in later
decades be replenished either by training children of existing personnel or
hiring from outside—German, French, and English being standard at the
new-model educational institutions or easily learned by nobles abroad or
from tutors—the Oriental ones required more deliberate effort. No regular

schools (of which there were few in a state where literacy rates remained in the single digits) taught Ottoman Turkish, Persian, or Chinese, and young nobles did not learn them; though Greek, Latin, and Italian were also essential in negotiations at Constantinople, they were not always enough. As a result, the College had constantly to take pains to ensure that it had a class of replacements in training in its embassies abroad, and its employees had the additional responsibility of taking charge of their own intellectual reproduction. This was not always easy. Premature death and, in the case of foreign hirelings, labor mobility constantly threatened to deplete the ranks of the specialists. Florio Beneveni, the polyglot Ragusan who headed the Oriental bureau at its creation, left Russian service in 1725, while the academic Georg-Jacob Kehr, hired as an Arabic, Persian, and Turkish translator in 1732, died eight years later at the age of forty-eight after training a half dozen replacements.[15] In short, despite the "institutionalization" of Oriental languages at the College of Foreign Affairs, everything continued to depend on the vagaries of individual lives.

Manchu and Chinese, two of the principal languages of the Qing Empire, posed unique problems of their own—even beyond the inherent hardships of gaining literacy in the latter. Many people in the Russian Empire spoke Persian and Turkish because of the dense mercantile diasporas that spanned their mutual frontiers.[16] In the Russo-Qing borderlands, by contrast, Mongol, in several dialects, was by far the most common tongue; although its script was the basis for the Manchu, linguistically it was of no use in understanding either of the more prestigious Qing languages, which had to be learned in China proper. In an attempt to reduce its dependence on the goodwill of its negotiating partners, the College repeatedly tried to institutionalize a system of training in which the occasional Qing exile or China-trained Russian student would educate a class of Russian youth in St. Petersburg. Such attempts fizzled out repeatedly over the course of the eighteenth century, never lasting beyond a single graduating class of highly variable quality. Oversupply could also be a problem: the Russian Empire rarely had use for more than one or two translators of Manchu and Chinese at any given time, and expensively trained specialists were sometimes squandered on menial careers.

The cornerstone of the College's strategy for training China specialists was the Russian Ecclesiastical Mission in Beijing, an institution so dysfunctional that it eventually came to stand in for the failures of Russia's China policy tout court. This mission existed in various forms from 1715 to 1954. It had been established nominally to provide for the spiritual welfare of a population of Russian captives taken from the town of Albazin near Nerchinsk when it was besieged and captured by Qing forces in the 1680s. These captives were enrolled as a company in the Qing Eight Banner system (which organized the privileged ethnic strata of the empire and set them apart from the Chinese population south of the Great Wall), given a quarter in Beijing, and provided with brides from other banner populations. However, they were also encouraged to maintain their traditional Orthodox religion, even if within a couple of decades nearly all were nominal Christians at best. Since they could not provide their own clergy, a group of missionaries was allowed to rotate in from Russia. After Savva Vladislavich's successful negotiations for the Treaty of Kiakhta in 1727–1728, the mission acquired the additional function of training students in Manchu and Chinese and serving as an unofficial Russian consulate in the Qing capital. It possessed two compounds (a primary one in the south of the Manchu Inner City, once the hostel for Inner Asian ambassadors, and a secondary one around the St. Nicholas Chapel in the Albazinian quarter in the northeast). Ten or twelve Russians, all men, lived in the primary compound at any given time, with several Qing-subject overseers and servants. No formal schedule of shifts existed in the initial period, but a new complement of personnel was rotated in every ten to fifteen years. For at least the next century, any Russian who spoke Chinese or Manchu probably learned it either directly at the mission or from one of its students.[17]

Two groups of Russians lived side by side at the mission. The first were the missionaries themselves: an archimandrite (similar to an abbot), deacons, priests, and lower-ranking clergy. Until the mission was massively restructured in 1818, these missionaries were underpaid, undertrained, and entirely ill equipped for their intended spiritual role, most notably because they were unable to communicate with most of their putative flock. Their employer was the Holy Governing Synod, Russia's supreme religious body; it was not yet particularly concerned about proselytizing to populations outside the empire and did not require the missionaries to learn the local languages. The other group were the students, who in theory were subject to the College of Foreign Affairs. Although it issued them with instructions and sometimes took charge of them upon their return to Russia, in most cases restrictions on correspondence between Beijing and St. Petersburg meant that the College had no day-to-day control over their affairs. On the ground, the functional differentiation and hierarchy of Petrine institutions often collapsed into ungovernable violence within and among the groups.

One reason for this chaotic environment was that almost none of the Russians wanted to be there. Jesuits and other Catholic missionaries regarded a China posting as a privileged opportunity and prepared for it for years; in Beijing they often had high-status roles at the court. Russians were chosen involuntarily and haphazardly with a few months' notice and in almost all cases dreamed of nothing more than to be allowed to return. They lived in dilapidated quarters and often suffered extreme poverty. Those who did not learn Manchu and Chinese stewed in utter social isolation from the city around them. Moreover, they were constantly drunk, a fact noted not only by hostile observers but by missionaries themselves. As one archimandrite put it, "Because of their endless and excessive solitude in Beijing and the insolence and insubordination of their subordinates, archimandrites develop melancholy [skuka], which produces great brooding [zadumchivost'], which induces them to drink much wine [i.e., vodka], the excessive consumption of which, though it produces great diseases and interrupts the life of many a drinker in Russia, produces these ruinous consequences in Beijing more quickly."[18] It was no surprise, then, that mortality for any of the mission shifts could reach 50 percent or more, even though the Holy Synod took pains to avoid sending anyone past his midforties, and the students and lower-ranking clergy were typically in their late teens or early twenties.[19] A missionary who did not die still risked being shut out of the systems of patronage and promotion that governed social advancement in the empire.

The Qing state, on the other hand, did take some interest in the students, which both gave them employment and placed them in an awkward position when the interests of the Russian Empire, the Qing, and the Jesuits were not in alignment. The Lifanyuan, the Bureau of Foreign Tributaries—essentially the Qing state's Inner Asian foreign ministry—had oversight over the Russian mission and was especially preoccupied with making use of its Russian assets.[20] The Lifanyuan had permitted students to be sent to Beijing in the first place partially in order to facilitate diplomacy between Russia and the Qing by providing Russia with Manchu speakers, thus bypassing Jesuit mediation and the need for Latin documents. In addition to learning the language, they served this function by teaching at the Manchu Russian School

(Eluosi wen guan), a Qing institution where Albazinian bannermen were taught to translate documents into and out of Russian.[21] Surviving homework from this school confirms the general impression that it did not produce graduates who were functionally literate in Russian, and the Albazinians' origins were no help: they "could not count to two" in their supposed native language.[22] The Russian and Qing foreign affairs bureaucracies did not always see eye to eye. When a graduate of the mission named Aleksei Vladykin was assigned to head a trade caravan to Beijing, the Lifanyuan announced that "it was not at all for the purpose of doing business [hūdašabumbi] that they were trained."[23] Still, whether they were translating Manchu correspondence into Russian in St. Petersburg or Russian into Manchu in Beijing, Russian students were central to Russo-Qing diplomacy. Latin translations, still obligatory in the 1720s, quickly became secondary and eventually stopped being generated entirely.

The mission was indispensable to post-Petrine China policy, from translation to intelligence to back-channel negotiations, but the paradox was that it could never be a well-ordered bureaucracy. The life and career of Russia's most skillful and prolific eighteenth-century China expert, Larion Kalinovich Rossokhin, is a vivid illustration of these constraints. He was born in 1717 in the village of Khilok near Selenginsk, east of Lake Baikal, the son of a parish priest.[24] At the age of eight his father enrolled him in a residential school of Mongol established the previous year by Antonii (Platkovskii), the archimandrite of Voznesenskii (Ascension) Monastery in Irkutsk. This decision linked the child's fate to the Qing Empire for the remaining three decades of his life. In 1729, when Platkovskii was appointed to head the Russian Ecclesiastical Mission, he took Rossokhin and two of his other students to Beijing. When he entered the Qing capital, he was only twelve years old. While Platkovskii claimed to know at least some Chinese and had some experience proselytizing across the border, as a leader he was disastrous.[25] Rossokhin reported that on the way to Beijing, the archimandrite forced him to act as his servant, confiscated his wages, and ruled over him with "coercion and beatings."[26]

The catastrophe of Platkovskii's mission was thoroughly documented in legal paperwork. As the missionary Feodosii Smorzhevskii wrote in 1751, "Upon our departure from Moscow, a Synod clerk . . . showing us the enormous pile of Platkovskii matters at the Synod, said: 'Watch out that all of you don't produce so many affairs in Beijing.'"[27] One of these documents, which have survived at the Synod archive, is Platkovskii's diary ("Register of various memorable notes"). He seems to have kept this in an effort to compile incriminating material for accusations against the other missionaries and students, but in October 1731 it was stolen from him by Rossokhin and the other students and given to the caravan director Lorents Lang, the former Swedish prisoner of war who eventually became vice-governor of Irkutsk. It is a truly remarkable work; written in a spare, laconic style, its 232 numbered entries reveal a litany of unceasing drunkenness, violence, and sexual misconduct:

55. Larion Rossokhin and Fedot [another student] were disgustingly drunk and Larion bit Feodot's hand 20th February [1730]
56. Larion did not know his lesson and cursed obscenely at the teacher Chenlao and I wanted to birch him but he fled to the deacon Ioasaf's cell and the deacon did not give him up
57. Mikhailo was disgustingly drunk and almost died of drunkenness Ioasaf the deacon cursed at me and grabbed my breasts and dragged my beard while the priest Ivan choked me while Feodot and Larion also pulled me by my breasts . . .
71. May 4th the priest Ivan being disgustingly drunk sent [the student] Luka Voeikov to me the archimandrite supposedly to take his confession and when I came to [Ivan] he pulled down his pants and pointing to his anus [*govennuiu dyru*] said "I can't [. . .], please give it your blessing so I can be healthy." Around the same time this priest almost stabbed me to death with his folding knife and I barely ran away . . .
74. May 21st the priest Ivan came to my cell and pissed in my tea and pissed all over my cell and befouled all my dishes[28]

Judging by the reports of the other members of the mission, Platkovskii was hardly an innocent victim of his disobedient subordinates. Before the archimandrite's arrival, Luka Voeikov and two other students had been operating under the authority of an imperial decree that confirmed their independence (as agents of the College of Foreign Affairs) from synodal oversight. Platkovskii ordered Voeikov, one of the diary's central antagonists, to "wipe his rear end with the decree," assumed absolute authority, and in the ensuing months "dishonored and crippled" him. The inability of Russian institutions to enforce their writ in Beijing licensed enormous abuses of power.[29]

"Dishonored," in this case, hints at the sexual violence that was a pervasive feature of Platkovskii's mission. In December 1729, a convert named Afanasii, whom Platkovskii employed as a servant, wrote a formal accusation in Chinese. He claimed that one evening the archimandrite asked him to fetch the student Ivan Pukhort, who refused and told him to go back because "the archimandrite is a bad man [*nedobrogo sostoianiia*], it is night and I will not come to him." Platkovskii, Afanasii claimed, asked him to "lie with me as if with a blanket." When Afanasii refused, the archimandrite attempted to compel him into his bed by force, eventually beating him and another Chinese servant with a stick. Rossokhin translated Afanasii's statement into Russian and submitted it to Lang; later, responding to the charges, Platkovskii claimed that his accuser was too old to be of sexual interest.[30] But Platkovskii himself accused the students and other missionaries of other forms of sexual violence.[31] The Synod was reluctant to either investigate or prosecute such cases, because the burden of proof was judged to be hard to meet, especially in Beijing. Even Afanasii's accusations, which were supported by several witnesses including the students, were dismissed as hearsay.[32] Charges of embezzlement proved much more galvanizing, since direct imperial interest was involved, and in 1736 Platkovskii was imprisoned and dragged back to Russia in chains.

Rossokhin, whose youth, language skills, and student status afforded him some autonomy from the mission's violence, began to strike out on his own. Platkovskii complained that Rossokhin disobeyed Lenten dietary rules, evaded his lessons, and spent the night in places he wasn't supposed to go. If he was neglecting his studies, so were his colleagues—in fact, their Chinese and Manchu teachers frequently refused to come to the mission compound, citing their fear of being assaulted with fists or knives by their unruly and inebriated students.[33] In 1734, Lang noted that aside from Pukhort, Tretiakov, and Voeikov, "there is no particular reason to hope that the other students will come to deserve the salary they have been granted by high imperial grace, for as I hear they have spent their time more in drinking than in learning languages for as long as they have been in Beijing." Platkovskii concurred: in 1736, just before he was arrested and brought back by that year's caravan, the archimandrite wrote to Tobolsk to request that Rossokhin and Mikhailo Ponomarev, another former Mongol school student, be "taken back to Russia and kept in fear in good hands, because these students are coming of age and acting out; specifically Ponomarev has taken to drinking, and Ros[s]okhin to being a rake [*molodetskaia okhota*] and if you do not deign to take them back to Russia soon they will lose themselves."[34] But Rossokhin remained in Beijing until 1740. Little is known of his early twenties except for the unexplained and perhaps exaggerated accusation, made by a missionary during a spat, that "the idler Ilarion Rossokhin cannot be trusted, for you [Deacon Ioasaf] yourself said that you lived in sin with him for two years or so, and that you jointly concerned yourself with whores shamelessly at the Mongol tribunal [Lifanyuan]."[35] Regardless of their veracity, such charges show how bitter the infighting at the mission could be and how wholehearted Rossokhin's role in it was.

Rossokhin's unruliness and his extramural activities in the Qing capital shaped his career and his outlook on Qing culture. In 1748, he was asked to annotate a manuscript of Spafarii's *Opisanie,* the hybrid Jesuit-Russian description of China that circulated so widely in manuscript. His comments are a cornucopia of details about everything from the varieties of Chinese liquor to the truth about dog eating in China (he thought this was a slander), though he never got very far outside Beijing.[36] More directly, his urban adolescence brought him into contact with the Jesuits from a Qing and not a Western perspective, since he appears not to have even known the Jesuits' Western names. (He referred to Matteo Ricci as Li Madou, for instance.) Rossokhin was not impressed with their Chinese literary achievements.[37] More concretely, Rossokhin discovered new sources of Qing secrets: as a teacher at the Manchu Russian School and a translator at the Lifanyuan, he discovered that the latter's archives contained a classified work called *Ūlet i unenggi sekiyen* (The true origin of the Oirats); decades later, back in St. Petersburg, he looked for a way to have an agent acquire a copy "secretly, by means of kindness and gifts," because it contained information about the Torghuts (Kalmyks) who lived under Russian sovereignty on the Volga.[38] In some ways more a Qing functionary than a Russian intelligence agent, Rossokhin did not fit neatly into his role in the Petrine bureaucracy.

Rossokhin was the only one of the three students who had come with Platkovskii to Beijing to survive into his twenties, but the College of Foreign Affairs did not know what to make of this strange young man. In 1738, after Lang had exercised his considerable patronage skills on his behalf, Rossokhin was granted the rank of ensign (*praporshchik,* rank fourteen) and a salary of 150 rubles as a reward for having obtained and annotated a map of the Qing

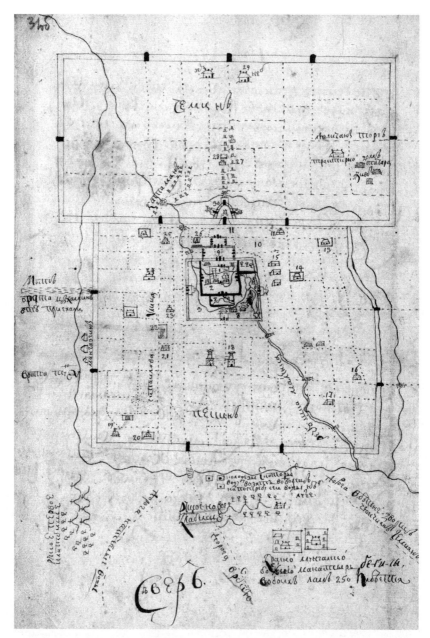

3.1 A Russian caravan map of Beijing, 1736. South is up. The main Russian compound is
     at 26, just south of the Forbidden City; the Russian cemetery is to the north. RGADA,
     fond 199, opis' 1, delo 349, chast' 2, l. 31v.

Empire (evidently a version of the Kangxi Atlas in thirty-two sheets). Although an insignificant position, it was the entry-level rank of the Table of Ranks and meant that he could continue to advance in status if he fulfilled his duties diligently.[39] But when Rossokhin arrived in St. Petersburg in 1741, the College decided it had no need of his services after all, in part because it already employed a baptized Manchu captive named Zhou Ge; the War of the Austrian Succession had clearly taken precedence over any ambitions the College may have had in Inner Asia.[40] Instead Rossokhin was sent to the Academy of Sciences to "translate Manchu and Chinese books and to teach the above languages to four students," though the Academy at first did not want him either.[41] Rossokhin clung to the paraphernalia of his official rank: in 1754, more than a decade after starting at the Academy, he was chastised for continuing to wear the military uniform that corresponded to his status rather than the appropriate but less prestigious civil outfit.[42]

Rossokhin may well have been the first Russian to be fully literate in Chinese and Manchu, at least in a way we can verify through his manuscripts. He was not a social elite like Nikolai Spafarii: he had gone from true obscurity in rural Siberia to an academic position in the capital, making full use of the Petrine reforms' opportunities for social mobility. Yet his fate also shows that the Petrine intelligence structure was only rational in theory. Despite the undeniable (if not first-order) importance of China to Russian imperial goals, the College could neither supervise the training of China experts nor allocate them efficiently. Rossokhin was not employed in the role he was trained for. Over the course of the rest of the century, these efforts would improve, but the basic contradiction between top-down structures and on-the-ground reality would never disappear.

The Making of China Experts

The College began to cultivate China experts as a narrowly circumscribed institutional role, neither intellectual nor decision maker. Aleksei Leont'ev, who achieved recognition in this role in a way Rossokhin never could, began with the advantages of prestigious schooling and ended with lavish state support, but in pushing up against the empire's glass ceilings he also demonstrated the limits of the expert's position. Even if they were later rewarded, these experts still fought their way through the chaos of the mission structure; as Pavel (later Archimandrite Pëtr) Kamenskii, who was in Beijing in the 1790s, put it, "for smart missionaries, Beijing is a wonderful school, heaven; for ignorant ones, it is a prison of torment—hell." Most were in the latter category. Kamenskii's experience, as we will see much later in this book, led him to formulate a comprehensive reform plan that aimed to finally render the mission useful and peaceable.[43]

Leont'ev was born in 1716, the son of a minor government clerk. Though his social origins were about as humble as Rossokhin's, he had one important advantage: he attended the Moscow Slavic-Latin-Greek Academy, the most influential school for both lowborn and aristocratic students in eighteenth-century Russia. (Rossokhin's Beijing contemporary Voeikov, among others, had also been a student there.) In 1739, when the Synod put out a call for volunteers not destined for the clergy to replace Rossokhin's class at the mission, Leont'ev and his classmate Andrei Kaniaev (a merchant's son) declared themselves "eagerly willing" to go to Beijing. In preparation, they were assigned to study with Zhou Ge, who taught them Manchu and possibly Chinese; Leont'ev, according to Zhou Ge's perhaps exaggerated report, had learned to write Manchu better than he did. The students arrived in Beijing, together with another student named Nikita Chekanov, only in 1743.[44]

St. Petersburg was fully aware of the mission's dysfunction. Leont'ev and Kaniaev had arrived during an interregnum in leadership, but in 1746 the archimandrite Gervasii (Lintsevskii) came to Beijing. Lintsevskii represented the Synod's attempt to renew the mission after the disastrous fifteen years of Platkovskii and his successors, for which a "skilled, learned, and temperate person" would be required. Lintsevskii would certainly end up as an improvement, though not a stunning success. The most serious charge against him was that he was a crypto-Catholic or at least a Catholic sympathizer, relatively mild in comparison to the charges of embezzlement, abuse, rape, and murder that haunted other archimandrites. Lintsevskii's principal antagonist among the clergy was his subordinate, the hierodeacon Feodosii Smorzhevskii, an intelligent and witty man who left behind a pile of sardonic notes eagerly devoured by future missionaries.[45] In denunciations, Smorzhevskii highlighted his superior's unbecoming fascination with the Jesuits, who went so far as to ask the archimandrite to come to their compound less often.[46]

Despite these squabbles, the missionaries were clearly improving their position in Beijing, even if one of the monks did "walk around at night with a pair of loaded pistols." Smorzhevskii's accusations themselves show that he and his colleagues enjoyed a great deal of contact with their European neighbors—unlike Platkovskii, who once turned down a Jesuit invitation "on account of their scheming."[47] Learning from Jesuits proved to be essential for Leont'ev's success. The famous Jesuit historian Antoine Gaubil, who knew several generations of Beijing Russians personally, even wrote him a letter of recommendation to the Russian vice-chancellor, as having "made good progress in Chinese characters and in the Chinese and Tartar languages."[48] Lintsevskii himself testified that "in both Manchu and Chinese [nikanskii] [Leont'ev] is very diligent, and has a natural inclination to that study. . . . Also, he reads Manchu books, dynastic histories, and other materials on his own and has read and annotated much." Like Rossokhin, Leont'ev taught at the Manchu Russian School. He also learned to play music in the Chinese style. Leont'ev's classmates were for the most part equally talented. Kaniaev, in addition to his language studies, learned to make and repair watches for Qing princes and other "honorable gentlemen." Kaniaev learned five musical instruments and played them "to chase away melancholy." Sakhnovskii, who had joined the others later, also learned the same skills but complemented them with hunting and painting. All in all, Lintsevskii wrote, "the three of them have become a sort of academy in the Russian compound in China, which had never been seen or heard of previously; and if in the future there be students from Russia, may God grant it would be again."[49]

This cultural flowering may have been satisfying, but it was of no particular value to the College of Foreign Affairs; nor did it cause the Russian state to take better care of its personnel on the ground. For almost a decade, no salary payments arrived from Russia; though this was caused by trade disruptions, neither the Synod nor the College took any steps to address the problem. Russian missions received a subsidy from the Qing court, but it was not enough to cover the students' or missionaries' material needs. They were forced to pawn their clothing and possessions or use them as collateral for loans at exorbitant rates. "News of their poor condition," Lintsevskii said, "has reached one of the great ministers here, who, ruing over their life at length, also asked how they live, the poor men, without any attention from their own?

I cite this deliberately to be decided by the College [of Foreign Affairs], for it seems to me that such speeches and regrets pertain to national honor; it would seem to be better and more honorable if such persons did not pity us." Moreover, the students complained that living too long in Beijing was bringing them close to "despair and regret for the loss of the years [best] suited to human life, during which they could have, like others, gotten married and borne children from their marriages, and from this there comes sorrow, and longing, and an obstacle to their business . . . just as [they say] the students who were there before us died from being here too long."[50] Kaniaev, for one, died of tuberculosis in 1755. His tombstone, located at the Jesuit Zhalan cemetery, survived at least into the mid-twentieth century, when a rubbing was made of it.[51]

The implication in Lintsevskii's report—that the students' condition was risking Russia's diplomatic prestige—made for a brief round of hand-wringing at the Synod and the College of Foreign Affairs, but in the end little changed except that salaries began to be paid more regularly. Yet the increasingly tense diplomatic situation meant that state bodies were developing a stronger interest in Qing affairs. Although Leont'ev was already forty years old by the time he returned to Russia in 1756, he was much better provided for by the College of Foreign Affairs than Rossokhin had been by the Academy: in 1757, Rossokhin complained that Leont'ev was already making four hundred rubles a year and had been raised to the rank of lieutenant (*poruchik,* rank twelve), while he had languished in career stasis for years.[52] By the time Leont'ev died in 1786 he had reached the rank of aulic, or court, councilor (*nadvornyi sovetnik,* rank seven). That meant he had achieved hereditary nobility, which was awarded at rank eight in the civil service. If not exactly meteoric, Leont'ev's rise showed that it was possible for a Qing expert to have a successful service career.

The College of Foreign Affairs afforded Leont'ev other opportunities for state service in addition to translating diplomatic documents. In 1768, he accompanied Colonel Ivan Kropotov to the Mongolian border for the negotiations surrounding an addendum to the Treaty of Kiakhta, during which he served as secretary and translator. Leont'ev retranslated the treaty from the Manchu, which allowed him to determine key inconsistencies between the Russian and Manchu texts; despite mutual accusations, this meant that neither the Russian nor the Qing side was strictly speaking in violation of the

3.2 Andrei Kaniaev's headstone in Zhalan Cemetery, Beijing, 1755. The inscription says "On February 23, 1755, here was interred the body of the Russian student of Manchu and Chinese, Andrei Kaniaev, son of Mikhail, who lived in Beijing for 12 years and was 33 years old." Ricci Institute, University of San Francisco.

treaty—though in the end, as we will see, this conclusion did not change the outcome of the negotiations. Leont'ev earned one thousand rubles for the trip, and Kropotov was instructed to "return this secretary here to the College as soon as your negotiations with the Qing have reached the desired conclusion."[53] He was now, finally, indispensable.

In 1761, Leont'ev, like Rossokhin and Zhou Ge before him, began teaching students Manchu and Chinese; funded directly by the College, his school was far better supported than Rossokhin's had been. The project seems to have been in large part Leont'ev's own initiative. He argued that "in order that Russia not run out of people who know the Chinese languages," he be assigned three young students who could then be used "in translations here, in various commissions with the Chinese at the border, and sent to Beijing with embassies and caravans." Institutional service, not intellectual work, was the objective.[54] One of his students, Iakov Korkin, did end up going to Beijing in 1770. There he made a reputation as a drunken lout "whose name Chinese mothers use to frighten their children when they cry."[55] At the same time, the College of Foreign Affairs found a place for another student of his. With the emergence of the Mongolian border as a major site of diplomatic interchange, it was no longer enough to keep the entire translation apparatus in the capitals. First Leont'ev's mission colleague Egor Sakhnovskii and then his student Mikhailo Antipov found employment in the Eastern Siberian administration, although first they had to learn Mongol from local Buriats.[56]

These successes in the foreign service notwithstanding, Leont'ev—despite being the most qualified Qing expert in the entire bureaucracy—had no impact on Russian decision making or intelligence gathering after the addendum. These were monopolized either by leading statesmen in St. Petersburg (who operated on the basis of preconceptions and wishful thinking about the Qing Empire rather than reliable data) or by local officials in Eastern Siberia, who nonetheless were increasingly losing touch with the informational landscape of the borderlands. There is no record of Leont'ev's being consulted during any of the foreign-policy crises that arose during the 1770s, such as the mass emigration of the empire's Torghut (Kalmyk) subjects to Xinjiang in 1771 or the trade interruption at Kiakhta in the decade's latter years. He is mentioned only twice (once as a student, once as Kropotov's secretary) in N. N. Bantysh-Kamenskii's 1803 history of Russo-Qing relations, written based on classified documents from the College of Foreign Affairs.[57] Despite having become acknowledged in Beijing, St. Petersburg, and even in Western Europe as Russia's leading expert on the region, Leont'ev did not shape Russian policy.

The students who graduated from the mission during the remaining decades of the eighteenth century suffered from the College's continued tendency to sideline its experts, as well as the repeated crises that threatened the mission's very existence. As a result of a growing diplomatic rift accompanying the Qing conquest of the Junghar Khanate, no students were allowed to enter with Amvrosii Iumatov, Lintsevskii's successor, in 1755. In 1759, the Qianlong emperor locked the gates of the mission compound with the remaining missionaries inside and posted an edict on them forbidding any Qing subjects to enter. (The Lifanyuan denied that anything like this had taken place.)[58] Even after the gates opened, the missionaries felt uneasy. In 1766, Iumatov reported that "he should go to the St. Nicholas Church [the northern compound in the Albazinian quarter] but not only he the archimandrite but even a hieromonk is ashamed to go there on foot . . . for the common people, seeing a man in foreign clothing, insult him, laugh, and spit, and could even crush him in the crowd due to their numbers."[59] The 1768 addendum to the Treaty of Kiakhta, which Leont'ev had helped negotiate, secured the mission diplomatically and provided for four students to be rotated with every shift, but its internal problems did not cease.

The College did realize that its presence in Beijing was a unique opportunity to gather intelligence in an age of permanently increased tensions. A new shift, led by the archimandrite Nikolai (Tsvet), arrived in 1771, when Iumatov and all but two of his colleagues had already died. Tsvet, a teacher of French and German from the Trinity Sergius Monastery outside of Moscow, brought with him three seminarians from Tobolsk: Aleksei Agafonov, Fëdor Baksheev, and Aleksei Paryshev. Leont'ev's infamous pupil Iakov Korkin also went with them; he died in Beijing in 1779. When the students returned to Russia in 1783, Leont'ev examined them and found their language skills middling at best.[60] Yet they did not come back empty-handed. They offered the state documents they "had acquired through careful student industriousness," including a Manchu report about the Kiakhta trade they sourced from a Lifanyuan clerk, maps, a description of Qing trade, lexicons, and military documents. Though the orders issued to them initially by the College have not survived, it is clear that they envisioned precisely this kind of intelligence gathering.[61]

The most impressive product of their time in Beijing was an intelligence journal they produced in 1771.[62] Here, Agafonov, Paryshev, and Baksheev compiled their contacts with Qing people and official bodies and the "secrets" they learned from them. In addition to documenting internal and external conflicts—such as the politically explosive undercurrent of Han nativism in the capital—and disorders with the mission itself, they also recorded more lighthearted encounters. One day, "two [Manchu] officers came to our compound . . . and among other conversations asked us, what sort of leather clothing our soldiers wear when they do battle with the enemy so that it cannot be pierced by bullets?" The students, "barely keeping from laughter," explained that it was the hide of a wondrous beast from the Arctic Ocean; later they found out the soldiers had been sent by Qianlong himself.[63] The journal, for all its local color, does not seem to have informed or influenced any decision the Russian government may have taken in the 1780s, a period of dramatically heightened interimperial tension. This is despite the fact that the students' most important function was determining if the Qing posed a military or political threat to Russia: after all, they had arrived immediately after the 1771 Torghut exodus. Turning up apparent (though dubious) evidence of precisely such a threat was not enough to overcome their underlying irrelevance.

As regional specialists and intelligence operatives, students who eventually became translators at the College could never break through the divide separating them from the senior officials who made decisions. But within those boundaries, a student could find a cozy niche for himself. One of the more successful eighteenth-century careers the mission produced was that of Anton Vladykin, although his failure as a would-be intellectual was far more poignant. He was born in 1761 among the Volga Torghuts, but when the exodus fractured the Torghut community in 1771, he remained in Russian territory. Vladykin was baptized in Astrakhan and at the age of fourteen entered the seminary at Trinity Sergius Monastery.[64] In 1779, as a new mission was being gathered under the leadership of Ioakim (Shiskhovskii) to replace Tsvet, Vladykin was attached to it as a student; the Synod authorities seemed to know only that he belonged to an "Asiatic people [*aziatskoi natsii*]." The journal Agafonov and his colleagues produced had evidently not dissuaded the Synod and the College of Foreign Affairs from pursuing the mission's intelligence possibilities. Shishkovskii's instructions specified that he was to tell the Synod "of the conditions and behaviors there," while the College attached an additional sheet. Its instructions demanded that he "discover whatever circumstances obtain in this distant state, which form their thoughts, behaviors, and the actions of their government, using this to keep a secret record to present to the College of Foreign Affairs upon your return," but "without raising the slightest suspicion among the Qing or giving them occasion to see you as an eavesdropper on their affairs."[65] Espionage remained at the forefront of the College's agenda.

Yet Shishkovskii appears to have done no such thing. Instead, he fell into the familiar habits of poor mission administrators: drinking and petty tyranny. One of his charges, the church servant Ivan Orlov, was first exiled to the northern compound around St. Nicholas Church; when it turned out that Orlov had made it into an idyllic little corner (complete with apiary), the archimandrite held him by the queue, beat him nearly to death, and ransacked his creation. Eventually Orlov managed to secure permission from the Lifanyuan to return to Russia, the most cherished dream a Beijing missionary could have.[66] The mission's students sent a letter with him to the Synod, in which they painted their Qing life in positive terms, with one exception: "Oh if only the Father Archimandrite's poor care for our well-being and certain oppressions would not bring us into faintheartedness!"[67] Orlov was lucky to have escaped. Vladykin was the only one of the mission's four students—none of whom had been over twenty when they joined—to make it back to Russia alive. Of the five dead, including the archimandrite, four had perished on the way back; a cryptic reference in the later archimandrite Kamenskii's reports to the Synod hints that they had died violent deaths linked to their own misconduct. (Other sources point to fevers or tuberculosis.)[68]

During his stay in Beijing, Vladykin composed a number of intelligence reports. One of these revealed the inability of the Manchu Russian School to produce competent translators: when a document supposedly sent by Russian officials to the Torghuts in Xinjiang was seized and threatened to cause a diplomatic crisis by revealing Russia's secret negotiations for their return, the Lifanyuan was forced to turn to the mission's students, not to the graduates of the Manchu school, to translate them.[69] His experience producing documents like these set Vladykin up for a successful career at the College of Foreign Affairs. Like Leont'ev, he reached the rank of aulic councilor, but also earned an Order of St. Vladimir.[70] He was also recognized as an expert within the College apparatus. When the next archimandrite Sofronii, a well-meaning but ineffectual busybody, proposed a series of reforms to the mission's customs and practices, Vladykin was consulted to evaluate them. He suggested that Sofronii had not tried hard enough to fit into Beijing culture and advised

cultivating "friendship and good acquaintance" with the Qing officer assigned as the mission's warden, "through which they can acquire more respect and honor from the people there, and their servants will scheme, dupe,
and insult them less."[71] Vladykin had accumulated enough credibility as a
specialist that when the doomed Golovkin embassy was assembled in 1805,
he was invited to serve as a Manchu and Chinese translator, one of its more
highly paid members—though the ambassador kept him on the sidelines and
did not seek his input.[72]

Vladykin was not the last of the China experts formed in the mold of the
mission, but he clearly illustrated the structures and limitations that defined
this role. The only survivor of a brutal and toxic mission environment, he had
clung to his career ladder and succeeded. This did not make him anything
more than a secretarial functionary, much like a translator of French or
German: the compromise between Petrine institutionalization and the real-
life process of training specialists only left a small degree of room to ma-
neuver. Yet the graduates had larger aspirations than simply producing
reams of unread manuscript reports. They wanted to be useful, to put their
skills to work informing a broader public. The place to do that was, supposedly, the Academy—but despite all the enlightened aspirations of the eighteenth century, there, too, Petrine structures constrained their emergence as
scholarly intellectuals.

Chapter 4

Scholarship and Expertise
at Home and Abroad

EIGHTEENTH-CENTURY RUSSIANS were interested in expanding public knowledge, not just secret intelligence. The structure of their institutions allowed space for that knowledge to be disseminated, but not everyone had equal access to the prestige and power of a formal intellectual role. In most cases, academicians whose names graced title pages in St. Petersburg bookshops were foreign-born and formally trained, with mastery of multiple European languages; they were not part-time dilettantes. This left the Russian Empire's lowborn, clerkish China experts in a bind and the Academy with a paradox. After all, the existence of the Russian Ecclesiastical Mission should not only have been a significant resource diplomatically but also a major intellectual opportunity for the Russian Empire, building on the legacy of the Muscovite contribution to the Republic of Letters. Russia was the only European country to maintain a permanent institutional presence in Beijing. Unlike the Jesuits and other Catholic religious orders, the personnel of the Russian mission were not in the direct service of the Qing emperors and could expect to return to Russia after about ten years in the capital; not a single secular European enjoyed the same privilege until well into the nineteenth century. Russia could thus have every expectation of becoming a major European center for scholarship about the Qing Empire, as it had for scientific studies of Eurasia and the North Pacific. Yet none of the experts that it produced became academicians; instead, their roles as public knowledge workers were as rigidly defined against prestigious scholarship as official policy making. Because of how the eighteenth-century knowledge regime envisioned the relationship between functionaries and institutions, eighteenth-century Russians would amount to no more than a footnote in the history of academic sinology.

Founded in 1724, a year before Peter's death, the Imperial Academy of Sciences soon came to be at the core of public knowledge in the empire, embodying Peter's push to promote the reading of newspapers and the growth of educated culture more generally. Even if some of its functions were technical and utilitarian—like the mapping of territory in the service of a cameralist vision of mastery over imperial space—others, like the study of antique numismatics, were less clearly so. Certainly the Academy facilitated the kind of learned culture that would ensure a steady supply of educated cadres for Peter's newly created institutions and, by encouraging the development of social distinctions around education, promoted the Westernized social hierarchy Peter admired.[1] But not least among the Academy's goals was the search for international prestige, akin to the emulatory impulse that drove Peter to build palaces such as Peterhof or allow himself to be crowned emperor in a ceremony deliberately meant to echo imperial Rome.[2]

These two faces of the Academy—pan-European acclaim and local enlightenment—were exemplified by the Academy's two publications. The *Commentarii* (later *Novi Commentarii*), a Latin-language periodical addressed to the learned world of Europe, was the main scholarly venue for the academicians' research. Sought after by savants from London to Berlin, it showcased the diversity of foreign talent Russia had been able to acquire and the ways in which its recruits were able to take advantage of their posting, from the mathematics of Leonhard Euler to the astronomy and geography of Joseph-Nicolas Delisle and the historical and Altaic studies of Gerhard Friedrich Müller. Its popular counterpart, various incarnations of which were founded by Müller starting in 1728, addressed a Russian-speaking audience through accessible essays and illustrations.[3] Although it did not oversee all of the empire's educational institutions, the Academy could fairly be described as a kind of College of Enlightenment whose core function was the dissemination of knowledge to an emerging—but still minuscule—reading public. In 1724, the Academy's senior officials Lavrentii Blumentrost and Johann Schumacher described its threefold mission as incorporating scientific work, scientific education, and pedagogical training.[4]

The Academy's midranking staff—its translators, traveling botanists, and correspondents—thus constituted public intellectuals of a kind, in that the end goal of their work was to serve a populace beyond the walls of their own institution. Just as the College of Foreign Affairs cultivated knowledgeable staffers to contribute their linguistic and regional expertise to the solution of diplomatic problems, so too did the Academy train Russians and hire foreigners to provide it with intellectual goods for wider distribution. For instance, Stepan Krasheninnikov, one of the Academy's first Russian-born success stories, became famous throughout Europe after traveling to Kamchatka as a student apprenticed to the academician Georg Steller. His main work, the *Description of Kamchatka,* was published in four languages across Europe.[5] Before Mikhailo Lomonosov became the first Russian-born academician in 1745, such figures were the Academy's principal means of showing itself off as an authentically Russian institution to both a domestic and a foreign audience; though it was prestigious to employ a luminary like Delisle, the progress of enlightened Westernization in Russia required some representation for cultivated indigenes, most of whom were found in the middle ranks. Yet there were limits to this. Krasheninnikov was able to make his career in large part because Steller had died in 1746. In few other cases were midranking figures allowed to outshine the academicians in the public eye. Considered as a whole, the Academy was an intellectual enterprise in which prestige accrued to the professors at the top and the tangible benefits of employment and patronage were distributed downward.

Publish or Perish

Larion Rossokhin's experiences with the Russian Ecclesiastical Mission and the College of Foreign Affairs showed the limits of China expertise as channeled through secret knowledge-making institutions; his academic career did the same for public knowledge. Like his successors from the mission, his formal position at the Academy was that of translator. Some of Russia's first men of letters, such as the poet Vasilii Trediakovskii, started in this role and continued to publish translations well after becoming cultural figures in their own right.[6] But these represented a minority; of the 317 entries in a biographical dictionary of Russian writers compiled by the enlightened publisher Nikolai Novikov in 1772, fewer than 10 percent were listed as having been employed as translators.[7] Regarded as subordinate intellectually, translators could assist senior academics in producing original work or prepare texts for publication, but they could rarely be authors in their own right. Although Rossokhin was probably more qualified than any intellectual in Europe then living to comment on Chinese life, this role meant that he could not do so publicly. It was not for lack of trying.

Rossokhin arrived at the academy at an unusually chaotic moment. In the wake of Empress Anna Ioannovna's death in 1740, the Academy had been dragged into the center of a bloody power struggle between rival court factions. In the academic context, the battle lines were drawn between the supposedly "pro-Russian" supporters of the ascendant Elizabeth and the "Germans," represented by the Academy's director Johann Schumacher. (Schumacher was, among other things, accused of suppressing native Russian scholarship.) The director was briefly placed under house arrest, but by December 1742 he was released and returned to his position, while the Academy languished without a budget.[8] Into this cataclysm stepped Larion Rossokhin, just returned from China and rejected from employment at the College of Foreign Affairs. Though an obvious candidate for promotion in the nativist Elizabethan environment, Rossokhin was denied assistants; when his salary was left unpaid, he was forced to pawn his clothes and dishes "to provide myself with daily food."[9] Matters improved slightly in 1743, when the Academy crisis had officially passed: the Academy bought out his pawned clothes, deigned to pay his rent for his shabby quarters on the Petersburg Side, and ordered his latest translation—a collection of "secret affairs of the Qing state," a statistical table of Qing provinces and banner forces—to be given a handsome French binding. This work survives in several manuscript collections, suggesting that it at least circulated beyond the Academy.[10] But thereafter, although Rossokhin continued to produce translations at an impressive rate, he was left largely unremarked on and unrewarded for his pains. Unlike his contemporary Lomonosov, who would become the premier Russian-born man of letters in the mid-eighteenth century, no amount of honest labor would raise Rossokhin from the level of the Academy's service class of copyists and translators.

The lack of institutional support undermined Rossokhin's efforts at pedagogy. Originally the teaching of Manchu and Chinese was meant to be a core
aspect of his appointment. He was supposed to have been assigned students
from Feofan Prokopovich's gymnasium, one of the era's most advanced Russian pedagogical institutions, and his pupils would arrive already knowing
Latin and German; failing that, they would come from the Academy's own
school. In practice he received half the original complement, and they would
come from the St. Petersburg Garrison School—an institution for the free-
born children of soldiers, who as conscripted serfs constituted the most downtrodden class of Imperial Russian society. Rossokhin performed his duties
willingly, though his four students not only attended class but also lived in
his apartment. Such an arrangement would have satisfied him but for the fact
that the house already had soldiers quartered on it, which he pleaded in vain
with the Academy to address.[11]

In his teaching, Rossokhin cleaved closely to the curriculum in use in Qing
schools, making him perhaps the first European to incorporate vernacular
Manchu into his teaching. Like pupils in all traditional Chinese institutions,
Rossokhin's students learned to read and understand Confucian educational
classics like the *Sishu* (*Four Books*) and *Sanzijing* (*Three Character Classic*). But
Rossokhin's curriculum had a distinctly Manchu spin. The versions of these
books he had brought from Beijing, quite likely those he had used himself
during his studies, were bilingual, and his students eventually produced trilingual versions with a Russian translation attached to the Manchu and Chinese.
Moreover, in his teaching he relied on one of the newest innovations in Qing
pedagogy: a text called the *Qingwen qimeng*, first published in 1730. Used for
teaching Manchu to bannermen, whom the imperial court judged to be in imminent danger of losing their native culture, this primer contained a casual,
entertaining set of conversations drawn from everyday life. It offered a stark
contrast to the ponderous pieties of the Confucian pedagogical classics.[12] But
conscientious and up-to-date as it may have been, Rossokhin's teaching could
not resolve the fundamental dilemma, which was that the Russian government
was willing to fund the education of Qing-language experts but not their continued employment. Even though they may have successfully completed their
studies, none of Rossokhin's students obtained relevant work; one later became
an Academy clerk, while the others disappeared from the historical record.[13]

Outside of the classroom, Rossokhin's role was more subservient. In 1747, he was placed under the supervision of the Academy historian G.-F. Müller, in effect as a research assistant. Though this position seemed to offer better use of his skills, in practice it only reinforced his separation from senior, professional scholarship. Müller, who made three times as much as his charge, sent Rossokhin questionnaires about such matters as Albazinian life in Beijing, the nature of Jesuit service in the Qing court, and the details of Buddhist beliefs, to which he dutifully responded; he was not invited to participate in the writing of original work.[14] When Rossokhin tried to strike out on his own, Müller filed a formal complaint that "the said translator Rossokhin has bypassed me, and . . . has submitted his translations and extracts directly to the chancellery, either because he despises me or for some other reason."[15] At least Müller and his colleague Johann Fischer were willing to occasionally credit Rossokhin in their works; Müller even called him "the most experienced of translators" and his historical translations "not the least achievement of our century."[16] In Fischer's case, however, a mere mention was an understatement of the translator's role: he used Rossokhin's "reliable information" to write an article about Chinese imperial titles, which the German professor had no linguistic capability to evaluate.[17] Rossokhin cited the "praise" he received from his "Professors" when he finally asked for a much-delayed promotion to the next rank in 1757, but it was clear that he himself would never be a professor.[18]

Rossokhin's reports to the Academy make it clear that he wished for a broader audience for his work. In 1747, submitting a translation of a historical work called *Panshi zonglun,* he asked that it be published "for the good of the Russian fatherland, so that the fruit of my labors would not be left without use"; he was refused "pending further consideration," and the work was forgotten.[19] In 1754, he informed the Academy chancellery that he had completed a Russian translation of the place names in a thirty-seven-map atlas, evidently a different one from the one he used in 1738. He argued that his transliterations of the names were far more accurate than in any European map he had seen, due to misleading inconsistencies in Western transliteration practices. "And if the chancellery . . . deigns to create one general map of the whole Qing state from this Atlas I have translated and send it to print," he wrote, "then in my feeble-mindedness I hope that no small glory would accrue to the Imperial Academy from this, especially because this Atlas is more complete than any other map of the Qing state in a European language." Schumacher ordered this to be done, but for some reason, nothing was ever published.[20] In both formal and informal ways, Rossokhin's aspirations to a public-facing authorial role were repeatedly discouraged.

Behind the scenes, Rossokhin used his local Beijing knowledge to help the Academy build one of the largest collections of Qing-language—especially Manchu—books outside of East Asia. Between his arrival in St. Petersburg and his wife's posthumous sale of his effects to the library, Rossokhin found and purchased dozens of Manchu titles.[21] The nature of the books he collected hints at his personal reading habits. In addition to various well-known linguistic, pedagogical, geographical, legal, and historical texts, he also collected books from Manchu vernacular print culture, like the "Eating Crabs" youth book, a humorous song pamphlet that poked fun at relations between Manchus and Chinese.[22] His later translations, including a compendium of household advice called "Chinese Secrets," indicate that he made use of the daily use encyclopedias (*leishu*) that circulated among ordinary people in Beijing.[23] All of these texts, together with another batch Rossokhin acquired from other Russians who had returned from Beijing, formed the core of the Academy of Sciences' Manchu and Chinese book collections. Judging by subsequent catalogs, a number of them survived at least until the nineteenth century and perhaps longer, though many of Rossokhin's original contributions were evidently lost during a 1747 fire at the Academy. Following titles and volume numbers is the only way to trace his contributions: no catalog mentions his role in curating the collection.[24]

The greatest opportunity for Rossokhin to make his name among the learned public came in 1756, when the members of the last Beijing caravan brought back a sixteen-volume book they thought was called "The History or Description of the Whole Qing State." The Senate, offering to foot the bill, sent the book to the Academy to be identified and translated in full—by far the largest Qing-language translation project ever undertaken in eighteenth-century Russia. Unfortunately, it turned out that the project was based on a misapprehension: the book in question, the /Baqi tongzhi/, was in fact a dry, specialized history of the Qing Eight Banner system. Yet Rossokhin managed to use his expertise to convince the Senate that the project was worth embarking on (at least, as the Senate put it, those portions that were "needed for Russia as well as the Learned World to know"). Müller, his superior, helped by testifying that its contents were not matched in any existing foreign text. Rossokhin even obtained the assistance of another Mission student—Aleksei Leont'ev, who had just returned from Beijing. On completion both were to receive a promotion in rank and a handsome financial reward. The Russian Senate, not known for its dedication to antiquarianism, had committed to a translation project as obscure as it was massive.[25] In 1762, Leont'ev announced that the translation was complete, and the Senate issued an order "to print it as soon as possible." Intra-academic squabbling, however, prevented this from taking effect, and the book was only dug up and published in 1784, two years before Leont'ev's own death.[26]

Rossokhin, however, had already died in 1761, having completed five volumes of the translation. He was forty-four years old and left behind his widow, Ekaterina (who received the substantial sum of six hundred rubles for his part in the work as well as a year's salary), his infant daughter, Aleksandra, and his eighteen-year-old son, Pëtr. Though there were thoughts of making his position hereditary, he had petitioned successfully for his son to be excused from any such studies, "him not having any inclination towards Manchu and Chinese, those being very difficult languages."[27] Not a single one of his dozens of works was published during his lifetime, although in 1764 Müller printed his annotated translation of Tulišen's Manchu-language travelogue of the Russian Empire.[28] Eventually Larion Rossokhin earned a two-line entry in Novikov's biographical dictionary, but under the name Ivan and mostly because Novikov was under the impression that he had authored the *Qingwen qimeng*. In other words, as a pure translator he could never count as a true man of letters, despite all his efforts, and a translator is what he remained.[29]

Defining the Limits of Authorship

Aleksei Leont'ev, unlike Rossokhin, did not depend on the *Baqi tongzhi* translation to secure his intellectual reputation. When his publishing career began in earnest, in 1770, it could not be ignored by anyone who followed the output of Russian presses. Between that year and his death in 1786, more than two dozen of his translations appeared in print (two more were released posthumously in 1788), a pace of production of China-related texts that had never been seen before and, proportionately to the size of the total book market, would never be again.[30] Yet Leont'ev, like his successors, was still not an academic or an author in the way Trediakovskii or Lomonosov were. He was known exclusively as a translator, he wrote almost no original works, and although he had a reputation abroad, he was not able to capitalize on it by engaging with foreign audiences directly.

The most controversial of Leont'ev's works has always been the very first. Published in the new journal *Pustomelia* (*Prattler*) in 1770, it was a translation of a text Rossokhin had brought from Beijing: the Yongzheng emperor's last testament, which settled the succession on his son, the future Qianlong. The year 1770 also happened to be the year Catherine II's son Paul reached the age of majority and hence ended his mother's nominal regency. A generation of Soviet scholars argued over whether the journal's editor, Nikolai Novikov, deliberately printed the text as a piece of political subversion connected to the majority crisis—and whether this act was the reason that the issue in which it appeared became *Pustomelia*'s last. Some have pointed out that the testament reappeared in an imperially supported translation two years later, while others draw attention to potentially crucial differences between the two texts. The debate, with the larger questions it enfolds about the political independence of Russian intellectuals, remains unsettled to this day.[31]

The potentially seditious implications of Leont'ev's translation are apt to obscure the larger picture. The source of Leont'ev's publishing success was for the most part not a receptive reading public primed by a growing interest in French *chinoiserie,* and certainly not a politically oppositional one; rather, it was substantial government support and investment. The years of Leont'ev's publishing career correspond almost exactly to those of the Society for the Translation of Foreign Books, a semi-institutionalized body created by Catherine II in 1768 and shut down in 1783. It was intended to promote the spread of the Enlightenment in Russia by providing state support both for the labor of translators and for the costs of printing their work. Initial forays were modest, but in 1769, the Society began to enroll translators employed at the Academy of Sciences. Leont'ev (sharing time with College of Foreign Affairs) was among them. Although the Society was technically responsible for only three of his books, the first of these was by far his most successful.[32] Likewise, though not formally affiliated with the Society, other Leont'ev publications were also printed at state expense, whether paid for directly by the empress or funded by the Academy of Sciences.[33] The Catherinian Russia in which Leont'ev made his career was a distinctly different place from the Elizabethan one in which Rossokhin made his; in Catherine II's time Novikov had effectively brought private publishing into existence.[34] But although Leont'ev undoubtedly benefited from the book market and print culture Novikov had fostered, he owed his success more to robust, flexible, and sustained state financing than to private popularity. This was something Rossokhin had never had.

To what extent was Leont'ev successful as a published writer? Unquestionably he had developed a certain respectability. By 1786, he had had a seal made for himself, a laurel-wreathed shield with his name and title in Chinese characters.[35] Two of Leont'ev's books were printed in multiple editions, an indication of commercial success, and he sometimes asked for copies "to give to my friends," which suggests that he was enmeshed in a literary community of some kind.[36] Though some of these publications were prominent enough to be reviewed or extracted in newspapers, others had to be pulped or had editions of later volumes reduced for lack of readership.[37] In the same period, Jean-Baptiste Du Halde's *Description . . . de la Chine*, translated from French, went through several editions.[38] Leont'ev, unlike Du Halde, had actually been to China, yet he was not able to draw on the same authorial credibility as the French Jesuit.

The same ambiguities obtain in the case of Leont'ev's international reputation, which like his domestic one was modest. The first edition of one of his books appeared in German translation in Weimar in 1776, published by the local printer Karl Ludolf Hoffmann; another edition emerged in 1796.[39] In 1782, the same book was retranslated in part and published in Paris as a small volume by one Levesque, part of a collection of "moral thoughts of various Chinese authors."[40] In 1774, the Nuremberg polymath Christoph Gottlieb von Murr, who had frequent contacts with the Imperial Academy of Sciences, asked the Academy's secretary Johann Euler in passing if he could "carry on a correspondence with Herr Leontiew for the discussion of Chinese literature" and if he could give him Leont'ev's address. No sign of a response or a correspondence has been recorded.[41] Aside from extracts in German-language publications in Russia, this appears to have been the sum total of Leont'ev's influence on the European scholarly community. Though he was better known in Western Europe than any other eighteenth-century Russian Qing expert, this amounted to little; by contrast, the works of a savant like Lomonosov had already been discussed and reviewed in such publications as the *Monthly Review,* the *Journal des Sçavans,* and the *Philosophical Transactions.*[42]

Intellectually, Leont'ev owed what success he had to the book collection and correspondence practices of his predecessors. Two of his translations, *Depei kitaets* and *Tian' shin' ko,* were based on books Jesuit correspondents had sent to the Academy of Sciences in 1737: Francesco Brancati's 1661 *Tianshen huike* and the Christian Manchu prince Depei's 1736 *Shijian lu.* Both books had been created in the context of the Jesuit attempt to spread Catholicism in Qing China by influencing elite opinion. Yet it is not clear that Leont'ev even knew what these books were; certainly the translated texts give no indication of their doctrinally problematic origin.[43] Leont'ev's most successful work, *Kitaiskiia mysli* (Chinese thoughts), was not a random assortment of Confucian staples, as the title might imply. Much of it seems to be drawn from a book of Yongzheng's edicts to the Eight Banners, which Rossokhin had sold to the Academy in 1741, while the rest was extracted from an anthology acquired in Beijing at Rossokhin's request.[44] Rossokhin's unsung labor as a Qing, and especially Manchu-language, bibliophile made Leont'ev's success possible, but that success was itself fleeting. After his death in 1786, Leont'ev seems to have been best remembered by Russian Freemasons, whose collections contain several copies of his works and who seem to have been drawn to them by their fascination with Eastern wisdom.[45] Leont'ev's translations effectively transmuted Qing Catholicism into Enlightenment Orientalia, but they had been made possible by Rossokhin's careful library building.

If Rossokhin's failure to become a public intellectual reveals the rigidity of the academic hierarchy in which he worked, Leont'ev's fleeting success shows how an adroit translator could take advantage of state support and official belief in the enlightening power of translations. But state support could not by itself turn a translator into a savant. Leont'ev's inability to make direct contact with figures like Murr, his dependence on the mediation of the academic bureaucracy for contact with learned publics, ensured that he remained not the distributor of intellectual patronage but its recipient. His contemporary Joseph Amiot serves as a useful point of comparison. A Beijing Jesuit, Amiot parlayed his personal friendship with the French secretary of

state Henri Bertin into an enormously successful career as an author, translator, and editor of China-related publications. In the process, his Russian
acquaintances charged, he was not unwilling to pass off the work of his Chinese collaborators as his own.[46] Leont'ev suffered from the opposite problem:
his name disappeared behind the work.

Leont'ev's successors followed directly in his footsteps. When the three students who had written an intelligence journal in 1770s Beijing tried to apply
their skills to achieving literary success, they found even less purchase than
they did in the foreign affairs bureaucracy. Baksheev, who had compiled a
manuscript Manchu dictionary while in Beijing, died in 1787, after having replaced Leont'ev for a year in St. Petersburg. Paryshev remained as a translator in Irkutsk. Agafonov came the closest out of any of them to a true literary career: five of his translations were published in 1788. But what was
responsible for his success was not his prowess as a self-made man of letters.
In 1785, the Irkutsk governor-general Ivan Iakobii sent three of Agafonov's
translations to Empress Catherine for her approval. Two of his publications
were labeled "translated in Irkutsk," with the first being explicitly linked to
the opening of the Irkutsk viceroyalty (namestnichestvo). In other words, Agafonov may simply have been the beneficiary of a burst of gubernatorial patronage intended as a means of demonstrating the province's literary achievements. After Iakobii was removed on suspicion of malfeasance, no other
publications by Agafonov emerged (although a reprint came out in 1795, a year
after his death).[47] Neither were any of his works reviewed or reprinted abroad.
In a compendious list of published Russian-language materials relating to the
Qing Empire, compiled by the academic I. Kh. Gamel' around 1830, his name
is absent.[48] Agafonov closes out the brief list of students from the Russian Ecclesiastical Mission who managed to convert their unique training and life
experiences into published scholarship. Their numbers are dwarfed by the
dozen or so of their classmates who did not make it back from Beijing.

Anton Vladykin, the Torghut-born student who at the end of the century
enjoyed the most flourishing career in state service, did not achieve comparable success as a public intellectual. Like his predecessors, Vladykin hoped
to make a broader impact with the training he had received. He even called
his manuscript books "A Manchu Abecedarium for the Benefit of Russian
Youth" and "A Manchu Grammar for the Benefit of Russian Youth." (A third
book, "Guide for Manchu Language Learners," contained a translation of the

Qingwen qimeng; like Rossokhin, Vladykin had been taught Manchu with it in Beijing.) Although he established a school at the College of Foreign Affairs in 1798, it existed for only three years, far less than the three previous attempts. After it closed, he attempted to find an audience for his translations. He sent a copy of a Chinese novel to an unnamed aristocrat. Nothing came of this.[49] In 1802, he presented a copy of a large Manchu dictionary, together with a smaller lexicon, to Chancellor Vorontsov—once again "for the further benefit of Russian youth who are studying." He hoped for "a presentation to His Imperial Majesty and a merciful petition [on its behalf] for high monarchical benevolence," presumably in securing state support for its publication. No response was forthcoming.[50] Vladykin died in 1811, having published none of his numerous manuscript works. The Russian youth on whose behalf he had labored would never see anything he had written.

Despite the dearth of publications by Russian authors, a young Russian growing up around the turn of the nineteenth century would have had ample opportunity to learn about China from published work like Du Halde's *Description*. A commonplace book likely kept in the 1810s by Aleksei Lëvshin, author of a famous study of the Kazakhs, includes material from a Russian translation of Amiot's *Mémoires concernant les Chinois* and the Abbé Prévost's *Histoire générale des voyages*—of a kind that suggested the reader was hungry for information about China, not just French opinions of it.[51] I. Kh. Gamel's list of sources on China from 1830, despite his relative familiarity with the work of Leont'ev and Rossokhin, includes four times as many French translations as Russian ones.[52] Even if the print runs of the Russian-language authors had been larger, the fact that they published almost exclusively translations, as opposed to original and synthetic works of history or geography, made them less accessible to ordinary readers than authors who wrote originally in French, but there was also far less writing in Russian all around.

The difference between the regime of authorship that constrained writers like Leont'ev and Vladykin from the one that would emerge in the nineteenth century is clear from the first-ever printed Russian description of China: Ivan Orlov's 1820 *New and Detailed Historical-Geographical Description of the Chinese Empire*.[53] If Orlov's name sounds vaguely familiar, it is because he was the same terrorized young church servant who was forced to leave China under Archimandrite Shishkovskii. Some three decades later, he tried to invoke his experience as a "native-born Russian and one who had lived in

China" as an argument for the relevance of his own book in a marketplace dominated by foreign texts:

> Many curious readers might be found who despite the title of this book will say that it does not deserve to be read because it is not new, because many descriptions of China have been published in foreign languages, and much is known of these from translations in the Russian language; but . . . those descriptions from which we have translations were composed, first of all, long ago, and second not by people who personally were and lived in China but composed them remotely while living in their homelands, e.g. France, Germany, and other places. . . . [Whereas] I lived in China myself and lived in its capital city Beijing with the ecclesiastical mission.[54]

Of all the Russians who passed through the Russian Ecclesiastical Mission in the eighteenth century, Orlov was a strange figure to represent the dawn of sinological authorship. After his return to Russia, Aleksei Agafonov had evaluated him as incapable of translating Manchu or speaking more than a few Chinese phrases, and his skills must have declined considerably since then.[55] In actuality Orlov's book is not much more original than Spafarii's had been. It is a hodgepodge of some original observational material and text directly plagiarized from his own missionary forerunners. Much of the text, especially those portions involving any knowledge of original Chinese sources, is adapted or copied word for word from Rossokhin's volume-length commentaries on the *Baqi tongzhi*.[56] Practically the entire second volume is an unacknowledged translation (by Orlov or somebody else) of the *Da Qing yitongzhi,* the same text Aleksei Leont'ev translated without claiming as his own in 1778.[57] The lines between appropriation, translation, and authorship were blurred, but this did not prevent Orlov from taking credit in a way none of his predecessors had.

Orlov's work exemplified changing norms around authorship, a process we will revisit in Chapter 10. His predecessors were bound by a different understanding of what it meant to be an expert. They had been trained by the post-Petrine Russian state to fill its need for functionaries with knowledge of Chinese and Manchu. Their work, unlike Muscovite hybrid texts, mostly failed to circulate outside of Russia, and despite addressing a wider internal reading public, their intellectual labor faded into the background: in the eighteenth-century knowledge regime, hierarchy superseded expertise as a way of organizing knowledge production. But these limited specialists were not the only group of people the state entrusted with Qing-related duties. In an evolving paradigm of Inner Asian commercial exchange, the Russian trade caravan to Beijing—staffed with its own class of specialized employees— would briefly emerge as a mobile nexus for institutionalized intelligence.

Chapter 5

The Caravan as a Knowledge Bureaucracy

IN 1694, A PRUSSIAN AGENT in Moscow observed that "the Muscovite people are entirely incapable of searching for . . . curiosities [*Curiositäten*], because they do not devote the slightest effort to anything that does not smell of money or bring some obvious benefit." He was apologizing for his inability to supply information of scholarly value to Gottfried Leibniz, who dreamed of a Westernized Russia as an intellectual link between the great civilizations of Europe and China.[1] But for eighteenth-century Russians, the Qing empire very much smelled of money, as did its curiosities. This meant that commerce—particularly in the post-Petrine era—went hand in hand with certain kinds of knowledge: not commentaries on Confucius or the intrigues of the Spring and Autumn Period but industrial technologies, military dispositions, and medical practices. The knowledge, in fact, was as material and mobile as the curiosities. Both depended on the physical and organizational carrying capacity of a caravan that traveled to China every few years. This caravan, and the configuration of intellectual and bureaucratic relationships it represented, was one of the central institutions for Russian intelligence gathering about China in the middle of the eighteenth century.

Trade was so important to eighteenth-century Russians that the caravan stood out against the general institutional landscape of the Russian Ecclesiastical Mission, the College of Foreign Affairs, and the Academy of Sciences. In general China in this era was not a first-order foreign-policy priority for the Russian state, but as a source of luxury goods for the court elite, its commercial value was significant. A diverse set of post-Petrine institutions thus built their strategies for engagement with China around the caravan, but in ways that were distinct from the public scholarship at the Academy or the expertise of translators at the College. Unlike the College, the caravan allowed for considerable creative initiative and autonomy from its intelligence personnel; unlike the Academy, it was not bound by the constraints of an elite-centered intellectual culture. Its distinctive form of knowledge production was industrial espionage, a persistent concern of eighteenth-century states. Russia in particular was a leading practitioner of early modern technology theft, largely by means of offering lucrative contracts to experienced foreign entrepreneurs who possessed trade secrets.[2] Qing craftsmen could not be lured away so easily, however, and Russian caravan personnel struggled to find other ways to lay their hands on Qing production methods. Their efforts demonstrate that secrecy and knowledge making were not just restricted to an educated elite.[3]

Between the 1650s and the 1750s, the Moscow-Beijing trade caravan was the most visible manifestation of Russo-Qing relations as far as any ordinary Russian or foreign observer was concerned. Although the caravan was more frequent and less official in the late seventeenth century than in the eighteenth, its underlying features were similar. It brought the pelts of tens of thousands of woodland creatures, carefully stockpiled in advance in Siberian depots, south to Beijing and brought back silks, porcelain, tea, and objets d'art for consumption by the imperial court and the nobility in the capitals. Before it was supplanted by the direct trade established at the border town of Kiakhta in the 1730s, this was the main commercial artery that connected the two empires. Yet financially speaking, the caravan was a break-even proposition for the Crown: even if the record books for a particular run showed a profit, this did not reflect the opportunity cost of the venture, the true cost of the furs being sold (since the state generally acquired these as tribute in kind), or the overhead required for maintaining the caravan's administrative support structure.[4] Thus its significance was not purely economic in the sense of generating an income from the state treasury.

Instead, the caravan was important because of the specificity of the commodities and the knowledge it carried. It helped fulfill the court's demand for specific goods, a vector for (paradoxically) the growing Westernization of elite Russian tastes, which like their French and British counterparts were beginning to include East Asian luxury commodities.[5] For the Qing customers who bought Russian furs in Beijing, on the other hand, they served as a marketable and prestigious signifier of Manchu frontier heritage.[6] Intelligence—secrets ranging from the geographic to the industrial—was another essential and nonfungible good. The longtime caravan director Lorents Lang, the former Swedish prisoner of war who later governed Irkutsk, by the end of his tenure accumulated a wide-ranging set of responsibilities involving knowledge and diplomacy, from keeping journals to reporting on conditions at the Qing court.[7] Finally, caravans also provided opportunities for impromptu inspections of conditions in Eastern Siberia. To understand why the Russian state spent so much effort sustaining its caravan, we should learn to see it as a multipurpose logistical platform for a variety of intellectual and commercial agendas: a bandwagon.

Commodities that were also compelling intellectually because of their East Asian origins and the techniques used in their manufacture were known in Russian as *kurioznye*. "Curiosity" was a common trope for early modern gentlemen-savants, but in Russia its seekers were more likely to be agents of the state.[8] In 1752, for instance, the caravan director Aleksei Vladykin was ordered to obtain "Chinese as well as Japanese goods needed for Her Imperial Majesty's court as well as for other highborn persons, and especially the best possible curiosities [*iz kurioznykh veshchei kak vozmozhno lutchikh*]."[9] A set of 1735 instructions to Lang spelled out in exacting detail what "curiosities" could and could not include. "Lacquered items of Japanese manufacture" were desirable, but porcelain "painted only in blue" was not, unless it was "very fine Japanese work"; "old curtains sewn on a black or white brocade" were not acceptable, "nor those with Chinese characters," unless "there are also flowers and people or birds."[10] When Vladykin's brother Eremei attempted to bring close to one hundred pieces of porcelain tableware and other objects back from Beijing, only to have them confiscated at an internal customs post, he argued—successfully—that these goods had been acquired *iz kuriozitetu* rather than for sale.[11] It is clear to us, as it was to the customs officials, that these were commodities and not simply individual items of artistic significance, but being curious raised them to a more exalted level. Curiosities underpinned the caravans' wholehearted pursuit of industrial espionage: the briefs of such spies as the Tobolsk silversmith Osip Miasnikov included a mandate to acquire any sort of "curious things" they might identify.[12] By contrast, when French Jesuits attempted to present their studies of curiosities, such as Chinese medicine or porcelain, the French Academy of Sciences was much more skeptical.[13]

But curiosity was only one of the motivations behind caravan-based intelligence gathering. Another major focus was strategic. After all, the caravan offered Russians their only opportunity to traverse spaces in the Qing realm that were not subjected to constant Qing surveillance and control, where they could assess potential logistical problems or evaluate local defenses in the event of a future military conflict. We have seen how Russian visitors like the ambassadors Baikov and Spafarii gathered information of this kind throughout the seventeenth century; in the eighteenth, as embassies became less frequent, caravan directors and their subordinates replaced them. The caravan's commercial activities, moreover, offered many opportunities to conceal the exchange of illicit objects, such as maps and documents. The Governing Senate and the College of Foreign Affairs did not fail to take advantage of such materials when their agents acquired them nor to duly reward the finder. Accordingly, any set of instructions issued to a caravan director bore the boilerplate warning that "any affairs which are subject to secrecy should not be discussed in personal letters, not [even] to him who sent you, aside from true [official] reports."[14]

Geography as Intelligence

In the eighteenth century, the caravan trade was becoming more centered on the commercial and intellectual priorities of the state rather than those of merchants. Nondiplomatic caravans began to travel from Russia to China after the 1689 Treaty of Nerchinsk, but the half dozen caravans that traveled between Moscow and Beijing from the 1727 Treaty of Kiakhta to the last caravan, which returned in 1755, were distinct in important ways. (Caravans still went to China from Russia in the second half of the century, but they originated at the border and were much smaller, meant mainly to resupply the Russian Ecclesiastical Mission.) They were limited by treaty to at most one every three years, a schedule aimed at keeping fur prices high as well as limiting Russian access to Beijing. They were also organized, staffed, and tightly controlled by state institutions. This was a sharp departure from the previous period, when Siberian merchants could use fictive diplomatic paperwork to launch unmonitored caravan ventures.

As a direct result of growing state control, the new caravans became a bureaucratic entity rather than a physical one. Our received image of a caravan—a line of camels crossing a dune against the setting sun—had nothing to do with the Moscow-Beijing caravan as it existed for most of its journey. In the Russian portion of its route, it relied on the postal system for travel, being issued a set number of drivers and carts at each station.[15] Only at the Mongol border were its hundreds of people and thousands of animals gathered, packed, and escorted through Qing territory to Beijing. For the most part, caravans with an official escort were not unduly hampered by bandits or lack of supplies, though such incidents did sometimes occur. A far more omnipresent reality was bookkeeping. Each post-1727 caravan had a treasury (*karavannaia summa*), which paid salaries to a director, a commissar, a suite of sworn Crown agents (*tseloval'niki*), a doctor, and so on, while its composition and instructions reflected the input and involvement of a number of government bodies: the Governing Senate as the administrative body of the empire, the College of Foreign Affairs as its diplomatic corps, the Siberian Bureau with oversight of Siberian commerce, local Siberian administrators, and the Academy of Sciences. Typically, preparations for a caravan would begin a year or more in advance; trained personnel would be requisitioned by the appropriate agencies and commanded to come to Moscow. The caravan would spend a year or more on the road, remain in Beijing for three to six months, then take another year to return, at which point its imports would be auctioned off. Often, outstanding disputes and investigations resulted in one caravan's books being open well into the tenure of the next.

The mobile bureaucracy of the Moscow-Beijing caravan responded to demands from a wide range of other bureaucracies. This fundamental heterogeneity was reflected in its intelligence-gathering practices as well. In a typical caravan, the director, following Siberian Bureau orders, oversaw the procurement of books, maps, and other privileged documents; the doctor, on assignment from the Medical Chancellery or the Academy of Sciences, acquired medical and technical know-how; a clerk might have been a disguised geodesist (on-the-ground surveyor) charged by the Senate with keeping a detailed journal with drawings of settlements and fortifications; one or two of the merchants might have been industrial spies from the Siberian Bureau; and students picked up from the Russian Ecclesiastical Mission in Beijing provided local knowledge and personal collecting skills for the benefit of the Academy of Sciences or the College of Foreign Affairs. Equipped with distinct, noncoordinated sets of instructions, these representatives of the Russian state pursued their missions without any regard for the others.

Not all of the knowledge assembled by caravan personnel was covert in nature. Instead, as in other venues like the College, caravan employees followed pragmatic considerations in gathering intelligence along a spectrum ranging from simple day-to-day meteorological and ethnographic observations to the secret and potentially risky bribery of officials for access to classified Qing documents. It is hard to identify a bright line between the two in the minds of the Russians. Yet they clearly regarded some forms of it as being riskier and hence worthier of reward than others. Such tasks figure as justifications in requests for promotions and raises, either before or after the fact.[16] On the other hand, official bodies were not unduly concerned about the qualifications of caravan employees and regarded with equanimity news that an assignment had been bungled due to laziness or drunkenness—though at one point Lang suggested that his chancellerist might "serve better with a sword than in the caravan with a pen."[17] The overriding motivation for the caravan's personnel, then, was not really the fulfillment of any specific information-gathering task. It was making as much use as possible of the opportunity provided by the caravan's motion through space: a clumsy early modern surveillance drone, it moved through Qing lands bristling with human sensors.

On the most basic level, the movement of the caravan took part in the Petrine era's massive expansion of geographical knowledge production.[18] As newly trained geodesists fanned out through the empire, members of the caravan helped to chart their particular path, which also followed the principal route between Moscow and Eastern Siberia. Travel journals and other forms of geographical intelligence were among the most well established of the caravan's intelligence practices. A mid-eighteenth-century *poverstnaia kniga* (gazetteer of postal routes) originating in the Astrakhan procuracy used data from Savva Vladislavich's 1725–1730 caravan journal to establish the official route from Moscow to the Qing border (via Verkhotur'e and Selenginsk).[19] The caravan's journal, kept by its main administrative personnel, contained

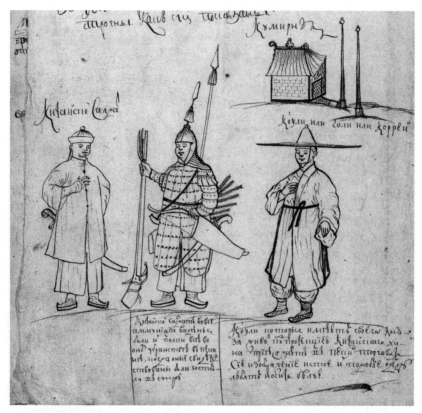

5.1 Two Qing soldiers, left, and a Korean, right, from a caravan journal, 1736. RGADA, fond 199, opis' 1, delo 349, chast' 2, l. 32v.

a great deal more secret information; it was explicitly meant to be more than a record of its journey. Travel impressions and drawings focused on questions that were likely to be of interest to military planners or other higher-level officials. They included descriptions of strategically-significant objects as well as plans of settlements and fortifications, such as the Great Wall crossings of Xuanfu and Kalgan (Zhangjiakou).[20] Though it was not always kept in a systematic way, the journal helped to translate the caravan's privileged vantage point in Qing territory into valuable intelligence.

The most explicit mission statement for the caravan's secret geographical activities was the set of instructions issued to the geodesist Eremei Vladykin for the 1752–1755 caravan. They went into great detail about why and how in-

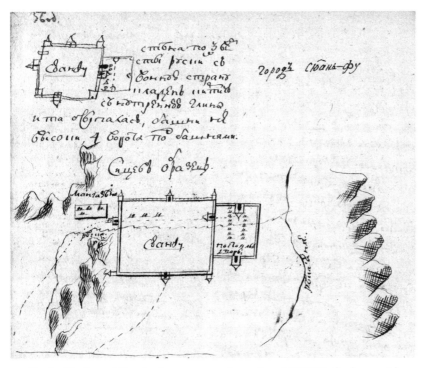

5.2 The fortifications at Xuanfu, from a caravan journal, 1736. RGADA, fond 199, opis' 1, delo 349, chast' 2, l. 56v.

telligence was to be gathered and how this was to be kept secret. They ordered him to survey the territories between Kiakhta and Beijing, "what people live there and what their numbers are, and where they obtain food and income, as well as where the rivers are, what they are called, and how distant they are from one another, and from where and to where they flow, describe all this thoroughly and map it." This could not be done openly, however, and it was concealed both from the Qing and from fellow caravan members: "While doing so this Vladykin is to conduct himself in an artful and secret fashion so that the Qing cannot discover or learn about this task from anyone or bear the slightest suspicion. And for this reason he is not to tell anyone that he is an officer of geodesy, but rather call himself a caravan commissar, and neither is he to disclose this to the Russians in the caravan, except for the director."[21] Vladykin's journal amply fulfilled these obligations. Some of his observations noted objective factors like distance (measured with a surveyor's wheel) and climate, but many focused on the details of military provisioning and interethnic relations.[22]

Vladykin supplemented his journal with a series of maps, as specified in his instructions. Some he evidently composed himself, but the majority (covering "the eastern side of the Qing state, which is quite unknown to the Russians but has been determined to be most valuable to know for future enterprises") he procured secretly from contacts at the "palace library" with the help of students from the Russian Ecclesiastical Mission. Vladykin and his assistant Bashmakov spent "day and night" furiously copying the maps, so they could be returned to the library's collections. The haul, which both Vladykins presented to the Senate on their return in 1756, included three maps of the Amur region (including Korea and some of the Japanese islands), three of Inner and Outer Mongolia, seven of various provinces, and one of the city of Beijing. All told, the collection cost 1,500 rubles to acquire—the equivalent of three years' salary for Vladykin, which the Senate was happy to compensate. The Amur maps were particularly crucial (and expensive), because the region was a focus of imperial expansion and because the Senate was in the midst of preparing a Third Kamchatka Expedition to sail down the Qing-controlled river.[23]

This was not the first set of maps acquired and turned in to the Senate by caravan intelligence. In 1738 (while Aleksei Vladykin was still a student at the Russian Ecclesiastical Mission), the caravan director Lorents Lang reported to Empress Anna that he had located "a geographic map of the entire realm of the Qing emperor on 32 sheets, which I obtained during my current stay in Beijing through the exertions of the language student Larion Rossokhin, on which by his own labors he has also marked the place names with Russian letters." For his pains, Rossokhin received a scant 150-ruble reward.[24] Did the Russian Senate and College of Foreign Affairs judge this map so inadequate or outdated that Vladykin had to retrace Lang's steps? Rossokhin's atlas was likely a version of the imperially commissioned Kangxi Atlas and hence would have represented one of the era's most reliable sources of geographical information about the Qing.[25] Most likely this collection of maps was simply forgotten by the time the 1753 caravan was due to be sent; Vladykin's instructions even claimed the region had not been surveyed by previous caravans. Like maps, books and texts that seemed to have geographical or strategic content were also in demand. The Russian state's appetite for intelligence about the Qing realm may have been voracious, but it was also indiscriminate and unsystematic.[26]

Trade Secrets and Objects on the Move

The caravan was, of course, not only a bureaucracy: it carried far more than paper. In certain cases, a courier might have done the same intelligence work as a caravan director. What he could not do was substitute for its ability to carry a wide range of material objects and service personnel. This feature made the caravan appealing to a number of imperial institutions, which hoped that it could give them a point of entry into the alluring realm of Chinese craft secrets. Russian officials hoped that one day they would be able to extract enough knowledge that China's unique exports could be replaced with local Russian equivalents. The Medical Chancellery, the Siberian Bureau, and—as we will see—the Academy of Sciences all seized the opportunity provided by this mobile platform.

Medical knowledge was one area in which Chinese expertise was particularly prized: rhubarb root, a highly regarded and expensive medicament, was one of the major goods in Russo-Qing commerce. (Russians transshipped the root to Western Europe at vastly inflated prices.)[27] Ironically, the initiative for the first Russian doctor to be sent to Beijing originated with the Kangxi emperor. When the Qing ambassador Tulišen met the Siberian governor Matvei Gagarin in 1713, he relayed Kangxi's request for a Russian surgeon; the Scot Thomas Garvine was assigned to accompany Lang's caravan to Beijing, where he successfully treated the emperor.[28] Garvine realized that he had as much to learn in the Qing capital as he had to teach: on the way back he carried medicine sent by the local Jesuits to the tsar, as well as a package of letters for the Holy Roman Emperor.[29] Subsequent caravans usually had a foreign-born official doctor, in part to deal with the habitual diseases that plagued travelers in Siberia and Mongolia but also to deliver Qing and Jesuit medical knowledge back to Moscow and St. Petersburg.

By the 1740s, this doctor's role was formally defined by the Medical Chancellery, the administrative body that managed medical personnel and gardens in the empire, to include investigations of medical and industrial secrets.

In exchange for a salary raise, one such doctor was instructed to "serve the medical craft by finding yet-unknown plants and medical information," though he had been apparently doing so already in the hope of a reward.[30] In 1744, he was replaced by a medic of Croatian origin named Franz Lukas Jellatschitsch.[31] Jellatschitsch (who also served as agent of the Academy of Sciences) had a much broader brief. In addition to his duties as a healer, the Medical Chancellery asked him to keep a journal, study Chinese medicinal practices with Jesuit help, and investigate manufacturing practices.[32] The chancellery's requests were not driven by its functional role in the imperial bureaucracy but by the opportunism of officials looking to leverage their participation in the caravan for competitive institutional advantage.

The Medical Chancellery's requests for kaolin and other craftwork materials betrayed no knowledge of the fact that the caravan was already serving as the staging ground for a wide-ranging project of industrial espionage in these fields. Although eighteenth-century Russia was constantly obtaining technological know-how in licit and illicit ways, it did so primarily by importing skilled workers from all over Europe, taking advantage of their expertise in high-technology areas such as mining. The foreign servitors who traveled to Beijing with the caravan, such as Lang, Garvine, and Heick, were one manifestation of this phenomenon: had Tulišen asked for a Russian-born doctor to attend Kangxi, it is unlikely that any of them would be found.[33] In the Qing context, however, Russian industrial espionage meant clandestinely observing working practices and strategically bribing craftsmen to reveal their trade secrets. It was in the development of industrial espionage that both the opportunities and drawbacks offered by caravan intelligence presented themselves most fully, for they were also about making the Russian empire useful: by involving personnel and resources from Eastern Siberia, the caravan could have acted to connect Siberia in new ways with both Russia and China.

This agenda was linked to the post-Petrine state's broader concerns about the Siberian economy. The Siberian Bureau had been revived in 1730 specifically because the Crown believed that "the Siberian guberniya, in which state profits mainly depend on Chinese and Mongol commerce and the collection of sables and other furs from iasak peoples, is no longer in the same condition and degree of oversight that it once was." Its mission was the restoration of Siberia to its former profitability through increased control over the caravan and anticorruption investigations.[34] Developing an industry that drew on Siberia in new ways, exploiting its skilled craftsmen and hitherto untapped natural resources, would have bolstered the Bureau's fragile claim to institutional relevance. But this depended on the successful acquisition of Chinese knowledge.

The most valuable secret to be gained was the recipe for Chinese porcelain, which depended on the use of kaolin and special high-firing kilns capable of maintaining temperatures over 1300° C. In 1712, the Jesuit François d'Entrecolles was conducting research into the process at the Jingdezhen porcelain factories in central China: although Lang was in Beijing in 1715 and was in close contact with the Jesuits, he did not mention the new research. In fact, the whole question should have been moot. In 1709 the German "alchemist" Johann Friedrich Böttger (or rather, more likely, his mentor Ehrenfried von Tschirnhaus) had finally discovered the secret of porcelain making, with Europe's first manufactory opening in the Saxon city of Meissen later the same year. Although Chinese-made porcelain continued to sell well in Europe until the mid-eighteenth century, in part because it was considered to be both cheaper and higher quality, the technical barriers to breaking the Qing monopoly had been lifted.[35] Peter the Great had extensive contacts in the German principalities, and the porcelain secret was not confined to Saxony for long; indeed, the Russian tsar employed a Saxon porcelain master named Peter Eggebrecht to import the craft just as Lang was arriving in Beijing. But nothing came of this. No porcelain manufacturing existed in Russia until the reign of Elizabeth, although one Ivan Grebenshchikov did manage to produce the cruder, less high-fired faience.[36]

Despite this earlier missed opportunity, between 1735 and 1755 the caravan managed to reinvigorate Russian interest in industrial espionage in the Qing Empire, including porcelain. In the former year, the historian and high official Vasilii Tatishchev reported to the Cabinet that while in the Siberian capital of Tobolsk he had met with a silversmith named "Maslov," "who had been in China." (His name, as subsequent reports clarified, was actually Miasnikov.) According to Tatishchev, "It is clear that he did not waste his time there. . . . He said he saw how they make vessels out of hard stone and would have worked himself but did not know what to call the materials in Russian, and had not brought any with him, so he asked me to send him there for a year. . . . He seems to be an intelligent man and no drunk." Miasnikov was dispatched with Lang's 1735 caravan to learn as much about Qing handicrafts as he could.[37] Although he achieved some success in studying metalwork and miscellaneous crafting techniques, Lang pleaded on his behalf that "he was not in a position to fulfill his duty entirely." Not only were Qing authorities so suspicious that they "never let Russian people leave the embassy compound without a guard for any reason," local Qing subjects also tended to avoid the caravan: "not only their artisans but any sort of people use any means to distance themselves from conversation [konversatsii] with Russians so as not to fall under suspicion." Nonetheless, in addition to the handful of local techniques he learned, Miasnikov managed to acquire samples of ore and other components; most importantly for the Russians, he discovered how to repair broken porcelain vessels using iron braces. Lang requested that Miasnikov be dispatched for a third trip to China with the next caravan.[38]

Although the Cabinet agreed with Lang that industrial espionage needed to be continued and expanded under Miasnikov's leadership, subsequent efforts were stymied by infighting.[39] Miasnikov located two pupils to help him, of whom one turned out to be an incompetent drunk. When the caravan returned in 1743 and the Cabinet attempted to determine whether Miasnikov had accomplished anything in Beijing, the silversmith denounced the new caravan director Erofei Firsov for refusing to buy precious stones for his research and for otherwise obstructing his work. He claimed he had found a Chinese porcelain master who was willing to share the secret for the astronomical sum of 2,000 taels (about 3,500 rubles), but Firsov had refused to pay, saying that the caravan was due to leave too soon to be of use. Consulted to adjudicate this accusation, the Siberian Bureau failed to respond for five years, leaving Miasnikov and his two students to draw pay uselessly in the capital. At last, in 1749 the imperial treasury staged a demonstration in the ballroom of the Winter Palace, at which the three craftsmen successfully repaired (with metal braces) a consignment of state-owned porcelain tableware. Of course, this left Russians no closer to the secret of porcelain manufacturing—after all, Miasnikov had supposedly learned the repair trick a decade before. Nothing else he had discovered in Beijing proved worthwhile.[40]

Yet the pursuit of Chinese industrial techniques became even more ambitious under the director of the next caravan, Gerasim Lebratovskii. When his caravan arrived in Kiakhta, he discovered a local resident named Andrei Kursin, who had been experimenting with kaolin deposits he had found in the area. Lebratovskii took him with him to Beijing. With the help of the mission student (and future caravan director) Aleksei Vladykin, Lebratovskii and Kursin managed to locate a porcelain maker who was willing to share the secret at a cost of 1,933 taels (3,286 rubles; the total cost of the director's experiments exceeded 5,200 rubles, enough to buy some seven hundred thousand pounds of rye grain).[41] He demonstrated the craft in an empty Buddhist shrine and provided Lebratovskii with a detailed set of written instructions. On his way home in 1746, Lebratovskii picked up Andrei Kursin's brother Aleksei and brought them both to St. Petersburg, where he set up an experimental porcelain factory near a brickworks.

This effort failed, probably due to the lack of the necessary kaolin, and the pressure to produce results led each participant in the project to blame the other. In a lengthy complaint, Aleksei Kursin claimed Lebratovskii's informant had provided faulty information, that the project was doomed, and that the director was simply trying to cover up the fact that he had wasted such a vast sum of the tsar's money; in the service of this lie, Kursin claimed, he had been forced to misrepresent how much he really knew about the process. Lebratovskii—whose letters as reproduced in the complaint really do show an escalating sense of desperation—insisted that they merely needed time and the proper materials to put the Chinese recipe into practice. The venture folded without ever having produced more than two prototype cups, and it is unclear how close to porcelain these actually were.[42] Lebratovskii, at any rate, had remarkably bad timing. In 1744, the Moscow metallurgists Gunger and Vinogradov successfully developed the recipe on their own and founded the Imperial Porcelain Factory, which remains in existence to this day. Chinese porcelain would play no part in its history.

The horizons of Russian industrial espionage were not limited to porcelain, however. In 1737, Lang was ordered to take on Stepan Dames, the son of the director of the Nerchinsk silver mines. Dames was expected to go to Beijing and, like Miasnikov, study Qing metallurgy—in particular, the means by which silver- and goldsmiths there extracted their own metal from raw ore on a piecemeal basis. Dames proved incompetent, and in any case, there were no convenient metallurgists nearby.[43] The graduates of the porcelain project were more enterprising. After their disappointment with porcelain, the Kursins went back to Beijing once more, together with Miasnikov's old pupil Dmitrii Popov. Along the way, they were overcome with enthusiasm for yet another industrial espionage project, which they seem to have conceived on their own: adopting Qing alcohol distillation techniques (of baijiu or another high-proof grain spirit) to the Russian market, since these were "much more convenient" than Russian methods. This and other efforts ended in utter failure, with the brothers alternately blaming the perfidy of the informants and the lack of appropriate materials. One, however, was a partial success—making what Russians call *finift'*, or enameled silverware, using the vivid mineral colors popular in China. The Kursins managed to create a finift' goblet and tray weighing approximately three hundred grams, but some of the colors and decorations they had learned to create were unavailable in Russia. As of 1758, they had been issued with a state-owned building in Moscow in which to carry on the trade, though what happened to Chinese enamel making in Russia subsequently is unclear.[44] The experience shows how a state commitment to funding industrial espionage projects had given experimentation a momentum of its own.

Linking Siberia into the Russo-Qing exchange was associated with a potentially even thornier question. Miasnikov's instructions on one of his trips to Beijing show how secrecy could be a tool of internal, not just external, security: it was essential to "keep this task entrusted to him secret or pretend that he is only spending his time in these tasks for his own curiosity, for if the common people and especially near the border discover that he is seeking ores for the good of the state, then it is likely that they will try to cause problems so that they do not find themselves being used for such work in time, and if the Qing discover [his efforts] then they may conceal their arts from us even more."[45] If industrial espionage could demonstrate the relevance of Siberian resource deposits for the manufacture of curiosities, this could result not only in the deeper integration of the Siberian economy but also in unforeseen tensions among already unstable border populations. In the end, the failure of this project negated these political dangers.

The motivations that led Russian institutions to pursue these industrial espionage projects—alongside other ways of using the caravan to produce intelligence—can easily be overshadowed by their lack of success. By the 1750s, the translators at the College exerted no influence on policy, the scholars at the Academy had published no scholarship, and the efforts of Russia's industrial spies had generated no usable innovations. These failures exemplify the challenges faced by the Russian Empire in assembling a comprehensive picture of its southeastern rival. Yet the motivations behind each of these projects matter, because they reveal how institutions competed for relevance in an era in which commercial advantage was paramount. The caravan bureaucracy, as it moved through Qing and Siberian space, combined multiple intelligence functions, the sheer length of its route serving not only to increase its inconvenience and expense but also to broaden the field of uses its mobility might potentially serve. This was why, no matter how often the caravan disappointed its taskmasters, administrators continued to incorporate intelligence requirements into the caravan's brief. By 1760 the situation had changed significantly: diplomatic tensions were escalating to such an extent that the College of Foreign Affairs concluded that "it is to be feared that the Qing will raid and despoil our caravan if it is sent at this time." What was to be a temporary halt turned out to be a permanent one two years later, when Catherine II ascended the throne.[46] This development halted not only Russia's doomed efforts to reconstruct the Chinese porcelain recipe but also another form of knowledge making. In the previous decades, a flourishing scholarly exchange had developed between the Imperial Academy of Sciences and the Jesuit community in Beijing. Despite their assertions of intellectual disinterestedness, it turned out that they, too, had depended on the material mobility the caravan had offered.

Chapter 6

The Commerce of Long-Distance Letters

IN THE FIRST HALF of the eighteenth century, Russians saw the Qing above all as a source of luxury goods. In the institutional ecosystem developed under Peter and his successors, experts were essential, but the caravan was paramount. Yet, just as experts operated in both secret and public-facing institutions, the caravan also had a dual role. Alongside cartographic and industrial espionage, it also facilitated the quintessential Enlightenment practice of learned correspondence between widely separated communities of experts. Between the 1730s and the 1770s, the Jesuit missionaries in Beijing and the professors of the Imperial Academy of Sciences in St. Petersburg carried on an extensive, if frequently interrupted, scientific correspondence. Both sides insisted that this "commercium plane nobilissimum" ("clearly the noblest commerce") was an exemplary case of learned men communicating with one another in the service of knowledge, and that the Russian empress's (indirect) support for it would redound to her glory. It would be easy to take them at their word: after all, this trans-Eurasian connection seems to have realized Leibniz's dream of Russia as a bridge between European and Chinese civilization in the form of an Enlightenment correspondence network.[1] Yet the letters were not disembodied communications flitting back and forth across four thousand miles of space. The correspondence remained dependent on the material infrastructure of the Moscow-Beijing trade caravan and on individualized ties of patronage and interest. This noble commerce was not distinct from intelligence gathering but interwoven with it; its rise and fall followed not the rhythm of

Russian involvement in Enlightenment learning but the fate of the caravan that made it possible.

Scholars of the Jesuit mission in China have sometimes paid attention to this route, but in a way that neglects this key material component. This is because, for nearly a century, work on this correspondence has relied on a partial set of letters copied and brought from St. Petersburg to Europe by the Jesuit François-Marie Gaillard around 1912. After the Russian Revolution, the Academy archives became comparatively inaccessible, and this archive emerged as an essential body of sources. Yet, in stripping away the logistical and ancillary paperwork that accompanied the letters, Gaillard's collection has contributed to the sense that these were idealized epistolary productions of the Republic of Letters. Even the correspondence of mainstream European savants was often as much about patronage and material acquisition as it was about the exchange of facts or interpretations.[2] The letters of Russian academicians were unusual, however, because they existed outside the postal infrastructure that sustained such networks in Europe. Instead, they relied on the Academy's ability to insinuate itself into the welter of institutions that surrounded the caravan to Beijing.[3]

The Russo-Jesuit relationship is an old one. In the Muscovite era, their presence had been associated with the foreign-policy aims of the Polish-Lithuanian Commonwealth; they were regarded with suspicion on that basis and repeatedly expelled.[4] Peter I treated them permissively and permitted the Jesuit use of the "Russian Route" (or "Siberian Route") for the dispatch of letters, which predated the Imperial Academy of Sciences by at least two decades. In 1708, Kilian Stumpf and Dominique Parrenin (a German and a French Jesuit respectively) visited a group of Russian merchants in Beijing to receive some letters from the Jesuit college in Moscow. The letters were delivered with the seals removed, leading Stumpf to conclude that "no one can write through this route except openly."[5] This violation of protocol, combined with the well-known Russian reputation for paranoia, made the Russian Route a poor choice for matters requiring confidentiality. But the challenges facing the Jesuit mission were often more public than that. In the late seventeenth century, Jesuits found themselves repeatedly embroiled in conflict with the papacy and European Catholic elites over their views on the compatibility of Chinese traditional practices with Catholicism. This episode, the Rites Controversy, revealed the route's utility for another purpose: the delivery of letters to Europe clarifying and defending the

Jesuit position, which were meant to be widely disseminated. Stumpf sent one such letter to the short-lived Moscow college of Jesuits in June 1712. It was accompanied by a brief description of China and a copy of the 1701 *Brevis Relatio;* not to be confused with a similarly named work from 1654, this text offered a glowing view of the Jesuit presence in the Kangxi emperor's realm. The letter seems not to have survived in Latin, but at least three manuscript versions dating to the mid-eighteenth century exist in Russian archives in Church Slavonic. This means that its circulation had not been restricted to its direct addressees, perhaps even that it found an eager public in the Russian clergy.[6] Another letter, addressed to Superior General Tamburini, was sent to Vienna via Moscow in 1717 and survives in a Latin version.[7]

The success of the Russian Route in this context was closely linked to the fact that the caravans employed a specialized staff that included educated Europeans. Although in theory Russian caravan merchants in Beijing could serve as couriers for the missionaries' correspondence as well as anybody else, in practice the Jesuits, from Stumpf onward, placed their trust almost exclusively in the Western Europeans in Russian service.[8] This applied particularly to the doctors, who were invariably of non-Russian origin, though foreigners such as the Swedish-born caravan director Lorents Lang also played courier roles. European servitors in Russia were in this period rarely of aristocratic or gentry origin, and indeed their willingness to abandon their old lives for what was likely a lifetime appointment in Russia testified to their marginal status. Yet their educational backgrounds and knowledge of Western languages made them more credible vectors for correspondence than the culturally alien Russians and Siberians who made up the bulk of the caravan. Moreover, as the leading French Jesuit scholar Antoine Gaubil discovered when he lent money to a missionary named Nikita (probably Chekanov), Russians were not always bound to the same standards of honorable gentility that prevailed among Westerners. An early modern European gentleman's word guaranteed his honor, and he could thus be trusted implicitly when he promised to carry a letter; this was not true for the clerks and petty bureaucrats who served in the caravan.[9] From the Scottish physician Thomas Garvine in 1715 to Franz Lukas Jellatschitsch in the 1750s, then, Western Europeans served as a bridge between Beijing and Moscow just as much as Moscow served as one between Europe and Beijing.

In Russia, the Jesuits fell victim to a diplomatic feud with the Holy Roman Empire and were expelled for the penultimate time in 1720.[10] The fact that

Jesuit establishments were forbidden on Russian territory until the First Partition of Poland in 1772 did not prevent Russian authorities from cultivating ties to Jesuits abroad. Three years after the Academy opened in 1724, the ambassador Savva Vladislavich arrived in Beijing in 1727 to negotiate the Treaty of Kiakhta. He was well received by the missionaries, to whom he offered a European atlas as a gift and whom he courted with vague (and empty) promises of free passage through Russia for the Society. It helped that he himself was educated in Europe and had "8 or 9 Catholics—Dalmatians, Venetians, Germans or Poles—in his suite," as Gaubil reported; "it must be admitted among the Russians there are a few who know what they're doing," he wrote to his superior Etienne Souciet in 1730.[11]

Private Careers and Institutional Goals

Yet Vladislavich's undeniable charms paled next to those of his subordinate Lorents Lang, who had known the Jesuits since his first trip to China in 1715. Lang was not just the superb administrator and agent he seemed to the Governing Senate: he also combined a fine Halle education with an extensive knowledge of European languages. Gaubil thought him "a true and well-regarded gentleman." More importantly, Lang was equally popular in St. Petersburg, where his expertise on Chinese matters, particularly related to trade, was widely acknowledged.[12] When he visited the Academy, the academic Gottlieb (Theophilus) Siegfried Bayer, professor of antiquities, took the opportunity to grill him for particulars about China. He then entrusted him to deliver a copy of his new book, *Museum Sinicium,* to the Jesuits in Beijing, along with a series of letters to Dominique Parrenin and others. In return, when Parrenin, Gaubil, and other Jesuits saw Lang in Beijing in 1732, they provided him with letters of their own.[13]

The Academy-Jesuit correspondence, then, did not begin as the official channel of communication between institutions—the Academy on one side and the Jesuit colleges on the other—that it would later become. It was an essentially private connection made possible by the ability of Lang to negotiate different social milieus structured by patronage relations and to leverage his position at the head of the Chinese caravan. This had concrete material effects. Lang's connections in Beijing allowed him to obtain Chinese objets d'art for his patron, Count Osterman (from whom they were later confiscated when he fell from power). His services to the Academy and personally to its president, Baron Korff, meanwhile, allowed him to procure a place for his nephew there. Personal and institutional relationships were often mingled. In 1737, for instance, Lang wrote to Korff on his way back from Beijing that "I have taken the liberty . . . of obtaining a very old Chinese Chronology from the learned Father Gaubil in Peking to humbly present to Your Excellency as one of the rarest antiquities, along with which there is another copy from this father to be forwarded to Monsieur Freret in Paris."[14] Lang, in other words, was able to deftly parlay his services as a middleman both to secure his Jesuit connections and to please his patrons at home. In fact, for the Jesuits, his intervention was indispensable, since they regarded sending any packages or correspondence through the hands of Chinese or Mongol intermediaries as exposing them to charges of treason, while—as later experience proved—Russian state servitors were untrustworthy.[15] As the preferred contact for the Jesuits, he also became a favored client of the academicians who wanted to correspond with them.

The academicians decided to offer a collective response. In September 1734, after delivering the Jesuits' return letters, Lang officially offered his services as a facilitator to a meeting of the Academy. The professors fell to it with gusto, with Bayer, the botanist Johann Amman, and the anatomist Du Vernoi assembling a list of books (which ran to dozens of titles, mainly works authored by seventeenth-century Jesuit missionaries) and questions for their new correspondents. Bayer himself was tasked with writing on behalf of the Academy, although his letters maintained the warm, personal tone of his earlier correspondence. It was only at the end of his letter to Ignatius Kögler, Andrea Pereyra, and Carel Slavicek that he noted that the Academy would not only "ordain your correspondence [*commercium*] with us with a most honorific decree" but would also transmit all the books it published "to your College."[16]

Yet there were also private motivations involved. After the 1730 publication of his *Museum Sinicum,* Bayer had extended his inquiries into Chinese chronology and began to compose a massive Chinese dictionary. According to a manuscript biographical sketch of Bayer, Osterman's patronage was key for this project: the count procured for him printed copies of the *Hai pian* and *Zi hui,* two seventeenth-century Chinese dictionaries, along with Parrenin's manuscript Chinese-Latin dictionary (given originally to Vladislavich).[17] Letters to and from Bayer deal largely with linguistic matters, with Parrenin attempting to walk the academician back from his doomed project of formulating a key to the Chinese language.[18] Bayer did not depend on the Russian Route and conceived of his letters as part of a separate process; he wrote that he would "ask the Vice-Chancellor [i.e., Osterman] to tell me if an occasion [to send letters] arises; if none does, I will give it to your Fathers in Pondicherry, who can send it on through Canton to your college."[19] Parrenin, who discouraged him from using the Indian route, also noted that he had "written in a small way to the Imperial Academy in the name of all the French Fathers in Peking, putting us forward as people looking to satisfy etc." The Jesuit, in other words, saw his personal interactions with Bayer as distinct from collective ones.[20]

Private correspondence could even work directly against the Academy's own interests. After 1732 Gaubil carried on an extensive exchange with the astronomer and geographer Joseph-Nicolas Delisle. Like Bayer, Delisle kept a firm line between private and institutional letters: "I will ask of you only what I need personally, and I will only send you things that depend on me and belong to me."[21] Yet unlike the German antiquarian, Delisle was recognized by the Jesuits even before he accepted his appointment in St. Petersburg.[22] In fact, Delisle had received Kögler's observations by means of an Italian correspondent a number of years earlier and had first written to him then.[23] As Delisle's letters to Gaubil show, he felt he had much more in common with the Jesuit savant than with his academic subordinates: "There is ... a great difference between mémoires that are exact and made by capable mathematicians, like those which emerge from the hands of Jesuits, and the majority of those that one can expect from the people of this country [i.e., Russia], who have only just begun to enter into the sciences and have not done so enough to produce an equivalent work."[24] Gaubil echoed his correspondent: "Certainly the Russians are greatly obliged to you and your brother de la Croyère. You'll make the whole land of this vast empire properly known, while here we'll devote all our efforts to giving you information about Tartary."[25] The strength of this personal connection endured not only after the initial Academy-Jesuit correspondence had broken down—as evidenced by a 1743 Gaubil letter in which he complained to Delisle that he had seen "no books, no letters, no news" since 1737—but also after Delisle stopped being part of the academy altogether, a departure soon accompanied by scandal.[26]

Delisle's correspondence with Gaubil had a geopolitical dimension: both astronomers, despite their current places of residence, owed their ultimate loyalty to the French crown. Throughout his time in Russia, the French astronomer secretly sent the French minister Maurepas copies of the maps he was hired to produce, referring to this as "the secret commerce we are carrying on together."[27] Whether he was driven ultimately by geopolitical considerations or by loyalty to the universalism of the Republic of Letters has been a matter of scholarly debate.[28] When he and Gaubil exchanged geographical information, they were engaged in matters of international importance. Particularly this applied to the geography of Kamchatka, which was kept secret as a matter of national security. Gaubil often asked for information on Kamchatka from Delisle.[29] Although this seems to have been fruitless, any discussions between the two men necessarily occupied the uneasy border zone between public scientific knowledge and privileged state intelligence.

By contrast, the letters the Academy produced and received as an institution belonged to a very different genre, one that was studiously officious. The most obvious distinction is length. Parrenin's June 1737 letter to the Academy runs to all of 160 words; his letters to Bayer average around 1,000. Their subject matter also had little in common. The Jesuits' letters to Bayer and Delisle were full of the raw material of sinology: astronomical observations, linguistic notes, discussions of history and chronology. The only topic treated at any length in their letters to the Academy (addressed to Korff) is the virtue, nobility, and honor of maintaining a long-distance commercium of this kind, with perhaps a smattering of scholarly news. Finally, though many of Bayer's and Delisle's letters are certainly genteel enough, the institutional missives are replete with performative exaggeration: Pereyra's 1736 letter to Korff calls the invitation to correspondence a "most benevolent" act of "munificence" and an "extraordinary favor" of which "we are barely worthy"— though the Academy in fact seems to have received by far the better end of the deal. In other words, the airy rhetoric of intellectual communion served to paper over the tangible commercial and material realities of the correspondence.[30]

The real value of the Academy's intellectual exchange with the Jesuits was not in the ideas expressed in letters but in physical objects, including books.

Along with Parrenin's letter, Lang carried three crates (*Kasten*) of books provided in response to the list drawn up by Bayer three years earlier, although
judging by the manifest, the final total was considerably less than the ambitious original request. (Some books seem to have been included individually.)
They included classic Chinese Jesuit works such as Guilio Aleni's catechism,
as well as more obscure texts by Chinese converts, such as an essay by the
Christian Manchu prince Depei. By the end of the century, all three books
had been translated into Russian—and Depei's work turned out to be something of a best seller.[31] In addition to being intellectual artifacts, these rare
books were specimens of Chinese printing and hence rarities in Europe; possession of them helped the Academy to build up the prestige of its library
collection. Botany, a major source of the Academy of Sciences' international
reputation and an important object of interest for Russian elites, was also an
important component of the Academy-Jesuit correspondence.[32] Lang carried
a collection of botanical materials for Amman, "both for safekeeping and to
be planted in the Academy's garden."[33] In his reply, Amman gave the Jesuits a full report on the results of their botanical dispatch. Twenty-nine of
them sprouted; listing them with their Chinese names, he seems to have
laboriously identified each by the grown plant it produced and provided a
reflection on why the remaining ones did not. In exchange, Amman sent
the Jesuits (specifically Parrenin) sixty-four seeds of his own.

The successful delivery of such physical objects, much more so than letters, required active institutional support, an area in which gentlemanly ca-
maraderie between Western Europeans would not be sufficient on its own.
On his way to Beijing in 1735, Lang wrote to Korff, "I reassure Your Excellency that the goods committed to my keeping by the Academy will remain
safe, but on the return to the borders, where the customs officials are, there
can be all sorts of difficulties and many objects can be damaged or even totally lost." He suggested that the Academy request a special edict from the
Russian Senate declaring its crates exempt from customs inspection.[34] The
Academy addressed its request directly to Her Imperial Majesty's Cabinet,
which granted it, with the certificates given to a courier who was to intercept
Lang before he reached the Qing border. This particular danger was averted in
a timely fashion.

Nonetheless, this did not resolve the central dilemma, which was the clash
between private and institutional interests. Lang had only by accident ended

up as both caravan director—and hence representative of the Russian Empire's material interests in the Russo-Qing trade—and as facilitator of the Academy-Jesuit correspondence. This helps explain why, after 1740, the correspondence ground to a halt. It certainly did not seem to be doing so at the time. In fact, the Academy had assembled quite a large package of responses, including Amman's seeds and an honorary member's diploma for Gaubil, which was ready to be sent in time for the next caravan's departure.[35] This turned out to be February 1740. Yet unlike the previous caravans, which had made the correspondence convenient, this one was headed by a merchant named Erofei Firsov. Lang, who was getting on in years, had accepted a position as the vice-governor of Irkutsk. (That is to say, he governed Irkutsk and hence oversaw all Russo-Chinese border trade but was subordinate to the governor of Siberia.) He had personally recommended the appointment of Firsov to take his place.[36] For the correspondence, this was a poor choice. As Gaubil put it in a letter to Delisle, Firsov "acquitted himself very badly in performing the commission you and the others had given him for us."[37] Gaubil could only write this in 1746, when the package was finally delivered; in 1743, after a series of Russian couriers and Firsov's caravan had passed him by without a single letter, he could only assume that the Academy had abandoned its correspondence with the Jesuits. This was, in fact, enough to effectively squelch the correspondence as it had been imagined by its initial participants. After all, by the time Gaubil's letter finally reached Delisle in Paris in 1748, every single Jesuit (except Gaubil and de la Charme) who was involved originally had died, and every single academician had either died or left the Academy.

The new director's failure to deliver only reinforces the centrality of Lang and the network of relationships he cultivated to the success of the Russian Route correspondence. This was only partially due to Lang's own mastery of learned sociability. Much of it could be ascribed to his social class. As a foreigner with special skills, he entered Imperial Russian society on the same level as the lesser nobility with whom he competed for patronage. By the time he ceased to direct the Beijing caravan, he had reached the rank of state councilor, which was the highest rank most foreigners could expect to earn. Firsov, by contrast, was an ordinary Siberian merchant, and his appointment to the directorship of the caravan—which meant direct responsibility for hundreds of thousands of rubles in merchandise and silver—brought with it only a promotion to collegiate assessor, slightly above a typical petty bureau-crat.[38] He could not have expected personal connections with the Jesuits to mean much for his career, and he certainly felt no personal attachment to the Jesuits as individuals. Perhaps more importantly, in 1741 Elizabeth as-cended the throne and sent Osterman into Siberian exile, while in 1740 Korff had been assigned to the diplomatic service in Denmark. There was, in short, little pressure on Firsov to keep up the patronage connections Lang had so laboriously built.

When Lang's own role shifted, so did his incentives for helping the Jesuits. As Irkutsk vice-governor, he actually turned out to be the proximate cause for the failure of the only 1740s attempt to reconnect with the Jesuits. Some-time in 1747, after the package entrusted to Firsov had arrived in Beijing, the Academy received a package from the Jesuits containing "some books, grasses, flowers, and other things that don't exist in Europe." (Records of these ma-terials do not appear to have survived, perhaps due to a fire at the Academy the same year.) "Because the Academy has always had a correspondence with the Fathers living in Peking," it was decided to assemble a set of Academy editions as well as botanical materials to send in return, per the Jesuits' re-quest. (It is unclear if this involved sending any letters as well; if it did, they appear not to have survived.) Many of the plants and seeds involved had been acquired at some cost in Europe, being unavailable at the Academy. But there turned out not to be a triennial caravan that year, and it seemed that the only solution was to send it to Lang in Irkutsk so that he could entrust it either to a courier or to a Chinese or Mongol trader for delivery to Beijing.[39]

But Lang was now more concerned about border affairs than about parcel shipping. Three years later, when the Academy was preparing a new package to be sent with the resumed caravan and wanted to know what had happened with the previous delivery, the Irkutsk Provincial Chancellery reported that the boxes were still in Irkutsk and there was no way of sending them except by caravan. Its circuitous report offered a few different explanations before settling on the real one, which was that "Jesuits . . . do not want to receive any Russian deliveries from Qing subject peoples, and hold this belief for an important reason, for if it is discovered or if the Qing person with whom that delivery will be sent reports it to the Chinese tribunal [Lifanyuan], they will not escape beatings for this, or will be considered suspicious."[40] Indeed, Gaubil and presumably others had warned the Russians of the danger of such

deliveries, and the original 1734 announcement in the St. Petersburg newspaper *Vedomosti* announcing the Academy-Jesuit correspondence had had to
be retracted to protect the Jesuits from charges of espionage. This was not
necessarily an idle concern; Gaubil himself regularly kept the Yongzheng
emperor informed of news items in European gazettes.[41] Though Lang no
doubt contributed to the safety of his friends in the Qing capital, the effect
was to impose another crushing five-year delay in the correspondence.

Knowledge as Commodities, Commodities as Knowledge

Lang's departure from facilitating the correspondence meant that the
Academy had to take a closer interest in the material value and infrastructure of its connection to China. When a new—and, as it would turn out, a
final—caravan to China was planned in 1751, the academicians' aspirations
became more ambitious. The man for the job was the doctor Franz Lukas Jellatschitsch, who had long been an academic employee and volunteered for
the job. He explained that he had been to Beijing and carried out a number
of intelligence-related tasks for the Medical Chancellery in 1744–1747. In the
process, he had evidently gotten to know the Jesuits well enough that he was
eager to see them again and serve the Academy at the same time.[42] The professors accepted eagerly. The key difference between Jellatschitsch and Lang
was that the latter, while acting on behalf of the Academy in conjunction with
his other roles, was never paid by the institution. Jellatschitsch, by contrast,
was the Academy's designated representative in the complex tangle of institutional interests any caravan involved. His role was to make it easier for the
Academy to stock its collections with Qing goods.

   The Academy, aiming to make the most of the opportunity to send an agent
to Beijing, charged him with a far weightier task than the simple delivery of
a few boxes and the collection of letters in response. Jellatschitsch's job was
to locate replacements for the hundreds of Qing texts, artifacts, and other curiosities that had disappeared in a 1747 fire. He was given a hand-drawn wa-
tercolor catalog of the destroyed collection so that he could identify similar
objects while on location.[43] It also contained an extensive list of books assembled by the Academy's Manchu and Chinese translator Larion Rossokhin,
who had once contributed dozens of Manchu books to the library himself.

This drew mainly on Etienne Fourmont's catalog of sinological collections in France, although Rossokhin used his own extensive Beijing experience as well.[44] Furthermore, Jellatschitsch's instructions enjoined him to collect naturalia, to prepare commentaries on the works of Samuel Gottlieb Gmelin and Du Halde, and to compose a sociological assessment of "the condition of the three colleges in China, by whom and how they are controlled, who among them has the most power, who is considered the most learned, and with whom would it be best to carry on scientific correspondence." In all of these purchases and investigations, he was to solicit the help of the Jesuits, in addition to securing the exchange of texts for the future.[45]

To accomplish his tasks, Jellatschitsch needed to become as much a merchant as an intellectual explorer. In his initial application, he had included a list of "objects in demand in China": scissors, pins, knives, soap, towels, and so on. He proposed that selling these would defray some of the cost of shopping for curiosities. The academy agreed; ultimately he would go on to exceed the allotted sum, making a profit of 163 rubles (about 100 taels) on an investment of 390. This defrayed only a small portion of the final cost of his purchases—800 rubles, equal to two years' worth of his salary. The Academy had also specified that he set aside a portion of the initial sum to buy gifts for the Jesuits in Moscow, while he himself suggested reserving some money for "gifts" to the Chinese, from whom "great things may be obtained through small expenditures."[46] Only the latter appears to have come to pass: none of the Jesuits who wrote to the Academy mentioned receiving anything besides the packages long since prepared for them.[47]

Jellatschitsch's mission, then, was something of a small caravan in itself: he went to Beijing with two fully loaded horses and a considerable sum of money and returned with three horses and several hundred rubles in debt from the vast collection he had acquired.[48] He proved to be an exemplary buyer. His manifest included 50 books and 274 other items, including clothing, braziers, games of cards and chess, mirrors, buttons, statuettes, prisms, "a doll depicting a wife beating her husband with a stick," "a Chinese cart with a horse upon which five dolls play a game while riding around the streets during the New Year," and much more. Many of the books he brought seem to still exist in the collections of the Institute of Oriental Manuscripts in St. Petersburg, and they certainly appear in Julius Klaproth's nineteenth-century catalog of the Chinese and Manchu manuscripts at the Academy

Library.[49] The packages he brought from the Jesuits contained still more books and sets of astronomical observations as well as botanical materials, for, as their letters testified, Jellatschitsch had successfully delivered the boxes of books and seeds that had been moldering in Irkutsk for five full years (though not all of the Jesuits knew this).

The Irkutsk boxes had been a major concern for the Academy's botanist Stepan Krasheninnikov. The "bulbs, roots, anemones, ramuncules and seeds" they contained had been obtained by the former academician Gmelin in Tübingen, and because they were European culinary herbs, which the Academy's gardeners did not cultivate, they could not be readily replaced (though with some effort they could be found among St. Petersburg's vegetable growers). Furthermore, botanicals, unlike books, were inherently time sensitive. As Krasheninnikov confidently declared, those sent in 1748 "were certainly no longer good for anything except being sent along with fresh ones to demonstrate to them how much the Academy is willing to exert itself to satisfy their requests." Yet even if Jellatschitsch were given a box of new botanicals to bring with the caravan, the bulbs would "grow along the way and then rot"; the roots, anemones, and ramuncules would go stale; and the seeds, presumably, would lose their vitality. They needed to be sent with a special courier or not sent at all.[50]

The purpose of the seeds was not to sprout, however, but to demonstrate the Academy's loyalty, so the old seeds in Irkutsk would have to suffice. To everyone's surprise, however, the Jesuit Pierre d'Incarville wrote to the Academy's new president Count Kirill Razumovskii in November 1756 that "the seeds I received by your last [letter], though they were very old, succeeded [in sprouting]." He also asked for more, and these were sent in December 1756; they included the seeds of more herbs, such as rosemary and thyme, which d'Incarville had asked for specifically, as well as those of peonies, lotus, and others, added by the new botanist Johann Hebenstreit of his own accord. The Russian requests were the same as two decades prior, mostly expensive cash crops: rhubarb, tea, and ginseng. (These were sent by the Jesuit Louis Desrobert, due to the death of d'Incarville, but he had no more useful information to offer owing to his lack of botanical knowledge.)[51] Against all odds, the exchange of seeds had succeeded, but it neither yielded any new knowledge nor led to any serious cultivation of Chinese botanical rarities in Russia.

This new correspondence seemed to permit a genuine attempt to exchange scientific news. On the Jesuit side, Augustin Hallerstein sent his astronomical work, while d'Incarville contributed a large natural-history compendium (published eventually by the Moscow Society of Naturalists in 1812).[52] Others passed along antique books and maps. In response, along with Hebenstreit's seeds, the physics professor G. V. Richmann—who would be killed in an accident involving an electrical experiment soon afterward—sent a long letter with an account of the latest electrical research, including Benjamin Franklin's.[53] The astronomer Stepan Rumovskii presented a critical analysis of some recent observations; this was an important time for astronomy, because a transit of Venus—one of the first occasions for truly global scientific collaboration—was due to occur in 1761.[54]

In 1760, however, the state caravan was abolished and, with it, the entire structure of Academy-Jesuit correspondence as it had functioned for three decades. The further exchange of letters would require the services of the couriers who traveled from Russia to Beijing frequently. (In fact, documents in Russian archives suggest that the exchange of angry diplomatic letters was ramped up deliberately to provide more occasions for couriers.)[55] Yet couriers were expensive and their entire purpose was to transmit letters quickly and efficiently; the Academy could not expect to be contacted and then to take six months or longer to prepare a package of gifts and letters, as it could with a caravan. Moreover, most of the couriers were sent from Selenginsk, near the Mongol border, rather than St. Petersburg, and the authorities there were utterly unconcerned with the convenience of institutions in the capital. In the end, although Razumovskii was a high-ranking nobleman and thus had a network of contacts throughout the empire, virtually no Academy correspondence ended up traveling by courier.

The last significant Academy package, which included the final shipment of seeds and letters, was entrusted to Vasilii Bratishchev, a diplomat who attempted unsuccessfully to negotiate access to the Amur River for Russian ships, in 1756. The Academy's leadership provided Bratishchev with letters of recommendation to the Beijing Jesuits, hoping that their place at the Qing court—which was habitually overestimated by Russian officials—would allow them to intercede on his behalf with the emperor. This expectation was not fulfilled, and any attempt to leverage the Academy-Jesuit correspondence for geopolitical ends was terminated for the time being.[56] Meanwhile, hopes for the continuation of the exchange were not high, as G.-F. Müller wrote to Gaubil and Hallerstein in 1760.[57] By that point Gaubil had been dead for over a year. His death marked the beginning of the end of the correspondence, but—contrary to Müller's expectations—not its absolute termination. The courier and diplomat Ivan Kropotov carried letters to Beijing and back in 1763, with three of the Jesuits (Hallerstein, Benoist, and D'Ollières) sending responses; only one Academy letter went east with him in 1766. Thereafter the courier line went dead.[58]

The correspondence did not end there, but its new form makes the distinctiveness of the midcentury exchange stand out in greater relief. In the final decades of the old Jesuit mission in China, the academicians primarily corresponded with Beijing not through the Russian route but through the French one. The Academy's voluminous correspondence books, which began to be kept in an orderly fashion after 1764, contain several letters from the 1770s by Hallerstein and the much younger Jesuit arrival Pierre Martial Cibot. Cibot's essay on a Chinese mushroom, together with a number of astronomical observations contained in letters from Jean-Paul-Louis Collas (which do not appear in the letter books), were also received and published in the Academy's learned commentaries.[59] In another letter, Cibot offered fulsome gratitude to Catherine II for her protection of the Society after the dissolution bull of 1773, claiming that "I have abandoned all my literary connections and apply myself more than ever to cultivate the ones I have with you [Leonhard Euler, the learned secretary in this period] and with the Academy."[60] These letters were sent through the Parisian bookseller De-La-Tour, individually rather than institutionally and as slim envelopes rather than boxes and bundles; even when Cibot said he had written *par le caravane,* what he had in mind was the much smaller caravan that escorted the Russian Ecclesiastical Mission to Beijing and back every decade or so.[61] The correspondence could no longer function to facilitate material exchange and accordingly drew little further interest from the professors.

A final ironic twist took place at the end of the eighteenth century. In 1798, Archimandrite Sofronii (Gribovskii) of the Russian Ecclesiastical Mission in Beijing found himself unable to send back news to St. Petersburg, owing to the habitual unwillingness of the Lifanyuan to pass along letters from missionaries. He was forced to turn to his friend, the bishop of Beijing, who instructed him to keep him missive brief so as not to arouse suspicion because of the increase in the volume of paper. (In fact, the Jesuits had been forbidden by the Jiaqing court to maintain relationships with the Russian missionaries.) Sofronii's letters were smuggled to Canton and thence to the Russian resident ambassador in Lisbon. The Russian Route had briefly been made to run in reverse.[62]

The Academy-Jesuit correspondence was not a triumph of learned Enlightenment exchange. It did not lead to great discoveries or to books showcasing the glories of cultural syncretism. Yet these letters offer us a new way to understand how and on what terms Russians participated in the eighteenth-century Republic of Letters. For these intellectual actors, science and state-based knowledge regimes were deeply intertwined. The books, objects, and plants received by the academicians from Beijing were not supplements to the letters that accompanied them: they made the letters worthwhile. It would therefore be a mistake to see the Moscow-Beijing trade caravan as engaging in industrial espionage and commerce on the one hand and facilitating intellectual exchange on the other. In the one case as in the other, curiosity and state interest drove a hunt for knowledge concretized in material form. But for the Russian state, the correspondence had a further advantage: it helped to link the intellectual agenda of the Academy with the search for a lever of influence at the court in Beijing, one that was imagined to belong to the Jesuits. If this had worked when Bratishchev sought Jesuit assistance in 1756, it would have been very timely: Eurasian geopolitics was about to undergo an epochal transformation.

PART III

REMAKING KNOWLEDGE *on* THE FRONTIER

Frontier Intelligence and the Struggle for Inner Asia

I N THE MIDDLE OF THE EIGHTEENTH CENTURY, the Russian Empire's understanding of its interests on the Chinese frontier began to radically change. In previous decades, imperial officials had assumed a state of equilibrium, which enabled them to launch the two experimental channels through which they pursued their studies into the Qing realm: the students at the Russian Ecclesiastical Mission in Beijing, who became translators at the College of Foreign Affairs and the Imperial Academy of Sciences, and the personnel of the Beijing trade caravan with their industrial and strategic espionage initiatives. All of these were linked to the institutional reforms of the Petrine and post-Petrine era, which had attempted to establish formal institutional hierarchies instead of relying on the ad hoc activities of ambassadors and Bukharan merchants. Though results were ambiguous, the stakes for St. Petersburg remained low: as long as the treaty settlements arranged at Nerchinsk in 1689 and Kiakhta in 1727–1728 held firm, Inner Asia would remain in balance, and Russian furs would continue to flow into Mongolia in exchange for Qing luxuries. This sense of security turned out to be a false one. A full-scale regional crisis was about to erupt that would necessitate not only the creation of a spy network controlled from the southeastern frontier but also a shift in the very significance of intelligence. No longer just a way of learning about the lands and customs of a still unfamiliar neighbor, it would now become the favored instrument for securing Russian hegemony in the border region.

This shift mirrors an analytical distinction in the study of intelligence. The intelligence scholar Michael Warner has distinguished between two ways of looking at the field: one that defines it as information gathering and the other as a form of "silent warfare," incorporating covert action as well as spying. The former, he argues, emerged from the ministerial logic of modern bureaucracy, while the latter describes the much older perspective of sovereigns in competition with rivals.[1] For the Romanovs and their high officials, the mid-eighteenth century saw the second perspective take its place alongside the first, as they were forced to turn their attention to an increasingly dangerous borderland—even if it was not as contested as imperial battlegrounds such as the zone between Western Russia, Poland-Lithuania, and the Ottoman Empire. If knowledge alone was no longer power, the people who delivered the knowledge could serve a variety of purposes: negotiate with frontier populations, manipulate events, and establish territorial claims. These changing functions shaped the course of Russo-Qing relations for the next century.

Borderlands have sometimes encouraged scholars to take a conflict-focused perspective: if a frontier existed, it must have been a current or imminent flashpoint for territorial warfare. The Russo-Qing frontier is considered a prime example.[2] Others have gone in the opposite direction, downplaying Russian territorial goals. Russian-speaking scholars (especially from the Soviet period) depict this era as one of peaceful, lawful Russian resistance to the "aggressive expansionist policy" of the Qing, while Anglophone historians characterize Romanov policy as being driven by commercial motivations.[3] None of these perspectives capture the nature of this frontier as it existed from the mid-eighteenth through the mid-nineteenth century. Open conflict was in fact quite rare—rarer, even, than conflicts within the interior of both states—but the threat of invasion and the lure of territorial aggrandizement were both important features of the political landscape. As a result, the relationship between Russia and the Qing took on the form of a slow-moving rivalry centered on intelligence. It became a cold war fought through spies, secret negotiators, and trade sanctions.

The trigger for the crisis that would begin this cold war was the Qing destruction of the Junghar Khanate (Confederation) in 1755–1757. Having carved out an overland empire encompassing at its greatest extent everything from southern Siberia to the northern reaches of Tibet, the Junghars posed a formidable threat to both Russian and Qing expansion. They formed the third

part of the regional configuration that had allowed Russia to remain relatively aloof from Inner Asian rivalries, as the outcome of the intermittent
Qing-Junghar conflict was seen to hinge on the intervention of Russia on
one side or the other. Under the Yongzheng emperor (1721–1735) this king-
maker role had secured for Russia the significant—and for a European power
unprecedented—trade concessions of the Treaty of Kiakhta in 1727–1728 and
two highly obliging Qing embassies a few years later. In the reign of Qianlong (1735–1796), however, a succession crisis crippled the khanate and led to
a massive Qing intervention. Russia's sparsely peopled and poorly defended
southeast now bordered a unified and triumphant Manchu empire, which,
Russians believed, could raise hundreds of thousands of soldiers for a single
campaign; any leverage the Russian Empire possessed had disappeared along
with the Junghar threat.[4]

But there were also intimations of an opportunity to be found in the crisis.
The new borderlands were restive, unfixed, and porous, suggesting to more
than one Russian official that a single push would be enough to pry them away
from Qing hegemony and perhaps even claw back Russia's seventeenth-
century concessions. This required a careful approach. Searching for a way
to counteract the Manchu advantage, the leaders of Russian institutions, such
as the College of Foreign Affairs, could not turn to the familiar strategies they
had used against their enemies in the western portion of the Eurasian steppe:
military conquest based on technological, numerical, or organizational superiority. Instead, they came to see "acting covertly and artfully"—by means
of espionage, deception, and secret diplomacy—as their only path to advancing imperial goals. Thus what appears to us as peaceful commerce in
fact concealed a wide-ranging strategy of deception.[5] By the middle of the
1760s, Russia had substantially expanded its diplomatic influence in the
former Junghar territories, and a network of intelligence agents and informers
began to extend from the trans-Baikal town of Selenginsk into the Mongolian and Manchurian frontier zones of the Qing Empire.

From Diplomacy to Intelligence

The immediate result of the Junghar collapse was a rapid deterioration in
Russo-Qing diplomatic exchanges. While the khanate had continued to exist

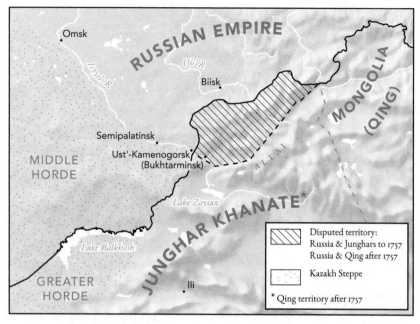

7.1 The Siberian Line frontier in the 1750s.

and even win substantial military victories in its wars with the Qing, the Kangxi and Yongzheng emperors kept Russia satisfied on the sidelines through treaty concessions. This even led to two Qing embassies to the Russian imperial court, during which the envoys kowtowed to Empress Anna in reciprocity for the Russian envoy Izmailov's adherence to the ritual in 1720.[6] With the Junghars' destruction, and with the murky role Russia played in their final crisis, the Lifanyuan—the Bureau of Foreign Tributaries in Beijing—had little reason to be obliging. It sent increasingly scornful letters, as in this 1764 exchange:

> You asked us in your letter to stop writing rude words to you. Take this under advisement: in any matter there is an undeniable truth, while every human has a natural conscience. We formerly always wrote to you in the manner that peaceful coexistence demands. But we started to write rudely to you and shame you since you began to violate the treaty provision about fugitives. . . . We were forced by necessity to respond rudely that you in every matter concoct excuses, do not do justice in

anything, and consider neither your face nor your buttocks [Ma. *dere ura be bodorakū,* i.e., you care neither about your honor nor your well-being].[7]

The most galling of the arguments offered by the Qing were based on the idea that it was ridiculous for "that woman of yours [*suweni emu hehe niyalma*]" to compare herself to the Qianlong emperor: "We have never heard of the lord of a foreign kingdom being a woman, not a man. . . . We laugh and have no words to continue such a discussion."[8] The tone fell short of a threat of war. The shift, however, was clear: the language of peaceful accommodation so typical under Yongzheng had been abandoned, and the Qing were seeing the Russians increasingly as rivals rather than silent partners.[9]

It would be easy to assume that this kind of language, so apparently similar to the famous response issued to the British ambassador Lord Macartney in 1793, was merely the default product of a xenophobic and "immobile" culture. Indeed, some have argued that the conquest of Xinjiang and the other manifestations of Qing ascendancy in the eighteenth century made the dynasty complacent and self-satisfied, lodging them in a "high-level-equilibrium trap."[10] Although it was informed by an ideology of cultural superiority, however, this type of scolding did not mean the Qing were unconcerned about Russian power or fully confident in their ability to resist Russian attacks. Instead, it was part of a conscious strategy to correct Russian rule breaking and acculture them to behavior that was "civilized" in neo-Confucian terms: after all, they had broken certain provisions of the treaty that bound the two states together. For the Qing, this was an attempt to avoid rather than provoke war, even if it was also about putting the Russians in their place in increasingly confrontational language. For its Russian addressees, however, it became a consciously felt grievance.

Russian officials cast about for another vocabulary with which to articulate a response. Catherine II personally drafted at least one reply to the Lifanyuan, in which she expressed "the surprise of the entire rational world" that "a people such as the Chinese, among whom even the last peasant . . . is taught his manners," might write so aggressively.[11] Other rejoinders were carefully framed in an effort to avoid sounding either too obsequious or too aggressive, while also implying that Russia did not fear confrontation. Though they accepted Qing claims to cultural greatness, they pointed to Russia's size and asked, "Will you not yourself become ashamed to compare us with Jung-hars and other Tartar hordes, whose miserable condition does not even permit them to be called states? . . . Our empire . . . is considered the greatest on earth, both for the extent of its lands and the number of kingdoms, prince-doms, and peoples under its scepter who were formerly independent and noble states."[12] When the Lifanyuan perceived some of these expressions to be threatening, it sardonically called the Russians' bluff; the College imme-diately backed down and said that it merely tried to defend Russian honor.[13] Diplomacy alone would not suffice to restore reciprocity in this relationship.

Although Western European diplomats were aware of rising Russo-Qing tensions, Russian officials were able to conceal the embarrassing nature of this correspondence in part through increasing diligence in handling secret archival documents. Secrecy was often honored in the breach: a 1767 decree upbraided a long list of provincial governors for sloppiness in dealing with secret papers, for instance, having them signed by subordinates who lacked the clearance even to view them.[14] But for matters that pertained to the Sibe-rian border, the eighteenth-century model of secrecy had profound conse-quences. In the pre-1730 period, foreign diplomats, Jesuits, and other Western figures had extensive access to materials produced at the highest levels of Rus-sian foreign policy toward the Qing. By the mid-eighteenth century the Rus-sian government seems to have achieved success in keeping such materials confidential. In 1764, the Earl of Buckinghamshire, the British ambassador in St. Petersburg, complained that "the greatest pains are taken to keep se-cret all the intelligence that comes from that part of the Empire," noting that "I have taken pains for some days past to get authentick information of the situation of the present disputes with China, as the greatest secrecy is ob-served in relation to everything that passes on that side."[15]

Secrecy also concealed the fact that Russian ambitions went beyond dip-lomatic reciprocity with the Qing. In 1754, the prominent official Fëdor Soimonov—soon to be governor of Siberia—arrived in Nerchinsk to prepare ships and personnel for a voyage down the Amur River and into the North Pacific. This was envisioned as a Third Kamchatka Expedition, following in the footsteps of Vitus Bering's earlier explorations. Russian officials had come to regard the Amur as crucial to their plans for the exploration and exploita-tion of fur-bearing territories in northeastern Siberia, the Pacific islands, and eventually Alaska. Without it, goods and supplies needed to be moved to the oceanic port of Okhotsk through the Stanovoi and Iablonovoi Mountains, a dangerous and ruinously expensive portage that precluded the building of large vessels. Anything that could not be carried by a donkey or packhorse was out of the question; anchors, for instance, had first to be divided into five parts.[16] In 1756, Vasilii Bratishchev went to Beijing to negotiate with the Qing court for permission to sail down the river; the letter from the College of Foreign Affairs he carried contained the pointed insinuation that the expedition was not to be abandoned in the event of Qing reluctance. According to a secret intelligence report from the Catholic missionary Sigismondo di San Nicola in Beijing, Qianlong had read Bratishchev's letter and exclaimed, "Cunning Russia . . . [implies] that they will sail with or without permission." Permission was denied, in part, San Nicola reported, because of a desire to protect the pearl fishery in the Manchus' ancestral domains.[17] Though the Russians regarded this as a flimsy excuse, the fishery was of tremendous economic and symbolic value for the dynasty.[18] Anticipating a rejection, Soimonov had been ready to sail down the Amur in force, but the College of Foreign Affairs found his proposal foolhardy and rejected it. Plans for the expedition were put on hold indefinitely.[19]

With the failure of diplomatic pressure to advance Russian interests, other routes began to seem more appealing. In 1763 the new empress Catherine II began to revisit the prospect of a military solution, which had first been proposed by Varfolomei Iakobii, the commandant of Selenginsk and the Russian spymaster on the southeastern frontier, in the 1750s. The Siberian historian Gerhard Friedrich Müller (Fëdor Ivanovich Miller) prepared a memorandum considering the justifications for a war: the "insults and contempt" shown by the Lifanyuan, he argued, provided ample grounds to renew pre-Nerchinsk Russian claims on the Amur and Mongolia. Like other proponents of a military option, of whom there were several, Müller argued that the conquest of the frontier would be easier than it seemed at first glance: vastly outnumbered by resentful Han Chinese subjects and facing discontent from Mongols who would abandon it for Russia at the first opportunity, the Qing Dynasty would, if not collapse like a house of cards, at least be easily pushed into an advantageous peace.[20] Qianlong, for his part, had also considered war with Russia: the Qing still maintained some claims over the region east of Lake Baikal and its Buriat and Evenki population (relatives of the Manchus and Mongols), and a Mongol spy reported to Iakobii in 1760 that a military council on the subject had taken place. According to the agent, the Qing generals were wary of the climatic difficulties of Siberian warfare and the uncertainties surrounding the Russian response.[21] Qianlong himself was reluctant to attack unless the war could be won at a single blow.[22] Though a military solution seemed possible, it was so risky that neither side wanted to make the first move.

Russia's military situation on the Qing frontier was more precarious than Müller realized. Though its aggressive expansion in the sixteenth and seventeenth centuries was driven in part by its military and technological superiority over the Siberian and steppe peoples it conquered, by the middle of the eighteenth century, Russia's military presence in Siberia was vulnerable to both Qing and Junghar attacks. An alarmed 1759 report from the Siberian governor Fëdor Soimonov pointed out that the two thousand miles between the easternmost Siberian Line fortresses on the Irtysh River and the border south of Irkutsk were entirely unguarded, so as to permit invasion "not just by cavalry but by wagons."[23] In 1763, Iakobii noted that only five thousand troops were available to guard the entire border of Manchuria and Mongolia, of whom fewer than half were regulars.[24] This meant that in an armed confrontation Russia would be at a minimum of a ten-to-one disadvantage and likely even more; worse, although the equipment carried by Qing troops was technologically somewhat inferior, Russia no longer had anything close to the near monopoly on firearms and artillery it had enjoyed in previous eras.[25] Thus neither party took any meaningful steps toward shattering the peace between the two empires, and Russia never committed to the required buildup of troops. In 1764, at the height of the tension, Russian military reforms doubled the border's theoretical complement of soldiers, but this was phrased in purely defensive terms and would in any case fall far short of the numbers needed for an invasion.[26]

With neither side committed to long-term peace but each unwilling to risk open conflict, an uneasy stalemate took shape in the Inner Asian borderlands. Intelligence and other forms of covert action substituted for military engagement and direct negotiation. As in other conflicts over hegemony, struggle for the loyalties of third parties became increasingly crucial—all the more so because the frontier was populated overwhelmingly by people who were neither Russian nor Manchu. Caught between the two empires, Eurasian peoples were themselves forced to choose between conflict and accommodation. In the mid-1750s, the Khalkha leaders of Qing Mongolia were corresponding with Iakobii about defection, the Kazakh Middle Horde and the Uriangkhai of the Altai Mountains were swearing fealty to both sides, and Junghar fugitives were demanding asylum in Russia in the tens of thousands. By the end of the period in 1771, most of the Volga Torghuts (Kalmyks)— Western Mongols like the Oirats who dominated the Junghar Khanate, some of whom had been Russian subjects since the 1630s and others who had recently fled the Qing conquest—defected across the border in a dramatic migration.[27] Meanwhile, Khalkha Mongols and Buriats whose traditional grazing lands lay near the northern Mongolian border made for ideal intelligence agents for Russia, and traders from Central Asia provided intelligence on Qing forces in the newly conquered territories of the future Xinjiang province.

Building Intelligence on the Xinjiang Frontier

The Russo-Qing cold war played out principally in two theaters: the mountains and steppes around the former Junghar Khanate—where the borders of modern Russia, Mongolia, Kazakhstan, and China meet—and the regions east of Lake Baikal, including northern Mongolia and Manchuria. They were never isolated from each other. Russian officials stationed in each theater routinely shared information and strategic deliberations, with Iakobii in his nominally insignificant town of Selenginsk serving as the key node for the collection and dissemination of intelligence along the entire Russo-Qing frontier; on the other hand, Qing armies and command staff sent to Xinjiang frequently included Khalkha Mongols or members of Solon, Daur, and other northeastern tribes.[28] Nonetheless, very distinct conditions obtained in each theater. Unlike the comparatively stable east, the western steppe was a region where Russia's imperial presence was still tenuous, characterized by ethnic and military volatility and lack of consensus on either empire's part about its legal responsibilities toward the other. Its geography was circumscribed by Russian settlement. On the Irtysh River, which flowed down into Junghar territory, Russia established a chain of fortresses known as the Siberian Line. These included, among others, Omsk, Semipalatinsk, and Ust'-Kamenogorsk, which would later become important regional towns. Here relatively small and isolated Russian garrisons interacted on a constant basis with Kazakhs,

Junghars, Bukharans, and, after the conquest, Qing representatives. Together, these groups worked out the terms of imperial condominium in Central Eurasia.

Russians had begun to create an intelligence network around the Siberian Line well before the Qing conquest, in an attempt to monitor the activities of the Junghars. Although formally the two states were never at war, small-scale warfare was a constant reality along the Irtysh and the upper reaches of the Enisei. In 1716, the Junghar leader Tsewang Rabdan captured the Swedish lieutenant J. G. Renat, who had been sent with other officers in Russian service to look for gold in Junghar territory, and put him to work mapping his lands and providing him with artillery to use in his wars against the Qing.[29] The Russian envoy Ivan Unkovskii, sent to investigate the potential for persuading the Junghars to accept Russian protection in 1722–1724, was also (or primarily) expected to gather intelligence and maps of Jungharia, as his report indicates.[30] Later, in the 1740s, Russians began to notice the Junghar threat to their iron production facilities around Kolyvan and Kuznetsk (now Novokuznetsk), which escalated as Galdan Tsereng attempted to develop his own iron industry. While Junghars did not attack the mines in force, they did attempt to lure the Russians working there into their own service.[31] Another serious threat was posed by Junghar claims to suzerainty over the Junior and Middle Juz Kazakhs, although a Russian embassy had partially neutralized these. In this region Junghar power could be as troubling as Qing proximity.[32]

As Galdan Tsereng fought the Qing in the 1740s, Russians kept a wary eye on the proceedings from afar. A Russian corporal stationed within the suite of Abulmamet (Abdul Muhammad) Khan of the Kazakh Middle Horde reported on the beginning of another round of hostilities in 1742.[33] The same year, a Bukharan Junghar subject named Aibaga Bakhmuratov, who was evidently trading in Tobolsk, gave the Siberian Provincial Chancellery a full report on "the Russians and Tartars that live in [Tsereng]'s domain and on other things which he could learn [rozvedal] during his residence in that land." Five years later, Bakhmuratov arrived with a caravan from Urga and secretly reported on the current situation in the Junghar lands in the wake of Tsereng's death in 1745. Most importantly, he announced that "they have no ill intent towards Russia but would like to remain in neighborly friend-ship, since at the moment they can barely handle their own people and have no need to enter into a quarrel with Russians."[34] Soon afterward, he reversed himself and abruptly warned the Russians that the Junghars planned a large-scale raid. Yet the College of Foreign Affairs dismissed this news, arguing that it was an attempt to draw Russia into a conspiracy against Galdan's successor.[35]

Still, when this new Junghar ruler was in fact overthrown in 1750, fears grew that the victor, Lama Dorji, planned to make good on Junghar claims to adjacent territories Russia had been gradually annexing since the early eighteenth century. The Orenburg governor Ivan Nepliuev was ordered to secretly support the bid for power of Lama Dorji's rival, Dawaci. As the College of Foreign Affairs explained to Empress Elizabeth in a 1758 postmortem, "the Junghar people, because of their power and the constant claims they made on Siberian border territories, were a dangerous neighbor, and therefore, because of future matters that may arise with this people, it was judged necessary to acquire the Junghar pretender Dawaci and another noble named Amursana for our own side."[36] But Nepliuev's courier was overtaken by events, Lama Dorji was killed by his own troops, and Dawaci ascended to the throne without Russian help in 1752.[37]

This victory was fateful, if short-lived. Dawaci's dissatisfied former ally Amursana defected to the Qing and in 1755 accompanied a triumphant Manchu army to defeat the new ruler. But the Qianlong emperor refused to make Amursana khan. Offended, the opportunistic noble rose up in revolt, together with the Khalkha Mongol prince Chingünjav.[38] It was this uprising that led to what has often been called the Junghar Genocide, although this characterization has recently been challenged.[39] What is clear is that Qianlong crushed Amursana's revolt, ordered the name of "Junghar" extirpated (in favor of "Oirat," the leading Mongol tribe in the Junghar Confederation), and commanded the killing or enslavement of perhaps 200,000 former Junghars. Yet Amursana himself, the final claimant to the khanate's throne, eluded him, and the furious emperor ordered a large-scale search.

It was here that the Russo-Qing cold war truly began to take shape. Amursana had taken refuge with the powerful sultan Ablai of the Kazakh Middle Horde, but in July 1757, he headed off in search of a more powerful protector, arriving at the Russian border fort of Semipalatinsk accompanied only by seven men.[40] He was promptly and in the utmost secrecy packed off to the Siberian capital of Tobolsk. In August, after repeated Russian denials, the

Mongol *zaisang* (midranking nobleman) Nurga arrived at the fort and announced that he had reliable evidence that Amursana was in Russian custody. The local commander, Major Dolgov-Saburov, told him that a party led by a Junghar claiming to be Amursana had attempted to cross the Irtysh River but that afterward they disappeared, and the only thing left behind was an overturned boat. Eventually, the Qing search party managed to fish a drowned corpse out of the Irtysh, but Dolgov-Saburov's scheme came to nothing when it turned out that the drowned man—unlike Amursana—wore his hair in a queue. The Qing now knew full well that Amursana was in Russian custody.[41] Qianlong's anger at the Russians was extreme, because of his suspicions that Russia was planning on using Amursana to advance its agenda in Jungharia. The Lifanyuan warned the Senate that if they had such plans, they should reconsider them, since he was likely to betray them just as he had betrayed the Qing and his fellow Junghars.[42]

Qianlong was right to worry. Dolgov-Saburov was acting on direct instructions from the Siberian governor Vasilii Miatlev, who had ordered that if Amursana tried to come over to the Russian side, he was to be "in a most artful and secret fashion, under heavy guard, conveyed to me in Tobolsk until further orders from the College of Foreign Affairs," while the official should "spread a rumor that he had perished under unknown circumstances."[43] But although the original justification for "acquiring" Amursana "to our side" had been countering Junghar claims in Siberia, the Qing conquest had made this strategy moot. The College of Foreign Affairs now wanted Amursana for his intelligence value: "to obtain from him, as a foremost participant and therefore more knowledgeable than anyone else, reliable information about the latest events and to see if anything of use to us can be gained from the complete conquest of Jungharia by the Qing."[44] Whatever role Amursana might have played in the dramatically altered post-1755 political situation in Central Eurasia, however, his death from smallpox outside of Tobolsk in September 1757 (only a few months after his defection) foreclosed it. It also nullified a contemplated Qing invasion of Russia, though it did produce a simmering dispute over the fate of the *noyan*'s remains.[45]

The Russian scheme to use Amursana as a cat's-paw had failed, but the Qing did not appear to show much interest in the territories that so worried the Russians. Russian authorities were therefore left to greet the Qing conquest of Jungharia with a mixed sense of relief, trepidation, and opportunity.

As a 1763 set of instructions to Lieutenant General Ivan Shpringer, assigned to manage the region's fortresses, put it, the Junghars' demise had saved Russia from their "claims" and moreover created "reason to hope that we may with time acquire for ourselves those lands stretching all the way to Lake Zaisan, which are quite valued, in hopes of procuring their rich mines," as long as the reactions of the "haughty" Qing state could be properly managed. The essential goal was to "act in a rather covert and artful fashion [*is podovol' i neskol'ko iskusnym obrazom*], so as not to alarm the already suspicious Chinese with great preparations." Shpringer was thus ordered to send a "reliable officer, especially an engineer," under the pretext of searching for fugitives or stray horses, to investigate the state of any Qing fortifications around Lake Zaisan and take any required measurements, "but do not equip him with any geodesic instruments so as not to arouse suspicion." If the officer was successful, "in the future you should under various pretexts send missions there from time to time, using officers and sometimes local peoples, so that the repetition of these missions will in some fashion accustom the Chinese to the idea that all these lands up to their new settlements belong to us." An unmanned outpost established in 1761 on the mouth of the Bukhtarma, which flows into Lake Zaisan, was burned down by Qing armies in 1764; in subsequent decades, it seems to have been rebuilt, for a 1798 document refers to a "fortified redoubt" there. Russian borders inched forward at a glacial pace, but their advance was real.[46]

Covert action was also the order of the day for dealing with the remnants of the Junghars themselves, who began asking for Russian asylum in individual groups in 1755. Consulting with local officials, the College of Foreign Affairs concluded that accepting the refugees was dangerous but unavoidable. They could not be trusted near the border or near any poorly defended region of Siberia, they could not pasture their animals in the colder parts, and they did not want to settle with the Torghuts (Kalmyks) on the Volga; on the other hand, if they were refused, they might attack the forts of the Siberian Line or, worse, take refuge with the already "insolent" Kazakhs.[47] The solution was for the Junghar refugees to be divided into small groups under the pretext of winter quarters, disarmed, and duped into joining the Volga Torghuts. At least five thousand of them, led by the zaisang Šereng, appear to have undergone this treatment by 1758, although a significant number seem to have bribed local officials and dispersed throughout the steppe regions of the empire. Many of the deportees died from disease, and the additional population strained Torghut society, already hemmed in by Russian settler encroachment.[48] Accepting the refugees demanded careful handling with the Qing, as the Treaty of Kiakhta strictly prescribed the handover of all fugitives on demand. Russian policy settled on two arguments: first, that the refugee Junghars were in fact the same Torghuts that had been Russian subjects since the early seventeenth century (in response to which the Lifanyuan asked facetiously what they were doing fighting the Qing in Jungharia); second, that in 1731 the Qing ambassador Toši had explicitly promised that his side would make no claims on Junghar refugees if Russia stayed out of the war with Galdan Tsereng.[49] No coherent response was ever offered to the second claim, perhaps because the 1729–1731 embassies had been scrubbed from Qing records; on the other hand, the Russian side had also selectively represented Toši's concessions.[50]

The case of the *dvoedantsy*, residents of the Altai and Saian mountains who historically were allowed to pay tribute to both Russia and the Junghars, was less straightforward to resolve, although intelligence ultimately decided the issue.[51] (In the wake of the conquest, the southwest portion of the Altai became Russian, while Uriangkhai land in the northeast became Qing territory; the latter has been a part of Russia's Tuvan Republic since its 1921 annexation by the Soviets.) In 1764, a Saian woman, who had "escaped from Mongol captivity" and encountered a Russian envoy in the borderland, reported her discovery that Mamut, a senior leader of the dvoedantsy, had "a concealed grudge against Russia" and had secretly gone to Beijing asking for troops to annex them to the Qing. Iakobii's sources repeatedly insisted that a Manchu and Mongol army was indeed on its way to the mountains to retrieve them.[52] As a result of this information, Shpringer ordered that Mamut's children and other dvoedantsy be relocated to the vicinity of Biisk fortress. Although his report stated that "he did not observe any desire to defect to Qing subjecthood," some degree of coercion can perhaps be safely assumed. Shpringer's quick response decided the issue: Qianlong decided not to risk withdrawing the dvoedantsy from the Russian interior by force, though this was now apparently no great loss as they were descendants of "worthless vagabonds" anyway.[53]

The Kazakhs posed an even thornier problem.[54] Historians, especially Russian and Soviet ones, tend to regard the Kazakhs of the Lesser and Middle

Hordes as at least nominal Russian subjects starting from the 1730s.[55] Yet Nurali Khan of the Lesser Horde, Abulmamet Khan of the Middle Horde, and Ablai Sultan, the Middle Horde's foremost chief and later khan, all swore allegiance to the Qing in the wake of the conquest of Jungharia even as they assured Russia of their continued loyalty—and it was far from clear that this was merely a false front.[56] Thus, in 1757 Ablai sent Qianlong a letter declaring, "Since the time of my grandfather and father, Eshim Khan and Janggir Khan, your edict has not reached to me. Now, hearing your edict, I am glad always to know [that you] have regard for us. I, that is Abulay, [my] sons and all the Kazakhs have become your *albatu* [slaves, subordinates]."[57] The Russians occasionally took Kazakh assurances at face value, but a "Description of the Kazakhs" composed at the College of Foreign Affairs around 1760 conceded that "they will join the side that is strongest, in hopes of plunder. . . . It must be admitted that the Kazakhs appear to have a better opinion of the Qing side than of ours." Lack of material demonstrations of Russian power had undermined Kazakh confidence.[58] The Lifanyuan even mocked the traditional Russian approach to the "vassalization" of steppe peoples, which it had followed religiously in the Kazakh case: "We have no such custom as some other countries to demand binding oaths and hostages from those lords who come to submit to us."[59] In 1758, to prevent the Kazakh drift eastward from proceeding any further, the College of Foreign Affairs ordered Orenburg officials to deflect Ablai from the Qing at all costs, while proclaiming to the Qing that letting Ablai send embassies to Beijing was a mark of Russia's mercy.[60]

Local translators from the Siberian Line forts, who also served as envoys and spies, were vital for this effort. In 1758, the Russian translator Arapov arrived just as Ablai and his chieftains were debating whether to accept the Qing offer to decamp to pastures in Jungharia and tried to persuade them to stay.[61] In 1760, a Bukharan named Alim Shukhov was sent in the guise of a trader to investigate conditions in Ablai's camp. Shortly afterward, he was followed by the translator Filat Gordeev, who happened to run into a Qing negotiating team, "pretended to be ill and did not leave," so he could observe the encounter. It became evident that the Qing envoy's poor translator impeded his communication with the Kazakhs, but Gordeev met with both groups and determined that the Kazakhs were above all terrified of a Qing attack—despite the fact that Kazakh leaders had assured the Russians of their cooperation in case of anti-Qing hostilities.[62] Information of this kind featured prominently in Catherine's 1763 instructions to Shpringer, who was ordered to use gifts (including swords and handsome salaries) and persuasion to drive home to the Kazakhs the dangers of Qing vassalage and the security to be gained under Russian protection.[63] In the end, although Ablai and the other Kazakh leaders continued to flirt with the Qing, they never permanently migrated as far as Ili, and their dependence on Russian trade at Orenburg and the Siberian Line fortresses kept them close to the Russian orbit.

In addition to translators, traders like Shukhov were an equally important source of intelligence, because as long as they did not openly claim Russian subjecthood, they possessed a virtually uncontested right to cross borders. A 1744 order from the College of Foreign Affairs specifically authorized petty traders to be sent using government funds as "spies" [shpiony] with a "small amount of goods, because with a heavy load they could not make haste themselves nor deliver a report promptly." It was inspired by the already significant activities of Aleksei Verkhoturov, who had provided information on events in Jungharia since the 1730s.[64] Among those authorized by the act was the intrepid Mikhail Voz'milov, who ventured to Bukhara and Xinjiang on intelligence missions in the 1760s–1780s.[65] By the end of the century, complaints had emerged that this provision was being exploited by actual traders spending thousands of rubles of their own money and having no real intelligence ends in mind; when these merchants were robbed by Kazakhs or encountered other difficulties in the steppe, it fell to local authorities to rescue them.[66]

Even when they were not setting out to spy, traders could have firsthand knowledge of events far from the border. In 1759, Qing troops began occupying the Tarim Basin, the southern portion of what would become Xinjiang.[67] In the process, they captured the Russian merchant Ivan Evseev and his partner, who told the whole story when he was returned to Orenburg. As a merchant from Tobolsk, he had done business in one of the Little Bukharan towns for fourteen years until it was captured by the rebellious Khoja Burhan ad-Din, who kept him in chains for a five-year period. When Qing troops arrived to crush ad-Din's rebellion, Evseev managed to escape from his custody, only to be captured by a Qing general and sent to Beijing for a threatening interrogation. Evseev concluded by saying that the Qing army "are the weakest, slowest, and most frantic people (except the Mongols, who are a little quicker). . . . They have rifles which are heavy and poor and wield them inexpertly, while their use of cannon is also inexpert, for they always place them in specially dug pits, while the people who fire them stand far away and turn their faces to the side."[68] Such comments from border crossers familiar with the armaments of both sides were one of the few opportunities Russians had to compare contemporary Qing military practices with their own, since local informants were generally unfamiliar with the details of Russian warfare.

It was not only Russians who gathered intelligence on the frontier. For imperial officials, counterintelligence also became part of their portfolio. In 1761 Major General Veimarn reported on a tense situation at the border, fearing Qing infiltration:

> The Bukharans are carrying on trade on the Ili River and . . . it would be good to send Shikhov [sic] there, but as there are Qing officers among them, it seems dangerous and doubtful to send Shikhov there alone, lest he be detained by them on the pretext of being a spy. . . . It also seems likely that the Qing are sending scouts to our borders, as in fact there were some among the Kazakhs at Troitsk Fortress, which the Kazakhs basically admitted to, as it is unlikely that they would have natural-born Chinese as their slaves. . . . Thus we have to be constantly wary of the Kazakhs without giving them any reason to be unhappy or distrust us.[69]

The suspected presence of scouts was not an isolated incident. In the 1770s, the Qing would embed a bilingual agent named Burud into the Kazakh Middle Horde. For four years, he would serve as a valuable source of information on their affairs and their relations with surrounding peoples. Though it is hard to say precisely how aware of each other's intelligence-gathering activities the two sides were, it was clear that this kind of knowledge production was a game with multiple players.[70]

A failure to predict the reactions of other communities and the long-term consequences of its own covert action policies underlay the most dramatic setback Russia experienced on the Irtysh frontier. In 1771, most of the Torghut (Kalmyk) nomads from the lower Volga plains migrated en masse to Ili in Qing Jungharia, at the cost of extreme suffering and loss of life (in part because they were pursued and massacred by Kazakhs, their longtime enemies). Some of them had been Russian subjects since the early seventeenth century, while others had only recently joined them from the former Junghar domains. The flight, however radical a measure it seemed at the time—and still seems today—was substantially overdetermined. Pressure from Russian colonists and land enclosures, excessive demands for military service, and blatant manipulation of the Torghut political system have all been cited as contributing factors to their decision to leave; in letters to Qianlong, Torghut leaders cited religious issues as a further motivation.[71] The presence of Šereng among the most vocal supporters of exodus was decisive, however. After all, he had been the leader of the group of 5,000 Junghar refugees who had been deported from the Siberian Line to the Volga, apparently against their will, in 1757–1758. Even beyond the Torghuts, however, the results of so much covert manipulation on the Irtysh were ambiguous at best. Russia may have acquired a few shreds of land, but its inability to carry on trade with Qing forts in Xinjiang directly left the region less useful economically than it had been before. Russians were forced to rely on Kazakhs as middlemen, who charged hefty fees and made the most of their crucial status. Hardly puppets of the great powers, the Kazakhs had managed to leverage their middle position to maintain their autonomy from Russia as well as the Qing—much as the Junghars had once done, but without permanent war.[72]

The flight of the Torghuts was not irreversible, at least as far as Russian officials were concerned. In the early 1790s the Irkutsk and Kolyvan governor-general Ivan Pil' attempted to take advantage of an opportunity to bring them back. In the spring of 1791, he heard from Major General Shtrandman of the Siberian Line. A merchant named Kurbanov, sent to spy "in the guise of a trader" to the Kazakh steppe, had met with the Torghut lama Khabun (or Gabun), who informed him that the Torghuts planned to return once more to Russia and were ready to bring with them a number of Mongols and former Junghars. In confirmation of this news, Khabun delivered a formal request to the Siberian Line commander soon after. By mid-April, with tacit authorization from the empress, Pil' had ordered preparations to begin in earnest to receive the Torghuts as soon as the weather became suitable for a mass migration. On April 30, however, he reported that the Qing authorities had captured Khabun and learned about the Russian plans from a letter the lama was carrying; if they learned the true extent of the Russian role, all the progress made in the Uladzai negotiations would collapse. But Khabun's letter was sealed with a Russian ruble coin instead of a proper seal. It was this circumstance that allowed the Senate to claim plausible deniability when the Lifanyuan demanded a response. Under torture, Khabun "confessed" that the letter and the entire plot was a forgery; the Qing, despite their suspicions, accepted this explanation, and the negotiations were allowed to proceed.[73]

This was not the last time the Torghuts would try to return to Russia, but whereas Catherine had been deeply committed to this goal—after all, the migration had been an embarrassment for her in the eyes of Europe as well as Beijing—her successors were decidedly lukewarm. In 1806, another attempt was delayed because it would conflict with the Golovkin embassy; subsequent orders demanded that no formal offers or promises of any kind be made to the Torghut leaders, but that "if they themselves come to us without aid on our part, do not oppose them." Due to this total official inaction, the matter died. Finally, in 1820, yet another Siberian Line commander heard from Torghut leaders about the potential for a return. He sent copies of the 1806 documents back to St. Petersburg as a pointed reminder that they had missed one opportunity but now had the chance to make use of another. He seems to have been entirely ignored. The Russian government's refusal to facilitate the return of its own former subjects was a measure of its increasing unwillingness to treat Inner Asia as the arena for covert action it had been during the previous century.[74]

Under Alexander I, merchants continued to circulate around the Irtysh, mostly to the indifference of the central authorities. In 1803 a merchant-spy named Sergei Urvantsov made a lengthy trip across the border; his superior officer's petition for a reward seems to have gone unanswered.[75] In 1809, Grigorii Glazenap, commander of the Siberian Line, reported to Foreign Minister Nikolai Rumiantsev about an unprecedented undercover expedition undertaken by the merchant Nerpin into the Kazakh steppe and Qing Jungharia, which appears to have successfully probed the possibilities for indirect cross-border trade between the Kazakhs, Qing, and Russians. Glazenap attempted to procure a reward for Nerpin, but it took over a year of repeated requests before Rumiantsev consented to give him more than token encouragement—despite the fact that trade with the Qing at the Irtysh border was an earnestly sought goal of Russian foreign policy.[76] These locally driven contacts would later contribute to the expansion of Russian prerogatives in western Xinjiang around the middle of the nineteenth century, but largely as a result of Qing disengagement rather than organized Russian pressure.[77]

The Qing conquest of the Junghars had briefly transformed the Siberian Line into a zone of opportunity for the Russian Empire, where covert action could accomplish what military buildup could not. By the last quarter of the eighteenth century, this was no longer true. The blowback to Russian policies exemplified by the flight of the Torghuts had led to long-term retrenchment. This did not mean that Russian officials ceased to think ahead: thus, in the 1780s the Irkutsk-Kolyvan governor-general Ivan Iakobii decided to encourage Old Believers, religious dissidents loyal to a seventeenth-century version of Orthodoxy, to settle illegally in the Altai in order to accustom the Qing to a Russian presence.[78] But there was no longer any expectation that the Qing conquest could offer new advantages to the Russian Empire. The region settled into a seemingly permanent stalemate. It came to resemble the stalemate that had already existed since the 1720s in the other major theater of the Russo-Qing cold war: Transbaikalia. Just as Russian plans on the Irtysh were gearing up in the 1750s, an even more comprehensive intelligence strategy was taking shape on the Mongolian border, one that used the region's fixed borders as a fulcrum for a covert action model of its own.

Chapter 8

Spies and Subversion in Eastern Siberia

A S THE STRUGGLE for hegemony unfolded in the former Junghar border-lands in the west, a parallel but very different process was taking place in the Russian territories bordering Mongolia and Manchuria in the east. In the former, the Russian Empire's policy was tentative, acutely conscious of the limitations of its military capacity and the fragility of its footholds on the Irtysh; in the latter, the new imperial configuration enabled frontier officials like Varfolomei Iakobii to dream of epochal shifts encompassing at their outermost limits the collapse of the Qing Dynasty and the absorption of Khalkha Mongolia and Manchuria into the Russian Empire. The paradox was that the border in this region had been fixed and stable for decades. It had been mostly delimited during the preparation of the 1727 Treaty of Kiakhta. Russians—notably merchants, Cossacks, and inmates of the vast convict-labor silver mines of Nerchinsk—had been living there since the middle of the seventeenth century. Interimperial interactions on this frontier were highly regularized, with well-defined protocols for dealing with cross-border raiders and fugitives. At the same time, the Russian-subject Buriats (northern Mongols) maintained religious and family ties with the Qing-subject Khalkha, which enabled constant cross-border interaction between them. It was in fact precisely these features of the frontier that enabled the Russian Empire to construct an intelligence network that drew on dozens of agents, spies, and informers in Mongolia. Its purpose was not only to determine the extent of the Qing military threat to Siberia but to probe and cultivate the likelihood of Mongol defection—an event that, if it could be arranged, would fundamentally alter the political landscape in the region.

What set the intelligence nexus that emerged in Eastern Siberia in the 1750s apart from the other components of the imperial knowledge regime was its geographical specificity.[1] This was an enormous strength: unlike the missionaries in Beijing or the employees of the trade caravan, local intelligence operatives east of Lake Baikal could draw on longstanding Buriat-Mongol ties and their own connections to achieve genuine inroads into the Mongol power structure. Yet the very local embeddedness that gave it such power as a knowledge-making apparatus also helped make its considerations peripheral in St. Petersburg. Local governors and officials developed endless plans to annex and divide the Qing borderlands, but for both Elizabeth and Catherine II, conflicts in the west always took precedence. By the end of the eighteenth century, the connections that had sustained Russian intelligence on the Qing frontier had begun to fray, but the divergence in goals and aspirations between center and periphery remained. It was only in the 1850s—as we will see later—that the ambitious new governor-general Nikolai Murav'ev was able to leverage this pent-up local initiative in a coup targeted almost as much at the imperial metropole as against the Qing Empire itself.

The intelligence network in Transbaikalia originated with Savva Vladislavich, the Russian ambassador responsible for signing the Treaty of Kiakhta with the Qing—and a onetime intelligence agent in Istanbul and other parts of the Ottoman Empire.[2] His embassy to Beijing (and status as plenipotentiary) also gave him the power and responsibility to reform Transbaikalia's political institutions to fit the new policies being established around the border, especially the management of Russo-Qing trade and the mutual tracking and return of fugitives and criminals. His intelligence expertise was an important asset for this project. His 1728 instructions to Colonel Ivan Bukholts, who had once led the Russian gold-seeking mission into Jungharia and was now appointed to manage the border, regulated the gathering of intelligence about Mongolia. He was to "keep a secret correspondence through Aleksei Tretiakov and through the interpreter Riazanov with the Mongol [i.e., Qing subject] colonel Galdan, who is a very good man and one very dutiful in the service of His Imperial Majesty." As long as he was paid on time, he would be a reliable source of inside information about Mongolia.[3] Similar instructions were reiterated in 1731 to the incoming Irkutsk vice-governor Zholobov. They included an added provision that he focus on "dangers to the Russian side, that is, preparations for war . . . and in all border

8.1 The Mongolian and Manchurian frontier in the 1750s–1760s.

places he should take firm precautions against the Qing, who are an inconstant people despite their cordiality [*laskovoe obkhozhdenie*]." They also enjoined the colonel to be wary of anyone sent to the Russian side by the Qing, "artfully watch over them and see if they are not spies, and in such a case take precautions to cut short their schemes through good escorting officers and so on." Intelligence was a core aspect of frontier governance.[4]

All such intelligence efforts would flow through the small town of Selenginsk and the Troitsko-Savsk fortress near the border, since Irkutsk was cut off by Lake Baikal (where couriers still drowned periodically) from any direct interaction with Qing Manchuria and Mongolia. Selenginsk had been specially rebuilt for that purpose with the help of the engineer Abram Gannibal, Aleksandr Pushkin's Ethiopian great-grandfather.[5] As a result of these administrative changes, the Russian intelligence network came to be concentrated in the hands first of Bukholts (who was made commandant of Selenginsk in 1731) and then his successor, Varfolomei Iakobii, a Polish-born veteran of Russian campaigns in Persia and the Ottoman Empire, who occupied the post from 1740 to 1769 (for the last few years in an unofficial capacity). It was Iakobii who, taking advantage of his position and the unique features of the frontier, made the post into an office with empirewide significance.

The most important sites for intelligence gathering in Transbaikalia were the border posts established by the Kiakhta treaty, where soldiers from the two empires routinely fraternized and exchanged information. Much of this naturally dealt with the day-to-day minutiae of horse theft and smuggling, but the frequent meetings offered opportunities to conduct more illicit traffic. For instance, in 1758, a Mongol lama named Luvan traveled to a border post for a conversation with the translator Pavel Gantimurov; when asked about military affairs, he "became afraid and said that if he reveals state secrets he risks execution"—but still told him that 50,000 men were being gathered, possibly for an attack on Russia.[6] These conversations generally took place in Mongolian, since translators formed the core of Iakobii's cadres.

The Manchus, too, saw the frontier as a useful vantage point on Russia. Sungyun's *Stories of 120 Old Men,* a late eighteenth-century Manchu work by a senior administrator on the border, literally mentions a post where "following a steep trail through the woods, you can arrive at a place opposite the Russian border where you can look down from above."[7] But Qing authorities also used the border-post system for more high-level forms of intelligence. In 1728, the Manchu official responsible for affairs on the Amur memorialized that a Russian named Danila had come to a Solon officer named Buju and, being questioned minutely about the news of his homeland, said that "after our khan [i.e., Peter the Great] died, his grandson [Peter II] being too small, his wife [Catherine I] took the throne, the grandson being raised by his uncle, [but] our high officials [*meni ambasa*], having said that a female khan would be greatly shameful before neighboring countries [*adaki gurun labdu, hehe han bici gicuke*], and the grandson having grown, made him khan, and he became khan in the seventh month of this year."[8] Such a framing, if Buju did not distort what Danila said, would have likely been punishable as lèse-majesté in the Russian Empire. Later that year, another Russian named Iakov (Yakub) reported on famine conditions in the Nerchinsk region as well as troop movements.[9] Yet Manchu and Mongol officers do not seem to have cultivated their informers in the same way that Iakobii did, and knowledge of Russian was not always a given for them, unlike knowledge of Mongol on the Russian side.[10]

The treaty's border institutions were stable and reliable; this meant they could be predictably exploited for intelligence purposes. An especially vivid illustration is the story of a convict named Mikhail Shulgin. In August 1754, Shulgin, who had lost both feet to frostbite and walked around "on bits of wood tied to his legs," stole a canoe, escaped from Nerchinsk, and "floated thievishly past all the border posts" established on the Amur and its tributaries. When he reached the Qing town of Aigun, he surrendered himself to its commander and announced that he had important news: four Russian regiments equipped with artillery and led by Fëdor Soimonov were assembling at Nerchinsk in preparation for an invasion of Manchuria the next summer. The Qing authorities questioned him about Nerchinsk, told him that they had more than enough soldiers to resist an invasion, and then finally had him caned three times until he confessed that he was lying (though in fact his report was mostly accurate) and handed him back across the border. Thereupon the Russian authorities, after three rounds of judicial torture, agreed that there was no conspiracy, only a desire to "live without want" in a foreign land. Though his treason carried a death sentence, it was later commuted to further exile in Nerchinsk. Local officials used Shulgin's attempted defection to interrogate him for information about the condition of Qing forces in northern Manchuria, while other intelligence agents determined that no preparations for war had been made in response to the threat. The Eastern Siberian intelligence network was resilient and multichanneled, with multiple agents and venues reinforcing and verifying each key piece of information.[11]

The Subversion of Mongolia

Though some aspects of the frontier intelligence apparatus had been in place for decades, the relative stability of Russo-Qing relations meant that there was little external impetus to turn this system into an apparatus for covert action. The Qing conquest of Jungharia in 1755–1757 changed the situation fundamentally. The Khalkha Mongols, already immiserated by Qing policies,

8.2 Qing Aigun, ca. 1700–1720. Library of Congress.

had provided most of the supplies and a substantial portion of the soldiers for the Qing campaigns in Jungharia; a smallpox epidemic in 1755–1756 brought them to the breaking point. When Qianlong executed Erinchindorj (the elder brother of the Jebtsundamba Khutukhtu, the most important Khalkha Buddhist religious leader) for failing to prevent Amursana's escape, the Jebtsundamba Khutukhtu's loyalties began to waver: not only was the executed man his brother, but his descent from Chinggis Khan had been thought to guarantee him a certain amount of immunity. The execution was also the last straw for the Mongol prince Chingünjav. In league with the still at-large Amursana, he rose up in revolt against Qing rule.[12]

Iakobii kept a close watch on events in Qing Mongolia and Jungharia, compiling information from border posts and from interpreter / envoys like Sava Frolov, who had received "secret orders to investigate and report" into "extracts" that were sent to the Senate on an approximately bimonthly basis starting at the latest from August 1754.[13] In the process, Frolov and his colleagues recruited informants among the Mongols. One day in March 1755, when Frolov was visiting the Tüsiyetü-Khan in Urga, he lingered on the pretext of obtaining Mongol medicines for the khan of the Volga Torghuts. He used the opportunity to give one of his frequent informants, a Mongol named Sharga, "a yellow fox pelt worth no more than a ruble" "because he, Sharga, always gives information to the interpreter about events in Mongolia and so he would be more eager to give such news in the future." Sharga accepted the pelt "happily" and promised to "always report all news related to Russia." Both Sharga and his father, taking care to meet with Frolov in private, reported on such matters as Mongol unhappiness with Qing demands and the fact that a shamanic vision showed a black dog baring its teeth at the Qing from Jungharia, for which they were rewarded with pelts three rubles in value.[14] By 1756, Iakobii had authorized his agents to give furs worth up to eight rubles, because of a new focus on information about Solon and Mongol troop movements in Mongolia.[15] For higher-ranking sources, like the general Batur Belei, more sophisticated gifts were needed: he asked for a high-quality hunting rifle (which constituted contraband) as well as a fox pelt from his Russian contact.[16]

As Chingünjav was beginning his rebellion and collecting allies— according to Batur Belei, his coconspirators had agreed that Russia would be their next destination after their revolt—news of other defectors began to reach Iakobii. An enormous group of 10,000 yurts demanded asylum in late 1755. In the spring of 1756, the interpreter Vasilii Sharin spoke with a *shabinar* (religious serf) of the Jebtsundamba Khutukhtu who suggested that other shabinars may want to defect as well.[17] Semën Surgutskii reported a more suggestive conversation that summer. Amid news of Qing setbacks in the west, he described the smallpox epidemic and the execution of Erinchindorj; he also said he had met with an old acquaintance—an elderly lama who had once been close to the Jebtsundamba Khutukhtu—who told him that "with further oppression the Mongols will certainly defect to the Russian side," and although Mongol leaders were not yet discussing this, commoners were confirming it to Surgutskii on a frequent basis.[18] Although Chingünjav's revolt, which never reached critical mass, was crushed by Qing forces in January 1757, plans for defection continued to develop. In July 1757, the border commissar Vasilii Igumnov reported that he had met with one Dorji Noin (Noyan?) Tsulai, who listed five Mongol notables with 23 *sumuns* (4,000–7,000 people) who were ready to defect. The crucial missing piece of the puzzle was the Jebtsundamba Khutukhtu; if he joined, Mongol informants agreed that even 49 Chakhar *jasaks* (banner chiefs) from Inner Mongolia would come over to the Russian side—and by the end of that summer it became clear that the other leaders were delaying any plans until the Jebtsundamba Khutukhtu's opinion was known.[19]

The collapse of the Mongol defection plan was the result of a carefully weighed analysis of the importance of enticing Mongol elites to the Russian cause and of assembling sufficient resources for the project.[20] Iakobii had been ordered to prepare a memorandum on the Mongol issue as early as November 1755, because accepting the defectors would be a clear violation of the Treaty of Kiakhta and therefore carried the risk of war; it certainly could not be explained away by a technicality like the Junghar refugee issue. In February 1756, he set out the basic problem with the requests for asylum that had hitherto come in: "they are currently all common people, while their leaders have not evinced such a desire."[21] He reiterated the point at the end of that year in a lengthier document: accepting the Mongols' defection would be beneficial only if the Mongol leaders, especially the Jebtsundamba Khutukhtu, were willing to defect but remain in place as Russian vassals, with the Russian army reinforcing them for the inevitable Qing attack. Any other solution would be a dramatic liability, as Russia was not just too weak militarily to hold off a Qing attack on Siberia but did not even have the power to keep a "flighty people" like the Mongols in line if they were invited into its borders. Even under the more favorable scenario, Iakobii recommended that 30,000 regular troops be sent to the Nerchinsk and Selenginsk border and two fortresses built on the Onon in Mongolia, with all the required artillery— something he must have known would be both utterly inconceivable for the Senate and impractical from a logistical point of view. Russia's involvement in the Seven Years' War (1756–1763) made this all the more impossible. When the Jebtsundamba Khutukhtu first refused to defect and then died under suspicious circumstances in 1758 (with the Qing ordering that his successor incarnation be found outside of Khalkha territory), there was no further benefit for Russia in pursuing the matter.[22]

Despite the failure of this attempt, the events of 1755–1757 had long-term consequences for the Russian intelligence network as the relationship between Russia and the Qing grew frostier. When Iakobii's agents cultivated cross-border ties, both new and preexisting, with Northern Mongolia, they forged lasting intelligence relationships. The most important of these involved a Mongol *jakirughci* (junior commissioned officer) named Chugan (in Russian; likely Ciwang in Mongol). He was apparently related to the Mongol *jasak* Chebak, who had declared his intent to defect, but he provided independent intelligence even before the crisis. In August 1759, long after any immediate possibility of defection had receded, the Russian agent Vasilii Sharin sent along a letter from Chugan (translated from Mongolian):

I hereby inform you that I have received Her Great Majesty's salary from your zaisang Vasilii on the 16th of the first autumn month consisting of two sables and five red-black foxes with tails and paws; and I performed obeisance for the health of Her Majesty in a hidden place while standing on my knees, three times to God, and nine times in the direction of Her Majesty, and once to God and thrice towards you for your health, Brigadier [Iakobii], in thanks. Moreover, I sincerely wish and ask God that he would place all of the peoples under the sky in these lands [Mongolia] under Her Majesty's hand and under her great and fortunate care, and this I desire and ask in the most sincere spirit. In the year of Enthroned by Heaven [i.e., Qianlong] 24, the 16th of the first autumn month.

Such a statement was of course openly treasonous to the Qing, and Chugan was already under suspicion: in the same meeting, he reported that during a council discussing the possibility of war with Russia, a Mongol general had said, "as if jokingly," that "[Chugan] knows [Russian] places well" and that it would be best to "keep to the better side, except they are unused to living in hot places and should not move there." The general was probably implying that Chugan would be accepted as a defector and then sent to the Volga like the Junghars had been.[23]

Despite this cloud of suspicion, Chugan became Iakobii's single most vital intelligence informant over the next decade, meeting with Russian contacts on a nearly monthly basis and sometimes providing written accounts. His services did not come for free. In August 1760, after a particularly fruitful meeting, he complained that his trips to Kiakhta were causing him financial expenses, pointed out that he was risking his own life and health, and said that even his father had once received two hundred rubles as a reward from Vladislavich. (This may suggest that Chugan was in fact the son of the Galdan mentioned in Bukholts's instructions.) After receiving permission from the Senate, Iakobii authorized his salary and the rewards given to others to be raised to one hundred rubles in pelts. Thus, over the course of five years, the budget allotted to one informant had risen fifteenfold.[24] For the most part, however, Russian informants were much lowlier (and less well rewarded). They included such figures as the petty trader "Deaf Baian" and the "gardener Namtui."[25]

Buriat and Mongol lamas, whose religious duties allowed them regular cross-border contacts, were an equally vital source of information.[26] One lama, Zaiaev, composed a travelogue and description of the monasteries in Tibet for Vasilii Igumnov during his pilgrimage there in the early 1770s, after having been a delegate to Catherine's doomed Legislative Commission.[27] Earlier, a Tibetan lama named Namjal had been a key source on Chingünjav's rebellion and a Mongol lama named Choinzhun had traveled to a border post to inform Igumnov of commercial developments in Mongolia.[28] These cross-border connections were not an unalloyed good from the Russian perspective, however: in 1764 Russia instituted the position of Khanbo Bandida lamas (of which Zaiaev was the first) in order to redirect Buriat loyalties away from the Jebtsundamba Khutukhtu. As the intelligence network decayed after midcentury, the impulse to sever cross-border ties rather than exploit them became stronger and stronger.[29]

The most consistently useful information—and the most striking report—came from a Buriat lama named Tsorzhi Sodbo Zasaev, who had family ties to the entourage of the Jebtsundamba Khutukhtu and cultivated them for intelligence purposes.[30] He happened to be at Urga in 1765, visiting a senior lama named Kanfa, when the governor-general (*jiyanggiyūn*) in charge of Mongolia, Sanzai Dorji, was found to be smuggling and illegally trading with Russia with the help of one of Kanfa's assistants (possibly a Russian informant himself). Soldiers were sent to fetch Kanfa and Zasaev for interrogation, but the two men found an excuse to talk and get their alibi straight: that Zasaev had come to negotiate his own clan's defection to the Qing. Although Qing officials were suspicious and issued "grave threats to tell the truth because he Tsorzhi is utterly at their mercy, even if he dies, there will be no one to find him," Zasaev replied that "even if they torture him or put him to death, he has nothing else to say." Zasaev was then interrogated about Russian affairs, to which he either pleaded ignorance or "not having anything else to say said false things that he had made up." Though the officials did not believe him, he insisted and at length managed to persuade them that he would be missed in Russia and therefore should not be sent to Beijing. Finally he was remanded back to Kanfa's custody. The Mongol provided him with detailed information about the size and composition of Qing forces in Jungharia and Mongolia and explained that the emperor was being advised on the military situation in Russia by a renegade Russian Kalmyk named Badashan.[31] News of Zasaev's supposed desire to defect even made it into the Qing *Shilu,* the official court record of the Qing Dynasty, although Qianlong never found out that the Buriat was lying.[32]

Iakobii's agents were the link that connected these informants to his office in Selenginsk. They were not specifically trained for intelligence work: as regular state servitors who happened to be issued secret orders to collect and investigate affairs beyond the border, they formed a miscellaneous crew. One, Pavel Gantimurov, was a descendant of the Evenki prince Gantimur, who had caused a diplomatic rupture by defecting to Russia in the seventeenth century. Some, like a Captain Tarskii, headed border posts; others, like Surgutskii or Sharin, were translators used routinely as go-betweens between Urga, Kiakhta, and Selenginsk. (They typically knew Mongolian, but not Manchu or Chinese.) Agents both cultivated local sources and collected their own observations on the spot, as when Sharin reported seeing "a dead Mongol body in all his clothes, and the Mongols said he had died of famine."[33] Such activities were apparently no mystery to the Qing authorities; in August 1765, at the height of the smuggling scandal, the courier Luka Ostrovskikh reported that "he could discover nothing as upon his arrival in Urga he was lodged in a yurt walled in with a palisade and they were not allowed to leave or receive visitors."[34]

Among these agents, the standout figure was Vasilii Igumnov. His father, a minor Siberian bureaucrat, was an official in the Moscow-Beijing trade caravan; he had been rewarded for it by Peter III with a wig, a watch, and a sword, but no apparent elevation of rank. Igumnov himself spent sixty years in state service from 1744 to 1803, and for at least fifty of those years, he was entrusted with intelligence duties. Yet, like Rossokhin, the promise of upward mobility embedded in Peter's Table of Ranks largely left Igumnov behind. Only in 1792, when he played a decisive role in negotiating a new border treaty, was he promoted from the lowest rank; by 1801 he was awarded hereditary nobility on the basis of an alleged "feat of influencing the Chinese government against the English ambassador Macartney," but this was too late to make a real difference to his life. As his son Aleksandr lamented, summing up this illustrious career, "he died in 1803 leaving behind no estate except his good name and his eternal memory"—though this was in part because he gave away his horse and cattle ranches to two Buriat and Evenki clans. An unusually talented product of the Eastern Siberian borderlands, for most of his life Igumnov escaped the notice of St. Petersburg entirely.[35]

Igumnov's local ties were his most important intelligence resource. Although he was primarily in charge of Russian border posts—and hence had plenty of clandestine meetings on the border—he was also assigned to escort replacement missionaries to Beijing in 1771, 1781, and 1794. He used these opportunities to visit Mongols he was friends with (he was evidently a fluent speaker of Mongolian, and the word "friendship" occurs frequently in his reports) and keep secret journals of events in the Qing Empire.[36] He even won the favor of the Jesuit missionary Joseph Amiot, who referred to him as "un fort aimable officier russe."[37] Though his intelligence is represented in many of Iakobii's reports and extracts, his name, like those of other agents, was omitted in printed collections. Igumnov's local role both enabled his career and cut him off from metropolitan sources of prestige.[38]

Unlike his informants, Iakobii succeeded in making himself visible and invaluable to the Russian government. His indispensable role is perhaps best represented by the fact that after 1764, when Catherine II decided to comply with repeated Qing ultimatums that he be relieved from his border-oversight responsibilities, he continued to send his reports as usual until his death despite theoretically having no official position.[39] He was not expected merely to aggregate intelligence reports but also to analyze and compare them and offer his opinion of their credibility. Thus, when the lama Luvan told Gantimurov that an army was assembling to march on Russia, Iakobii decided this was "doubtful" since other agents had not confirmed any such preparations and sufficient time had already passed to discount the news. (He recommended vigilance anyway.)[40] Iakobii's extracts and reports therefore represent the documentary output and material trace of a wide-ranging, well-honed system for sourcing, gathering, collating, and analyzing frontier intelligence. His reports reached a number of addressees. The Senate, the College of Foreign Affairs, and the governor of Siberia were typically mandatory recipients, but often the official in charge of the Siberian Line fortresses and the College of War also received copies. (Although the Siberian Line had its own intelligence resources, none were as consistent or intimately informed as Iakobii's sources.) To the extent that the imperial administration had a mental picture of events on the other side of the border, it was largely painted through Iakobii's efforts.

In the middle of the 1760s, signs of strain began to emerge in this system. The bellwether was Russia's most trusted agent, Chugan. In 1766, although Russian sources initially reported that he had been sent to Urga for questioning in a smuggling case, it emerged that he was in fact going to be elevated in rank, either to *meiren i janggin* (lieutenant general) or even higher. He was in fact only made a colonel (*jalan i janggin*).[41] In 1767, Chugan came to visit Major Kopylov in Kiakhta "for no apparent reason, but most likely because he was sent from the amban Soli to gather intelligence." The major asked "if, once he leaves and if he visits the amban, whether he would not tell him everything, and [Chugan] replied that if he asks then he will not forbear."[42] As recently as 1766, Mongol leaders told Russians they still intended to defect in the event of war.[43] Chugan's promotion and his new role as a double agent indicate that the Qing policies that had once alienated the

Mongols and driven them to seek Russian protection were beginning to be accepted by the population, especially after the removal of the unpopular Qing governor-general Sanzai Dorji (though he was later reinstated with less authority). To the extent that Russian strategy relied on maintaining the spark of potential defection in the hope that it would be kindled by some later crisis, it was increasingly becoming obsolete.[44]

More broadly, the smuggling crackdown in the wake of Sanzai Dorji's dismissal drove Mongolia and Russia further apart. Qing officials had always been leery of the cross-border ties the Kiakhta trade had encouraged: one of them had complained about illegal Russo-Qing trade in 1762, "facilitated by the fact that their Qing people live at Kiakhta for ten or twenty years or more, fraternize with the Russians, and moreover due to this long residency come to live in sin with [Russian] women, from which some of their merchants have lost their livelihoods and become poor."[45] When Qing authorities stopped the Kiakhta trade in 1764, arguing that Russians had been illegally enclosing border territories and charging tariffs in violation of the treaty, the College of Foreign Affairs specifically encouraged Iakobii to promote border smuggling.[46] Soli, however, by means of the aggressive clearing and monitoring of border areas, appears to have succeeded in minimizing this.[47] By 1767, Iakobii confessed that very few goods were being brought in illegally, which he saw as a deliberate plot on the part of Soli to pressure Russia into petitioning for trade to be reopened.[48]

The test of Iakobii's network in the wake of changes in cross-border ties would have to come with the signing of a new addendum to the Treaty of Kiakhta.[49] In 1767, weary of the trade interruption and the apparent escalation of interimperial animosity, Catherine sent Colonel Ivan Kropotov to the border to finally negotiate a resolution to the Lifanyuan's complaints. He had been an envoy in Beijing four years earlier, albeit to little substantive effect.[50] With him Kropotov brought Aleksei Leont'ev, the most successful of the surviving students of the Russian Ecclesiastical Mission in Beijing. Although his instructions did not contain any intelligence-specific provisions, he was instructed to consult regularly with Iakobii and given wide discretion to resolve matters in such a way that trade could be reopened while maintaining Russian dignity. The issues facing Kropotov were the alleged Russian appropriation of Qing lands through enclosure with fences; the annulment of old cases and claims related to cross-border raiding by Buriats, Evenki, and Mongols, which would have entailed a heavy restitution be paid by Mongol authorities; and the practice of charging duties on trade goods, which Russia had no intention of abandoning and which therefore required special finesse.[51]

Soon after the commencement of negotiations in May 1768, it became clear to Leont'ev that underlying the disagreement about tariffs and fences were differences in the Manchu and Russian texts of the treaty: the latter did not specify duty-free trade and adopted a different formulation of the border line. At the same time, he and Kropotov began receiving secret visits from the Mongol Tüsiyetü-Khan, one of the four most important Khalkha leaders and a party to the negotiations alongside the Manchu *ambans.* He also obtained copies of the Lifanyuan's instructions to its ambans and other documents, passed along by the Mongol officer Bandzar through the Russian merchant Pëtr Volkov. Bandzar received merchandise (including a watch) worth nearly one hundred rubles as a reward. Eventually, the Tüsiyetü-Khan sent a letter through Bandzar offering his "friendship" to Kropotov. The letter left little doubt what this implied: "But since no one can be suspicious of the officials of two great states having a friendship with one another, so we can also henceforth send messages to each other with gifts and with information [*s vest'mi*] as good friendship demands." Kropotov got the hint and sent the khan a rifle and a brace of pistols. By mid-October, Kropotov wrote in the official journal that "the Tüsiyetü-Khan, having become great friends with the commissar [Kropotov] through mutual gifts and correspondence, secretly sent a man to the commissar to tell him that the conclusion of the treaty had gone to a vote," three to one in favor of the Russian proposal.[52]

Yet in the end, this extraordinary intelligence coup changed nothing whatsoever for the Russians, who still had no leverage to exert against the Qing. Although Russia had a plausible claim that the Russian text of the treaty was just as binding as the Manchu one, Kropotov ultimately surrendered on all three of his major points, with the exception of a small amount of fenced-in territory and some concessions related to the mission in Beijing: the fences were torn down, old cases were annulled, and duties were declared illegal. (In practice, the customs office was merely moved slightly deeper into the Russian interior.) His unprecedented access to the deliberations of the Qing side had yielded no advantage in the negotiations: Russia remained too weak militarily and too unconvincing diplomatically to present a serious alternative.

The combination of success and gridlock was the central paradox of Russian intelligence on the Mongol border. Although intelligence was intended as a substitute for war, advancing imperial goals in the absence of credible military or diplomatic force, by the end of fifteen years of increasingly intensive penetration of Qing Mongolia, Russia was no closer to achieving these goals than it had been at the outset. In the meantime, the Mongol loyalties that had once so threatened Qing rule in Mongolia now foreclosed the possibility of a Russian takeover. As Qianlong put it, rejecting the prospect of an invasion of Russia: "If the Russians wished to cause trouble they would have done so long ago, when Chingünjav and the Khalkhas were in confusion and wavering. . . . Since they did not move in the past, they certainly will not cause trouble now."[53] It would be nearly a century before Russian ships sailed down the Amur, and Mongolia would remain firmly in Qing hands until the twentieth century.

Eastern Siberia Dreams of Empire

After the deaths in 1769 of both Iakobii and Kropotov—who had been expected to use his plenipotentiary powers to continue reforming matters on the frontier—the Eastern Siberian intelligence network began to decay, but the officials who controlled it, especially Iakobii's son Ivan, continued to build on the conquering aspirations of the 1750s. Isolated on the empire's distant periphery, these local administrators constantly sought to make the case for their relevance to the distant metropolitan establishment. They were motivated in part by dreams of glory but also by a persistent feeling of vulnerability. With their intelligence apparatus decaying, they did not know if a Qing invasion was on the horizon, and information from across the border was contradictory if not deliberately misleading. Although the Russian Empire still saw the struggle for regional dominance with the Qing as important, additional military resources were always more needed elsewhere. Plans for attack were also a means of defense.

The immediate successor of the Selenginsk spymaster was Major Semën Vlasov, who had experience serving in Kiakhta under his predecessor. His 1770 instructions to his border patrols made clear that he meant to continue expanding his intelligence network. Point 12 specified that "important de-

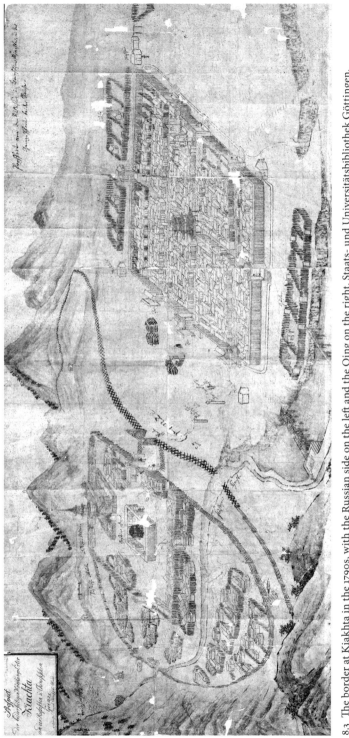

8.3 The border at Kiakhta in the 1790s, with the Russian side on the left and the Qing on the right. Staats- und Universitätsbibliothek Göttingen, Von Asch collection, 269.

fectors, if they report substantively about hostile Qing intentions towards the Russian empire . . . should be sent in all haste and with extreme secrecy and care to this chancellery, and in case of demands for them from the Qing side excuses should be made in a concealed fashion." Point 13 demanded that couriers should be sent immediately in case of "secret and important matters," while less important ones would be reported by extract monthly. Anything said by Qing personnel stationed at the border should be written down and likewise sent in monthly.[54] But neither Vlasov nor his successors ever had as much success as Iakobii with developing the cross-border intelligence network.

One reason was yet another paradox. Pursuant to reforms intended to strengthen Siberia in the face of the Qing threat, Irkutsk and the eastern part of the vast Siberian landmass became its own province. In the process, after specific demands from the Qing side, the governor in Irkutsk became responsible for interactions with the authorities in Urga. The problem of Lake Baikal remained, however, and because governors rarely ventured east of the lake and had many more pressing duties, it was no longer possible for them to have close contact with agents. The Russian intelligence network was now fully subordinate to the governor and had virtually no influence or access to resources beyond the province; in practice it was run out of the Troitsko-Savsk fortress outside of Kiakhta by an official who enjoyed much less authority than Iakobii had. Even the archival records show a notable decline in the density and sophistication of intelligence reports.[55] This was not because information was less necessary: recurrent foreign-policy crises continued to plague the area. As the College of Foreign Affairs put it in Archimandrite Shishkovskii's 1779 instructions, his information "cannot but be curious, given the increasingly few means we have for reliable information about events there."[56]

One of these crises itself illustrates the problem. In 1778, trade was briefly interrupted when a Russian named Grigorii Sharin, in training as a Mongol translator, was caught sneaking across the border from Kiakhta into the Qing trading settlement (*maimaicheng*). Although he claimed he was merely drunk, the Mongol authorities accused him of plotting with several of their soldiers to smuggle horses. They kept him in chains and refused to surrender him for several months, during which tensions continued to escalate; ultimately Sharin spent several years being shuttled around the Chinese interior. The whole episode was in marked contrast to the 1750s and 1760s, when Mongol interpreters like Sharin's relative Vasilii crossed the border seemingly at will and negotiated with Qing subjects over matters much weightier than horse smuggling, including outright espionage. The kinds of cross-border contacts that had allowed Russian intelligence connections in Mongolia to flourish were now being much more rigidly policed, which was reflected in both the reduced number and variety of reports filtering through to the center.[57]

In 1783, a further administrative reform seemed to portend major changes for the Russian Empire's approach to its Qing neighbor.[58] Catherine II created the governor-generalships of Irkutsk and Kolyvan—covering the entire southeastern frontier zone—and placed them both under the leadership of Ivan Iakobii, a Potemkin protégé who had extensive governing experience already. Few men seemed better suited for the job: Ivan Iakobii was not only the son of Varfolomei but had also been in Beijing several times as a courier. Yet the empress seems to have given little thought to how a single man might effectively rule two provinces cut off from each other by endless mountains and thousands of miles of almost ungoverned space, and Iakobii complained about not being able to deal with the problems of both provinces at once. Clearly, the desire to have the whole Qing frontier under unified control superseded any considerations of efficiency.

Ivan Iakobii's major test came almost immediately. In 1784, a gang led by a Russian Buriat named Uladzai robbed and murdered a Chinese merchant. They were captured by Russian authorities, caned, fined, branded, and sentenced to hard labor, without any consultation with the Qing official in charge of frontier matters. The Qing protested that Uladzai should have been executed per the 1768 treaty. Yet the Russian authorities replied that this was impossible, because capital punishment had been abolished in the Russian Empire during the reign of Elizabeth. The two sides were unable to reach agreement: the Russians not only refused to execute Uladzai but even insisted that hard labor was in fact a more severe punishment than death. Catherine's prestige as an enlightened monarch was, of course, a major consideration. In March 1785, the trade at Kiakhta was once more shut down by the Qing side, which marked the closing by firing a cannon. The interruption would last for over six years, the most grueling such episode in the history of the Kiakhta trade.[59]

Catherine and her officials were so perplexed and alarmed at the outcome of the Uladzai incident that some contemporaries concluded that she was formulating and implementing a plan for an offensive war against the Qing, one that was derailed only by a new Russo-Turkish war that erupted in 1787.[60] Russian military preparations on the ground, however, were defensive in nature, the result of the radical uncertainty induced by the decay of Russian intelligence capabilities on the Mongolian border. In June 1785, Catherine sent a series of decrees to Potemkin and other high officials, all beginning with a variation on the same sentence: "We have received word from Lieutenant General Iakobii that the Qing have closed their trade and marked this by firing a cannon. Although it is difficult to assume for many reasons that they will start a real war with us, prudence and care demand that we take measures to prevent against a sudden attack."[61] Just before the trade closed, Iakobii had passed along a report from the Kiakhta commissioner Lady-zhenskii that allegedly "revealed the fiendish plans of the Qing [to attack]." Before long, another letter revealed that the informant had been lying in hopes of a reward.[62] That same summer, Iakobii attempted to "maintain unceasing vigilance against these neighbors and find any appropriate measures to determine their further plans" by sending a merchant accompanied by two translators, in reality intelligence-gathering agents, across the border. The merchant's contact failed to show, and the enterprise resulted in almost no useful information, except the predictable news that reinforcements had been sent to Qing border posts. The Russian state no longer possessed any effective way of determining the significance or goals of Qing military movements.[63]

Iakobii's now manifestly inadequate intelligence network did not stop him from making grand schemes against the Qing state. In February 1785, he composed the initial version of a plan for an invasion. He intended this to substitute for defensive preparations, which his list of troops revealed to be utterly futile: nearly every border post under his command was less well staffed in 1785 than it had been in 1763, at the height of the previous crisis. Instead, he hoped for a massive infusion of troops from European Russia, with whose help he would take Manchuria and push the Mongols into open defection.[64] In 1787, he augmented this plan with an ethnographic component. In 1782, he wrote, he had been ordered to "accept into Your Majesty's subjecthood those [peoples] of the Qing state who wish to enter into it," and "in the event of an open rupture . . . I conducted matters in such a way that this would end with a whole [piece of territory] rather than small and unimportant pieces, and this would be followed by an agreement with the Beijing court." He then listed a range of frontier Qing subject peoples, from the Nivkh (Giliaks) of northeast Manchuria to the dvoedantsy of the Altai Mountains, claiming that he had conducted extensive investigations into the willingness of each of them to defect. Since no actual intelligence documents were included, this claim is difficult to evaluate. At any rate, there is no sign that Catherine ever intended to act on Iakobii's wildly optimistic proposal, and the 1787–1792 Russo-Turkish War put an end to any such possibility.[65] The end of the immediate crisis did not prevent Iakobii from continuing to develop the plan, and eventually he produced a much lengthier and more ambitious document, which remained ignored just like the previous ones had.[66] He had the leisure to do so, because in 1788 he was ordered to return to St. Petersburg for an investigation of his conduct as governor; although he was eventually cleared, he would never return to Siberia.

Of the sixty separate accusations in the indictment, most reflected Iakobii's failure to successfully deal with local elites in Irkutsk. But one of the charges he took most seriously suggested that he had attempted to initiate war with the Qing with the expectation of profiting from the resulting military procurement. Iakobii's response to this allegation indicates that he was far less sanguine about the prospect than his strategic scheming suggests. "I shudder at the very thought of such a thing," Iakobii wrote in his letter of appeal, "but thankfully the circumstances . . . clear me of such a woeful suspicion . . . which has almost brought me to my grave, and my very innocence could hardly lift my spirits, brought low by this horrible accusation."[67] Besides, he wrote later, who would even want to be part of such a war, with only 4,799 men, "most of them elderly, removed from their regiments for insubordination and repeatedly punished, as well as those Buriat heathens who are border guards in name only and who share a faith with the Mongols?" He pleaded, "Would I not have to bear the responsibility for the thousands of my countrymen who would have become the victims of my madness or shameful self-interest, before God, my monarch, and my fatherland?"[68] Iakobii was clearly terrified that his conduct would be interpreted as provoking war: although his conquering aspirations were ambitious, they were very much rooted in the reality of his remote, underfunded frontier province.

Iakobii's clarification of the actual events in this case makes clear that what had happened was another result of the growing weakness of the Russian intelligence network. In August 1785, after the merchant-espionage scheme had failed, Iakobii tried to sneak an agent named Iusupov across the border south of Lake Baikal. Iusupov was equipped with an open-ended set of instructions to "collect intelligence . . . wherever you find it most convenient," but which especially encouraged him to recruit local Mongol informants in the time-honored fashion of the 1750s. Unlike Varfolomei Iakobii's agents, there is no indication that Iusupov spoke Mongol or had any contacts across the border, and in any event, he was recalled before he even crossed into Qing-controlled lands. In the interval between the dispatch and the recall, two of Iakobii's subordinates independently hatched a plan to provoke a small Mongol raiding party to attack into Russian territory and have Iusupov intercept them, thus generating a casus belli and triggering a military response from St. Petersburg. (As Iakobii pointed out, this plan was absurd, since the Mongols would simply be tried by Qing authorities as bandits and executed as so many had been before them.) Their letter was copied and sent as part of an anonymous accusation against Iakobii. In the governor-general's telling, when he dismissed his subordinate for this highly incriminating proposal, the latter committed suicide and apologized for his transgression with his dying breath. Even if this was just gilding the lily, the episode stands as a monument to Russia's growing inability to successfully pursue covert action against the Qing.[69]

After Iakobii's departure, the threat of war appeared to temporarily recede. In 1792 his successor, Ivan Pil', negotiated a new treaty that brought matters back to the status quo ante. The newly relaxed international climate in Inner Asia, amid escalating revolutionary conflict in the West, briefly returned the Kiakhta trade to its peak. This paralleled an immense rise in the power of the head of the Kiakhta customs office, Pëtr Vanifat'ev, who occupied his post for some two decades starting in 1790. As the Russian ambassador Iurii Golovkin would later learn, this would have grave consequences for any centrally directed intelligence policy that had the potential to damage his interests. Meanwhile, any remaining Russian intelligence informants within Qing Mongolia had apparently disappeared. In the journals of the Committee of Ministers, Alexander's supreme cabinet body, the reports on the Eight Trigrams Rebellion that swept through northern China in 1813 are entirely derived from the conversations and correspondence of Siberian merchants rather than state agents and are rather out of date. Yet local officials like

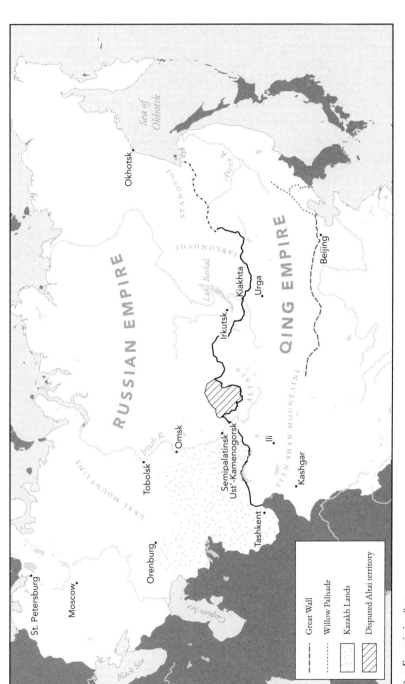

8.4 Eurasia in 1800.

Aleksei Kornilov, the civilian governor of Irkutsk, continued to draw up plans for attacking and annexing Qing territory. Stability did not mean an end to regional rivalry.[70]

By the early nineteenth century, the Eastern Siberian structure of intelligence and borderland administration that had coalesced under the pressure of the 1750s crisis still existed, albeit in a shrunken form. It retained both its isolation from the resources of the metropole and its standing as a distant outpost for ambitious "proconsuls," but not its close connection to events across the Qing border. It seemed unlikely that it could ever support a fully realized bid for territorial aggrandizement: relations between Russia and China had coalesced into a relatively stable pattern.[71] Yet within a few decades, just such a bid, launched from the governor-general's seat in Irkutsk, would fundamentally reshape the region's geography and power structure. It became possible because St. Petersburg elites were beginning to see the region from a newly globalized, maritime perspective. As the Inner Asian land frontier seemed to recede in importance, another zone of encounter emerged to take its place: the Pacific coast, the rich maritime zone that bordered it to the south, and the vast North American landmass that faced it across the Bering Strait. The sparsely settled backwater of Kamchatka was suddenly at the epicenter of a whole new set of geopolitical calculations.

PART IV

INTELLIGENCE *and* SINOLOGY *in* SEARCH *of* WORLD POWER

Chapter 9

Imperial Encounters in the North Pacific

IN THE LAST QUARTER of the eighteenth century, the perspective of St. Petersburg elites on the Russian Empire's relationship with the Qing shifted rapidly and fundamentally into a new frame of reference. For Muscovite rulers and officials, China had been an aspect of the broader Siberian problem, to be addressed through intermediaries like loosely controlled Cossacks and Bukharan merchants. In the Petrine and post-Petrine era, it was a problem of Inner Asian competition in which the administrative and intelligence tools of modern empire were deployed in a regional cold war. In the 1770s, a new set of considerations entered the picture: the global ambitions of Russia's main Western rivals: Britain, France, and eventually the United States. From St. Petersburg—unlike Irkutsk—the Qing empire and its borderlands now looked increasingly like an adjunct of the North Pacific, and the North Pacific itself like a new theater of the worldwide imperial contest.[1]

This new framework was not based on a new set of facts on the ground. No British invasion force yet arrived to threaten Kamchatka; no French colonies were established on the Alaskan coast. Instead, what changed was the sense of threat that policy makers gathered from their intelligence sources and transmuted into concrete diplomatic and military acts. As a securitization theorist might put it, the *referent object* (Russia's sphere of influence in the Pacific) and the *referent subject* (the imminent danger of foreign challenge) were constructed together and at the same time, with the help of transnational intermediaries and practices of covert action.[2] This was true of the British and French themselves just as much as of Catherine II and the Russians. Far from clarifying the geopolitical situation, intelligence (true as well as false) made imperial competition seem more threatening, improbable long-distance schemes more lucrative, abrupt decisive action more urgent. Conspiracy theories emerged to fill in the gaps, because they formed a way to connect isolated pinpoints of data: it was easier for France, Britain, and Russia alike to believe that a large-scale plot was afoot when sources of information were as thin and sporadic as they were in the North Pacific. Empires took action on the basis of these kinds of theories, and thus real threats gradually emerged as responses to imagined ones. By the beginning of the reign of Alexander I, this sense of global encirclement had become the driving force of Russian policy toward China.

The orientation toward security in a global arena also changed the internal institutional dynamics of Russia's China policy. Industrial espionage efforts were not renewed except, decades later, as an afterthought. Little effort was made to rebuild Russian intelligence capacity on the frontier in Mongolia and Xinjiang or to allow freer rein to the ambitions of local administrators. Instead, Catherine and her officials put more and more stock in international diplomacy and long-distance naval expeditions from St. Petersburg, projects that needed to be coordinated from the capital rather than driven by events on the periphery. Longstanding Russo-Qing institutions like the Russian Ecclesiastical Mission were reimagined by both Russians and Westerners as unique sources of leverage—not against the Qing but against other European rivals who lacked such contacts. In the eyes of people who knew little more about the North Pacific than its contours on painstakingly obtained maps, even geographical features like the Kamchatka peninsula became freighted with imaginary significance as beachheads and strategic bulwarks of empire.

These changes in the mental maps and informational horizons of Russian officials went hand in hand with Russia's changing structural role in the international system. Under Empress Elizabeth, a period of growing Russian involvement in Europe was capped off by a successful intervention in the Seven Years' War (1756–1763), although it was prematurely terminated after Elizabeth's death in 1762. When Catherine II overthrew and assassinated Elizabeth's successor (and her own husband), Peter III, in July of that year, the Russian Empire began to rapidly gain power and influence abroad. By the mid-1770s it had clearly emerged alongside Britain, France, Prussia, and Austria as one of Europe's great powers; its decisive victory over the Ottoman Empire in 1774 and the first partition of Poland-Lithuania in 1772 solidified this status at the expense of its formerly imposing neighbors.[3] No longer constrained to defend its immediate frontiers, Catherine and her successors sought ways to gain power and influence even across the Atlantic. In the eighteenth century, maritime power was global power.

The Pacific was an especially significant arena of competition because, especially in the north, it had not yet been settled and partitioned by colonial troops. Of the new "pentarchy" of great powers, only Russia, Britain, and France had significant colonial possessions outside of Europe and the means to contest control of them. The Seven Years' War had been a truly world war, with important theaters in North America, the Caribbean, and the Indian subcontinent; there was every reason to think the Pacific would be next. Explorers like Louis-Antoine de Bougainville and James Cook were already plying its waters in the service of their empires, bringing back voluminous and highly influential reports. As the stakes of great power competition rose in Europe, the risk that it would spill over into Russia's vulnerable Pacific backwater grew in tandem. Neither could the contenders ignore the growing commercial value of the China trade, which the British East India Company had come to dominate after midcentury.[4] With furs one of the few reliable import commodities on the Chinese market, tracing the important connection between Canton and the fur-bearing regions of the Pacific North—all the way from the Columbia River valley on the ocean's northeastern shore to the Sea of Okhotsk in its northwest—did not require a sophisticated understanding of geopolitics. Driven onward by the gradual extinction of fur-bearing animals in Siberia, for Russia a confrontation with its North American rivals seemed inevitable.[5]

The space of the Pacific imposed significant constraints on imperial expansion. Over the course of the early modern era, attempts to send battleship fleets into the ocean were frustrated by supply problems, storms, and poor navigational aids: George Anson's 1740 expedition left Portsmouth with six ships and almost two thousand crew and returned with one ship and one-tenth of the original complement, none of the losses having resulted from enemy action.[6] As a result, instead of a space of cohesive geographical borders and clear lines of demarcation, it became a web of indigenous travelers, merchants, whalers, scientific explorers, ambitious projectors, nonnative fauna, commodities, and disease microbes.[7] Instead of dampening interimperial conflict, however, the tenuousness of these connections amplified the anticipated risks and potential of regional dominance. For many imperial

9.1 The North Pacific around 1800.

actors, an obsession with the future of the North Pacific long preceded any ability to impose their will on it from a distance.

Geographical "discoveries" in this region gained significance because they identified likely areas of confrontation between imperial powers. Already in 1759 the Jesuit José Torrubia published a pamphlet arguing that Spanish colonies in California were in danger from Russian seafarers. It was intended primarily as an intervention in a long-running debate about the geography of the North Pacific region and the existence of a Northwest Passage from the Atlantic.[8] This was never merely an academic question. The Russian government took steps to ensure all cartographic material pertaining to Kamchatka and the territories to the east was kept secret, fearing an attack on the poorly defended settlements by European powers. Thanks to Joseph-Nicolas Delisle, working for both France and Russia at once, the French government managed to get its hands on copies anyway. In 1752, several years after he left Russia for good, Delisle published a map of the North Pacific that included a relatively accurate depiction of Kamchatka alongside a series of other landmasses in distorted form. He may have had bad information, or his goal may have been to provoke the Russians into publishing more accurate maps as a correction. Like other great powers, the French government regarded this area of geography as a matter of state concern.[9] The links between the geopolitical and informational dimensions of this imperial rivalry were clear to everyone involved.

The Russian Threat and the Art of Intelligence Failure

For France, calculations about the future of the Pacific seemed especially urgent. It had decisively lost the Seven Years' War to Britain, while the Russian Empire's gains in Europe came at the expense of what the French had regarded as their "eastern barrier" against Russian power, which included Poland-Lithuania, Sweden, and the Ottomans. Its foreign policy was torn in two directions, between the pro-Habsburg alliance policy of the official foreign ministry and the anti-Austrian, anti-Russian, and anti-British policy of the clandestine network of royal correspondents known as the Secret du Roi. The struggle extended not only into the world of elite diplomacy—via such figures as François-Michel Durand de Distroff, the French plenipotentiary in St. Petersburg in the early 1770s and a member of the secret clique—but also into the realm of ideas and intellectual culture. In the 1760s, Catherine II had responded to a critical travelogue of Russia by an *abbé* linked to the Secret with a series of blistering pseudonymous pamphlets.[10] The Secret's own conspiratorial nature and sense of embattlement helped to predispose Louis XV and his closest advisors—themselves deeply invested in the Franco-Russian competition—to trust in conspiracy theories and dubious intelligence reports, which validated their own anxieties about the Russian threat.

There was no figure better suited to take advantage of this than a soi-disant Hungarian nobleman named Móric Benyovszky, one of the eighteenth century's many transnational grifters.[11] In 1768 he was captured in Poland while fighting against the Russian army as part of the Confederation of Bar. He was released on the condition that he no longer bear arms against Russia but soon was captured again and imprisoned in Kazan. He escaped and made his way to St. Petersburg, where a ship captain turned him in to the authorities. Finally, Catherine's government decided to exile him to Kamchatka, where he could in theory make no further trouble. Together with a party of other exiles, Benyovszky arrived at the fort of Bolsheretsk (west of Petropav-lovsk) in 1770. He soon proved that he was far wilier than the Russians could have imagined. After enrolling all the local exiles into a conspiracy to escape—ostensibly on behalf of Prince Paul's claim to the throne—he murdered Ka-mchatka's commandant, overpowered the small garrison, and took control of the peninsula. On April 30, 1771, he and his coconspirators boarded the galliot (corvette) *St. Peter* and set sail for points south. He arrived in Macao on September 12, after having made a whirlwind voyage around Japan (where he claimed to have met with a "King Ulikamhy") and Taiwan.[12] There he found an attentive audience of French officials, ideal targets for the con that would happen next.

Benyovszky was not the first European to have highlighted the strategic value of Russia's Pacific possessions, but he was the first to conceptualize them as a zone of current and ongoing geopolitical conflict. Unlike Torrubia, he did not do so in the form of a conceptual reflection about geography. Instead, he produced an official document so authentic in appearance and troubling in content—apparently freshly looted from the Kamchatka chancellery he had just raided—that it was no surprise the French representatives were im-mediately taken in. The letters sent by supercargoes at Canton to the Naval Ministry suggest that they had come to believe that returning the escapees to France was an "indispensable necessity for the French nation," even though none of them were French.[13] On August 9, 1772, the French foreign minister the duc d'Aiguillon wrote to Durand in St. Petersburg that "Monsieur Benj-owski, whom the newspapers have talked so much about, has given me a document, whose translation I feel obligated to send you."[14]

The document that followed was a letter, dated September 5, 1770, and marked "top secret," from the Okhotsk chancellery to the main Kamchatka chancellery at Bolsheretsk. It contained copies of orders issued by the Senate to the governor of Irkutsk. Fifteen thousand soldiers had been ordered to assemble in Kamchatka for a vast naval expedition against an unknown enemy. Worse, the expedition was to be closely coordinated with British ves-sels; the Russian troops were to "obey the British commanders as if they were their own officers"; if the British brought any prisoners, they were to be held under guard in various parts of Siberia. D'Aiguillon's immediate as-sumption was that the Russians and the British aimed to attack the Spanish territories in North America—although "the situation of Kamchatka seems suited to be the *point d'appui* or the meeting point for various equally dangerous expeditions. They might indeed have views either on China or Manila and the other Spanish islands." Because "this Hungarian could not give us a satisfactory idea," the minister instructed Durand that "the King desires, Monsieur, that you find any possible means of obtaining clarification on this subject."[15]

Over the course of the ensuing six months, Durand devoted much of his energy to ferreting out the Anglo-Russian conspiracy Benyovszky had supposedly unearthed—even though Russia was then in the midst of trouncing the Ottomans in a war whose consequences would reverberate throughout the world. In a coded letter, he revealed that something possibly even more earthshaking had happened: "Commerce, like empire, has its revolutions. For several years, one has been silently in preparation, which cannot be an indifferent fact for Europe." Russia, Durand believed, had discovered a "Northeast Passage to America and even has settlements on the coast of this continent." Asking for "secrecy" from his correspondent, he explained that "Russia will not delay extending its sphere of claims and connections. It will enter into everything that passes in America and in the Indies and in enlarging the theatre of the world it will increase the number of stages for intrigues, quarrels, and wars."[16] Durand even found a young "Kamchadal" officer named "Popow" who confirmed the existence of the Northeast Passage, although he also clarified the geopolitical concerns involved: Russia was clashing not with the Spanish, as Durand thought, but with the Hudson's Bay Company on the other side of the passage.[17]

Even more importantly, Durand identified the target of the coming Russo-British campaign: China. His survey of Russo-Qing relations combined true grievances (like the Torghut exodus) with false ones (the supposed execution of Kropotov by the Qing) to argue that "[Russia] is preparing in silence the means of a vengeance as useful as it would be stunning."[18] This was nothing short of a secret plan to attack China. The academic Peter Pallas would travel there to produce a pretext for war, at which point Russia would attack, "enrich itself from the spoils of China, and put them to use in extinguishing the debts of the Crown."[19] (Pallas had, in fact, been close to the Qing border and even planned to travel to Beijing as a kind of diplomatic attaché but was too uncomfortable with taking on a formal role and ultimately refused to go at all.)[20]

D'Aiguillon forwarded these documents, starting from the one provided by Benyovszky, to Secretary of State Henri Bertin—a man whose deep pre-occupation with China and extensive correspondence with Beijing Jesuits made him especially well suited for resolving the situation. The information provided by Benyovszky and Durand filled Bertin with dread—all the more so as the number of Russian troops became steadily inflated as the document wound its way through the French bureaucracy. Bertin also seems to have concluded that the British merchant James Flint, who had provoked a scandal with the Qing when he sailed to Tianjin in 1759, had ended up in St. Petersburg and was working for the Russians as a navigator.[21] This mounting evidence made it clear to him that the Russian armies on Kamchatka were being gathered for a pincer attack on the Qing, and he could anticipate what would happen next. However "impressive in their height, their power, and their equipment," even Ottoman troops had "proved unable to resist [Russian] battalions bristling with artillery, resembling more walking fortresses than groups of soldiers . . . aiming to exterminate humans in as large a quantity and with as much rapidity as possible." Bertin worried "that an expedition of 24,000 men would seem to the eyes of the court of Beijing as a vain effort. . . . But one should not doubt that the armies of China could be annihilated by this formidable artillery." Russia was now a terrifying global threat.

There are numerous such panic-stricken passages in his January 1774 missive to Ko and Yang, two Chinese-born Jesuits who had toured France and then returned to Canton. Bertin's desperate solution was to send along copies of Europe's most current strategy manuals, including books by Puységur (the 1747 *Art de la guerre par principes et par règles*) and Guibert (the just-published 1772 *Essai général de tactique*), as well as special *mémoires* dealing with French military ordnance, castrametation, and organization. If Ko and Yang could only make Qianlong listen and persuade him to rapidly reorganize his army on the French model, the Qing would have a chance at resisting the Russian onslaught.[22] In December 1775, Yang replied. He was deeply concerned about the contents of Bertin's letter, but all his attempts to persuade someone to report to the emperor had failed. He could only hope that "the Russians in Beijing, informed about the victory [we] have achieved over Great and Little Tibet, will persuade their compatriots to desist from the plan they have formed against a country which has begun to be warlike."[23]

In the midst of this apocalyptic reasoning, it did not occur to anyone from Louis XV on down that neither Benyovszky nor Durand's information was credible. We know as they did not that no Northwest or Northeast Passage existed, still less one under Russian control. Although the alleged Kamchatka document is a plausible imitation, both internal and external evidence leave no doubt that it was a forgery pasted together from fragments of real documents. One paragraph, for instance, refers to the "Governor of Siberia," a post that had not existed since 1764 (and could not coexist with the "Governor of Irkutsk" mentioned elsewhere), while another mentions an "Irkutsk Voevoda Chancellery," which could not have existed at the time.[24] As someone who had captured the peninsula with a few dozen ragtag convicts, Benyovszky must have been well aware that it had neither the supplies nor the facilities for an army of 15,000—even if such a thing could be scraped together in Siberia, which was impossible. None of this dented the plan's perceived credibility. By 1776, the document resurfaced in a new context: d'Aiguillon had apparently come to believe that Russia and Britain were targeting Japan, not the Qing.[25]

The conspiratorial reasoning induced by Benyovszky's forgery was uniquely appealing to the elites of an embattled empire like France, surrounded by perceived enemies and grappling with its inability to challenge its rivals on a global scale. Indeed, his choice of targets, Britain and Russia, was probably intended deliberately to exploit French anxieties. But France was not the only state to be engulfed by conspiracy theory. As the North Pacific became a real and not merely a theoretical arena of imperial encounter, the elites of the Russian Empire were seized with a preoccupation with a powerful European threat. In his memoirs, published in London in 1790, Benyovszky wrote that "the arrival of the first foreign vessel will produce a revolution in Siberia. . . . This event cannot be far distant, and Russia will find herself, by a stroke of this nature, deprived of all that support which alone enables her to play a principal part in Europe." Though his speculations were fanciful, nobody was more aware of the fragility of Russian rule there than Russian officials themselves.[26]

The British were the first foreign power to directly observe the Russian presence in Kamchatka and conceptualize its connection to the rest of the Pacific maritime trade zone. After James Cook's death in Hawaii in February 1779, his remaining crew aboard the ships *Resolution* and *Discovery* limped north to Petropavlovsk under his lieutenant Charles Clerke. When he died of tuberculosis in August, he was buried near the port. Bem (Behm), the commandant of Petropavlovsk, was immediately suspicious of the foreigners' goals, scientific or not: Kamchatka had never before seen a foreign vessel, and the settlement was in unusually bad shape, having suffered through a fire and a smallpox epidemic in the previous decade (in addition to Benyovszky's revolt). He provided the explorers with free tea and sugar, but when they asked for a more substantial set of supplies, both Bem and his successor Shmalev dithered. In the meantime, the Kamchatka officials asked Irkutsk for an urgent shipment of cannon and arms to reinforce the settlement's defenses, which consisted of a total of 398 soldiers throughout the entire peninsula, most of them lacking even basic firearms. By the end of the year, the Irkutsk governor Klichka had received official word from Senate Procurator-General Viazemskii that Kamchatka needed to be "brought into defensible shape without fail, because the way there has become known to foreigners."[27]

Despite Bem's suspicions, Clerke felt well treated and left the Russian commandant with a highly obliging letter.[28] For Russians anxious to promote the empire's standing as a European intellectual great power, Cook's voyages soon became a frequent point of reference.[29] The unexpected friendliness of the encounter served just as well as any confrontation to heighten British interest in Kamchatka and hence ramp up the scale of contact and competition between the two empires. In 1786, a small vessel (snow) called the *Lark*, under the command of a Captain Peters, called at Petropavlovsk with a selection of trade goods. It had sailed from Macao and carried with it a letter signed by the British East India Company supercargoes there. Explicitly invoking the precedent of the Cook voyage, the letter proposed "to form a Commercial Intercourse between India & China & Kamschatka" and pointed out that goods shipped via India would be much cheaper than the "tedious Route" they currently required. Peters's attempt came to nothing, as he was shipwrecked soon after, but the Irkutsk governor-general Ivan Iakobii thought the proposal was worth considering even as he recognized the "mobility and precision" of British commerce.[30]

By the late 1780s, however, the relationship between the two empires was becoming much more antagonistic; while Britain's longstanding economic connections with Russia convinced the British of the need to challenge Russian expansion, the Russian Empire's push to the Pacific afforded some autonomy from British commercial power.[31] When Sweden declared war on Russia in 1787, the British brig *Mercury* began assaulting Russian-subject Aleuts while flying the Swedish flag.[32] In 1790, the British trader John Meares—instigator of an armed Anglo-Spanish standoff at Nootka Sound the previous year—published *Voyages Made in the Years 1788 and 1789*. It argued explicitly that Britain could and needed to challenge Russia for control of the China trade in the Pacific.[33] From the Russian perspective, the British were even sending spies to Kamchatka overland. Using false documents claiming authorization from Catherine, an American named John Ledyard—who traveled the world out of curiosity and a desire to satisfy his ethnographic theories but was not acting as a formal agent of any state—had made it all the way to Irkutsk in late 1787. When Iakobii met with him, he decided immediately that he was probably looking at a British spy: he displayed "avid curiosity" about islands in the North Pacific and used "elaborate means of questioning" to pry for information. At the end of their conversation, Ledyard was incautious enough to announce that "[the power] whose strength will be the greatest will certainly have the most right to occupy those islands." Iakobii decided to send him to the remote town of Iakutsk, where he would be unlikely to obtain any useful information, and when Ledyard returned to Irkutsk, he was arrested and escorted all the way back to the Polish border.[34]

Russian officials seemed to have a clear pattern before them. The first foreign vessel in Kamchatka was a British ship; the British were sending spies to investigate the poorly defended Russian territories; the British East India Company had a clear design on the Qing fur trade; British vessels were capturing North American territory and privateering. All this was soon augmented by a brief diplomatic crisis in Europe, when the British prime minister William Pitt the Younger threatened hostile action if Russia did not return the captured Ottoman fortress of Ochakov. Yet in its way, the seemingly obvious conclusion that Britain was Russia's main enemy in the Pacific was just as misleading as the dramatic errors made by the French court in the 1770s. After all, Ledyard had no connection to Britain, and the *Lark* was so minor that it does not even appear in the East India Company's Canton factory records.[35] Over the next few decades, it would be the Americans, not the British, who would take the leading role in the emerging maritime fur trade between Canton and northwestern North America.[36]

Nevertheless, Catherine's officials felt increasingly threatened and conscious of the need to reinforce Russian claims against feared British encroachments. In 1784, William Coxe, the British author of a widely popular book about Russian discoveries in the Far East, proposed a new expedition there; headed by Joseph Billings, it would be in action until 1795.[37] A more explicitly political project soon followed. In a 1787 memorandum, the State Council argued that Russia's previous "discoveries" in the Pacific north of the fifty-first parallel had not been publicly attested using the now-accepted protocols of European empire (such as durable spatially specific plaques confirming the Russian presence) and that, as a result, Cook had been able to claim them for Britain. To rectify this, an official map would have to be issued—shifting from a regime of secrecy to a regime of publicness for the region. More concrete steps would have to follow, most prominently sending a naval expedition to erect metal imperial crests along the coastline and patrol the region for foreign vessels.[38] The expedition, due to be headed by Grigorii Mulovskii, was canceled due to the outbreak of a new Russo-Ottoman war. But the same year, Grigorii Shelikhov, a merchant already busily engaged in colonizing the islands near Alaska, published the first detailed map of Russia's Pacific acquisitions. In 1799, after Shelikhov's death, his enterprise became the Russian-American Company with exclusive rights to North American trade.[39]

After planning the Mulovskii expedition, the Crown became increasingly eager to support other far-reaching initiatives to link the North Pacific to China and the southern islands. In 1789, it approved a quixotic circumnavigation project proposed by one Pierre Torckler, a Russian subject living at the French port of Lorient. Torckler wanted to equip a ship for trade between Kamchatka and Nanjing, with the goal of establishing an enduring trade route—apparently unaware that foreigners were not allowed to trade outside of Canton, and no Russian ship had gone even there.[40] In 1793, Torckler arrived in Kamchatka flying a revolutionary French flag and wearing a cockade; "the greater part of the cargo consisted of spirituous liquors."[41] By 1803, he had ended up in Calcutta, where he proposed yet another project, this time to establish Russian consulates throughout the East Indies; while there, he inspired Kruzenshtern to launch his own more famous expedition, the first Russian round-the-world voyage.[42] In 1791 Erik Laksman, a Swedish-born botanist and priest, proposed a more ambitious project. His son Adam would command an expedition to Japan carrying a Japanese shipwreck survivor, the merchant Kōdayū, whose repatriation would provide a convenient excuse to establish stable commercial relations with the Japanese. Laksman intended the expedition to secretly sail down the Amur and establish a harbor, without any regard for Qing approval or the feasibility of such an enterprise. At a stroke, he believed, Japan would augment or even replace China in Russia's Far East economy.[43]

The final piece of the Pacific puzzle—its emergence as an integrated conceptual space connecting Russo-Qing diplomacy with the global rivalry against Britain and other powers, Alaskan colonization, and the fur trade—was now sliding into place. Laksman warned that the British and Dutch, too, were trying to get their hands on Kōdayū. The latter were obviously trying to curry favor with their longtime trading partners, but the involvement of the former bespoke a more serious threat: a new embassy to China and Japan that promised to cement British dominance in Pacific trade. It was to be led by Lord George Macartney, the former British ambassador in St. Petersburg.[44] The Russian resident at the Court of St. James's, Semën Vorontsov, knew of the plans for the Macartney embassy almost as soon as they were hatched, at the latest by January 1792. He and his brother Aleksandr, who was the head of the College of Commerce, corresponded in detail about the British scheme. As Semën put it, echoing the sentiments of Catherine and her high officials, "I would be very angry if this matter were to be regarded with indifference. If the English succeed, we will see, but too late, what sort of harm this will do to our commerce." The overriding objective of Russian policy in the region would now be to checkmate the British effort to gain a greater foothold in China.[45]

The plan Catherine and the Vorontsovs developed brought in a number of moving parts.[46] The most important were the Jesuits. In 1773, after decades of increasing pressure from Catholic governments, Pope Clement XIV formally dissolved the Society of Jesus with the breve *Dominus ac Redemptor*. Russia had just annexed the Livonian and Belarussian portion of the Polish-Lithuanian Commonwealth in the First Partition of Poland. These areas had a substantial Jesuit presence, and the order was central to the educational system. Hoping to render them beholden to the Russian crown, Catherine forbade *Dominus ac Redemptor* from taking effect on her territory. Thus the Society of Jesus survived only thanks to the protection of an Orthodox monarch.[47] In 1777, the Beijing ex-Jesuit and naturalist Pierre-Martial Cibot registered his gratitude for Catherine's deed in a letter to the Academy of Sciences.[48] Since the days of Spafarii, Russian elites—just like Henri Bertin—had been convinced that Jesuit missionaries had the ear of the Qing emperors and wielded massive influence at court; in reality, there is little reason to believe that the few missionaries who remained had any substantial input on matters of state, as previous experiences in the 1720s and 1750s should probably have suggested. For the Vorontsovs, however, they seemed to be ideal vectors for an anti-British message, especially considering Britain's anti-Catholic and anti-Jesuit political stance.

In June 1792, the Jesuits Gabriel Gruber and Manswet Skokowski were summoned from the central college at Polotsk to the imperial residence at Tsarskoe Selo and instructed to compose a letter with very specific contents. They were to reassure their Beijing colleagues of Catherine's support for their mission and especially its scientific endeavors, inquiring in particular about their material need for instruments and supplies. Only once this was done could they introduce the real topic of the letter, which concerned the imminent threat of the British embassy. The British had wormed their way into the heart of the Mughal Empire and subjugated it; how could they fail to do the same in China? Having been persuaded of Russian friendship and British iniquity, the Beijing Jesuits would then be expected to procure the court's permission for a Russian counter-embassy, laden with scientific devices and gifts, as well as reinforcements for the Jesuits themselves, who had largely ceased being replaced with new cohorts. Finally, and least importantly, "to this they might add in their letter, something about their order, and of its present condition," largely to camouflage the real purpose of the text. This was clearly no simple letter from one college to another: it was a vehicle for the Russian geopolitical agenda.[49]

The other part of the plan, alongside Semën Vorontsov's information gathering in London and the Jesuit preparations in Russia, was the actual delivery of the Jesuit letter to Beijing. This was in some ways the most complicated part of the process, yet it was also the one to which Aleksandr Vorontsov devoted the least thought. Once the letter had arrived in Irkutsk, he assumed, it would be straightforward to deliver it to Beijing through the standard communication channels. Jesuits had never been able to use Qing couriers for their letters, an enormously risky gamble—one of the reasons that their correspondence with the Academy had relied so heavily on the caravan and withered so quickly once it was shut down. Neither were Qing subjects willing to act as couriers for Europeans.[50] Instead of a letter to Beijing, Vorontsov's message had to be entrusted to Vasilii Igumnov, the border intelligence agent whose contacts in Mongolia had become so extensive in the 1760s.[51] Igumnov did, it seems, succeed in meeting with the Urga ambans and persuading them of the value of his information, or at least Russian officials seemed to think so a decade later. (Among other things, it was enough to earn him a long-delayed promotion.)[52] The Qing official record says only that "Captain Wasili" had come to notify Qing authorities about the British embassy, a notification that arrived only on March 1, 1793; Macartney was almost in China by then, and the warning did not deter the officials.[53] The remnants of the intelligence establishment stagnating on the Siberian frontier thus proved crucial in realizing a plan that had been hatched without consulting or involving it in any way, for which international diplomacy had seemed to supersede frontier horse trading.

On the other side, the British embassy was also a product of the tension between the ambitions of global empire and the commercial objectives of frontier interests—which were mutually reinforcing only in part. The East India Company had been the primary driver of the project to send an embassy to the Qing emperor; the instructions issued in 1787 to Lord Cathcart, the original ambassador, stressed "the measures lately taken by Government for drawing the tea trade out of the hands of other nations" and "attention to the prosperity of our territorial possessions in India." But Cathcart was not to be merely a commercial agent: he was also to keep records attending "to every Article likely to throw a light upon the present Strength, Policy, and Government of that Empire, now less understood in Europe than they were in the preceding Century," as well as to China's foreign relations.[54] Five years later, Macartney's embassy took place in part against the objections of the East India Company, and the concessions it received (if any) would not be exclusive to the company.[55] By this point, the British struggle against the French ally Tipu Sultan in India, whose proximity to the Qing border in the Himalayas made it relevant to Macartney's mission, had added new geopolitical implications to the project.[56]

But Macartney was challenging Russia, not just defending the East India Company. A manuscript in his papers, probably written by an MP named

John Sinclair in 1787, declared that "the Russians . . . are not satisfied with their dominions in Europe, and Asia, but are already grasping in Idea, rich and extensive Possessions in the American Hemisphere." To achieve this goal, the Russian Empire needed to both expand its presence in the North Pacific and conquer the Amur from the Qing, for "without possessing it, the Empress can make no successful attempt either for Trade or Conquest, on America."[57] Japan was a key theater of conflict: the Vorontsovs' intelligence was correct that the fate of the Japanese castaway Kōdayū, and hence the possibility of opening European trade with Japan, was a major concern for the British. As the embassy was being prepared in 1791, Charles Whitworth, the British ambassador in St. Petersburg, kept in close contact with Peter Pallas about the possibility of abducting the castaway and handing him to Macartney, though the "precautions" taken by the Russians to prevent Kōdayū's capture proved too extensive to proceed.[58] Despite this failure, Whitworth still managed to acquire and send Macartney several letters exchanged between the Senate (or rather the College of Foreign Affairs) and the Lifanyuan concerning the Uladzai affair, to give him insight on "what an opinion [the Chinese] entertain of the Russians . . . and there is no doubt, but that the Japanese, if they enter with their views, will soon have reason to use the same reproachful language, and perhaps with still more Cause."[59] Rising Russian power in the Pacific framed both the goals and the preparations of the embassy.

The Russian context not only raised the stakes for the British; it was also key for determining the form of the British approach to the emperor.[60] A substantial travel literature had emerged around European diplomacy in China, but each of the existing accounts had its problems for a mission of the kind Cathcart and Macartney were facing. Nieuhof's 1665 account was old and, because it described a Dutch East India Company embassy, was not quite suited to British goals.[61] Mezzabarba's 1720 legation was unsuccessful and involved religious matters.[62] As for the 1753 Portuguese embassy led by Pacheco, "no public account . . . has come to my knowledge, nor did I ever hear that any further relation of that Embassy was published than what appeared in a Newspaper."[63] This left one embassy and one account: John Bell's 1763 journal of his overland voyage to Beijing with the 1720 Izmailov embassy and the Lorents Lang journal that was published with it. Here was a lushly detailed eyewitness report that paid attention to ceremonial minutiae, provided information on the nature of trade at Beijing, and described an embassy by a state that, like the British, was deeply concerned with maintaining its honor in the face of Qing claims to universal kingship.[64]

In James Cobb's "Sketches Respecting China and the Embassies sent thither," prepared for Macartney in 1792, Bell's and Lang's accounts were summarized at length ("none are deserving of more attention") and provided with context on the Russo-Qing trade drawn from the Abbé Raynal's *Histoire des deux Indes*.[65] Cathcart's and Macartney's expectations and horizons were deeply shaped by the Russian experience. Not only was Macartney equipped with stolen diplomatic correspondence about the Uladzai case; Russia was also cited as evidence against the idea that "the Chinese in general are studious to avoid any intimate connection or intercourse with Europeans."[66] In formulating the list of people who would travel to Beijing in Macartney's entourage, Russian precedent proved dispositive.[67] Already in Beijing, when Macartney requested that a British agent be allowed to remain in the city, along with students, he referred to the precedent set by Lang and to the Russian Ecclesiastical Mission: it became the template for the British Empire's diplomatic requests.[68]

Above all, it was Russia that determined Macartney's response to the supreme ceremonial question: whether or not he could kowtow to the Qianlong emperor, which would have been politically unacceptable but without which he could not expect to succeed. The initial letter composed by Thomas Fitzhugh for Cathcart's benefit in 1787 (which was later passed on to Macartney) seemed to suggest a way out. Fitzhugh said that Izmailov "was informed, in mitigation of so humiliating a custom, that whenever the Emperor sent an Embassador to Russia, his orders would be to conform to their forms and regulations."[69] In other words, the Qing court was willing to accept the possibility of a reciprocity of ritual rather than unilateral submission. It was to this that Macartney turned when the kowtow issue finally arose, proposing a kind of mediated reciprocity in which a Qing representative would himself kowtow to an image of King George. Macartney's account of this episode makes clear that he desperately wanted and expected this proposal to succeed; when it was first accepted, then rejected without explanation, he was crestfallen.[70] Although another compromise was later found, in which Macartney bent to one knee nine times rather than performing a full kowtow, one of the envoy's own Jesuit translators believed that failure to kowtow had caused the embassy's collapse.[71]

For both Russia and Britain, this attempt at projecting their mutual struggle into the East Asian space was grounded in mutual misapprehensions and intelligence failures. Russian elites believed that the British were setting their sights specifically on capturing control of the Kiakhta trade, when this was not even mentioned in the embassy documents. When a correspondent offered Macartney some views on the embassy, pointing to Russo-Qing tensions as a potential pressure point, the ambassador was reticent. "It is true," he wrote, "that in case of a rupture, the aid of Great Britain might be of essential use to the Chinese against Russia, but it is a point of too great delicacy and intricacy to be insinuated to the Court of Pekin, without the utmost caution and circumspection. Occasion may nevertheless occur when it would be true policy to assist them, upon terms of certain advantage to ourselves."[72] The British were convinced that it would be even easier for them to gain a hearing in Beijing than the Russians because of the lack of a clash of frontier interests. What they did not understand was that in the Yongzheng era, Russo-Qing relations had been shaped by their mutual involvement in Inner Asian politics and the need for the Qing to forestall a Russo-Junghar alliance. No such consideration impelled Qianlong to meet Macartney halfway.

Russia's response was ultimately belated, but it established a short-lived link between Eastern Siberia and the emerging Pacific context. Igumnov finally delivered Vorontsov's letter to the ex-Jesuits in Beijing in 1795, two years after his initial warning, along with a payoff in furs. In exchange the Jesuits— including José Bernardo de Almeida, Macartney's translator—sat down with him repeatedly over "tea and snacks" and explained what Macartney had asked for and what had gone wrong for him at the imperial court. They also offered information on the Dutch embassy that had come to visit at the same time.[73] The skills of this frontier agent had thus been successfully redeployed in the pursuit of a wider global agenda that went far beyond the Mongol border that had once been Igumnov's sole ambit. He was the exception that proved the rule: the rest of the infrastructure that had once supported him—the diplomatic and intelligence network set up in Eastern Siberia, once the key node in relations with the Qing—was becoming less and less relevant to Russian ambitions.

Russian Intelligence in a Global Key

The Macartney embassy accelerated the transformation of Russian knowledge making about China into a globalized, metropolitan phenomenon, in which the purpose of intelligence was to advance Russian positions in a worldwide quest for influence. This meant rethinking both the location and the nature of knowledge. Increasingly, Russian officials perceived Eastern Siberia as a provincial annex of a much larger struggle. From St. Petersburg, they reached eastward to transform what they saw as the obsolete methods and narrow horizons of frontier intelligence. The shift would be far-reaching: henceforth, great-power competition in Europe would govern both Russia's foreign-policy goals in the region and its knowledge-making institutions.

The intellectual climate surrounding this shift and the conspiratorial thinking that accompanied it were effectively encapsulated by the career of a onetime Irkutsk merchant named Fëdor Shchegorin. With the collusion of one of the court eunuchs, as a member of Igumnov's caravan he had disguised himself as a Chinese servant to spy on the just-arrived Dutch embassy of Isaac Titsingh. Although he learned nothing useful, and indeed his identity was revealed during the mission, the taste for skulduggery seems to have gone to his head.[74] After his return from Beijing, Shchegorin went to St. Petersburg, where he began to market himself at court as a secret agent with a treasure trove of highly valuable smuggled-out Qing court documents. One of the first texts he circulated was what purported to be a summary of the deliberations of the Qing Grand Council about the Macartney embassy. Shchegorin skillfully played on the anti-British anxiety in the Russian capital: the British, he claimed, had offered the Qing an equal supply of furs to that coming from Russia at half price, on the condition that they receive a monopoly. After strenuous debate, in Shchegorin's telling, the emperor himself rejected this proposal as giving the British too much power over the trade. (Macartney's records do not mention any such offer, and it is doubtful that Britain could then have fulfilled such an undertaking.)[75]

In subsequent years, Shchegorin's mystifications became more and more preposterous and elaborate. In 1798–1799, he submitted a "secret" "Project on the China Trade." The first part, which may well have been genuine, consisted of the Lifanyuan's supposed instructions to its merchants at Kiakhta; Shchegorin wanted the Russian government to create a company or cartel that could effectively counter their joint bargaining strategy.[76] The second, which was apparently meant to make the case for an even broader reform, claimed to be a comprehensive commercial regulation from the era of the Yongle emperor. The State Council agreed to hear the proposal but decided it amounted to "the compositions of an overheated imagination."[77] This did not deter Shchegorin. In December 1799, he made yet another proposal, this time offering some "Confucian" secrets with the help of which the entire Russian imperial government would be remodeled to protect against subversion.[78] Incredibly, he continued to survive and work on this until at least 1826, by which point his proposal had accumulated several more "secret translations," including a "report by Confucius to his emperor." Confucius, of course, did not serve an emperor, and in fact this was clearly an à clef rendering of contemporary European politics.[79] Another component pitched this "Confucianism" as a solution to Masonic conspiracies; others offered technological solutions such as a telegraph and a hydrometer to protect against floods.[80] In his obsession with linking the old relationship with China to Russia's civilizational mission in a world haunted by the French Revolution, Shchegorin was picking up on a broader trend in the culture of the period.

This preoccupation also prevailed at the top of the imperial hierarchy. In 1804 Alexander I, who had become emperor three years earlier after the assassination of his father, Paul, returned to the decade-old plan to send a massive embassy to China, in part on the advice of the Jesuit superior general Gabriel Gruber. The Russian ambassador, Count Iurii Golovkin, was not a native Russian speaker. He had grown up in Switzerland and Paris as the descendant of a family of exiles who had intermarried with European nobles. By the time he received the embassy assignment, he was one of the empire's most powerful aristocrats. Such a significant figure needed a large suite. In contrast to Savva Vladislavich's 120 or so attendants, Golovkin aimed to bring 242, among them soldiers, doctors, secretaries, and academics—including the future influential sinologist Julius Klaproth. All in all it was to cost over half a million rubles.[81] The goals of the embassy were both familiar and new, grounded in an expansive vision of a unified Pacific and Inner Asian commercial landscape. Golovkin was to demand the right of navigation on the Amur but also the opening of a new trade entrepôt on the Bukhtarma in Jungharia and (very optimistically) permission for a Russian trade expedition to go to India through Tibet. In addition, he would try to coordinate with

Kruzenshtern's contemporaneous around-the-world voyage to secure trade access to Canton. Finally, following the original anti-Macartney plan, three Jesuits—now Giovanni Grassi, Norbert Korsak, and Jan Stürmer—would travel to Beijing by sea, conduct intelligence on Golovkin's behalf, and establish a Russian Jesuit college there on the French model.[82] (This last project lurched on for five years but eventually collapsed after a failure of negotiations with the papacy; none of the Jesuits made it to China.) The Golovkin embassy concerned not only China but the world.

Yet despite these ambitions, Golovkin was not very popular, and the Europeanized aristocrats in his suite inspired further distrust. Grumblings about the embassy began before it even departed. Aleksandr Vorontsov called it a "gang," said Golovkin lacked "moral character," and expressed the wish that "the Qing emperor would decide it all for them and, in his anger about the engineers they are bringing to make plans and profiles of their fortresses, would order them all to be flogged from the first to the last and then turned out of his domains."[83] But there were deeper issues at stake as well. The new trade post at Bukhtarma, which would be closer to Moscow and more convenient for merchants, threatened the Kiakhta trade and the entire Eastern Siberian economy; the same might be true of Russian trade at Canton.[84] The Kiakhta trade was economically significant for Khalkha Mongolia as well, making any changes politically tricky for Qing authorities. Navigation on the Amur was a far more complicated question than it seemed and would not suffice by itself to make the river useful.[85] In short, the embassy had odds against it from the very beginning, even without considering the possible objections of the Jiaqing emperor.

These potential difficulties were one reason the embassy was deeply concerned with updating and modernizing its intelligence apparatus. Several of its members had associated intelligence-gathering functions, including the academics, but it seems clear that the unofficial head of intelligence was twenty-seven-year-old Count Iakov Lambert, son of the French émigré Henri-Joseph de Lambert and the embassy's second secretary. In preparation for departure Lambert collected all the existing documents he could find in the central archives having to do with Russo-Qing relations. This included not only N. I. Bantysh-Kamenskii's 1803 compilation *Diplomaticheskoe sobranie del...*, still one of the principal sources for historians of the period, but also a wide range of secret materials, including a number of the documents cited here.[86] After consulting Igumnov's 1794–1795 journal, either Lambert or one of his assistants wrote a contemptuous memorandum dismissing the information he had reported. "This brief note," he wrote, "clearly proves that aside from the countless advantages our scholarship could obtain from our mission in Beijing, we could also have the singular chance of learning much from the escorting officers we send, if only the government would deign to inquire into the advantages Russia has possessed for so long in obtaining knowledge about the Qing State versus other European powers."[87] In addition to Lambert, the embassy also employed the best Qing experts in the empire: the former mission student Anton Vladykin, Vasilii Igumnov's son Aleksandr, and several others. These played a subsidiary role, however. The embassy's approach to intelligence relied on the notion that Russia's previous efforts in that area had been terminally hidebound and lacked the expertise that could only be provided by the leadership of Western-trained specialists. This new vision would be realized most coherently in the package of espionage instructions issued two years later to the new missionary archimandrite Iakinf (Bichurin), though evidence suggests that they mostly fell by the wayside.[88]

For all his preparations, Golovkin's embassy was a failure, due in large part to problems of knowledge. In January 1806, having just entered Mongolia after a humiliating series of reductions in his entourage demanded by the Urga amban Yundondorji, he was invited to a feast where the amban demanded he kowtow to an image of the emperor. Although Golovkin was ready to kowtow in Beijing, such a demand in Urga was utterly unacceptable to him, and the embassy was at an end. A leading Russian scholar has suggested that the Qing government had no use for the embassy and sought for any excuse to turn it away.[89] While this may or may not be true, Golovkin had also been misled by his intelligence service. In November 1805, the embassy's first secretary Lev Baikov interviewed a Bukharan rhubarb supplier named Abdaraim at Kiakhta. Abdaraim informed the diplomat that both Yundondorji and the Tüsiyetü-Khan had recently been reprimanded by the emperor and that both their reputations were on the line. According to Abdaraim, Yundondorji's demand for suite reductions was an attempt "to demonstrate his service to the emperor," but "if this embassy retreats from the border, then *all the fault will fall on him* [i.e., Yundondorji] and he will suffer great wrath."[90] A misapprehension of the stakes involved for the Mongol had clearly contributed to Golovkin's miscalculation.

Another source of disruption was Pëtr Vanifat'ev, the Kiakhta customs director who had gained so much power due to imperial neglect of the Mongolian frontier. He had a clear motive to disrupt Golovkin's progress, both to protect the exclusivity of the Kiakhta trade and his own immunity from supervision. Golovkin's letters to Lambert make it clear that he regarded the director as a significant obstacle to his plans.[91] According to the memoirs of F. F. Vigel', one of the members of the entourage left behind after the reductions, Vanifat'ev had pulled him aside when the embassy crossed into Mongolia and whispered, "Don't worry, brother, they won't get past Urga; they'll dance in the cold for a month and a half or so, and what will they see? Almost the same things as here."[92] After the embassy returned to Irkutsk, Lambert tried to salvage matters by sowing disinformation about Russian military reinforcements arriving in Transbaikalia with the hope of convincing the Mongol authorities that Russia planned an invasion if its embassy was not accepted.[93] In June 1806, Vanifat'ev indignantly reported to the commerce minister Nikolai Rumiantsev that he was being persecuted by members of the embassy—and that they were spreading rumors of war, which he was doing his best to dispel.[94] Deliberately or not, Vanifat'ev had repeatedly blocked any attempt to make good on the embassy's promises. Golovkin had found no way to tame this particular local authority.

One final threat was an imaginary one, fueled by the same conspiratorial mentality that had shaped the Russian approach to the region since the 1780s. Golovkin and his entourage believed that one reason the embassy failed was that the British were scheming against them. According to the jaded and skeptical P. N. Struve, the most accomplished diplomat in the suite, they even put forth the notion that Yundondorji had been bribed by the British.[95] Based on the records of the British factory at Canton, it is unlikely that the British knew anything concrete about the embassy or its future plans. But in fact, they did the Russians a major service. In November 1805, Kruzenshtern's two ships arrived at Canton to trade, without making any effort to coordinate with Golovkin (who cited this as yet another factor in his failure). Although they were able to exchange their goods, the local Qing officials were suspicious and ordered the vessels impounded until the receipt of a resolution from Beijing. Only with the wholehearted help of the local East India Company supercargoes was Kruzenshtern able to disentangle his ships—and when the edict finally arrived, it shocked both the Russians and the British with its severity. Russians were to trade only at Kiakhta, and their use of any other entrepôt was strictly prohibited. It was China, not Britain, that obstructed Russo-Chinese trade.[96]

Ultimately, the Golovkin embassy failed because of an accidental confluence of circumstances, not because it was undermined or betrayed; as we will see, it ultimately contributed to a series of shifts in the Russo-Qing knowledge regime. Politically, however, Russo-Qing politics remained at a stalemate for nearly half a century, and Golovkin's embassy was the last significant diplomatic endeavor for many decades. In 1810, after British soldiers briefly occupied Macao, Qing officials tried to contact the Irkutsk civil governor Treskin with an offer encouraging the Russians to try again. Russia was adamant, however, that a return embassy from the Jiaqing emperor would have to be sent first, and the proposal was permanently dropped.[97] The Golovkin embassy also had longer-term consequences for the other players in the global drama. In 1816, William Amherst's embassy collapsed in part because Qing officials imitated Yundondorji's precedent in demanding that he kowtow not just in Beijing but in advance of his audience. Both sides explicitly invoked Golovkin in the process.[98] Amherst's failure would eventually contribute to the perception that Qing diplomacy was fundamentally intransigent, boosting the British faction that favored a militarized approach—the gunboat diplomacy of the Opium Wars.[99]

Despite Golovkin's failure, St. Petersburg elites continued to see the Russo-Qing relationship through the lens that had given rise to his embassy in the first place: as one aspect of the broader struggle for superiority in the Pacific. Even as neglect of the Inner Asian frontier continued, the obsession with extending Russian power into the ocean remained. In 1812, the American merchant Peter Dobell arrived in Petropavlovsk with a shipment of foodstuffs. In 1813–1814, he submitted a detailed plan for the creation of a triangular trade between Kamchatka, Canton, and the Philippines: "the Chinese will bring to Manila everything that they can sell to the Russians, so that Russia can make use of all the benefits of their trade without suffering from their caprice and insolence."[100] Alexander's government approved the plan, and Dobell was sent to Manila to serve as the Russian consul, though the mission proved abortive.[101] In 1821, Alexander I issued a decree claiming Russian sovereignty over territory on both sides of the Pacific north of the fifty-first parallel (a substantial increase over the previous claim, which lay four degrees north) and attempting to exclude foreign vessels from the area. The move immediately provoked an American response declaring hegemony in the New World, which became the famous Monroe Doctrine of 1823.[102] While the age of the great Pacific projects had ended, the ocean would never again return to being a distant Russian lake in the minds of the tsars and their high officials: the globalized competition for control over it was now a permanent feature of the landscape.

From the perspective of the well-ordered intelligence institutions set up under Peter the Great and his successors, the landscape of knowledge surrounding Russo-Qing relations had become unruly indeed. No longer was China a conceptually well-bounded problem, to be addressed either from a caravan, from the mission, or from the frontier. Now all kinds of dilettantes and foreign experts weighed in despite their lack of specialized training: the struggle for the Pacific had made Russia's relationship with China an apparently larger and more open-ended question. Thus, knowledge making about China became defined by frequent intelligence failures but also mounting ambition and prestige. At the Imperial Academy of Sciences, these growing aspirations would soon lead to a fundamental transformation of what it meant to study China in the first place.

Chapter 10

Making Russian Sinology in the Age of Napoleon

B Y THE TURN of the nineteenth century, Imperial Russian officials like Aleksandr Vorontsov had come to see their relationship to the Qing Empire through the lens of global rivalry between European empires rather than borderland conflict or Eurasian trade. This meant that knowledge production, too, would have to be politicized in a new way. In the Russian context, it had always been oriented toward pragmatic ends, generally quite immediate ones, which is why most intelligence gathering was conducted through administrative rather than academic institutions. But academic knowledge about the East was beginning to acquire a quite explicit political dimension in Europe. In 1790, the leading French Manchu scholar Louis-Mathieu Langlès published a pamphlet on "the importance of Oriental languages" addressed to the new National Assembly. Language learning would not simply serve to enrich the learning of the revolutionary state, he argued, but to promote French commerce in the widest possible sense. Had not the British "unceasingly built new establishments on the ruins of those built by other Europeans"? Was not the particular attention they paid to Oriental languages "proof of the utility which they derive from it for their commerce, their political or their military operations"? France needed to follow their example.[1] For their part, the British saw Oriental knowledge as key for countering the universalism of the French Revolution.[2] Russians, too, came to see their encounter with China in the context of their European rivalries. Russian sinology was born in the nineteenth century out of the need to compete with other imperial powers.[3]

This new incarnation of the imperial knowledge regime took the form of a discipline, a specific type of intellectual configuration that was beginning to emerge in the early nineteenth century. Before the rise of disciplinarity, a historian might easily draw on jurisprudence or moral philosophy and frame the result as an essay for the benefit of lay readers. Now, however, scientific and humanistic fields were increasingly bounded conversations with more or less well-defined traditions, methodologies, and specialized institutions. These disciplines were made up of a new kind of practitioner, an author with a "disciplinary self." Where an earlier version of the Enlightenment ideal had emphasized polymathy and encyclopedism, the disciplinary expert embraced specialization as a claim to authority. He (this figure was almost always male) was formed internally through seminars designed to cultivate a particular affinity for a field of study and externally through the display of pedigree, academic credentials, and publications in learned journals. Disciplinarity was the hallmark of what Europeans saw as the modern, sophisticated way to produce knowledge, so the Russian intellectual encounter with China became modern by becoming the discipline of sinology.[4]

Oriental studies in particular became a key site of disciplinary knowledge formation, as the literary-philosophical exercises of earlier Orientalists gave way to language-intensive, archival, and institutionalized scholarship, often by practitioners directly linked to European imperial projects. While the study of India or the Middle East was harder to cleanly separate from its eighteenth-century predecessors, in the study of sinology and its cognate fields—including, for instance, Manchu and Inner Asian studies—the shift from a "traditional" to a "modern" approach was much more obvious and distinct. This is because eighteenth-century European scholarship on Chinese history and culture had remained dependent on Jesuit intermediaries. By 1814 the last members of the former Jesuit mission in Beijing were dead. The leading sinologists in the West would henceforth be secular academics with research posts, particularly Jean-Pierre Abel-Rémusat, who was appointed to the first chair of "Chinese and Manchu languages and literatures" at the Collège de France in 1814, and eventually his Berlin colleague Julius Klaproth. State-sponsored institutionalization paralleled the creation of academic societies, like the Société Asiatique, which Abel-Rémusat founded in 1822, or the Royal Asiatic Society, established in London the year after, as well as their affiliated scholarly journals.[5] European sinologists took advantage of the interest of state patrons and developed a discipline centered on a handful of key players and institutions.

By the middle of the century, a similar process had taken place in Russia as well, although neither sinology nor Oriental studies became as centralized as in Britain or France. Instead, these efforts were dispersed more widely, leading to the formation of academic-bureaucratic nodes like the Asiatic Department of the new Ministry of Foreign Affairs, regional language schools, manuscript libraries, and faculties in universities like Kharkov and Vil'na. Of these the most important was at Kazan University, where local Tatar scholars worked with German-speaking academics to create a prominent and durable Orientalist establishment. In 1837, Kazan would host the empire's first department of Chinese studies. (Manchu would be added seven years later.)[6] In the Russian context, the emergence of authorship also reconfigured academic hierarchies, creating new opportunities for people from nonelite backgrounds to lay claim to the status of intellectuals. For instance, Grigorii Spasskii, the founder of the journal *Sibirskii vestnik* (later *Aziatskii vestnik*)—a Russian-language cousin of Abel-Rémusat's *Journal asiatique*—was a junior clerk and mining engineer, not an academician.[7] This transformation undermined the Academy of Sciences's emphasis on social hierarchy, helping to bring the study of China out of the shadows of bureaucratic secrecy.

The emergence of disciplinary sinology took place against a backdrop of changing attitudes to China. Over the course of the eighteenth century, the bien-pensant European view of China gradually shifted from the mostly positive image long propounded by missionaries and the philosophes toward the sino-skepticism that would define the following era.[8] In particular, this reflected the growing relative significance of science and technology in determining civilizational hierarchies. By the early nineteenth century, China's backwardness and failure to modernize economically and militarily seemed axiomatic to European observers.[9] Though sinologists echoed many of these arguments, the emerging sinological discipline was also defined by its self-conscious sobriety in evaluating the value of Chinese history and literature. Abel-Rémusat's stance was that its glory was a distant mirror for the present-day triumph of French culture; while rejecting what he considered the uninformed accounts of recent critics, he was far from taking the glowing view that had been mainstream in the eighteenth century.[10] Even a missionary like Robert Morrison, who considered the Chinese classics godless, avoided making normative evaluations of the culture as a whole. Here the scientific self-image of the discipline took precedence over the more explicitly colonial rhetoric of political actors.[11]

Russians routinely saw their own sinological achievements as lagging behind British or French scholarship, even though their claims to intellectual priority and continuity with past sinological research were in some ways stronger than any other European state. As the Catholic missions withered, Russian Ecclesiastical Missions continued to be sent, and students continued to learn Manchu and Chinese in the Qing capital, a far greater degree of access than any of Russia's rivals possessed. But just as metropolitan foreign-service officials like Iakov Lambert were casting a critical eye on the achievements of eighteenth-century intelligence, so were academically trained scholars starting to regard their own missionary predecessors with skepticism. As Nikita (Iakinf) Bichurin, archimandrite of the ninth mission, wrote in 1817, "The century-long existence of the Russian Mission in Beijing has yielded . . . no benefit either for the sciences or for the arts."[12] In fact, the logic of backwardness was built into the context of imperial competition, which defined valuable knowledge precisely in the disciplinary terms that had just been established as normative by Western European pioneers. To overcome their newfound lag, Russians had to jettison the legacy of the eighteenth-century knowledge regime that had once defined the Russo-Qing encounter and rebuild sinology from the ground up.

Reforming the Ecclesiastical Mission

The Russian Ecclesiastical Mission had been central to both secret and public knowledge production about China in the first half of the eighteenth century, and as the imperial knowledge regime wrenched into a new track it became central once more. To transform the study of China in the Russian Empire from an intelligence enterprise centered on the Inner Asian frontier to an academic one framed by a network of European scholarly institutions, the mission needed to be made into a professionalized school for sinologists, which required integrating it more deeply with Beijing life. Due to his experiences in the Qing capital, Bichurin's name more than any other came to be associated with the newly established discipline of Russian academic sinology, giving him a lasting reputation as a pioneer.[13] But the real story is more complicated. As an academic celebrity in the 1830s, Bichurin successfully capitalized on the regime of authorship that the new intellectual culture would produce—but as the head of the mission decades earlier, he had been the emblem of everything that seemed not just archaic but shameful in the old mission structure.

Bichurin's role as leader emerged from the 1805 Golovkin embassy to China. This abortive venture, as we have seen, was the most concrete manifestation yet of the state's newly globalized way of thinking about China. This applied just as significantly to its scholarly aspects. Never before had the Imperial Academy of Sciences been so deeply and deliberately engaged in the process of shaping a diplomatic mission to China. The last time one of its agents (Jellatschitsch in 1755) had gone to Beijing, it was as a caravan doctor, his responsibilities to the Academy being of little concern to the caravan director or the College of Foreign Affairs. For its part, the Academy showed little interest in sinological field research. In the 1770s, a plan to send the academic Peter Simon Pallas to Beijing in the guise of an envoy was quickly abandoned, in part because Pallas was unwilling to go.[14] Now, however, the Academy (headed by a personal friend of the young emperor) joined the imperial project with relish, eagerly proclaiming the "great benefit . . . for the sciences generally" its participation could bring.[15] Five researchers would accompany Golovkin to Siberia: an astronomer, a zoologist, a mineralogist, a botanist, and, finally and most importantly, the young Orientalist Julius Klaproth.

Klaproth had come to Russia specifically in pursuit of this opportunity. In 1803, in Berlin, he had met the Polish aristocrat-literatus Count Jan Potocki.[16] Klaproth was then twenty years of age and had apparently taught himself Chinese using the St. Petersburg Orientalist Gottlieb Bayer's 1730 *Museum Sinicum,* a failed attempt at a Chinese grammar and lexicon by a scholar whose own knowledge of the language was deeply imperfect.[17] This achievement and a few publications made Klaproth a minor academic celebrity in the German states; the fact that he was unencumbered by professional or familial obligations made him an ideal candidate for recruitment to the St. Petersburg Academy. Potocki's ties to the Russian court allowed him to secure an adjunct position in Oriental languages at the Academy for his protégé; assigned to supervise the academic activities of the Golovkin embassy, Potocki could watch over his young charge directly. In 1804, Klaproth arrived in St. Petersburg with every expectation of being able to use Russia's special relationship with the Qing as a springboard to a successful sinological career—particularly as he would be the embassy's only liberal-arts academic.[18]

This would not work out quite as he had imagined it. The Qing authorities in Urga, the Mongolian capital, decreed that the embassy would need to reduce its personnel by nearly half, and in December 1805 Klaproth (to his "contemptuous outrage") drew the short straw; eventually, three of his colleagues would have to be cut as well.[19] After the embassy's failure Klaproth would retaliate with a pseudonymous German pamphlet excoriating most of the embassy's participants, perhaps not without reason, as vain and hapless fools.[20] This did not prevent him from turning his prematurely terminated journey into the foundation of a future scholarly career. In Irkutsk, he acquired the former missionary and translator Anton Vladykin's massive library of Qing-language manuscripts, from which he would publish translations for the rest of his life, and employed the services of a shipwrecked seaman from Japan to learn Japanese. Over the course of the next year, Klaproth traveled back and forth along nearly the entire length of the Russo-Qing border, studying Mongol, Buriat, and Kalmyk customs, visiting Buddhist temples, and collecting texts. He was richly rewarded in St. Petersburg and in subsequent years authored influential studies of the Caucasus in addition to his work on China and Inner Asia.[21]

It would not be the Imperial Academy of Sciences whose prestige would ultimately benefit from Klaproth's activities. In 1810, having traveled to Berlin to commission Manchu fonts for a published grammar, he decided not to return: despite his nominally high pay in paper rubles, the poor exchange rate in silver in Russia meant he was making less money every year.[22] Klaproth chose the most provocative way possible to burn his bridges. Having long overstayed his leave in Berlin, in June 1812 he wrote a letter to the Academy president in which he accused the institution of having cheated him out of his salary and announced his resignation. "What the Academy loses with my departure, neither it nor I can judge," Klaproth wrote. "May the learned world judge of that. Until then this matter will be unresolved, and the [Academy] Conference can comfort itself with the thought that it will thereby save 1400 paper rubles annually, which it can use to maintain a Gottorp Globe or run a tavern [*einer харчевня*]."[23] Predictably, the Academy was furious. At a meeting in August, the Conference decided "not only to dismiss him, as he demanded in his reckless letter while making utterly baseless and absurd claims, but to issue him a dishonorable discharge from the Academy, as one unworthy of holding the post of Academician and the rank of Aulic Councillor that came with it."[24] (Publicly stripping Klaproth of his rank deprived him of hereditary nobility, in theory even the "von" he had inserted into his name.) But there was a more serious problem. Upon his departure from St. Petersburg in 1810, Klaproth had taken a number of valuable manuscripts from the Academy's library, and the librarian spent the next ten years fruitlessly trying to track them down all over Europe. At one point, the Russian consul in Florence informed him that Klaproth had left behind a safe deposit box as collateral for some unpaid debts after departing the city, but while this box did prove to contain some books, they were not the ones he was looking for. A decade after Klaproth's defection, the new Academy president Sergei Uvarov was still complaining that "there can be no doubt that Klaproth looted the library of the Academy of Sciences in the most brazen possible way."[25]

The Klaproth experience was so galling in large part because the strategy of recruiting early-career scholars from the German lands and turning them into Russian intellectuals with international reputations had been a long-established strategy for the Imperial Academy of Sciences (though this was not the first time it had fallen through). In the emerging international economy of academic sinological prestige, the loss of such an investment was acutely felt. Worse, Klaproth continued to exploit his Russian experience to further his career in Europe. In 1814, he wrote to the famous German publisher Johann Friedrich von Cotta offering a collection of his travels in Siberia and Inner Asia. "As I traveled in the service of the Russian Crown," he wrote, "it was easy for me to assemble new and authentic information. My language skills enabled me to create descriptions of Inner Asia, including Tibet, Little Bukhara, Jungharia, and of the Mongols and their steppe domains, which no other traveler was in a position to do."[26] Like Strahlenberg and Witsen before him, Julius Klaproth parlayed his direct access to sources from the Russian Empire into professional success abroad. This left room for some prevarication as well. Klaproth claimed that he had, in fact, crossed the Qing border into Mongolia, and most of his biographers took him at his word.[27] On one occasion, he even invented a document—a map and travelogue of Kashmir—by claiming that he had obtained it from an official Russian source. He was obviously relying on the fact that no Westerner was in a position to challenge him on this score, and the gamble paid off: the fraud was not discovered until decades after his death.[28] The Golovkin embassy, which had been intended to elevate Russia's standing within the European intellectual world by finally capitalizing on the empire's unique geographical and diplomatic position vis-à-vis the Qing, had instead given the Academy a well-connected and personally aggrieved rival in Paris and Berlin.

Relying on the foreigner Klaproth had clearly been unsuccessful, but there was another member of the embassy whose role in Russian sinology would turn out to be even more significant. In 1806, Count Golovkin persuaded the Ministry of Foreign Affairs and the Synod to replace the archimandrite scheduled to be sent to Beijing in 1807. This archimandrite, the twenty-five-year-old Apollos, had fit in badly with the ambassador's entourage and failed to impress him with his intellectual achievements. His replacement, Father Iakinf (Bichurin), was a French-speaking epicure who was much more personally appealing to the Western-educated envoy, and he also provided the embassy with valuable information about Golovkin's 1720 predecessor, Izmailov.[29] There was only one obstacle: Bichurin was being held under guard at a monastery in Tobolsk as punishment for his role in a riot that broke out during his previous appointment, as archimandrite of Voznesenskii Monastery in Irkutsk. Some younger monks had discovered that Bichurin was keeping a girlfriend in his suite disguised as a young acolyte, and the archimandrite barely escaped with his life as they stormed his quarters. Golovkin was hardly deterred by this piquant episode and eventually prevailed on the Synod to set aside Bichurin's penalty.[30]

Troubling reports about Bichurin's behavior began filtering in soon after he arrived in Beijing. In 1813, a denunciation signed by three mission students arrived in St. Petersburg, containing upward of twenty distinct accusations against Bichurin, both individually and together with his hieromonks. Some of these would hardly be calculated to inspire outrage either for contemporary readers or for the libertines in Alexandrian officialdom: Bichurin was charged with hunting birds with a rifle, attacking the mission's escorting officer, and calling him a "son of a bitch." But the others were more disturbing. The students claimed the archimandrite had become a connoisseur of the local sex trade; he regularly spent the night in brothels, and the hieromonks suffered from venereal disease. Qing visitors to the mission compound were shocked by the state of the impoverished young boys and girls Bichurin ordered sent to him, "saying that they remembered the arrival of three missions but never had they seen one with a leader like this." To pay for all this, Bichurin and the hieromonks appropriated salary funds set aside for future years.[31] A. N. Golitsyn, the Synod procurator, was skeptical; he blithely responded that "if the Father Archimandrite's behavior were as outrageous as the students describe, and as openly known to the public . . . then the Qing Government would not have left this unnoticed and would have written to our Senate, but no complaints against Archimandrite Iakinf have come in."[32] Six years later, this complaint finally arrived, from the director of the Kiakhta customs office on the Mongolian border. "To my great regret and shame," the director wrote, a Qing border official gave a "highly unflattering report" about the mission and asked, "why are people who are unable to behave themselves sent to Beijing? Asking this question with a revealing expression, he awaited my reply with a look that testified to his great curiosity."[33] It was clear from the director's letter that this was no longer simply a question of missionary misconduct of the kind that had plagued the Russian Ecclesiastical Mission since the beginning: it was starting to have wider effects that imperiled the mission's function as an intelligence-gathering and diplomatic institution. A comprehensive reform agenda would need to be adopted to curb the abuses to which Bichurin's leadership had clearly led.

The goal of reforming the mission did not just come out of this particular case but also out of a broader sense of urgency surrounding Russia's mounting competition with European rivals, of which Bichurin himself was keenly aware. Imperial officials increasingly concluded that they could no longer afford to treat the mission as an afterthought, since it represented one of the few intellectual and diplomatic trump cards the empire possessed over Britain and other powers. Even before Bichurin left for Beijing, it was becoming clear that the Russian Ecclesiastical Mission could not satisfy either the academic or the religious demands placed on it by state institutions. In the long term it could not even expect to maintain the existence of the Beijing Albazinians—the Russian-descended Manchus who supposedly constituted its flock—as a cultural, much less a religious, community, and hence it was in danger of losing even the pretext for its existence. In 1806, even Klaproth weighed in with a proposal to make the mission actively "useful for the sciences" as opposed to merely producing "mechanical translators."[34] In 1809, having just returned from Beijing, Archimandrite Sofronii submitted a lengthy reform plan that emphasized intensified Orthodox proselytization, along with increased budgets and centralization, as the key to the mission's future survival.[35] A few years later, Bichurin himself submitted a reform proposal in hopes of getting permission to stay on for another decade. In contrast to Sofronii, Bichurin judged the mission to be a primarily intellectual enterprise. He therefore encouraged student salaries to be raised and students to be sent to the mission already trained in "Russian literacy and in part in many other sciences," among which would be knowledge of Tatar and Mongol. The hieromonks and hierodeacon would spend their time researching Chinese, art, and the material culture of the area. Since the central axis of Bichurin's plan was his own guiding role—he was to shepherd the arriving missionaries through their initial years of studying the basics of the language and then act as academic director for the remainder of the decade—the reform made little sense without him. When the Synod decided not to leave the archimandrite in Beijing, no doubt as a result of the controversy already swirling around him, Bichurin's reform plan was shelved.[36]

The restructuring proposal that ultimately won favor with the state apparatus, including Emperor Alexander himself, was the work of a former mission student named Pavel Kamenskii. Long regarded by Soviet scholars as a doctrinaire religious conservative, Kamenskii was in fact a highly paradoxical figure, as much secular Enlightenment idealist as pious monastic; his proposal combined religious goals with intellectual ones and Jesuit influences with vaguely liberal concepts.[37] He was born in 1765 near the major Volga trade center of Nizhnii Novgorod, the son of a village priest. Kamenskii received a partial seminary education—though there is no sign he intended to join the clergy—and then a year at university in preparation for a civil service career. After a brief stint as the overseer of an orphanage in St. Petersburg, Kamenskii learned that a new mission was going to China and asked to be attached to it as a student.[38] His resolve did not last long: when the mission was already in Irkutsk, Kamenskii tried to use the recent death of his brother as an excuse to be relieved of his duties, but by the time the request was received, it was already too late.[39]

Although Kamenskii was known in Beijing as an industrious, well-behaved student, his experiences at the mission came close to destroying him psychologically. In one of his voluminous notebooks, he described his experience as a colossal waste of human life:

> We all suffered for 14 years. For many reasons related to this service, we deserved attention and pity. We lost, one might say, our best years. . . . There, we suffered contempt by the mores of that nation; having returned to our homeland, with the blunting of our abilities and with our inevitable ignorance of customs here, we must at the very least find ourselves at a distance. Our marriageable years passed without estate, without skills in service, and therefore there is no hope to obtain the common happiness of humanity. This is what China has rewarded us with! . . . This mission costs so much, but bears so little fruit. We ourselves are embarrassed to look at our translations.[40]

According to this somewhat melodramatic account, Kamenskii's fourteen years in Beijing had robbed him of a chance to have a normal life by the standards of early nineteenth-century Russian elite society. His service record to some extent belies his own bleak assessment. In 1809 he was appointed translator for the College of Foreign Affairs (together with his fellow student Stepan Lipovtsov); in the next few years, he became part of high-profile organizations like the Russian Bible Society, the Free Economic Society, and the Imperial Benevolent Society, and in 1816 he finally earned hereditary nobility. Yet he clearly believed that the skills he had acquired in China had been wasted on an ungrateful Russia.[41] One reason for this was that Kamenskii consistently found that the intelligence he compiled, much as Agafonov and Rossokhin had before him, inspired little interest in St. Petersburg. While still in Beijing, Kamenskii composed a series of notes and translations for the benefit of the Golovkin embassy, but these were never used or acknowledged in any way; neither were the miscellaneous strategic suggestions he continued to compile after his return.[42]

If the Russian Ecclesiastical Mission was going to train experts with real intellectual clout, this needed to be planned out in advance and in close, structured consultation with state authorities. Kamenskii's proposal, accordingly, envisioned an explicit division of labor for missionaries. One of the vergers would study the Tibetan language as well as Buddhist practices. The four students would each study Manchu and Chinese as well as their own specialized research subject: medicine, philosophy, history and political economy, arts and crafts. (The medical student would also act as a mission doctor and endear himself to Beijing dignitaries by treating them with European methods.) Each student would be assigned an organization to affiliate to in St. Petersburg, from which they would be issued instructions—the Medico-Surgical Academy, the Academy of Sciences, and the Free Economic Society. These institutions occupied very different social locations: the Medical-Surgical Academy was a formal part of the state bureaucracy, while the Free Economic Society was a nominally autonomous public organization.[43] For Kamenskii, this mattered little, despite his own experience in the Free Economic Society and other associations: he saw the imperial knowledge regime with all its off branches as a coherent whole with a common interest in developing a competitive sinological industry.

Kamenskii also envisioned fundamentally reorganizing the mission's structure. He wanted a predictable schedule to be put in place in advance to reward missionaries for diligent labor either in proselytization or research so that they would not find themselves lagging behind their peers in terms of social advancement. At least one member of the mission would be persuaded to stay behind on a voluntary basis to guide each new rotation through its initial years in Beijing.[44] Most importantly, the leadership of the mission would be vested in a "secret bureaucratic office [*prisutstvennoe mesto*] equal to eparchial consistories, which has as its sole task the glory of God, the good of the Sovereign and the fatherland." The office would hold votes and keep a journal, the ecclesiastics taking on roles as secretary and treasurer. With this new institution, Kamenskii hoped to replace the authoritarian rule of the archimandrite by a bureaucratized collective government—a kind of constitutional revolution imagined for a tiny society of ten in the middle of the Qing Empire.[45]

Over the course of his decade back in Russia, Kamenskii continuously drafted and evolved his reform plan for the mission as both a religious and an intellectual organization. To do so, he needed to take inspiration from the only other approach he knew to have worked in the Qing Empire: that of the Jesuits. "The Roman church," Kamenskii wrote, "does not suffer expenses in vain. Its mission, also consisting of no more than 10 people, works enviably. It would be good if ours could imitate them at least in part. Their preachers are first trained so well in their faith that they not only sacrifice their leisure, abilities, and properties for it, but are also willing to sacrifice their lives. . . . The Chinese are cunning, but [the Jesuits] are no simpletons either." Specifically, Kamenskii cited the Jesuit practice of training young Chinese students in their seminary to use as translators or catechists, as well as the generally better material conditions of their mission. He believed that during an anti-Catholic persecution in 1805, he and the other Orthodox students saved the ex-Jesuits from complete destruction by providing the Lifanyuan with a favorable translation of captured correspondence.[46] Although Kamenskii's opinion of Jesuit learning was low, he admired them greatly as authors of liturgical texts. Matteo Ricci's *Tianzhu shiyi* was in his view "the best book for the conversion of pagans." He went on to list four other Jesuit texts he had also translated for the use of the Russian mission because the Russian mission lacked texts of its own. These included a children's scripture, Giulio Aleni's *Wanwu zhenyuan*, and other material especially adapted for the use of new converts. Kamenskii asked that these translations be "in time, looked over and ordered to be given to new and converting Christians." To the extent that Kamenskii's reformed mission would refocus its activities on spreading Orthodoxy among the Albazinian and other Beijing populations, it would be using materials and approaches borrowed from the Russians' Catholic rivals.[47] The final version of the draft omitted any reference to the Jesuits, camouflaging Kamenskii's inspiration behind general-sounding phrases.[48]

In contrast to other proposals that stressed either the religious or the secular aspects of the mission's work, then, Kamenskii's drafts envisioned the new mission as combining both functions in a mutually reinforcing way, much as the Jesuits had once done—with the crucial difference that their activities would be under close state supervision. Studying Qing languages and books gave missionaries something to do and kept them from boredom and idleness, which generations of commentators had identified as key causes of the drunkenness, violence, and melancholy that plagued each successive mission. Language skills enabled the missionaries to create and participate in an urban religious community, which broke down the walls of isolation around the mission, while successful proselytization provided them with native connections and informants. Such an approach also reflected the tactics of a mounting wave of British Protestant missionaries in China, which combined Christian preaching with the kinds of sinological practice (like lexicography) that were needed to craft effective appeals to converts. Robert Morrison, the first of these missionaries and the compiler of the first comprehensive Chinese-English dictionary, had begun his activities in Canton in 1807 inspired by a program remarkably similar to Kamenskii's.[49]

A set of instructions reproducing Kamenskii's proposal in every meaningful sense, if not quite word for word, was approved by the emperor in July 1818. The search for an archimandrite had already begun. In the minds of Golitsyn and Foreign Minister Nessel'rode, there could only be one possible candidate: Kamenskii himself. In September 1817, he accepted—but just as he did during his first departure for Beijing, he immediately developed second thoughts. In January 1818, Kamenskii wrote to Nessel'rode, "Your Excellency, by insisting on my opinion, has forced me to declare that service in Beijing, in terms of private and personal good, compares to service in the depths of the fatherland as a long and unalterable period of suffering compares to a long period of pleasure. To voluntarily choose the worse is contrary to nature, and therefore I refuse to go." But in the absence of any other suitable candidates, over the course of a year, Kamenskii was finally prevailed upon to agree. (The promise of a second-degree Order of St. Anna, formally awarded to him by the tsar in December 1819, no doubt played some part in his decision.) On May 3, 1819, less than two months after accepting the position, the collegiate assessor Pavel Kamenskii became the monk Pëtr; on May 8, he was raised to hierodeacon; on May 9, to hieromonk; and finally, on May 15, he became an archimandrite and was awarded a diamond-studded pectoral cross.[50] It took almost another year and a half for the mission to enter Qing territory.[51]

On arriving in Beijing, Kamenskii immediately found confirmation of the worst accusations against Bichurin, as well as "much else that is serious that was not mentioned there, especially things in which the denouncers themselves took part. To describe everything in detail would be, in my opinion, to befoul my very pen; I will only say that Arch. [Bichurin] in his person combines the qualities and properties of Cicero's Antony and Seneca's Hostius and Latro."[52] The ambiguity of this encoded classical description encapsulates Kamenskii's attitude to his colleague. Like (Mark) Antony, he is utterly amoral and unprincipled; like Hostius (Quadra), his sexual appetites have driven him to shocking and criminal extremes; like Latro, he is justly renowned for both eloquence and dissolution. Kamenskii never cast doubt on Bichurin's sinological achievements: what he perceived was a failure of morality combined with a profound failure of leadership. The new archimandrite did not, in the end, shrink from "befouling his pen." In sixteen large pages of tiny hand-writing, he cataloged Bichurin's countless transgressions, from the sexual (sleeping with rent boys in the church altar) to the murderous (torturing or causing students to be tortured to death) to the merely ecclesiastical (not holding church services for years at a time) and administrative (destroying a bell tower because it offered an unobstructed view of the garden in which his festivities took place). Kamenskii also made it clear that this was all common knowledge in the Qing capital. On one occasion, a rent boy of the hieromonk Serafim's was lured off the property and returned to the Lifanyuan, where-upon the child was sent into exile and "the whole capital roared with laughter." The most concrete manifestation of the Bichurin mission's obviously toxic re-nown were "inscriptions, insulting and dishonorable to the name of Russians, posted above the gates [of the mission compound]." Bichurin, in Kamenskii's view, was not simply an archimandrite like any other, content to drink him-self into oblivion and descend into sporadic violence and illness. He had taken the absolute power of the head of a Beijing mission, effectively restrained nei-ther by Russian nor by Qing law, to the furthest possible extreme.[53]

Most of the specific charges contained in the students' and Kamenskii's reports never made it into the final indictment announced against Bichurin in January 1823. Church regulations had strong protections against hearsay, and as no material evidence or witnesses could be presented in St. Petersburg to support many of them, the worst accusations were never investigated. Still, on his way home from Irkutsk, Bichurin was found to have abducted a twelve-year-old boy whom the church enforcers found in his cell when they came to confront him. In the end, although Bichurin was found guilty on eight sepa-rate points, his punishment was comparatively lenient; just as in the case of Platkovskii in the 1730s, the Russian Orthodox Church took a lax view of sexual crimes if they were not proved by ironclad eyewitness testimony. Ia-kinf Bichurin was stripped of his ecclesiastical rank and condemned to live for five years as a simple monk at a remote monastery, though Golitsyn made sure this would be the relatively hospitable Valaam in Karelia rather than the forbidding Solovki. In fact, he would not serve even that long.[54]

The solidity of Kamenskii's new institutional arrangements in Beijing was put to the test almost immediately. In addition to the discovery of the true state of Bichurin's mission, which sent him into a panic, his handpicked hierodeacon Izrail turned out to be a conman who, "being still an untonsured commoner, hiding under the mask of impenetrable hypocrisy, insinuated himself into the staff of this Mission with the long-term plan of enriching himself and departing with the money for further improvements of fortune." A decision of the newly established council voted to dismiss Izrail from the mission's ranks.[55] Once the panic subsided, Kamenskii's letters from Beijing began to report a uniformly flourishing mission whose material state, intellectual achievements, and conversion activities continually reached new heights. Though these were clearly not unbiased observations, the fact that no one in his mission died either a natural or unnatural death during that decade was a significant—and hitherto unparalleled—development in the history of the Russian Ecclesiastical Mission in Beijing.[56]

Intellectually, the impact of Kamenskii's reforms was more ambiguous. Unlike Bichurin, who soon took advantage of his connections in the capital to build a new career for himself, Kamenskii never became a public intellectual—instead, after his return from Beijing in 1830, he refused all honors, retreated to a remote monastery, and remained there until his death in 1845.[57] Indeed, in a sense Kamenskii had failed to shape the intellectual agenda even of his own mission. His ideas about the sort of knowledge a missionary sinologist was expected to generate were quickly reframed by the Academy of Sciences and the Ministry of Foreign Affairs' newly established Asiatic Department in ways that paralleled the emergence of professional sinology in Paris, London, and Berlin. Kamenskii's thinking belonged to the eighteenth century, but his superiors in St. Petersburg would make sure the mission's work belonged to the nineteenth. Their primary tools in this regard would be the mission library and the intellectual agenda set forth for the missionaries by the Academy of Sciences.

The New Questions of Academic Sinology

Two proposals for the mission's library represent the divide between the old Enlightened learning and the new professionalized discipline. When he was made archimandrite, Kamenskii immediately assembled a list of books he thought the mission would require. He was a prolific reader of both sinological and general literature; this is reflected in his many notebooks, which contain detailed commentaries on Bentham, Amiot, Raynal, Macartney, Müller, and Chulkov (author of a lengthy work on Russian commerce).[58] He was most vociferous, however, in rejecting Amiot's approach to sinology, which through the vast collection *Mémoires concernant les Chinois* had shaped the terms of China-related discussion in eighteenth-century Europe.[59] "It cannot be said that the work of the Jesuits in publishing their Chinese Memoirs does not deserve much public approbation," Kamenskii wrote. "But the truth demands an acknowledgment that in flattering Europe with news, and trying to be useful to it, they supported their conceptions with excessive decoration— these Memoirs are written eloquently, but cannot be relied upon except as similar to truth." In Kamenskii's view, the Jesuits had deliberately concealed how much they relied on direct adaptations of texts from native informants with their own biases and then further exacerbated the problem by adding their own Christian bias. This both reflected and contributed to a dramatically mistaken sinophilia, which had systematically exaggerated how enlightened the Qing Empire really was: "Not knowing their holy books, [a reader] would consider [their true contents] a fairytale contrary to reason or a libel against this famous people. In China, reason never had the chance to work independently."[60] In this way, Kamenskii was echoing the sino-skeptical position that was beginning to define European views of China.

The alternative vision Kamenskii presented, however, was still of the eighteenth century. His selection of books revealed his expectation that the missionaries would, like himself, strive to be men of letters in the Catherinian vein: his original list included works by Adam Smith, Hugo Grotius, Francis Bacon, the Abbé Mably, Cesare Beccaria, and Adam Ferguson, as well as a wide and generalist selection of less famous compositions, especially travel and historical literature. The Synod immediately regretted giving Kamenskii authority over the mission library. Assigned to evaluate his choices, Archbishop Filaret of Tver' concluded that "what is needed is not to correct the list but to make it anew," for Kamenskii had chosen "anti-Christian" works of Enlightenment and Protestant theology instead of reliable Orthodox texts.[61]

The list would have to be rewritten from the ground up by representatives of the imperial knowledge regime. It was to be composed by the Moscow Ecclesiastical Academy in cooperation with the Asiatic Department, but the latter institution—which had until recently employed Kamenskii himself and still employed his friend and colleague Lipovtsov—took the leading role. Paradoxically, the new library was both much larger, amounting to some three or four hundred distinct books, and much more specialized. With the help of Filaret and Foreign Minister Nessel'rode, most traces of generalism were utterly expunged, including many works on recent Russian history and literature as well as guides to Russian-language style. On the other hand, Kamenskii had conspicuously omitted some of the most renowned recent sinological works, including books by Abel-Rémusat, Langlès, Klaproth, and Morrison. This omission was now decisively rectified, and the library fairly groaned under the weight of specialized Qing-related reference works and linguistic compositions. Philosophy and theology—the domain of the Ecclesiastical Academy—were well represented, but the historical and natural-scientific portion overwhelmingly reflected the priorities of European Orientalism. The only major group of sinological scholars not represented were Russians. Only a single translation by Leont'ev—his collection of Qing laws—made it into the mission library, and on a supplementary list at that. The main list featured a book Klaproth published using Leont'ev's name as a pseudonym (*Lettres sur la littérature Mantchoue traduites du Russe du M. Leontiew*) and the deeply obsolete, century-old *Museum Sinicum*, but not a single work by anyone ever previously associated with the Russian Ecclesiastical Mission. Forgetting the legacy of the past was a key part of building a disciplinary future.[62]

At the Academy of Sciences, this process of reinvention reflected the prevailing sense that what mattered was taking part in an intellectual agenda framed in Western Europe. In December 1819, the Academy began to compose a "detailed instruction" in academic matters for the mission's four students, which would require a committee of four academicians to be convened.[63] Longer and more substantial than any previous Academy engagement with China, the 1819 instructions dealt with history, antiquities, astronomy, geography, zoology, political economy, and mineralogy; most were composed first in German and then translated into Russian. The page count was weighed disproportionately toward historical and source-critical questions drawn from European debates. Even the astronomical section, written by Vikentii Vishnevskii, was primarily focused on the history of Chinese astronomy, a field pioneered by the Jesuit Antoine Gaubil. The antiquarian Christoph Frähn (Fren), subsequently the core of the Kazan University China program and a frequent correspondent of Klaproth's even after the latter's self-imposed exile from the Academy, composed what amounted to a lengthy essay. In contrast to the queries for the Jesuits issued to Lorents Lang by the academicians in 1734, which were composed off the cuff and without consulting any of the available published sources, the 1819 instructions relied on close and critical readings of the entire spectrum of printed Western scholarship about the Qing Empire. Even the mineralogist's questions referenced specific reports and asked students to address questions previously raised by European scholars.[64] Running to nearly 20,000 words, this package of instructions was less a set of general queries than a massive programmatic statement about the state of Qing studies in the early nineteenth century.

The section on political economy, written by the Baltic German Genrikh fon Shtorkh (Heinrich von Storch), was the most obviously revealing part of the document. If in the seventeenth and eighteenth centuries China was often considered by European philosophes to be a well-governed commonwealth in which pacific emperors and literati arranged policies for the benefit of all, Shtorkh, like Kamenskii, used China as a foil for narratives of Western progress. "Information communicated to us by travelers to China contains many contradictions with respect to the political condition of this country," Shtorkh wrote. "If our travelers find occasion to resolve these contradictions or explain the essence, then they will not only enrich our information about the Qing Empire unknown to us in many respects, but will also serve to explain the theory of political economy with important examples." Shtorkh was far more interested in the latter than in the former: his very first question—"How widespread is the division of labor in China?"—contained a basic explanation of Adam Smith's political economy, borrowing the famous pin factory example nearly word for word (though Shtorkh reduced Smith's 48,000-pin figure by an order of magnitude). He made it clear that what he expected was not an objective resolution of the assorted contradictions in existing accounts but proof that China's agrarian economy was more primitive and inefficient than industrializing Europe: it "distances itself from its own goals and obstructs the activity that it aims to encourage." Jesuit observers, in Shtorkh's view, had blinded Europeans to the fatal defects of the Qing political and economic structure, and the Russian missionaries were well placed to refute them.[65]

Rather than simply gathering texts and information, then, the Russian missionaries were expected to provide ammunition for intellectual quarrels between European academics. This was made equally clear in the instructions on history, written by Philipp Krug. Krug's interest was above all in one task: confirming Joseph de Guignes's hypothesis of an identity between Buddhism (the religion of Fo, the Chinese word for "Buddha") and Christianity, which Krug believed to be "supported by well-founded reasons."[66] Not content to let the students learn from the historical material they found on the spot, Krug provided them with a strongly Guignesian capsule version of Chinese and Eurasian history incorporating references to classical European as well as Arabic sources.[67] Fren, the antiquarian, made this kind of preparation, in which European compositions were to be the point of departure for any new research to be conducted by the students, an explicit part of his instructions: "If I were to undertake a voyage to China, I would not only consult with the few learned men spread out through Europe who have dedicated themselves exclusively to Chinese literature and ask them to turn my attention to subjects hitherto considered doubtful or unworthy of respect; I would spend at least half a year carefully examining all the lengthy compositions related to China and its history." Like Krug, Fren was focused on confirming or disconfirming the work of De Guignes, Gaubil, and de Mailla, prominent French writers who had taken an interest in Inner Asian history and the conquests of Chinggis Khan. This meant, above all, providing "a true and complete translation of a substantial and full work" about the Mongol Yuan Dynasty and its Chinggisid antecedents. The study of historical Chinese numismatics and inscriptions was to form an ancillary focus for this work, along with research into material culture like bronzes, weapons, and so on.[68]

These questions, especially Fren's, may seem like obvious points of departure for young scholars who would, in all likelihood, have neither basic Qing-language training nor any kind of specialized historical preparation. What better tool to guide research than questions about lively current debates? Yet, as with the list of books for the Academy's library, what each of the academics ignored was the entire previous century of Russian knowledge production about the Qing Empire. Making use of this would not have even required consulting the Academy's new ex officio corresponding member, Archimandrite

Pëtr Kamenskii, who as Qing-language translator would have access to the papers of the Ministry of Foreign Affairs—or, indeed, Bantysh-Kamenskii (no relation to the monk), who had just assembled those papers into a substantial book.[69] All the Academy would have to do was to consult its own library and archives, which contained the whole surviving corpus of the works of Larion Rossokhin, Aleksei Leont'ev, and numerous other graduates of the Russian Ecclesiastical Mission. The Academy had printed dozens of volumes of Leont'ev's work a few decades earlier. None of the existing Russian sinological material was even consulted in the process of assembling these instructions, though the academicians assembled citations to sometimes obscure Western publications. In the case of Fren's attempts to procure Russian translations of historical works on Inner Asia, this was a particularly glaring omission: thanks to Rossokhin's immersion in the Manchu-inflected book culture of Yongzheng-era Beijing, the Academy had long possessed unique original and translated works of Inner Asian history. Many of the Academy's questions had already been answered, but what mattered was the new context in which they were asked.

As envisioned in the Academy's instructions and in the books with which the mission was now equipped, the rebirth of Russian sinology entailed the wholesale abandonment of its eighteenth-century past and a reorientation toward the debates felt by St. Petersburg academics to be the truly important ones—that is to say, those that academics like Klaproth carried on in Paris, London, and Berlin. For the mission to become "useful to the arts and sciences," it needed to not only undergo massive structural reforms but to conform to an unexpectedly specific definition of intellectual usefulness. As written retrospectively by Russian-speaking historians, the history of the emergence of all disciplines, including sinology, in Imperial Russia tends to be framed as a struggle of great men against a conservative establishment—but it was the changing form of the imperial knowledge regime that set up the problems to which the new framework became a solution. The dawn of Russian sinology had little to do with Kamenskii or Bichurin as individuals and everything to do with the collective decisions of state-linked, institutionalized official bodies.

It is hard to say that any of the research goals set forth in the Academy's instructions were actually realized. Graduates of Kamenskii's mission, like Kamenskii himself, published little; they went on to largely minor careers teaching Manchu and Chinese at the new educational institutions, like the Kiakhta language school, that began to open in the reign of Nicholas I. In doing so they helped bring into being the most important long-term consequence of Kamenskii's reforms: the creation of a unified continuity between different mission rotations and between the mission and its surrounding institutional landscape. Between Kamenskii's mission and 1917, every mission included at least one member who had taken part in the one before, while departing members were routinely channeled into established academic bodies as opposed to ad hoc, short-lived pedagogical experiments (like the schools of Rossokhin, Leont'ev, and Vladykin). Although the missions did not remain free from scandal, they ceased to be a perennial embarrassment to Russia.[70] Sometime after 1825, an anonymous Siberian poet even composed a verse "On Meeting the Returning Ecclesiastical Mission in Kiakhta," which congratulated the unnamed "venerable elder" who leads the mission for having served "with honor and benefit" and now proceeding to "certain reward" from a tsar who recognizes "the fruits of mind / Of labors so immense."[71] Needless to say, such a poem could hardly have been written about almost any of the missions before Kamenskii's, certainly not Iakinf Bichurin's.

The Synod and the Ministry of Foreign Affairs began preparing for the 1830 mission well in advance. Their new instructions displayed complete confidence in Kamenskii's arrangements, but with even more elaborate provisions for preliminary linguistic training. Ironically, this was one of the reasons Bichurin was able to reenter professional life as a sinologist: he was one of the only people judged capable of teaching the future missionaries Chinese. With Nicholas I's accession to the throne at the end of 1825, Bichurin's brief period of punishment was first lightened and then brought to an end entirely. In 1829, he was appointed honorary librarian at the Imperial Public Library in St. Petersburg, his first salaried position post-Beijing.[72] State patronage proved equally crucial for Bichurin's early publications. The same year, Nessel'rode wrote to the Ministry of Education to encourage the dissemination of two of Bichurin's works to schools and universities across the Russian Empire.[73]

As of 1830, Russia's bid for world academic prominence seemed in danger of faltering. In 1824–1827, Egor Timkovskii, the escorting officer for the 1822 mission, published his travel journals along with a number of works by Bichurin, first in Russia and then in Germany, Britain, and France. The French publisher, from whom the British edition was sourced, hired Julius Klaproth to act as consultant, and Klaproth proceeded to savage Bichurin's translations. The reviewer for the *Asiatic Journal* was not impressed, describing his remarks as "splenetic and illiberal" and noting that "in the present work he has displayed an unusual share of ill-humour." Yet he did not omit first to say, "As inaccuracies seem so abundant in this publication, while novelty and interest are so rare . . . we shall here take leave of the original author, expressing our disappointment and regret that his work contains so little to gratify curiosity."[74] Being the victim of a transparently unjust attack did not give either Bichurin or Timkovskii any more intellectual credibility in the eyes of Western European sinologists.[75]

It took until the second half of the century for the Russian Empire's investment in its new mission to pay off in international academic prestige. Although Bichurin had made a successful career in Russia, Klaproth helped make sure his work was sidelined in the West by emphasizing the supposedly slavish adherence to Qianlong-era editorial practices in the texts he published. It did not help that Bichurin defended demonstratively false hypotheses about Inner Asian history.[76] The first Russian sinologist (as opposed to Mongolist) whose international reputation was on a comparable level was I. I. Zakharov, member of the Russian Ecclesiastical Mission from 1839–1850. In the 1870s, after having served as Russian consul in Kulja, he became a university professor and published a Manchu grammar and dictionary that proved superior to anything then available in any language other than Chinese, superseding existing references in Russian as well. These became standard tools for Manchu scholars (manjurists) in Europe. "But why use the native [Chinese] works at all," asked the German manjurist Paul von Möllendorf in 1886, "since all of them have been condensed and placed in our hands in the form of Sacharoff's admirable complete lexicon? Of course you will say, it is in Russian! Now-a-days no excuse; for students of Manchu, Mongol, and other Asiatic subjects a knowledge of Russian has become a conditio sine qua non." Russian sinology had finally achieved the international recognition it had craved for so long.[77]

In 1825, the Orientalist Aleksandr Rikhter published an article in *Aziatskii vestnik* surveying the state of Oriental studies in the Russian Empire. "Russia's power in Asia," Rikhter wrote, "must encourage its sons to labor more than other Europeans in obtaining knowledge about the creations of this vast territory and the peoples that inhabit it." Up to that point, however, Russia had consistently disappointed Europe's expectations. Only recently had signs of hope begun to emerge. The founding of *Aziatskii vestnik*'s predecessor, the *Sibirskii vestnik,* by Grigorii Spaskii in 1818, had been one of them; dictionaries by Bichurin and Kamenskii were another. Yet Rikhter also listed as legitimate achievements of Russian sinology numerous works by Leont'ev and Agafonov. "The venerable Leont'ev, who had rendered so many services to his fatherland by means of his translations, is now almost forgotten," Rikhter lamented; even for him, Rossokhin and Agafonov barely merited a passing mention. Their era was now clearly over. To equal the achievements of its Western colleagues, Russia needed to develop an "Oriental Society, such as those in Paris, London, and Calcutta." The way forward seemed unambiguously to point west.[78]

By 1830, then, Russian authorities had definitively reoriented the production of knowledge about China toward a European mode of public scholarship buttressed by recognized, prestigious personalities and represented by publications, societies, and academic debates. As a modern discipline, Russian sinology was more similar to the nineteenth-century sciences than their humanistic counterparts in the resoluteness with which it cast away its own archive.[79] Bichurin, the first Russian sinologist to come of age as a scholar in that period, was the first beneficiary of this new intellectual culture. Here, to a great extent, lies the explanation for his later prominence in the grand narrative of Russian sinology. The system of academic authorship, unlike that in which Rossokhin and his colleagues had languished in the eighteenth century, dictated that the career of the scholar be given as much prominence as the texts that scholar produced. Bichurin, with his social graces and skill at networking, was better positioned than anyone else to take advantage; Kamenskii, having retreated to a distant monastery, was hardly a real competitor. Ironically, in the 1840s, Bichurin, by then a member of the Société Asiatique, complained that his Russian contemporaries "preferred French fibs to Russian truth" and that Russian-language studies of the Qing had been unjustly neglected. He did not seem to realize how integral this forgetting had been for the scholarly era he represented.[80]

Chapter 11

Conspiracy and Conquest on the Amur

IN 1860, THE RUSSIAN EMPIRE formally annexed from the Qing about a million square kilometers of territory north and east of the Amur River, the future Russian Far East. Framed by two successive, entangled global conflicts—the Crimean War and the Second Opium War—the final settlement marked the apogee of China's shift, in the eyes of Russian officials, from an Inner Asian competitor to an object of global rivalry with Britain and the United States. Just as Russian academics now followed their Western colleagues in imposing a nineteenth-century Orientalist framework on China, so too did officials come to regard the Qing as defined by helpless backwardness. Although such institutions as the Russian Ecclesiastical Mission would survive and officials would long continue to invoke the legacy of Russia's "special relationship" with the Qing, the conquest changed that relationship irrevocably, both in intellectual and in diplomatic terms. The territorial stability and languid war of position that had persisted on the frontier since 1689 collapsed, turning Russia into just one of many colonial powers fighting over slices of the Qing pie. This would eventually become part of a more general tendency; as Russian armies pushed forward across the empire's borderlands and reform transformed its metropole, Western models became increasingly alluring blueprints for imperial rule.[1] Diplomacy, scholarship, and intelligence would now be underwritten by superior military force instead of substituting for it.

Though the annexation is often seen as a reaction to Russian defeat in Crimea in 1856—a rapid "swing of the pendulum" from West to East—it built on more than a century of plans, schemes, and fantasies nurtured by imperial administrators on the frontier.[2] Already in 1731 Savva Vladislavich was imagining the possibility of a war that would lead to the reconquest of the Amur and, if pursued with more forethought, to the dissolution of the Qing governing apparatus along ethnic lines; he believed this to be an unwise though not an implausible course of action.[3] For Varfolomei Iakobii in the 1750s and his son Ivan in the 1780s, as we have seen, vague plans had given way to concrete proposals. These continued to be revised further: soon after the failed 1805 Golovkin embassy, the former Irkutsk governor Aleksei Kornilov developed an outline for a joint naval and military expedition down the Amur that hinged on the recruitment of a militia from Siberia's own people, an effort to sidestep the need for central involvement. It was not far removed from the actual sequence of events that led up to the annexation, though a collapse in the prestige of Qing power would have to happen in the intervening decades.[4] De facto occupation of the Far East, under Eastern Siberia's governor-general Nikolai Murav'ev, began a decade before the 1860 Treaty of Beijing, when the start of the Crimean War was still three years away.

Instead of creating a predictable path to annexation, however, the long buildup set up a fundamental antagonism between imperial institutions. In the late eighteenth century, the reorganization of Russia's knowledge regime had left the Eastern Siberian periphery of the empire as a neglected outpost of a network now more heavily centered on St. Petersburg. The interests of officials in Irkutsk had long been focused on gaining enough attention from the center to concentrate a large military force on the frontier and instigate a conflict with China, but by the reign of Nicholas I (1825–1855), there was even less sympathy for this project at the court than there had been in the 1790s. Instead, the emperor and his foreign minister Karl Nessel'rode favored a project to advance into the Pacific indirectly by way of the Russian-American Company, without risking a border war. They turned out to be more significant antagonists for Murav'ev than the vast Qing army once feared by Vladislavich. The annexation hinged more on this internal conflict than any armed confrontation between Russian and Qing troops.

Murav'ev's success depended on his ability to persuade the emperor that formal, not informal, imperialism was required in the Far East. To do so, he would have to rely on his mastery of the knowledge regime, which allowed him to manipulate the information that reached the center, cultivate a sense of foreign threat, and leverage the works of intellectuals themselves increasingly

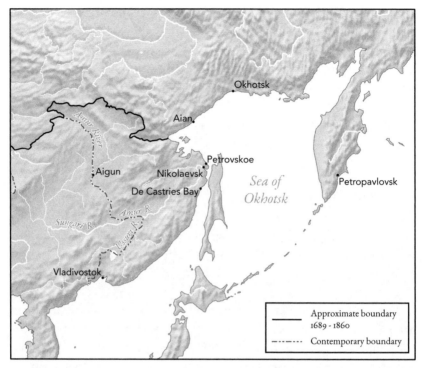

11.1 The Amur frontier in the 1850s.

committed to claiming the Amur for Russia. Generations of Russians inherited a heroic narrative of the conquest with Murav'ev at its center, a story that took shape as a byproduct of these efforts.[5]

The Retreat from the Amur

If Murav'ev is made to be the hero in the story of the annexation, its villain is usually Karl Nessel'rode. Born in 1780 to a globetrotting German diplomat, this elder statesman dominated Russia's Ministry of Foreign Affairs from 1816 until his forced retirement in 1856. In the annexation drama, he is traditionally regarded as passive almost to the point of treason, so dedicated to maintaining stability in the Concert of Europe that he missed ripe opportunities for conquest. Yet his reign as foreign minister saw Russia vastly expand its possessions at the expense of Persia and the Ottoman Empire in the south and finally become embroiled in the catastrophic Crimean War. He was not dogmatically committed to avoiding conflict but sought ways to grow Russian power without risking its reputation abroad.[6]

Nessel'rode saw the stability of the Russo-Qing frontier as a welcome respite from the welter of imperial rivalries elsewhere. The Qing, preoccupied with a gradually mounting internal crisis and certainly lacking any impetus to pursue further territorial gains in Inner Asia, were more than happy to oblige. On the other hand, the Ministry of Foreign Affairs' approach to the "Amur question," as it would soon be called, was in place well before Nessel'rode became foreign minister. In 1806, it took a decisive stand against efforts to exploit the vagueness of the 1689 Nerchinsk agreement for territorial aggrandizement: although "unquestionably the Treaty of Nerchinsk possesses [doubtful points whose] explications offer an opportunity to extract benefits," they could not be used, because "we would have to start a war before making the declarations proposed by the Ministry of Commerce. . . . We would need fifty thousand troops ready to march and above all to suffer the complete extinction of the Kiakhta trade."[7] Not for another century, after the construction of the Trans-Siberian Railroad, did active Russian troop numbers on that frontier even begin to approach this figure; as decades of experience had shown, St. Petersburg would never dedicate sufficient resources to this cause. In effect, as the ministry well knew, the note meant that no revision of the Amur question could ever take place barring fundamental changes on the other side of the border.

Merely obtaining the right of free navigation of the Amur, which the Russian court had imagined as a solution since the 1750s, created as many problems as it solved.[8] As Golovkin himself wrote in 1805, for such a concession to be useful, the Amur would need to be provided with a port at its mouth to transfer goods from river- to oceangoing vessels, as well as supply stops along the thousand-mile course of the river. Then, to protect the goods deposited there, a military force would need to be stationed at each of these points, which would create a permanent source of military tension. Having to rely on Qing subjects or indigenous peoples to sustain an enterprise that would effectively benefit only Russians would make the entire enterprise uneconomical. Even in the highly doubtful event that a purely diplomatic solution to the Amur question could be found, then, there could be no meaningful way for Russia to gain the use of the river without a vast cession of territory.[9] In the absence of any real prospects for gains, there was no justification for ramping up frontier tension.

The effects of Nessel'rode's strategy of détente resonated far beyond the frontier itself. Despite the efforts of the Ministry of Foreign Affairs and the Synod to reform the Russian Ecclesiastical Mission in Beijing in the 1820s, the mission suffered the brunt of the policy's effects. In fact, the reform had ensured that the mission could not be entirely in keeping with the spirit of the diplomatic agreements that facilitated it. For instance, sending bona fide scholars and scientists instead of twentysomething acolytes as "students" and "church servants" was inherently suspect, since the Qing authorities were always adamant that the purpose of the students was to learn languages, no more (and no less, because the students also helped translate diplomatic paperwork at the Lifanyuan). The ministry now decided to minimize any possible objections. Rather than obscuring a campaign of espionage and anti-Qing subversion as it once had, secrecy became an end in itself. In May 1839 the missionary Veniamin Morachevich informed the ministry that he had been asked to serve as executor for the estate of Caetano Pires Pereira, the last Catholic bishop of Beijing. Such a role was in keeping with the mission's century-old tradition of cooperation with Jesuit and other Catholic missionaries in China; in the past, officials had encouraged such contacts as a way of promoting Russian influence at the heart of the Qing state. But its response to this message was furious. "We are deeply disappointed to learn that you have taken upon yourself a task which pertains neither to the Mission nor to its members," the Asiatic Department's vice director L. G. Seniavin wrote to Morachevich that November. "All contacts between the Mission and the Catholic missionaries who secretly reside in China are forbidden by the government. . . . The slightest misstep could have harmful consequences for the Mission."[10] At the very same moment that British authorities were turning to an aggressive military solution to their trade conflict with the Qing, Russians sought to dampen sources of conflict on their end.

Nessel'rode's policy of caution also stretched to include the mission's role in Russia itself. All mention of the possible scientific function of the missionaries was censored from the press for decades. In 1831, Karl Liven (Lieven), the Minister of Education, reprimanded a St. Petersburg censor for not having banned an article in the *Northern Bee* containing letters from the road to Beijing. The accused censor objected that the article had no political content whatsoever, only a description of Mongol customs and medical observations, and that the author was not even a secretly dispatched scientific expert but a mere physician's assistant.[11] In effect, the mission, which was supposed to represent Russia's contribution to the learned world of European sinology, was being black-boxed in the name of preserving stable relations. In 1840, the Academy of Sciences itself was forbidden from naming V. P. Vasil'ev—soon to be one of Russia's most prominent sinologists—as its agent in any journals or publications. "Such a title," Nessel'rode wrote, "if it somehow became known to the Chinese, could excite their suspicions and have harmful consequences for the Mission."[12] No Qing official had ever publicly evinced any knowledge of, much less concern about, the Academy of Sciences or what relationship the missionaries had to it. Though it was, from a certain point of view, pragmatic, Nessel'rode's obsession with secrecy reflected a deep sense of disbelief that any change in Russo-Qing relations could possibly be to Russia's benefit.

Over the course of this long deadlock, impetus for annexation began to build outside the Ministry of Foreign Affairs, bolstered by the work of geographers and other experts—though largely not the Orientalists who had been so laboriously trained under the auspices of the Academy's sinological turn.[13] One axis of the argument was administrative: Was a physical border actually represented on the ground, and if so, did it match Russia's official maps? In 1844–1845 the geographer Aleksandr Middendorf, a prominent supporter of imperial expansion into the Amur region, exceeded his instructions by extending a scientific expedition into the future Far East. Middendorf claimed to have located an entire line of Qing border markers running south and not north of the lower extension of the Stanovoi Mountains, almost up to the Amur delta, a region amounting in his view to some 50,000 additional versts of Russian territory.[14] Yet as he himself must have known—having referred specifically to the first clauses of the Nerchinsk treaty a few pages above— there could be no such thing, since the demarcation had never taken place. Later, Nikolai Akhte claimed to have found evidence justifying even larger claims, which soon turned out to simply be stone cairns used by indigenous people to mark mountain passes.[15] The basically paradoxical argument from border revision in the context of a region explicitly lacking a clear border became a key assumption of the annexationist wing of Russian policy.

The other axis of the argument was ethnographic and historical. It was not merely the location of the putative border markers that determined a Russian claim to the area; it was the attitude of the local population and the legacy of Russia's seventeenth-century colonization project. At one point Middendorf encountered a party of Siberian Cossacks who, it appeared, had been successfully gathering tribute in furs from local indigenous people for some time—which they were able to do by timing the arrival and departure of Qing inspection parties on the river.[16] Unlike subsequent writers on the topic, Middendorf did not deny that the Qing regularly visited the area, collected tribute, and traded with the locals nor that the Qing-subject Evenki (Tungus) regarded themselves and their territory as such. Instead, his argument was that sovereignty was differentiated by terrain, with the lowland peoples adhering to Qing rule and highland Sakha (Yakut) and Evenki ranging freely from Russia across the border. This was in line with his proposal that the border be drawn along the southern edge of the mountains.[17] Middendorf's attitude was equivocal when it came to the question of Russia's historical claims to the region and the loyalty of its inhabitants. He blamed the "terrorism" of the region's seventeenth-century Cossack occupiers for the dismal outcome of the war with the Qing. The central lesson here was not that they had abdicated Russia's claims but that the defeat had been a contingent one—in other words, the region was not necessarily fated by historical destiny to belong to the Qing. This argument would soon be pursued further by proponents of annexation.[18]

Geographical concerns about the navigability of the Amur were more ambiguous and suggested a different, nonterritorial outcome; after all, if the Amur could not be used to transport goods and people from Siberia to the Pacific, it was not worth risking a war to get it. Debates over the river in the 1840s focused on three points of dispute: whether Sakhalin was an island or a peninsula (and hence whether the mouth of the Amur was accessible to ships entering from the north or the south), whether it was too marshy or filled with sandbars to allow entrance, and whether the river itself possessed obstructions to shipping.[19] Each was key to determining the river's value as an economic and logistical engine, and opinions on each shifted repeatedly over the course of the nineteenth century. (Golovkin, for instance, already assumed the river and its mouth were both navigable, an opinion that would seemingly be disproven by subsequent explorations.) An expedition by the

Russian-American Company navigator A. M. Gavrilov in 1847 appeared to confirm that Sakhalin blocked the entrance to the Amur from the south, though it did also show that the river itself was navigable. Contrary to later mythmaking, this did not lead Nicholas I to dismiss the prospects of Far East expansion entirely.[20] It did, however, lead Karl Nessel'rode and his allies to articulate an alternative plan to gain influence in the Pacific.

The Russian-American Company would serve to anchor the plan. Founded in 1799 and given a monopoly over the fur trade in Alaska and other territories outside the Siberian mainland, this organization quickly developed trading outposts and interests all over the North Pacific, from California to Eastern Siberia.[21] The Company was clearly seen as playing a major role in whatever Pacific policy would emerge in the 1850s, especially since it stood to be the major beneficiary: since the eighteenth century, imperial officials had believed that once it was acquired, the Amur's main function would be to facilitate the supply of Russia's Pacific establishments, including both Kamchatka and Alaska.[22] The Company's pursuit of trade and supply routes gave it not only a justification but also a network from which to pursue an agenda of Pacific growth. Perhaps more importantly, its commercial agents were plausibly deniable representatives of the Russian state vis-à-vis Qing authorities but would be able to stake claims to territory on the Amur if European rivals came calling.

In 1843, a special committee was formed under the emperor's oversight to determine courses of action regarding the Amur question; the Nessel'rode alternative soon began to take on a relatively coherent shape, as expressed in a set of instructions sent but not delivered to the Amur explorer Gennadii Nevel'skoi in the summer of 1849.[23] Since the Amur itself seemed to be unpromising, the instructions focused on Sakhalin as a site for settlement—though claimed by the Japanese, it would also be a less problematic location because it did not interfere with Qing territory. (It would eventually be settled in parallel to the Amur delta.) The overriding goal was to maintain secrecy in relation to the Qing but defiance in relation to other foreigners.[24] At the same time, the Company itself was ordered to organize an overland expedition to establish trade with the Nivkh (Giliaks)—the indigenous people who inhabited the Qing-controlled lower Amur.[25] Both Nessel'rode and Nicholas I appeared to be in agreement that this course of action maximized the advantages and minimized the risk of a confrontation; other plans, like an expedition down the Amur or naval patrols around Sakhalin, were rejected as too ambitious.[26] The methods of informal imperialism seemed to offer the best mixture of profit and security.

Annexation in Theory and Practice

The emperor's favored strategy did not win out, however. An influential group of scientific and political actors was already articulating a more ambitious agenda, stressing the need to annex the Amur and not just to expand informally. They included socialists and other political dissidents, but also much more powerful figures—like the tsar's own son Konstantin, who would become head of the Naval Ministry in 1853. In their rhetoric, the absorption of a vast chunk of Qing territory could be a recipe for Siberian social regeneration or for geopolitical revival. More directly, Russia's competitors were also growing bolder. Britain's victory in the First Opium War in 1842 brought it sweeping trade and territorial concessions in the Treaty of Nanjing, and throughout the mid-1840s, a steady drumbeat of other agreements—including those with France and the United States, longtime rivals in the Pacific—made Russia's exclusion from the imperialist partitioning of China painfully obvious. The officials who had established Russia's foreign policy in the region a half century earlier, like Golovkin and Aleksandr Vorontsov, had seen the failure of the 1793 Macartney mission as a reprieve from the British threat. Now this was over: even if the Ministry of Foreign Affairs was still clinging to the old status quo, the Kiakhta trade, which it was so eager to protect, would be doomed without further action.[27] To critics of Nessel'rode, the question no longer revolved around commercial dominance in the North Pacific but the global future of the Russian Empire itself.[28]

The Qing, too, now looked less threatening. Savva Vladislavich and his successors once feared the military force that the Qing could deploy to overwhelm Siberia's frontiers, but the consolidation of Orientalism around sino-skeptical ideas of Chinese backwardness now made victory much more conceivable than it had been in the past. With industrial production and technology now seen as key to military dominance, Qing mastery of large borderland armies and logistics no longer seemed sufficient to counter European might. Discourses of backwardness seemed amply confirmed by the unexpectedly easy British triumph in the First Opium War (1839–42) cast doubt on the idea that southward expansion would require a difficult military campaign. As the erstwhile circumnavigator Ivan Kruzenshtern put it in an 1843 memorandum, "the Chinese government has already agreed to retreat from many of its ancient rules relating to trade with European powers, it will of course concede to its powerful close neighbor the right of free navigation along the Amur, so necessary to Russian trade."[29] China seemed ripe for direct Russian intervention.

The man who brought together these diverse political and intellectual developments into an aggressive policy of formal annexation was Nikolai Nikolaevich Murav'ev, soon to receive the cognomen Amurskii and the title of count for his role in "resolving" the Amur question. Born in 1809, Murav'ev was still a toddler when Nessel'rode took the reins of the empire's foreign policy. After serving with distinction in Russia's brutal counterinsurgency campaign in the Caucasus, he was appointed governor-general of Eastern Siberia in 1847.[30] As soon as he arrived in the province, he set out to reverse the trends that had made it peripheral to imperial diplomacy for decades.

Everything that took place in the thirteen years that followed is veiled in so many layers of self-mythologization and propaganda—not only from Murav'ev but also from his allies and agents—that historians have found it difficult to avoid following in the tracks of the narrative they themselves laid down. In 1860, a visitor to Siberia named Markelov commented skeptically to his relative in an intercepted letter: "The hollowness and insignificance of these fatuous muses is in such contrast to the great work that is supposedly being done in their name that we can only trust in the fortunate star that carries our people where they need to go. In Irkutsk a fatuous gang of comme il faut dandies is playing an unfathomable comedy, a legendary farce known as the governance of Eastern Siberia and the colonization of the Amur."[31] A week later, having met Murav'ev personally, Markelov was already raving that "there is no one more genteel and charming among the greats of this world. . . . This capital of the future great and powerful Siberia contains such troves of human will and intelligence."[32] This was typical of the raptures that greeted Murav'ev at the height of his career and have influenced his reception since, obscuring the pathways that actually led to his celebrated colonial achievements.[33]

Previous frontier administrators with an imperial bent, like the Iakobiis, chafed under the limitations of governing a forgotten borderland. Even though his previous links with the region were minimal, Murav'ev too developed a world view in which Eastern Siberia was Russia's unjustly ignored geopolitical pivot. In 1852, for instance, he complained to his friend Iakov Rostovtsev that "Petersburg rests on its European laurels and cannot inquire into this far-off place," calling himself a "cry in the desert." "Russians who love their fatherland," he argued, must not ignore the mounting influence of Americans and the precariousness of the Qing Dynasty.[34] The following year, as the Crimean War was breaking out in the West, he wrote to Grand Duke Konstantin arguing that "no matter how alarming it would be for us to fight a war with Turkey, England, and France, Russia is so united with its unconditional loyalty to its tsar that no danger can threaten it from that quarter," so the Far East was where its attention should be concentrated instead. This was, of course, a colossally bad prediction.[35] But if St. Petersburg was unwilling to follow his lead, he was happy to take the initiative. By 1854 Murav'ev managed to sideline the Asiatic Department almost completely in dealings with officials in Mongolia and Manchuria.[36] In effect he had recovered all the autonomy Varfolomei Iakobii had possessed a century earlier but with vastly more resources at his disposal.

Murav'ev saw Far East expansion as a zero-sum game: either he would win and end up as the proconsul of a vast new riverine territory, or the Russian-American Company, together with its patrons in the Ministries of Finance and Foreign Affairs, would lead the process and turn the Amur into a mere trading post, short-circuiting the rejuvenation of Siberia. To persuade the emperor to reject the Company, Murav'ev needed to prove the imminence of a foreign military threat, the low risk of a military confrontation with the Qing, and the legal defensibility of a formal territorial annexation; he also proposed various schemes to defang the Company administratively, such as putting it under his control.[37] In 1849, thanks to the support of Murav'ev, Prince Dmitrii Men'shikov, and a few other key figures, an unofficial expedition to the Amur delta was prepared. Its leader would be Gennadii Nevel'skoi, a ship captain assigned to the bark *Baikal* then being built in Kronstadt for transfer to Kamchatka service; Nevel'skoi would carry out his nominal task, the delivery of supplies to Kamchatka, and then sail south and explore Sakhalin and the region around the Amur mouth. The Amur Committee had intended its own secret instructions to be delivered to Nevel'skoi as well, but the ships failed to rendezvous—and the captain already had very definite plans. In the summer of 1849 Nevel'skoi, now Murav'ev's main ally, discovered the full navigability of the Amur and established that Sakhalin was an island. (This meant that navigation was possible, not that it was easy—a distinction that would prove crucial in the coming decades.) This revelation upended the terms of debate in the emperor's special committee.[38]

Nevel'skoi's goal was now to prevent his discovery from being co-opted by the Company, as he made clear to his deputy Dmitrii Orlov in a letter almost comically self-incriminating in tone:

See for yourself after reading this paper what kind of caper I'm pulling. The dirtbags [*podletsy*] at the Main Directorate [of the Russian-American Company], spies of that dirtbag the Minister of Foreign Affairs [Nessel'rode], they'll get squat [*shish*]. My friend Dmitrii Ivanovich, adopt the rule that the more we see a man as an enemy the more politely we have to act. . . . I promise you that if everything is good, i.e. peaceful, calm, your actions brave, etc., as I wrote, and we discussed—*A ship came up; the Giliaks demand vassalization; we were forced to occupy Cape Kuegda*—we will be showered in honors. Your family will be provided for. For Christ's sake courage—and politeness to whomever necessary (Koshevarov [director of the Russian-American Company facility at Aian] and the Company), let them take their pennies. Let the sheep be whole and the wolves be sated . . . P.S. Destroy this letter and do not keep it lest someone gets his hands on it. Care is needed everywhere.[39]

In the context of ongoing events, the letter's elliptical phraseology is easily decodable. In the summer of 1850 Nevel'skoi established an outpost on Cape Kuegda on the Amur, which would later become Nikolaevsk, and raised the Russian naval flag there. Orlov was left behind at Petrovskoe in Shastya Bay, north of the Amur. With the first postal vessel, he was to send Murav'ev a report, whose principal contents were prepared by Nevel'skoi well in advance and would form the basis of the argument for annexation: (1) a foreign vessel was seen approaching the mouth from the south, which could only mean a British or American ship aiming to seize the delta; (2) the local Nivkh were demanding that the tsar take them under his protection both from Qing tribute collectors and foreigners; (3) the occupation of Nikolaevsk had been necessitated by a forced wintering whose survivors were now experiencing extreme hunger and would need to be supplied by an expedition down the Amur. Murav'ev would then dispatch this report to St. Petersburg to justify a further occupation of Qing territory. The first two points did indeed feature prominently in the governor-general's reports.[40] The third, which was to provide a diplomatic pretext for the Amur expedition, was kept in abeyance until the expedition itself could be prepared—but by that time the Crimean War and the (soon justified) desire to protect the Amur delta from Anglo-French attack offered a more convenient rationale.[41] Manipulating the intelligence that reached St. Petersburg about the Amur delta was essential for countering the Russian-American Company.

Nevel'skoi accompanied his scheming with tight control over the information that emerged from the lower Amur. Everyone capable of writing a firsthand report was brought into the plot as a confidant; the detail about the Amur provisioning expedition, for instance, seems to have originated with the Kamchatka commandant and longtime Russian-American Company hand Vasilii Zavoiko.[42] Others were placed under stringent observation. In May 1850 Nevel'skoi informed Murav'ev's deputy Mikhail Korsakov of his order that any Cossacks with a knowledge of the Sakha language were to be excluded from the expedition and sent back because their gossip could not be controlled: "During the winter they will drink a bit and start telling God knows what stories. . . . Besides there are already two retired Cossacks snooping around that region."[43] His letter to Orlov made clear that it was essential to send reports to Murav'ev via private letters only, because otherwise an official of the Russian-American Company with the right to read his reports might learn about his activities and report them to Nessel'rode.[44] This obsession with secrecy applied only to fellow agents of the Russian Empire—specifically those aligned with the Nessel'rode faction as opposed to Governor-General Murav'ev. According to his own testimony, the captain made no similar effort to conceal his activities from Qing or foreign actors; in fact, he strove to make them as obvious as possible to any visitor to the area. For this purpose he gave the local Nivkh a proclamation proudly informing "all foreign vessels" that the entire region—including not only the Amur but the entire future Far East down to the Korean border—was now officially Russian territory.[45] In St. Petersburg, by contrast, any mentions of "navigation on the Amur," including Russia's territorial claims to these lands, were censored from the press even in 1855.[46] The informational rift between

St. Petersburg and Eastern Siberia enabled a system of differential secrecy to bolster the fait accompli being created on the ground.

Making Russia's claims explicit to the locals was also key for establishing a legal basis for the annexation. While agreeing with Middendorf that it was ultimately the shortsightedness of the Muscovite state that had allowed the region to be lost, Nevel'skoi nevertheless argued that "simply by means of establishing themselves on [the Amur]'s shores, [the Cossacks] gave Russia the incontrovertible right to reclaim this country." This right was supposedly substantiated by the geographical nuances of the 1689 treaty, the geophysical relationship between the Amur and the trans-Baikal region, and finally by the failure of the Qing to construct any fortresses east of Aigun. By not doing so, "they left the middle and lower Amur with its tributaries in the same position in which Poiarkov had found them in 1644, that is, free [svobodnym]."[47]

This was why Nevel'skoi's very first concern upon arriving in the delta was securing a formal attestation of Russian rule from the local Nivkh (Giliaks). In his famous account of his disembarkation, he "came up to the senior Manchu, whom the Giliaks called a janggin, which means rich old man or merchant." After a circular discussion about each man's "right" to be there, Nevel'skoi "took out a double-barreled pistol, pointed it at the Manchus, and announced that if any of them dared to move to carry out his order they would immediately be killed." Thereupon, the Nivkh, in this telling, took the side of the Russian, and the Manchu was forced to admit at gunpoint that he was there without official authorization and that there were no Manchu fortresses in the area of the delta at all.[48] Nevel'skoi is an unreliable narrator: janggin denotes the rank of captain in Manchu, suggesting that his opponent was in fact a representative of the Manchu state, despite the implication that it did not claim the settlement. Moreover, we know from Zavoiko's correspondence that Nevel'skoi had to beat and abuse his Nivkh allies, presumably to extract from them the request for Russian protection he already knew he needed.[49] It is no surprise, then, that when he described his secret plan to Orlov, he stressed that the officer must write in his report that "the Giliaks demand vassalization," as he himself did in his own reporting.[50]

Nevel'skoi and Murav'ev had to work equally hard to establish the existence of a foreign threat to the Amur. This was, of course, a perennial obsession of Murav'ev's, one that was apparently borne out by the preparations for

Commodore Perry's expedition to Japan in 1852.[51] In May 1852 Nevel'skoi reported that his scouts had learned of foreign missionaries "who spread unfavorable rumors about us among the locals and Manchus, that we want to massacre or enslave them, that we are sending whole armies of cannibals."[52] The reports of the missionary in question, almost certainly a member of the Missions Étrangères de Paris named Venault, have survived—but his attitude to the Russians was different from Nevel'skoi's menacing picture. When he heard rumors among the locals that "the Russians were going to take possession of the country," he wrote that he regarded this possibility as an act of "Divine providence"; like many European agents, he preferred the rule even of a schismatic Christian power to unpredictable heathen caprice.[53] There was as yet little concrete evidence that a French or British threat was imminent.

For the moment, this campaign to construct a foreign threat along with indigenous legitimacy was unsuccessful. At a meeting of the Amur Committee in February 1851, Nevel'skoi was chastised for his unauthorized establishment of the outpost of Nikolaevsk; although the tsar disagreed with Nessel'rode and the other commissioners and rewarded Nevel'skoi handsomely, he nonetheless supported the reversion of the outpost to the Russian-American Company. The understanding that the Company would retain at least nominal leadership in the Amur project persisted until 1854, though Nessel'rode and the tsar lacked any practical means of withdrawing Nevel'skoi's conquests from the governor-general's de facto control.[54] Both sides seemed to be scoring points. In 1853 Nicholas decreed unilaterally that the Russian border would now include the territory occupied by Nevel'skoi.[55] But that same year, Nessel'rode waited until Murav'ev had left the country to issue a note to the Qing Bureau of Foreign Tributaries (Lifanyuan) in which he reasserted the ministry's longstanding interpretation of the Treaty of Nerchinsk: that rivers running north of the mountain chain east of the Gorbitsa River belonged to Russia and rivers to the south of it were Qing property—in other words, that the entire Amur was acknowledged as Qing territory. The note made no mention of any new claims on the Amur mouth.[56]

The Crimean War proved to be the factor that most decisively undermined Nessel'rode's case. By 1854 Murav'ev was already testing the waters by sending expeditions down the Amur. These were intended in equal measure to facilitate the military reinforcement of Russian ports in the region, to test the river's navigability for large-scale shipping projects, and to demonstrate that the Qing would not put up resistance to the attempt. A projected demarcation meeting with Qing officials in those years failed in part as a result of communication problems and in part because Murav'ev deliberately evaded it.[57] Instead, he argued to local Qing authorities that he needed to anticipate a planned British occupation of the Amur delta and therefore urgently needed to reinforce Russian outposts there with more armaments and supplies. The spring 1854 expedition was brilliantly timed to forestall an Anglo-French raid by a small flotilla, which took place in August of that year and was defeated in part because of the reinforcements Murav'ev had shipped to Petropavlovsk via the river. (The ships had arrived in pursuit of a Russian vessel, and there is no indication that the British became aware of Russian settlements in the delta until the following year.)[58] The same justification was then offered for the next expedition. On both occasions, Qing border officials allowed the Russians through, vainly specifying that this was to be a one-time arrangement, since they had no military resources with which to resist an advance; for Murav'ev, this was merely evidence that the Qing were on the brink of being convinced to give Russia control of the entire left bank of the Amur and the maritime region east of the Ussuri. In fact, it was nothing of the kind: imperial edicts to the Heilongjiang governor-general continued to reaffirm the importance of protecting the area from Russian seizure.[59] On the Russian side, however, the arrival of foreign attackers had wholly justified the notion of a foreign threat and convinced everyone involved that an informal policy was no longer practicable.

The next step was to formalize the Amur establishment as a Russian administrative unit. Murav'ev had earlier received official approbation and a medal from the Russian Geographical Society for abolishing the port of Okhotsk and moving its facilities to Petropavlovsk. (The humiliatingly poor conditions at Okhotsk had long been a byword for the empire's languishing Pacific policy.) When the pro-annexationist tsar Alexander II ascended to the throne in 1855, the next step lay open. Despite the Kamchatka port's successful defense against enemy attack, in 1856 Murav'ev was able to persuade the emperor that it too was unsustainable and indefensible; it had been evacuated after the repulse and was ransacked by Anglo-French troops. Nevel'skoi's progress in the lower Amur meant that Nikolaevsk was already set up to replace Petropavlovsk. It is likely that this had been planned since the very beginning, since a major port at Petropavlovsk could not be made agriculturally self-supporting; all pretense of Nikolaevsk being a commercial outpost was now abandoned, while Nevel'skoi himself was speedily put out to pasture as a dangerous loose cannon. The new city was made the capital of the new Primorskii Krai, which now incorporated Kamchatka and the entire Pacific coast.[60] Nessel'rode had already been dismissed from his post a few months earlier by the new emperor. The Russian-American Company, meanwhile, lost almost 150,000 rubles from its participation in the Amur project, a contributing though not a decisive factor in its gradual decline as a viable commercial entity.[61] The strategy of formal annexation had won out, but the entire Pacific strategy of the Russian Empire had now come to hinge on a territory it did not yet formally possess.

Power without Knowledge

"After taking [the Amur]," wrote an American observer of the conquest, the Russians "contrived to have it ceded to them by treaty. . . . Honest Uncle Sam has occasionally acquired territory in much the same way."[62] But making the seizure official required a different set of tools from the intra-Russian wrangling that had allowed Murav'ev to defeat the Russian-American Company. To formalize the annexation of the Far East, Murav'ev would have to turn his attention away from St. Petersburg and toward Beijing. Like Varfolomei Iakobii before him, he had already secured for himself the right to carry on frontier negotiations with Mongolian and Manchurian authorities. The problem now was how to translate this authority into success at the Qing court. With the Ministry of Foreign Affairs pushing from the west and Murav'ev from the north, Russo-Qing diplomacy was fragmented and contradictory; though the Russians knew more than the Qing, who believed that Russia had soundly defeated Britain in the Crimean War, Russia's intelligence remained flawed and its image of Qing politics at odds with reality.[63] As Russian troops set up permanent residence on the Amur, the empire's diplomats convinced themselves that they were on the brink of a historic Russo-Chinese rapprochement.

Murav'ev's case for annexation had been strongly bolstered by the apparent absence of a formal response from his counterparts on the other side of the border, despite multiple formal notifications. The Qing authorities in the

Amur region—particularly the governor-generals of Sahaliyan Ula, stationed at Aigun—made no concrete effort whatsoever to resist their gradual dispossession, although they were certainly aware of it as it was taking place (if not perhaps of the full dimensions of the crisis). In large part, this indecisiveness stemmed from their near-total abandonment by Beijing, which constantly urged them to stiffen their spines without providing any troops, resources, or guidance for how far they should go in doing so. With all significant Qing military assets engaged in fighting the Taiping forces and subsequently (after the outbreak of the Second Opium War in 1856) the Western invaders to the south, an armed response was hopeless, and the Russians could hardly be expected to leave the Amur peacefully.[64]

It was not until 1860, ten years after the initial Russian occupation of the delta, that the Qing Dynasty finally surrendered its northeastern territories. It was the culmination of an arduous and deception-filled diplomatic process that led to disappointment for three successive Russian negotiators and an arguably accidental victory for the fourth. In 1857–1858 Evgenii Putiatin first failed in getting the Qing government to admit him as an envoy and then made himself invaluable to the Anglo-French invaders and rode their coattails to sign the trade-oriented Treaty of Tianjin. In 1858 Murav'ev gained what he thought was formal cession of the Amur and the Maritime Region from the Aigun governor Yishan. In 1858–1859 his translator Perovskii was sent to secure final Qing ratification of both treaties but instead witnessed the repudiation of Murav'ev's Aigun agreement by the emperor. At last, in 1860 the new resident ambassador Nikolai Ignat'ev artfully maneuvered between the Western armies besieging Beijing and the Qing court, persuading each that his mediation was to their benefit; his reward was the Treaty of Beijing, which not only formally ceded the Far East but guaranteed Russia unprecedented commercial and diplomatic access to Qing territory.[65] The overall outcome of this unequal treaty represented the outermost limit of what the Russians could have hoped for in 1849, especially once the Ussuri region's southern tip (never mentioned by anyone before the treaties were signed) became the major Russian port on the Pacific, Vladivostok, in the decades after 1860. Russian officials and the liberal reformists who hoped for so much from their new possession could also take pride in having achieved a conquest that was effectively bloodless, even when their hopes for the territory began to decline.[66]

The Treaty of Beijing did not benefit from the expertise of the reformed Russian Ecclesiastical Mission. The Asiatic Department's training policies had gained Russia new successes in Xinjiang thanks to Ivan Zakharov and Egor Kovalevskii, mission graduates who helped negotiate advantageous new treaties in the region in the 1840s. But in Beijing, Archimandrite Palladii (Kafarov) struggled to escape the information vortex of the capital and provide useful advice.[67] He was also hemmed in by Putiatin's formal authority. Approached by Qing negotiators, he noted in his diary that "circumstances had brought them to the false conclusion that I have some influence over the Count. False hopes!"[68] For over a century Russian intelligence had been expected to serve as a substitute for coercive power; now, when power was available, knowledge seemed increasingly redundant.

It was secrecy in relation to other Europeans rather than intelligence in China that meant the difference between failure and success at this juncture. As Ignat'ev wrote in his final report, one of his principal objectives was "bearing in mind that the English expedition was effectively directed against us, to turn their attention away from our unfinished business with China."[69] In this, Russian diplomats were entirely successful, even if their British counterparts had come to the negotiations equipped with a copy of Iakinf Bichurin's map of Beijing.[70] Just as the Earl of Buckinghamshire had complained about his inability to secure reliable intelligence about Russo-Chinese relations in the 1750s, a century later both Lord Wodehouse (1857) and Sir John Crampton (1860) would find themselves unable to pierce the "system of secrecy" that protected "the proceedings of [the Russian] Government on its Asiatic frontiers."[71] As a result, the British were never in a position to understand just how much Russia stood to gain or lose from its negotiations with the Qing or how much their own unwitting cooperation was assisting their geopolitical rivals.

Yet the Russians were not the masters of the situation either. Murav'ev was driven not by concrete intelligence but by the idea that what he was doing was both justified and desirable for the Qing and that his imperialist policy could be a form of anti-imperialist solidarity grounded in a sense of Russia and China's special relationship.[72] When it came to the occupation of the Amur delta, Murav'ev seems to have been sincerely convinced that the Qing would also find it desirable to protect it from British encroachments through Russian occupation—but "if the Chinese will not desire to understand the sincerity of our considerations and will resist them in an English spirit [*uzhe v dukhe Angliiskom*], then, of course, there will be no injustice on our side in opening this necessary route for us by military means." Only if the British had succeeded in subverting Qing thinking, in other words, could the Qing emperor find fault with the Russian proposal.[73] As Murav'ev's successes in the region mounted, so did his aspirations for the unequal Russo-Qing alliance he fully expected would result. On two occasions in 1858, he sent envoys to Urga, the Mongolian capital, with explanations of his position. The first offered Russian mediation in the Second Opium War.[74] The second, sent after the conclusion of the Aigun negotiations, was more loquacious and direct in its logic. Because of the "helplessness and indifference" of the Qing government, it needed a "support" in Russia to prevent the "greedy" English from seizing Qing territory, which would certainly happen "if the Chinese government does not unite with Russia and persists in being suspicious of its actions and demands." The entire Amur episode had now been rewritten in the language of anti-imperial imperialism—an altruistic Russian effort to protect its neighbors, who were unable and unwilling to protect themselves.[75]

The framework of anti-imperial imperialism was also built into the calculations surrounding the eventual Treaty of Beijing. In 1858 the Russian envoy Putiatin had offered the Qing a significant shipment of modern weapons and artillery, which was agreed to and then rejected as Russo-Qing negotiations fell apart. Putiatin had envisioned this as the beginning of an effort to "form a regular army with orders to fortify the principal points of the state against external invasion," with a naval component to follow. In effect it would be the kernel of a military occupation whose goal would be to "bring China into a position, not at all fearsome to European powers, but such that a handful of foreigners could not shake the current government to its foundations at will, as well as offering it the means to prevent disastrous internal uprisings."[76] With the demise of this initial overture, the next negotiator, Nikolai Ignat'ev, concluded that the best way to drive the point home and shock the Qing out of their noncommittal attitude would be for the Anglo-French allied forces to teach the Qing a "hard lesson" that would "finally convey to the Manchu government a sense of its own powerlessness." As he eventually put it to a commission of Qing high officials, "It is time for you to understand . . . that Russia alone can save you." Ultimately, the final treaty, as signed by Ignat'ev in Beijing in 1860, did include a provision for weapons shipments; training was conducted on the Mongolian border in 1861, at which point the Qing government withdrew from the program.[77] As Qing diplomats realized, Murav'ev's fantasies about Russia's paternal embrace were not as benevolent as they seemed to be.

Even the large-scale strategic views of Russian diplomats were strikingly disconnected from reality, envisioning a much more extensive entanglement between Russia and the Qing than circumstances dictated. Putiatin projected a limited Russian military protectorate accompanied by the establishment of a vast network of Orthodox schools and relying commercially on a major expansion of overseas trade. The Russian Ecclesiastical Mission would then serve as the nucleus of Russian political and diplomatic influence in the capital. In the near term, the most serious concern was securing Russian participation in an Anglo-French expedition to suppress the Taipings, which Putiatin judged to be imminent. Nothing of this ultimately came to pass.[78] Ignat'ev's more modest 1861 reflections on the means for properly implementing the Treaty of Beijing were somewhat more realistic, but he still envisioned Chinese merchants circulating through Siberia and Russians acting "as one" with the Qing against the powerful khanate of Khoqand in Central Asia. Not only did this not happen, Russia's most accomplished negotiator in Beijing also entirely failed to anticipate the Treaty of Tarbagatai, signed three years later, by which Russia acquired a vast swath of western Xinjiang— an additional land grab that derived from a creative interpretation of his own treaty's second article.[79] The future of Russo-Qing relations would involve ever-growing colonial aggression, not a new era of Eurasian unity.

With Russian coercive power on the rise, the significance of "soft power" institutions began to fade. Despite optimistic predictions of an Orthodox network in China, the Russian Ecclesiastical Mission was not due for a massive expansion of its portfolio (even if it did begin to acquire converts in greater numbers). Archimandrite Palladii constituted the apex of the mission's influence on Russo-Qing diplomacy. In December 1860, after the ratification of the Treaty of Beijing and Ignat'ev's attendant return to Eastern Siberia, the new archimandrite Gurii (Karpov) attempted to step into his predecessor's shoes and make policy in the Qing capital. He sent Ignat'ev a memorandum outlining future ways to assume the role of imperial protector of the dynasty, guaranteeing external loans and training Qing armies to defeat the Taipings. He also attempted to obtain an audience with Prince Gong, the primary Qing negotiator of the Treaty of Beijing, and was summarily refused.[80] Gurii's reports did not impress Ignat'ev. "The leader of our Ecclesiastical Mission in Beijing is entertaining desires of having the same influence in the Chinese capital as the Russian envoy had under extraordinary circumstances," he wrote in a memorandum, "but he should keep in mind that the objective of the mission is ecclesiastical and scientific, not political; the leader of our mission should not enter into open political relations with the Chinese government."[81] Ballusec, Ignat'ev's successor as Beijing resident, was then instructed to take charge of the mission and ensure that none of its members caused "misunderstandings, idle talk, and unfounded actions that can have an unfavorable effect on affairs" by entering into any sort of formal contact with Qing officials.[82] After a century and a half, the role of the mission as a central mediating diplomatic force between Russia and the Qing had come to an end.

When the Russian Empire annexed the future Far East, it seemed to resolve the basic contradictions of Russian intelligence on the southeast frontier. There was no longer any need to decide whether to strengthen Eastern Siberia for an Inner Asian war of conquest or to counter British actions in the Pacific. Although both direct and indirect routes seemed to be available in the 1840s, Murav'ev had skillfully manipulated the internal structures of the imperial knowledge regime to show that only the former could connect these two paradigms of Russian intelligence, convincing the emperor to ratify a conquest that was already underway. Yet the count and his allies were themselves trapped in the framework of anti-imperial imperialism, a conceptual scheme that was increasingly out of touch with the reality of Russian colonial expansion in East Asia. As Russians moved back into the territory their ancestors had left behind in 1689, they had more power but not much more knowledge.

Conclusion

In 1925, the Soviet Union's most prominent Orientalist scholar—the turcologist V. V. Bartol'd—criticized his colleague Sergei Ol'denburg for claiming that "Russia, the Orient's neighbor, always knew and understood it well." He thought it would be more accurate to say that "Russia, the Orient's neighbor, despite their proximity, often preferred reading bad Western books about the Orient to studying it directly."[1] Such a view would not have seemed unduly pessimistic to a Russian engaged in the study of China after the mid-nineteenth century. In fact, reading Western books—bad or good—was what defined Russian sinology as a discipline. It had emerged out of the same rivalry with Britain and other great powers that made the annexation of the Russian Far East seem inevitable and urgent. Intellectual preeminence, commercial advantage, and territorial aggrandizement wove together into a vision of global supremacy, in which the Qing Empire was increasingly not the opposing team but the ball. Knowledge—parallel transnational economies of secrets and of academic prestige—lay at the heart of this vision.

To a seventeenth-century Muscovite, this construction would have appeared disconcerting. Russia's business was not in dominating the globe; it was in probing and strengthening its connections to the "first part of the universe," the Asian world abutting its new Siberian hinterland. This required collecting and assembling knowledge from many different sources—Jesuit scholars and educated diplomats alongside all sorts of nonelite informants, often people themselves of Inner Asian origin. The purpose of the resulting knowledge was not to showcase Russia's splendor to Western Europeans but to facilitate its control over Siberia and the enrichment of the Muscovite state. If Western Europeans sought access to what the Russians produced, this was a potential source of danger, not proof of Muscovy's cultural maturity. And interested they were. Perhaps at no point before 1860 were intellectuals in England and the Netherlands more diligent in finding and translating Russian texts about Northeast Asia than they were in the seventeenth century. Seeing them as the raw material of ethnographic investigation, they adapted them for use in landmark compendia like Nicolaas Witsen's *Noord en oost Tartarye*. Russian secrets had become public in Europe without ever having been public in Muscovy.

An eighteenth-century Russian working in the system produced by Peter's reforms would have been equally puzzled by both the nineteenth-century and the seventeenth-century models. In that era, China emerged as both a regional rival and an important commercial partner; the improvised, pluralistic approach of the Muscovites had become an institutional bureaucracy where experiments were tempered by rigid hierarchy. It developed expert translators at the Russian Ecclesiastical Mission, but they would not be permitted to develop into autonomous, high-status intellectuals. Small wonder, then, that the "salons of St. Petersburg" preferred what "Montesquieu or Voltaire, or Jesuit letters" had to say about China to "anything Ilarion Rossokhin could ever expect to write."[2] The "noblest commerce" of intellectual exchange between the Academy of Sciences and the Jesuits developed with wide ambitions, but it remained a subordinate part of the much larger knowledge-making apparatus aimed at the Qing empire. The Moscow-Beijing trade caravan, its most concrete manifestation, became a nexus of multiple institutions with overlapping and sometimes conflicting intelligence goals.

The stakes for this new intelligence regime rose abruptly in the middle of the eighteenth century. As Qing armies overran the lands of the Junghars, the Russian Empire began to build out a frontier intelligence network aimed not only at gathering information but at subverting Qing control over the borderlands. Knowledge, as produced by an array of indigenous informants, merchants, spies, and local officials in Eastern Siberia and the Siberian Line fortresses, seemed to offer the key to regional hegemony without risking a war that would overwhelm Russia's fragile garrisons. It was not to be public in any sense; on the frontier, secret negotiations and covert cross-border infiltrations offered the possibility of spectacular coups. None of them materialized. Qing consolidation crushed the personal links that had tied Kiakhta to Mongolia and forestalled Russian efforts to make gains in Xinjiang; by the time the Torghuts (Kalmyks) fled eastward in 1771 and secret Russian efforts failed at returning them, it had become clear that knowledge was no substitute for power.

The apparent failure of intelligence to give Russia a decisive advantage in Inner Asia, far from making intelligence irrelevant, accelerated the consolidation of a new politics of knowledge that redefined and centralized its role. As momentum waned on the eastern frontier, the empire's rapid ascent to world power status under Catherine II encouraged Russian elites to see their relationship with China in global terms. At the same time, Russia's most ambitious rivals—Britain and France—began to regard the North Pacific as a new arena of imperial competition. Globe-spanning conspiracies, like Móric Benyovszky's tale of a planned Anglo-Russian assault on China, haunted the dreams of imperial policy makers; plots and counterplots snaked between Paris, London, St. Petersburg, Beijing, Kyoto, and Alaska. They became a substitute for the deployment of significant armed forces, because no European state yet had the capacity to dominate the region militarily. Ultimately, these efforts at achieving dominance without open war terminated with the failed Macartney and Golovkin embassies of 1793 and 1805.

With the globalization of Russo-Qing relations, the last piece of the nineteenth-century model fell into place. The main audience for Russian knowledge making about the Qing was no longer the empire's internal bureaucracy but the European scholarly community, envisioned through discourses of both prestige and utility as key to the colonial project. At the same time, Eastern Siberia under Nikolai Murav'ev reclaimed its role as a frontier of covert action by manipulating the bureaucratic structures of the empire and conjuring up an imminent foreign threat to justify the annexation of the Russian Far East. Even at this late date, however, knowledge did not become power—even if secrecy could. Russian diplomats operated on premises about the Qing that turned out to be groundless but were aided by the inability of the British to discern Russian intentions. Few of the basic features of eighteenth-century intelligence—its uncertainty, its trust in high-level narratives over low-level operatives, its institutional diversity—disappeared as the Russian Empire's colonial agenda became more explicit. What had changed was its relative position in the Imperial Russian knowledge regime, now dominated by professional, disciplined academics with their eyes on Western books.

IN 1932, the Soviet historian M. A. Polievktov argued that "the scholarly vanguard of Russian capitalism's colonial assault on the Caucasus, the 'academic' caucasology of the eighteenth and nineteenth centuries, had its direct antecedent in the caucasological investigations carried out by Muscovy in the seventeenth," leaving the nature of their "mutual entanglement with each other and with the policy of Russian capitalism" as an exercise for future scholars.[3] In *Spies and Scholars,* I have tried to reconstruct this relationship for a different region, one that would mostly never fall under the Russian Empire's control. To explain the transition, I have focused on changes in the organization of knowledge, using the overarching model of a knowledge regime. Knowledge regimes encapsulate the entire complex of state-based, autonomous, and semiautonomous institutions that allow a state's policy makers to make decisions; they evolve in unpredictable ways, responding both to broader shifts in intellectual climate and to changes in relative standing between individual people and institutions. Unlike a focus on states and networks, the knowledge regime model stresses that they are both heterogeneous, distributed, and structured by a relationship to state power.

The figure at the heart of the imperial knowledge regime was the expert. Early modern experts have been central to much recent scholarship in the history of science, which focuses on the ways in which they negotiated relationships between different domains of knowledge—for instance, by creating theoretical frameworks around fields of specialized craft knowledge and by offering themselves to state patrons as high-status representatives of those fields.[4] In fields such as medicine or mining, the expert's privileged position at the hinge of early modern craft and modern technoscience appears straightforward. But the Russian Empire's experts on China did not have the autonomy or the marketable skills associated with scientific experts, because no one except the state was buying what they were selling. They were products of the internal processes of the bureaucratic order, which controlled their training, their employment, and the destination of the intelligence they manufactured. The knowledge regime was inherently dependent on these actors but also trapped them in constricting institutional frameworks. Only in the early nineteenth century did Russian experts gain the prestige and autonomy associated with modern scholars and academics, and this shift was consciously driven by a new state orientation toward the marketplace of academic knowledge.

The imperial knowledge regime controlled and housed experts, but on a higher level, it also structured relationships between institutions and types of knowledge—especially, in the context of Russia's intellectual encounter with China intelligence and scholarship. One was made in bureaucracies such as the College of Foreign Affairs, without the expectation of public access and with the overall goal of protecting the security of the state. The other, concerned with theoretical abstractions and other findings lacking immediate practical use, was produced and circulated in outward-facing public institutions such as the Academy of Sciences. The emergence of the latter as a dominant paradigm was neither inevitable nor a corollary of modernization or Westernization. Indeed, scholarship had played significant roles in the seventeenth and eighteenth centuries (albeit mostly, in the former case, through non-Russians), but in both eras it was consciously subordinated to other priorities. These choices resulted most significantly from the Russian Empire's changing sense of its place in the world.

To fully understand the role of intellectuals in the European colonial project, then, we need to understand the emergence of intellectuals as a contingent historical category. In the Russian Empire, this emergence was made possible by constructions of state interest that went beyond the quotidian motivations of needing useful personnel to staff a bureaucracy. Autonomy—the factor that subsequently made it possible for them to stake out positions against or at a distance from colonialism—was part of the complex of traits associated with an ideal intellectual, along with social status and the ability to generate prestige through academic authorship on a transnational scale. Scholarly conversations about the participation of Russian Orientalists in Russia's imperial expansion in its Asian borderlands, or their resistance to it, need to take into account the two centuries in which that participation was an inherent assumption of the imperial knowledge regime and offered the ultimate motivation for intellectual work.

Despite their newfound autonomy, however, nineteenth-century Russian intellectuals mostly proved eager to endorse Russia's assumption of colonial tutelage over the Qing. In the course of the nineteenth century, the history of the Russo-Qing relationship began to be rewritten as a morality tale about the failure of eighteenth-century Russians to understand and seize the moment for state advantage. The first systematic, documentary historical overviews, composed by N. N. Bantysh-Kamenskii around 1803 and by Pavel Divov around 1804, tell the story of a diplomatic connection like any other, in which periods of calm followed periods of crisis and where one party or the other gained the upper hand at different moments.[5] Thereafter, a new kind of emplotment came to the fore: the past two hundred years had been a series of missed opportunities to prevent the loss of the Amur, establish a relationship of diplomatic equality, and forestall the ascendancy of British competition. In an essay written in 1818, Stepan Lipovtsov and Pavel (not yet Pëtr) Kamenskii bemoaned the precedent set by a century of Russian bowing and scraping and declared that no diplomatic attempt to extract concessions from the Qing could possibly succeed.[6] Nevel'skoi treated the earliest Russo-Qing interactions as a promissory note to be redeemed by future encounters and the entire eighteenth century as a failure to do so, save for the proposals of a few brave visionaries.[7] By the time the Russian Far East was annexed in the 1850s, the seizure had come to be seen as the telos of the entire relationship. In 1859, the prominent sinologist and missionary V. P. Vasil'ev compiled a study of the eighteenth-century treaties and found it puzzling that the Russian Empire had allowed itself to be bound by such "humiliating" terms; at the time, there was "no one to see things clearly," and therefore these "omissions and mistakes" had been allowed. By contrast, as he had written earlier, the Treaty of Tianjin's "opening" of China was a greater victory for "the common enlightenment of humanity" than Poltava, Austerlitz, Waterloo, and the conquests of Alexander the Great. Henceforth Russia's world-historical greatness would be vouchsafed by having China as its junior partner.[8]

This triumphalist narrative, in which Russia's colonial dominance over China after 1850 was seen as absolving the sins of past neglect, became the prevailing understanding in the late imperial period.[9] Even the Russian Ecclesiastical Mission had finally achieved its destiny after the 1860 Treaty of Beijing, because Murav'ev's heroism left it free to pursue religious goals without being rendered "humiliated," "downtrodden," "rightless and defenseless" by its ambiguous position in the capital.[10] The Buriat doctor and intellectual Pëtr Badmaev reinterpreted the post-1850 era as the culmination of three centuries of peaceful coexistence between the "Russo-Christian" and

"Buddhist-Bogdykhan" worlds; Russia's intervention in the Second Opium War and its willingness to return Ili in 1881 after having seized it during the Dungan Revolt was final proof of its essentially benevolent attitude toward China.[11] Whether seen in revanchist terms or as a demonstration of the "special relationship" Russia had to China, Russian colonialism was returning matters to their rightful place after the anomaly of the post-Nerchinsk era.[12] When V. M. Florinskii—an obstetrician who turned to history to promote his racialized historical theories—published Bantysh-Kamenskii's work in 1881, it was to demonstrate the importance of Russo-Chinese relations to the centuries-old project of the "dissemination of Western Aryan civilization to the Asiatic East." The book became one of the most frequently referenced source compendia in later historiography.[13]

Unsurprisingly, Soviet historians did not at first share the views of late imperial writers on the Amur annexation. One of the most influential early Soviet writers on the initial period of Russo-Qing relations, B. G. Kurts, took a judicious approach to the question, concluding that while the Russian objective in the eighteenth century had been commercial rather than territorial, declarations about the peacefulness of Russian gains were "obviously not applicable" to the subsequent period. Kurts seems to have been responding to a widespread early Soviet assumption that the Russian attitude was uniformly (rather than episodically) imperialist and territorially expansionist; he also took pains to emphasize that at the time of its signing the Muscovite state was fully satisfied with the Treaty of Nerchinsk despite its territorial concessions.[14] For a state concerned about overcoming the legacy of tsarist imperialism in other ways, a skeptical attitude to past annexations was a natural consequence.

It was in the 1950s, as Sino-Soviet disputes heated up on the world stage, that the study of Russo-Qing diplomacy began both to flourish in the Soviet Union and to take a characteristically pro-Russian position. Pëtr Kabanov's 1959 study of the Amur question, still one of the most highly referenced works on the annexation period, sketched out the outlines of this approach. Writing before the formal Sino-Soviet split, Kabanov emphasized how the Far East was now home to "two great socialist states marching forward on the path to communism. A great process of construction is now taking place on both sides of the Amur, on both sides of the border set up a hundred years ago." It was the fact that the 1850s demarcation was "peaceful" that had enabled this to take place.[15] Like Nevel'skoi, Kabanov was careful to argue that "the Muscovite state had every reason to consider the Amur territories its property both de facto and de jure." He echoed nineteenth-century points about the legal status of the borderline but offered a more Leninist twist on their arguments about the loyalties of the indigenous population. "Inclusion into the Russian sphere of influence," he wrote, "was more favorable for the peoples of the Amur than keeping them under the yoke of Manchu officials and merchants, who did not represent the true culture of the Chinese people." Because these Manchus were "a narrow circle of the exploiting elements of [China and Japan]," they did not uplift these people beyond the "last stage of the clan-based order"; to the extent that Murav'ev and his successors had failed in the Amur, it was because they had failed to fully sever the Amur from its dependence on Qing exploiters.[16] Hence Marxist arguments about socioeconomic progress proved to be perfectly compatible with Imperial Russian ones about the shallow footprint of Qing control.

By the 1970s and 1980s, such nuances were no longer necessary. In the preface to A. I. Alekseev's *Delo vsei zhizni*—a young-adult book about Nevel'skoi by a leading scholar of the period—A. P. Okladnikov wrote that the captain had been driven "not by greed for wealth and money, not desire for power, but the glory of Russia, the basic interests of our state and people in the East." The fact that they "belonged to the ruling class" did not detract from their heroism in carrying out their "historical mission."[17] Alekseev himself, both here and elsewhere, emphasized the fact that the only solution of the Amur question was "the return to Russia of its inherent [*iskonnykh*] territories in the Amur region, which was discovered, explored, and settled by Russian people." Indeed, the Russianness of these territories confirmed that it was not an imperial conquest. Citing the pro-Russian views of Marx and Engels on the Second Opium War, Alekseev argued that "Russo-Chinese relations were being built on a foundation of mutual benefit and equality."[18] For the earlier period, Alekseev cited V. S. Miasnikov's argument that the Nerchinsk treaty had been "violently forced upon" Russia—an argument that constituted a volte-face from Kurts's view that it had been mutually beneficial and guided by economic interests.[19] Miasnikov's 1969 edited collection of documents on the treaty was prefaced with a comprehensive essay that aimed to expose the entire Chinese historiography on the topic as a biased, nationalist distortion. Nerchinsk, in this now hegemonic view, had been an unequal treaty; the agreements that had sealed the Russian annexation of the Amur, on the other hand, had not been.[20] Still active as an academic, Miasnikov is easily the most influential scholar of Russo-Chinese relations in all of Russia; his students have carried on the project after him, while translations of his work and publications in English have spread his influence beyond the former Soviet Union.[21] Subsequent work has gone further in defending Russian claims. A. Iu. Plotnikov, for instance, argues that by not annexing the entirety of Manchuria, Russia was "firmly adhering to the principle of peaceful and friendly policy toward China and nonintervention in its internal affairs, rejecting the efforts of Western countries to draw it into a military conflict with its Far Eastern neighbor."[22]

Such a normative outlook would have seemed utterly foreign to anyone working in eighteenth-century Russia's intelligence apparatus on the Qing frontier. Though even Catherine II complained of being unfairly slandered in Qing diplomatic correspondence, she did not shy away from potential invasion plans. What governed the Russian Empire's conduct in this period was expediency, not a benign commitment to peaceful coexistence: there were simply not enough military resources to commit to a campaign against Qianlong. In their absence, intelligence was decisive. It helped fill in gaps between capability and aspiration, allowing imperial officials to dream about overcoming their limits through guile instead of force. At key moments it also reassured them that a conflict or a surprise attack was not imminent, though sometimes this meant ignoring intelligence reports as well as listening to them.

For much of the pre-Murav'ev era, however, the fate of intelligence registered the tensions in the Russian mode of understanding frontier territories. It was never an orderly apparatus where everyone was agreed on what the purpose, methods, and limits of intelligence should be. Instead, it was a collection of competing institutions staffed by a small, often disregarded service class and brought into action by conflicting cultural and geopolitical imperatives. The system it replaced had been dynamic but porous and ad hoc, reliant on chance encounters between skilled foreign servitors and varied but unreliable informants; the system that replaced it deployed the tools of disciplinary academic knowledge making alongside a modern imperialist framework embraced by powerful sectional elites. The Russian Empire needed all its senses to understand the world; again and again it woke to find that they revealed the world anew.

Appendix: Reign Dates

Muscovy and the Russian Empire

Mikhail Fëdorovich 1613–1645
Aleksei Mikhailovich 1645–1676
Fëdor Alekseevich 1676–1682
Ivan Alekseevich and Pëtr Alekseevich (Sophiia Alekseevna, regent) 1682–1689
Pëtr Alekseevich (Peter I) 1689–1725
Catherine I 1725–1727
Peter II 1727–1730
Anna Ioannovna 1730–1740
Anna Leopol'dovna 1740–1741
Elizabeth 1741–1762
Peter III 1762
Catherine II 1762–1796
Paul 1796–1801
Alexander I 1801–1825
Nicholas I 1825–1855
Alexander II 1855–1881

China (reign names)

Ming Dynasty

Wanli 1572–1620
Taichang 1620
Tianqi 1620–1627
Chongzhen 1627–1644

Qing Dynasty

[Nurhaci 1616–1626]
[Hong Taiji 1626–1643]
Shunzhi [1643] 1644–1661
Kangxi 1661–1722
Yongzheng 1722–1735
Qianlong 1735–1796
Jiaqing 1796–1820
Daoguang 1820–1850
Xianfeng 1850–1861

Abbreviations

PSZ   *Polnoe sobranie zakonov Rossiiskoi imperii.* 45 vols. St. Petersburg: Tip. II Otdeleniia EIV Kantseliarii, 1838.

RKO XVII   Demidova, N. F., and V. S. Miasnikov, comp. *Russko-kitaiskie otnosheniia v XVII veke.* 2 vols. Edited by S. L. Tikhvinskii. Moscow: Nauka, 1969–1972.

RKO XVIII   Demidova, N. F., V. S. Miasnikov, A. I. Tarasova, and G. I. Sarkisova, comp. *Russko-kitaiskie otnosheniia v XVIII veke.* 6 vols. Edited by S. L. Tikhvinskii. Moscow: Nauka, 1978–2011 [vols. 3–6 published with Pamiatniki istoricheskoi mysli].

RKO XIX   Davydova, M. B., I. T. Moroz, V. S. Miasnikov, and N. Iu. Novgorodskaia, comp. *Russko-kitaiskie otnosheniia v XIX veke.* Edited by S. L. Tikhvinskii. Moscow: Pamiatniki istoricheskoi mysli, 1995.

Notes

Introduction

1. AV IVR, f. 7, op. 1, d. 38, l. 12–37.

2. See the overview in Nancy S. Kollmann, *The Russian Empire 1450–1801* (Oxford: Oxford University Press, 2017), 335–354.

3. Bernard S. Cohn, *Colonialism and Its Forms of Knowledge: The British in India* (Princeton, NJ: Princeton University Press, 1996).

4. James Louis Hevia, *English Lessons: The Pedagogy of Imperialism in Nineteenth-Century China* (Durham, NC: Duke University Press, 2003).

5. Suzanne Marchand, *German Orientalism in the Age of Empire: Religion, Race, and Scholarship* (New York: Cambridge University Press, 2009).

6. Productive recent attempts to preserve the critical kernel of Saidian thought while rethinking some of its characteristic approaches include Michael Dodson, *Orientalism, Empire, and National Culture: India, 1770–1880* (Basingstoke: Palgrave Macmillan, 2007); Priya Satia, *Spies in Arabia: The Great War and the Cultural Foundations of Britain's Covert Empire in the Middle East* (Oxford: Oxford University Press, 2008); Aamir R. Mufti, "Orientalism and the Institution of World Literatures," *Critical Inquiry* 36, no. 3 (2010): 458–493.

7. For example, SPb ARAN, f. 3, op. 1, d. 225, l. 431–445.

8. Clifford Foust, *Muscovite and Mandarin: Russia's Trade with China and Its Setting, 1727–1805* (Chapel Hill: University of North Carolina Press, 1969); Mark Mancall, *Russia and China: Their Diplomatic Relations to 1728* (Cambridge: Harvard University Press, 1971); Eric Widmer, *The Russian Ecclesiastical Mission in Peking during the Eighteenth Century* (Cambridge, MA: Harvard University Press, 1976); Barbara Maggs, *Russia and "Le Rêve Chinois": China in Eighteenth-Century Russian Literature* (Oxford: Voltaire Foundation, 1984); Susanna Soojung Lim, *China and Japan in the Russian Imagination, 1685–1922: To the Ends of the Orient* (New York: Routledge, 2013); Alexander Lukin, *The Bear*

Watches the Dragon: Russia's Perceptions of China and the Evolution of Russian-Chinese Relations since the Eighteenth Century (Armonk, NY: M. E. Sharpe, 2003).

9. While mostly neglected in the Russian context, early modern intelligence has increasingly been a subject of interest for historians. Nadine Akkerman, *Invisible Agents: Women and Espionage in Seventeenth-Century Britain* (Oxford: Oxford University Press, 2018); Lucien Bély, *Espions et ambassadeurs au temps de Louis XIV* (Paris: Fayard, 1990); Emrah Safa Gürkan, "Espionage in the 16th Century Mediterranean: Secret Diplomacy, Mediterranean Go-Betweens and the Ottoman Habsburg Rivalry" (PhD diss., Georgetown University, 2012); Robyn Adams and Rosanna Cox, eds., *Diplomacy and Early Modern Culture* (New York: Palgrave Macmillan, 2011); Alain Dewerpe, *Espion: une anthologie historique du secret d'état contemporain* (Paris: Gallimard, 1994).

10. John L. Campbell and Ove Kaj Pedersen, *The National Origins of Policy Ideas: Knowledge Regimes in the United States, France, Germany, and Denmark* (Princeton, NJ: Princeton University Press, 2014), 3. Compare Peter Wehling's similarly named concept, which emphasizes norms and practices rather than institutions: "Wissensregime," in *Handbuch Wissenssoziologie und Wissensforschung,* ed. Rainer Schützeichel (Cologne, Germany: Herbert von Halem Verlag, 2018), 704–713.

11. Campbell and Pedersen, *National Origins,* 326.

12. James C. Scott, *Seeing like a State: How Certain Schemes to Improve the Human Condition Have Failed* (New Haven, CT: Yale University Press, 1998); a somewhat similar perspective on the role of the Enlightenment is Larry Wolff, *Inventing Eastern Europe: The Map of Civilization on the Mind of the Enlightenment* (Stanford, CA: Stanford University Press, 1994).

13. The network approach is now pervasive in the history of knowledge. See, for example, Markus Friedrich, "Archives as Networks: The Geography of Record-Keeping in the Society of Jesus (1540–1773)," *Archival Science* 10, no. 3 (October 2, 2010): 285–298; David Lux and Harold Cook, "Closed Circles or Open Networks? Communicating at a Distance during the Scientific Revolution," *History of Science* 36, no. 112 (1998): 179–211; the central figure in inspiring this turn was Bruno Latour, especially *Science in Action: How to Follow Scientists and Engineers through Society* (Cambridge, MA: Harvard University Press, 1987).

14. For a thorough attempt to apply the Foucauldian model to a similar set of questions, see Denis Volkov, *Russia's Turn to Persia: Orientalism in Diplomacy and Intelligence* (Cambridge: Cambridge University Press, 2018).

15. Campbell and Pedersen, *National Origins,* 29; John L. Campbell, "Institutional Analysis and the Role of Ideas in Political Economy," *Theory and Society* 27, no. 3 (1998): 377–409.

16. For a genealogy of the concept of "image" in this context, see Stefan Gaarsmand Jacobsen, "Chinese Influences or Images? Fluctuating Histories of How En-

lightenment Europe Read China," *Journal of World History* 24, no. 3 (2013): 623–660.

17. Ingrid Maier and Daniel C. Waugh, "How Well Was Muscovy Connected with the World?" in *Imperienvergleich. Beispiele und Ansätze aus osteuropäischer Perspektive. Festschrift für Andreas Kappeler,* ed. Guido Haussmann and Angela Rustemeyer (Wiesbaden, Germany: Harrassowitz, 2009), 17–38; on flows in the Ottoman context, see John-Paul A. Ghobrial, *The Whispers of Cities: Information Flows in Istanbul, London, and Paris in the Age of William Trumbull* (Oxford: Oxford University Press, 2013); see also Ann Blair and Devin Fitzgerald, "A Revolution in Information?" in *The Oxford Handbook of Early Modern European History, 1350–1750,* ed. H. M. Scott (Oxford: Oxford University Press, 2015), 1:244–268.

18. Marc Raeff, *The Well-Ordered Police State: Social and Institutional Change through Law in the Germanies and Russia, 1600–1800* (New Haven, CT: Yale University Press, 1983).

19. Andre Wakefield, *The Disordered Police State: German Cameralism as Science and Practice* (Chicago: University of Chicago Press, 2009).

20. A similar example in a different context is Simon Werrett, "The Schumacher Affair: Reconfiguring Academic Expertise across Dynasties in Eighteenth-Century Russia," *Osiris* 25, no. 1 (January 2010): 104–126.

21. Bottom-up approaches focusing on individuals within imperial institutions include some of the essays in Stephen M. Norris and Willard Sunderland, eds., *Russia's People of Empire: Life Stories from Eurasia, 1500 to the Present* (Bloomington: Indiana University Press, 2012); Anna Joukovskaïa, "Unsalaried and Unfed: Town Clerks' Means of Survival in Southwest Russia under Peter I," trans. Yelizaveta Raykhlina, *Kritika: Explorations in Russian and Eurasian History* 14, no. 4 (2013): 715–739; Erika Monahan, *The Merchants of Siberia: Trade in Early Modern Eurasia* (Ithaca, NY: Cornell University Press, 2016), 254–301.

22. Anna Joukovskaïa, "Le service diplomatique russe au XVIIIe siècle: genèse et fonctionnement du Collège des Affaires étrangères" (PhD diss., EHESS, 2002), 420–424 (most translators worked from two or more foreign languages).

23. Simon Schaffer et al., eds., *The Brokered World: Go-Betweens and Global Intelligence, 1770–1820* (Sagamore Beach, MA: Science History Publications, 2009); Emrah Safa Gürkan, "Mediating Boundaries: Mediterranean Go-Betweens and Cross-Confessional Diplomacy in Constantinople, 1560–1600," *Journal of Early Modern History* 19, no. 2–3 (April 21, 2015): 107–128.

24. On the role of middle strata in the imperial social order, see Elise Kimerling Wirtschafter, *Structures of Society* (DeKalb: Northern Illinois University Press, 1994); Alison K. Smith, *For the Common Good and Their Own Well-Being: Social Estates in Imperial Russia* (Oxford: Oxford University Press, 2014); Catherine Evtuhov, *Portrait of a Russian Province: Economy, Society, and Civilization in*

Nineteenth-Century Nizhnii Novgorod (Pittsburgh, PA: University of Pittsburgh Press, 2011).

25. On "administrative entrepreneurship," see Igor' Fediukin, "Rol' administrativnogo predprinimatel'stva v petrovskikh reformakh: navigatskaia shkola i pozdnemoskovskie knizhniki," *Rossiiskaia istoriia*, no. 4 (2014): 80–101.

26. Matthew W. Mosca, "Empire and the Circulation of Frontier Intelligence: Qing Conceptions of the Ottomans," *Harvard Journal of Asiatic Studies* 70, no. 1 (2010): 147–207; Matthew W. Mosca, *From Frontier Policy to Foreign Policy: The Question of India and the Transformation of Geopolitics in Qing China* (Stanford, CA: Stanford University Press, 2013).

27. Works inspired by New Qing History approaches include Mark C. Elliott, *The Manchu Way: The Eight Banners and Ethnic Identity in Late Imperial China* (Stanford, CA: Stanford University Press, 2001); Pamela Kyle Crossley, *A Translucent Mirror: History and Identity in Qing Imperial Ideology* (Berkeley: University of California Press, 2000); James A. Millward, *Eurasian Crossroads: A History of Xinjiang* (New York: Columbia University Press, 2007); Johan Elverskog, *Our Great Qing: The Mongols, Buddhism and the State in Late Imperial China* (Honolulu: University of Hawai'i Press, 2006).

28. Matthew W. Mosca, "The Qing State and Its Awareness of Eurasian Interconnections, 1789–1806," *Eighteenth-Century Studies* 47, no. 2 (2014): 103–116; Mosca, *Frontier Policy*.

29. David Mungello, *Curious Land: Jesuit Accommodation and the Origins of Sinology* (Honolulu: University of Hawaii Press, 1989); Florence Hsia, *Sojourners in a Strange Land: Jesuits and Their Scientific Missions in Late Imperial China* (Chicago: University of Chicago Press, 2009); David Mungello, *The Great Encounter of China and the West, 1500–1800* (Lanham, MD: Rowman & Littlefield, 2009); critical perspectives include Huiyi Wu, Alexander Statman, and Mario Cams, "Displacing Jesuit Science in Qing China," *East Asian Science, Technology, and Medicine*, no. 46 (2017): 15–23; Mario Cams, *Companions in Geography: East-West Collaboration in the Mapping of Qing China (c. 1685–1735)* (Leiden, Netherlands: Brill, 2017).

30. See my introduction to Ieromonakh Feodosii Smorzhevskii, *Notes on the Jesuits in China [Ob Ezuitakh v Kitae]*, trans. Gregory Afinogenov (Chestnut Hill, MA: Institute of Jesuit Sources, 2016); as well as "Jesuit Conspirators and Russia's East Asian Fur Trade, 1791–1807," *Journal of Jesuit Studies* 2, no. 1 (February 24, 2015): 56–76.

31. On the relationship between the research program of the history of science and a more general "history of knowledge," see Lorraine Daston, "The History of Science and the History of Knowledge," *KNOW: A Journal on the Formation of Knowledge* 1, no. 1 (March 1, 2017): 131–154; David Armitage, "The International Turn in Intellectual History," in *Rethinking Modern European Intellectual History*, ed. Darrin M. McMahon and Samuel Moyn (Oxford: Oxford University Press, 2014), 232–252; James A. Secord, "Knowledge in Transit," *Isis* 95, no. 4 (December 2004):

654–672; see also Alain Blum, "Circulation, Transfers, Isolation," *Kritika: Explorations in Russian and Eurasian History* 9, no. 1 (March 10, 2008): 231–242.

32. For example, Anne Goldgar, *Impolite Learning: Conduct and Community in the Republic of Letters, 1680–1750* (New Haven, CT: Yale University Press, 1995); Richard B. Sher, *The Enlightenment and the Book: Scottish Authors and Their Publishers in Eighteenth-Century Britain, Ireland, and America* (Chicago: University of Chicago Press, 2006); Lawrence Brockliss, *Calvet's Web: Enlightenment and the Republic of Letters in Eighteenth-Century France* (Oxford: Oxford University Press, 2002).

33. Huiyi Wu, *Traduire la Chine au XVIIIe siècle. Jésuites traducteurs de textes chinois et le renouvellement des connaissances européennes sur la Chine (1687–ca. 1740)* (Paris: Honore Champion Editions, 2017); Isabelle Landry-Deron, *La preuve par la Chine: la "Description" de J.-B. Du Halde, Jésuite, 1735* (Paris: Editions de l'Ecole des hautes études en sciences sociales, 2002); Paul Hazard, *La crise de la conscience européenne: 1680–1715* (Paris: Fayard, 1978); Rhoda Rappaport, *When Geologists Were Historians, 1665–1750* (Ithaca, NY: Cornell University Press, 1997); Julia Ching and Willard Gurdon Oxtoby, eds., *Discovering China: European Interpretations in the Enlightenment* (Rochester, NY: University of Rochester Press, 1992).

34. Gary Hamburg, *Russia's Path toward Enlightenment: Faith, Politics, and Reason, 1500–1801* (New Haven, CT: Yale University Press, 2016); Max Okenfuss, *The Rise and Fall of Latin Humanism in Early-Modern Russia: Pagan Authors, Ukrainians, and the Resiliency of Muscovy* (Leiden, Netherlands: Brill, 1995); Cynthia Whittaker, *Russian Monarchy: Eighteenth-Century Rulers and Writers in Political Dialogue* (DeKalb: Northern Illinois University Press, 2003); Elise Wirtschafter, *Religion and Enlightenment in Catherinian Russia: The Teachings of Metropolitan Platon* (DeKalb: Northern Illinois University Press, 2011).

35. Michael D. Gordin, "The Importation of Being Earnest: The Early St. Petersburg Academy of Sciences," *Isis* 91, no. 1 (March 1, 2000): 1–31; Simon Werrett, "An Odd Sort of Exhibition: The St. Petersburg Academy of Sciences in Enlightened Russia" (DPhil diss., University of Cambridge, 2000); Yuri Slezkine, "Naturalists versus Nations: Eighteenth-Century Russian Scholars Confront Ethnic Diversity," *Representations*, no. 47 (July 1, 1994): 170–195; David Moon, "The Russian Academy of Sciences Expeditions to the Steppes in the Late Eighteenth Century," *Slavonic and East European Review* 88, no. 1 / 2 (January 1, 2010): 204–236; Ryan Tucker Jones, *Empire of Extinction: Russians and the North Pacific's Strange Beasts of the Sea, 1741–1867* (Oxford: Oxford University Press, 2014).

36. RKO XVIII, 6:331–348; see also Yan Guodong, "18 shiji Eguo hanxue jia de Zhongguo lishi wenhua guan," *Jinan xuebao (Zhexue shehui kexue ban)* 36, no. 7 (2014): 122–129.

37. Works exploring the relationship between secrecy and authorship include Pamela O. Long, *Openness, Secrecy, Authorship: Technical Arts and the Culture of*

Knowledge from Antiquity to the Renaissance (Baltimore: Johns Hopkins University Press, 2001); Daniel Jütte, *The Age of Secrecy: Jews, Christians, and the Economy of Secrets, 1400-1800*, trans. Jeremiah Riemer (New Haven, CT: Yale University Press, 2015); Paola Bertucci, "Enlightened Secrets: Silk, Intelligent Travel, and Industrial Espionage in Eighteenth-Century France," *Technology and Culture* 54, no. 4 (2013): 820–852.

38. Max Weber, *Economy and Society: An Outline of Interpretive Sociology* (Berkeley: University of California Press, 1978), 2:956–1005; here I agree with John LeDonne, for example, *Absolutism and Ruling Class: The Formation of the Russian Political Order, 1700-1825* (Oxford: Oxford University Press, 1991), ix.

39. Jacob Soll, *The Information Master: Jean-Baptiste Colbert's Secret State Intelligence System* (Ann Arbor: University of Michigan Press, 2009).

40. C. A. Bayly, *Empire and Information: Intelligence Gathering and Social Communication in India, 1780-1870* (Cambridge: Cambridge University Press, 2000).

41. Kollmann, *Russian Empire*, 2–7 and passim; Il'ia Gerasimov, Marina Mogilner, and Sergey Glebov, "Glava 7. Dolgii XVIII vek i stanovlenie modernizatsionnoi imperii," *Ab Imperio*, no. 1 (May 28, 2015): 387–447.

42. Nathaniel Knight, "Grigor'ev in Orenburg, 1851-1862: Russian Orientalism in the Service of Empire?" *Slavic Review* 59, no. 1 (2000): 74–100; Adeeb Khalid, "Russian History and the Debate over Orientalism," *Kritika: Explorations in Russian and Eurasian History* 1, no. 4 (2000): 691–699, and the other contributions to the Kritika debate; Austin Jersild, *Orientalism and Empire: North Caucasus Mountain Peoples and the Georgian Frontier, 1845-1917* (Montreal: McGill-Queen's University Press, 2002).

43. David Schimmelpenninck van der Oye, *Russian Orientalism: Asia in the Russian Mind from Peter the Great to the Emigration* (New Haven, CT: Yale University Press, 2010).

44. Vera Tolz, *Russia's Own Orient: The Politics of Identity and Oriental Studies in the Late Imperial and Early Soviet Periods* (Oxford: Oxford University Press, 2011); Ian W. Campbell, *Knowledge and the Ends of Empire: Kazak Intermediaries and Russian Rule on the Steppe, 1731-1917* (Ithaca, NY: Cornell University Press, 2017).

45. The last wave of archival research in this period predated the Russian Revolution. See Gaston Cahen, *Histoire des relations de la Russie avec la Chine sous Pierre le Grand (1689-1730)* (Paris: F. Alcan, 1912); Gaston Cahen, *Le livre de comptes de la caravane russe à Pékin en 1727-1728* (Paris: F. Alcan, 1911); John F. Baddeley, *Russia, Mongolia, China* (London: Macmillan, 1919).

46. P. E. Skachkov, *Ocherki istorii russkogo kitaevedeniia* (Moscow: Nauka, 1977); P. E. Skachkov, "Znachenie rukopisnogo naslediia russkikh kitaevedov," *Voprosy istorii*, no. 1 (1960): 117–123; G. F. Kim, *Istoriia otechestvennogo vostokovedeniia: do serediny XIX veka* (Moscow: Nauka, 1990); V. P. Taranovich, "Ilarion Rossokhin i

ego trudy po kitaevedeniiu," *Sovetskoe vostokovedenie*, no. 3 (1945): 225–241; T. A. Pan and O. V. Shatalov, *Arkhivnye materialy po istorii zapadnoevropeiskogo i rossiiskogo kitaevedeniia* (St. Petersburg: Sankt-Peterburgskii filial Instituta vostokovedeniia, 2004); T. K. Shafranovskaia, "O poezdkakh Lorentsa Langa v Pekin," *Sovetskoe kitaevedenie*, no. 4 (1958): 155–159; T. K. Shafranovskaia, "Puteshestvie Lorentsa Langa v 1715–1716 gg. v Pekin i ego dnevnik," *Strany i narody vostoka* 2 (1961): 188–205; see also V. V. Kopotilova, "Izdanie kitaiskikh proizvedenii predstaviteliami rossiiskoi obshchestvennosti (konets XVIII–pervaia polovina XIX vv.)," *Vestnik Omskogo universiteta*, no. 2 (1998): 60–64.

47. A useful general overview is E. O. Poliakova, "Otechestvennaia istoriografiia russko-kitaiskikh otnoshenii XVII v.," *Dokument. Arkhiv. Istoriia. Sovremennost'*, no. 11 (2010): 11–26; major works in the contra-Chinese vein include P. I. Kabanov, *Amurskii vopros* (Blagoveshchensk, Russia: Amurskoe knizhnoe izd-vo, 1959); E. L. Besprozvannykh, *Priamur'e v sisteme russko-kitaiskikh otnoshenii: XVII–seredina XIX v.* (Khabarovsk, Russia: Khabarovskoe Knizhoe izd-vo, 1986); V. S. Miasnikov, *Dogovornymi stat'iami utverdili: diplomaticheskaia istoriia russko-kitaiskoi granitsy XVII–XX vv.* (Khabarovsk, Russia: Priamurskoe geograficheskoe obshchestvo, 1997).

48. B. G. Kurts, *Russko-kitaiskie snosheniia v XVI, XVII i XVIII stoletiiakh* (Dnepropetrovsk, Ukraine: Gosudarstvennoe izd-vo Ukrainy, 1929).

49. Aside from RKO XVII, XVIII, and XIX, see also I. Ia. Zlatkin and N. V. Ustiugov, eds., *Russko-mongol'skie otnosheniia, 1607–1636: sbornik dokumentov* (Moscow: Izd-vo vostochnoi lit-ry, 1959); F. N. Kireev, ed., *Kazakhsko-russkie otnosheniia v XVI–XVIII vekakh: sbornik dokumentov i materialov* (Almaty, Kazakhstan: Izd. Akademii Nauk Kazakhskoi SSR, 1961); B. P. Gurevich, G. F. Kim, and S. L. Tikhvinskii, eds., *Mezhdunarodnye otnosheniia v Tsentral'noi Azii: XVII–XVIII vv.: dokumenty i materialy* (Moscow: Nauka, 1989).

50. Classic imperial-era works include Kh. Trusevich, *Posol'skiia i torgovyia snosheniia Rossii s Kitaem* (Moscow: Malinskii, 1882); P. A Badmaev, *Rossiia i Kitai* (St. Petersburg: Izd. red. "Novago Zhurnala literatury, iskusstva i nauki," 1905); Nikolai Adoratskii, *Pravoslavnaia missiia v Kitae za 200 let eia sushchestvovaniia: opyt tserkovno-istoricheskago izsledovaniia po arkhivnym dokumentam* (Kazan, Russia: Tip. Imperatorskago universiteta, 1887); especially valuable publications of sources are N. N. Bantysh-Kamenskii, *Diplomaticheskoe sobranie del mezhdu Rossiiskim i Kitaiskim gosudarstvami s 1619 po 1792-i g.*, ed. V. M. Florinskii (Kazan, Russia: Imperatorskii Universitet, 1882); E. I. Sychevskii, *Istoricheskaia zapiska o kitaiskoi granitse, sostavlennaia sovetnikom troitsko-savskago pogranichnago pravleniia Sychevskim v 1846 godu*, ed. V. N. Basnin (Moscow: V Universitetskoi Tipografii, 1875).

51. I. L. Maiakovskii, *Ocherki istorii arkhivnogo dela v SSSR* (Moscow: Glavnoe arkhivnoe upravlenie NKVD, 1941), 159–183.

1. Muscovy on the Knowledge Frontier

1. Perspectives on the intellectual history of early European colonialism in Asia include works as diverse as Robert K. Batchelor, *London: The Selden Map and the Making of a Global City, 1549–1689* (Chicago: University of Chicago Press, 2014); Ananya Chakravarti, *The Empire of Apostles: Religion, Accommodation, and the Imagination of Empire in Early Modern Brazil and India* (New Delhi: Oxford University Press, 2018); Steven J. Harris, "Jesuit Scientific Activity in the Overseas Missions, 1540–1773," *Isis* 96, no. 1 (2005): 71–79.

2. For example, V. V. Postnikov, "Knizhnyi pamiatnik istorio-geograficheskikh znanii v Rossii XVII v.," *Oikumena. Regionovedcheskie issledovaniia*, no. 1 (2012): 133–137.

3. For studies of the Timur legacy, see Beatrice Forbes Manz, *Power, Politics and Religion in Timurid Iran* (Leiden, Netherlands: Cambridge University Press, 2007); Lisa Balabanlilar, "Lords of the Auspicious Conjunction: Turco-Mongol Imperial Identity on the Subcontinent," *Journal of World History* 18, no. 1 (February 27, 2007): 1–39; John Darwin, *After Tamerlane: The Global History of Empire since 1405* (New York: Bloomsbury, 2008).

4. Millward, *Eurasian Crossroads*, 70–72; Peter Perdue, *China Marches West: The Qing Conquest of Central Eurasia* (Cambridge, MA: Belknap, 2005), 51–129; For an accessible introduction to Inner Asia more generally, see Svat Soucek, *A History of Inner Asia* (Cambridge: Cambridge University Press, 2000).

5. Elverskog, *Our Great Qing*, 14–62; Perdue, *China Marches West*, 133–161.

6. Elliott, *Manchu Way*, 39–78; Crossley, *Translucent Mirror*, 145–167.

7. Junko Miyawaki, "The Chinggisid Principle in Russia," *Russian History* 19, no. 1 (January 1, 1992): 261–277; Charles J. Halperin, *Russia and the Golden Horde: The Mongol Impact on Medieval Russian History* (Bloomington: Indiana University Press, 1987); Donald G. Ostrowski, *Muscovy and the Mongols: Cross-Cultural Influences on the Steppe Frontier, 1304–1589* (Cambridge: Cambridge University Press, 1998); but on a cautionary note, see Lawrence N. Langer, "Muscovite Taxation and the Problem of Mongol Rule in Rus'," *Russian History* 34, no. 1/4 (2007): 101–129.

8. Matthew P. Romaniello, *The Elusive Empire: Kazan and the Creation of Russia, 1552–1671* (Madison: University of Wisconsin Press, 2012), 117–45.

9. Songyun, *Emu tanggū orin sakda-i gisun sarkiyan*, ed. Giovanni Stary (Wiesbaden, Germany: Otto Harrassowitz, 1983), 421.

10. Yuri Slezkine, *Arctic Mirrors: Russia and the Small Peoples of the North* (Ithaca, NY: Cornell University Press, 1994), 11–46.

11. Monahan, *Merchants of Siberia*.

12. For the history of a Bukharan trading family from Siberia, see Monahan, *Merchants of Siberia*, 254–301; see also G. L. Penrose, "Inner Asian Influences on the Earliest Russo-Chinese Trade and Diplomatic Contacts," *Russian History* 19,

no. 1 (January 1, 1992): 361–392; Audrey Burton, *The Bukharans: A Dynastic, Diplomatic, and Commercial History, 1550–1702* (New York: St. Martin's, 1997).

13. RKO XVII, 1:40–49.

14. RKO XVII, 1:60–68.

15. William Rowe, *China's Last Empire: The Great Qing* (Cambridge, MA: Belknap, 2009), 11–30.

16. RKO XVII, 1:140–144.

17. Mancall, *Russia and China,* 33–64.

18. Morris Rossabi, "The 'Decline' of the Central Asian Caravan Trade," in *The Rise of Merchant Empires: Long-Distance Trade in the Early Modern World, 1350–1750,* ed. James D. Tracy (Cambridge: Cambridge University Press, 2010), 367–369; Kurts, *Russko-kitaiskie snosheniia,* 3–15, 39–57; on Lake Yamysh, see Monahan, *Merchants of Siberia,* 175–208.

19. Zlatkin and Ustiugov, *Russko-mongol'skie otnosheniia,* 81.

20. RKO XVII, 1:99.

21. RKO XVII, 1:79–90; Baddeley, *Russia, Mongolia, China,* 2:66–70; Penrose, "Inner Asian Influences," 364. In a departure from his cataloging, Petlin even found the time to note that "the female sex there is very gentle to the male, with girls and women like these I would live my whole life and finish out my days, if only it were possible not to part from them before I die." This passage was not well received by the recording clerk, who noted "written accurately, but it is inappropriate to write such things in a diplomatic deposition." OR RNB, f. 775, d. 4968, l. 425.

22. RKO XVII, 1:161–162.

23. On early modern descriptions of Muscovy, see Marshall Poe, *A People Born to Slavery: Russia in Early Modern European Ethnography, 1476–1748* (Ithaca, NY: Cornell University Press, 2000).

24. Samuel Collins, *The Present State of Russia In a Letter to a Friend at London; Written by an Eminent Person Residing at the Great Czars,* ed. Marshall Poe, 1671, 14–15, http://ir.uiowa.edu/history_pubs/1.

25. Grigorii Kotoshikhin, *O Rossii v carstvovanie Alekseja Mixajloviča* (Oxford: Oxford University Press, 1980), 65–66.

26. Borivoj Plavsic, "Seventeenth-Century Chanceries and Their Staffs," in *Russian Officialdom* (Chapel Hill: University of North Carolina Press, 1980), 19–45; Peter B. Brown, "How Muscovy Governed: Seventeenth-Century Russian Central Administration," *Russian History* 36, no. 4 (November 1, 2009): 459–529.

27. Filippo de Vivo, *Information and Communication in Venice: Rethinking Early Modern Politics* (Oxford: Oxford University Press, 2007), 58–74; Garrett Mattingly, *Renaissance Diplomacy* (London: Cape, 1955), 207–216.

28. The European context of these kinds of diplomatic works is represented in, for example, Adams and Cox, *Diplomacy;* and Vivo, *Information and Communication,* 48–85.

29. See, for instance, the reports collected in *Puteshestviia russkikh poslov XVI–XVII vv.: stateinye spiski* (Moscow: Izd-vo Akademii nauk SSSR, 1954).

30. James Forsyth, *A History of the Peoples of Siberia: Russia's North Asian Colony, 1581–1990* (Cambridge: Cambridge University Press, 1992), 28–108; Perdue, *China Marches West,* 133–173.

31. Joseph Sebes, ed., *The Jesuits and the Sino-Russian Treaty of Nerchinsk (1689): The Diary of Thomas Pereira* (Rome: Institutum Historicum S. I., 1962); Peter Perdue, "Boundaries and Trade in the Early Modern World: Negotiations at Nerchinsk and Beijing," *Eighteenth-Century Studies* 43, no. 3 (2010): 341–356; RKO XVII, 2:38.

32. See the discussion in Kurts, *Russko-kitaiskie snosheniia,* 136–141.

33. RKO XVII, 2:257.

34. AV IVR, R. I, op. 1, d. 5, l. 44. See also Andrey V. Ivanov, "Conflicting Loyalties: Fugitives and Traitors in the Russo-Manchurian Frontier, 1651–1689," *Journal of Early Modern History* 13, no. 5 (2009): 333–358.

35. RKO XVII, 1:270–271; Michel N. Pavlovsky, *Chinese-Russian Relations* (New York: Philosophical Library, 1949), 127–144.

36. The work of A. I. Andreev is the most comprehensive discussion of this new genre; see A. I. Andreev, *Ocherki po istochnikovedeniiu Sibiri: XVII vek* (Leningrad: Izd-vo Glavsevmorputi, 1939); and A. I. Andreev, *Ocherki po istochnikovedeniiu Sibiri: XVIII vek* (Leningrad: Izd-vo Akademii nauk SSSR [Leningradskoe otd-nie], 1960).

37. Valerie A. Kivelson, *Cartographies of Tsardom: The Land and Its Meanings in Seventeenth-Century Russia* (Ithaca, NY: Cornell University Press, 2006), 117ff; Daniel C. Waugh, "The View from the North: Muscovite Cartography of Inner Asia," *Journal of Asian History* 49, no. 1–2 (2015): 69–95; more generally on Russian mapping, L. A. Goldenberg and A. V. Postnikov, "Development of Mapping Methods in Russia in the Eighteenth Century," *Imago Mundi,* no. 3 (1985): 63–80; Steven Seegel, *Mapping Europe's Borderlands: Russian Cartography in the Age of Empire* (Chicago: University of Chicago Press, 2012), 23–44.

38. For the contemporary American equivalent, see Katherine Grandjean, *American Passage: The Communications Frontier in Early New England* (Cambridge, MA: Harvard University Press, 2015).

39. Denis J. B. Shaw, "Mapmaking, Science and State Building in Russia before Peter the Great," *Journal of Historical Geography* 31, no. 3 (July 2005): 409–429.

40. Leo Bagrow, "A Russian Communications Map, ca. 1685," *Imago Mundi,* no. 9 (1952): 99–101; Leo Bagrow, "The First Russian Maps of Siberia and Their Influence on the West-European Cartography of N. E. Asia," *Imago Mundi,* no. 9 (1952): 83–93.

41. Another version of the Godunov map spells "Euchan" as "Suchai" (the two sets of letters are very easily confused in Muscovite handwriting), and both are po-

sitioned roughly where Suzhou would be. See Kivelson, *Cartographies of Tsardom,* plate 18.

42. P. E. Skachkov, "Vedomost' o Kitaiskoi zemle," *Strany i narody vostoka,* no. 2 (1961): 206–213; Andreev, *Ocherki po istochnikovedeniiu Sibiri: XVII vek,* 15ff; for Ablin in Tobolsk, see RKO XVII, 1:256.

43. OR RGB, f. 344, n. 123, l. 148–155. On the Manchu origin myth, see Elliott, *Manchu Way,* 44ff.

44. OR RGB, f. 256, n. 294, l. 19–24. For other similar texts, see OR RGB, f. 236, n. 31, l. 328ff. The text cited here along with others was published imperfectly in the nineteenth century. See A. A. Titov, *Sibir' v XVII veke: sbornik starinnykh russkikh statei o Sibiri i prilezhashchikh k nei zemliakh* (Moscow: G. Iudin, 1890).

45. Andreev, *Ocherki po istochnikovedeniiu Sibiri: XVII vek,* 24–91; Kivelson, *Cartographies of Tsardom,* 133ff. Andreev's reproduction of this map is my source, but I have been unable to locate a higher-quality copy. See also OR RGB, f. 256, n. 346 (the Chertezhnaia kniga).

46. See Kivelson, *Cartographies of Tsardom,* plate 20.

47. OR RGB, f. 256, n. 294, l. 1–19. For the published version, see *Sibirskiia letopisi* (St. Petersburg: Tip. I. N. Skorokhodova, 1907), 367–395.

48. For another important instance of this, see Nikolaos A. Chrissidis, *An Academy at the Court of the Tsars: Greek Scholars and Jesuit Education in Early Modern Russia* (DeKalb: Northern Illinois University Press, 2016).

49. This famous if inconclusive adventure has been extensively treated elsewhere. For instance, see Baddeley, *Russia, Mongolia, China,* 2:203ff; Mancall, *Russia and China,* 65–111; Pavlovsky, *Chinese-Russian Relations,* 99–145; Ye Baichuan, "17–18 shiji Eguo lai hua shi chen yanzhong de Beijing cheng," *Lishi dang'an,* no. 4 (2014): 81–88.

50. On the fate of these books, see Noël Golvers and Efthymios Nicolaidis, *Ferdinand Verbiest and Jesuit Science in 17th Century China: An Annotated Edition and Translation of the Constantinople Manuscript (1676)* (Athens: Institute for Neohellenic Research, 2009), 55–76 and passim; on Martini more generally, Paul Begheyn, "Dutch Publications on the Jesuit Mission in China in the Seventeenth and Eighteenth Centuries," *Quaerendo* 49, no. 1 (March 26, 2019): 49–65.

51. The only existing published version, despite the high quality of the reproduction, is missing both the Amur text and the translation of *De Bello Tartarico* because its manuscript original is unique in omitting both; this gives a distorted picture of the book. Nikolai Spafarii, *Opisanie pervyia chasti vselennyia imenuemoi Azii, v nei zhe sostoit Kitaiskoe gosudarstvo s prochimi ego gorody i provintsii* (Kazan, Russia: Imperatorskii Universitet, 1910). I am grateful to Evgeny Grishin for his assistance in locating a copy.

52. Many of these have not hitherto been recognized as being in fact copies of the *Opisanie.* My sources here include the following: OR RGB, f. 96, n. 35; f. 205,

n. 102; f. 92, n. 107; OR GIM, Muzeinoe sobranie, n. 3998; Zabelin, n. 311; Chudova m-ria, n. 361; RGADA, f. 181, d. 223; f. 196, op. 1, n. 1615; OR BAN, 16.2.9; 32.12.6; 17.9.10; Tek post 90; 32.6.18; PD DKh, op. 13, n. 182; op. 23, n. 223; SPbII, f. 36, op. 1, d. 289; f. 36, op. 1, d. 290; OR RNB, f. 550, F-IV-141; f. 550, F-IV-179; f. 550, Q-IV-1; f. 550, F-IV-87; f. 550, F-IV-289; f. 550, Q-IV-384; BNF, Fonds Slave 35.

53. OR RGB, f. 96, n. 35, l. 200ff.

54. OR RNB, f. 550, F-IV-289, l. 1v.

55. OR RNB, f. 550, F-IV-87; PD, Peretts Collection, op. 23, n. 223.

56. See, for example, Iu. K. Begunov, "Rukopisnaia literatura XVIII veka i de-mokraticheskii chitatel' (Problemy i zadachi izucheniia)," *Russkaia literatura,* no. 1 (1977): 121–132.

57. Baddeley, *Russia, Mongolia, China,* 2:209–212.

58. OR RGB, f. 92, n. 107. There are a number of reasons to conclude that this is, in fact, the original. First, after the Amur chapter, there is a Latin line reading "Laus Deo, qui concessit incipere, et finite" [Blessed be the Lord, who allows us to begin and complete (a work)]. It is much easier to imagine the Western-educated Spa-farii writing this than a Russian churchman. Second, everything including num-bering and dates is consistent with a seventeenth-century text. Third, the hand is quite similar to verified Spafarii autographs (see O. A. Belobrova, "Ob avtografakh Nikolaia Spafariia," *Trudy otdela drevnerusskoi literatury,* no. 36 [1969]: 259–65). Finally, there are the marginalia. In the passage about lychees on l. 126 the mar-ginal note "We ate these in Beijing and brought some back with us" is rendered particularly awkwardly in a different, later manuscript (OR GIM, Zabelin 311, l. 170). The copyist has taken the marginal note from this manuscript and incorporated it brutally into the body of the main text, without regard for grammar or meaning. The same phenomenon can be seen in a number of other manuscript versions of this passage, with the quote being inserted at different points in the text, and can be observed for other marginalia as well. This leaves little doubt that this is the original from which the copies were ultimately derived.

59. See Leo Bagrow, "A Few Remarks on Maps of the Amur, the Tartar Strait and Sakhalin," *Imago Mundi,* no. 12 (1955): 127–136.

60. OR RGB, f. 92, n. 107, l. 157v–161.

61. OR RGB, f. 92, n. 107, l. 88, l. 160, l. 126.

62. Spatharios Map, Leo Bagrow Map Collection, Houghton Library, Harvard University. See Leo Bagrow, "Sparwenfeld's Map of Siberia," *Imago Mundi,* no. 4 (1947): 65–70.

63. See, for example, Hsia, *Sojourners*; Alexander Bevilacqua, *The Republic of Arabic Letters: Islam and the European Enlightenment* (Cambridge, MA: Belknap, 2018).

64. Ashley Eva Millar, *A Singular Case: Debating China's Political Economy in the European Enlightenment* (Montreal: McGill-Queen's University Press, 2017).

2. Seeing China through Russian Eyes

1. Jarmo Kotilaine and Marshall Poe, eds., *Modernizing Muscovy: Reform and Social Change in Seventeenth-Century Russia* (London: RoutledgeCurzon, 2004); Angela Rustemeyer, "Systems and Senses: New Research on Muscovy and the Historiography on Early Modern Europe," *Kritika: Explorations in Russian and Eurasian History* 11, no. 3 (2010): 563–579.

2. See Jan Hennings, *Russia and Courtly Europe: Ritual and the Culture of Diplomacy, 1648–1725* (Cambridge: Cambridge University Press, 2016).

3. Frederik Vermote, "Travellers Lost and Redirected: Jesuit Networks and the Limits of European Exploration in Asia," *Itinerario* 41, no. 3 (December 2017): 484–506.

4. See Sebes, *Diary of Thomas Pereira*, 88–105.

5. Jodocus Crull, *The Antient and Present State of Muscovy: Containing a Geographical, Historical and Political Account of All Those Nations and Territories under the Jurisdiction of the Present Czar [. . .]* (n.p.: A. Roper and A. Bosvile, 1698), 61ff.

6. Jodocus Crull, *The Compleat History of the Affairs of Spain, from the First Treaty of Partition, to This Present Time* . . . (London: Jos. Barns, 1707).

7. See also Blair and Fitzgerald, "Revolution in Information?" 244–268; Ann Blair, *Too Much to Know: Managing Scholarly Information before the Modern Age* (New Haven, CT: Yale University Press, 2010); Mary Poovey, *A History of the Modern Fact: Problems of Knowledge in the Sciences of Wealth and Society* (Chicago: University of Chicago Press, 1998).

8. A comprehensive discussion of the early modern use of such "morsels" is in Blair, *Too Much to Know*, 2.

9. R. D. Bedford, "Jodocus Crull and Milton's 'A Brief History of Moscovia'," *Review of English Studies*, n.s., 47, no. 186 (May 1, 1996): 207–211.

10. Philippe Avril, *Travels into Divers Parts of Europe and Asia: Undertaken . . . to Discover a New Way by Land into China* (n.p.: Goodwin, 1693), 137ff.

11. For more on copying as an early modern intellectual practice, see Fred Schurink, "Manuscript Commonplace Books, Literature, and Reading in Early Modern England," *Huntington Library Quarterly* 73, no. 3 (September 1, 2010): 453–469; Ann Blair, "Humanist Methods in Natural Philosophy: The Commonplace Book," *Journal of the History of Ideas* 53, no. 4 (October 1, 1992): 541–551; William H. Sherman, *Used Books: Marking Readers in Renaissance England* (Philadelphia: University of Pennsylvania Press, 2009); Kevin Sharpe, *Reading Revolutions: The Politics of Reading in Early Modern England* (New Haven, CT: Yale University Press, 2000).

12. Laurence Sterne, *The Life and Opinions of Tristram Shandy, Gentleman* (n.p.: R. and J. Dodsley, 1761), 3:175–178.

13. The phrase comes from Mungello, *Great Encounter*.

14. Batchelor, *London,* 64ff.

15. For a general overview, see T. Armstrong, "In Search of a Sea Route to Siberia, 1553–1619," *Arctic* 37, no. 4 (December 1, 1984): 429–440, and the other articles in this issue. (Until global climate change opened the passage in recent years, the ice was too thick to permit this kind of navigation.)

16. Justin Stagl, *A History of Curiosity: The Theory of Travel, 1550–1800* (Langhorne: Harwood Academic, 1995); Joan-Pau Rubiés, *Travellers and Cosmographers: Studies in the History of Early Modern Travel and Ethnology* (Aldershot: Ashgate, 2007); Joan-Pau Rubiés and Manel Ollé, "The Comparative History of a Genre: The Production and Circulation of Books on Travel and Ethnographies in Early Modern Europe and China," *Modern Asian Studies* 50, no. 1 (January 2016): 259–309.

17. Samuel Purchas, *Hakluytus Posthumus: Or Purchas His Pilgrimes: Contayning a History of the World in Sea Voyages and Lande Travells by Englishmen and Others* (Glasgow: J. MacLehose and Sons, 1905), 14:272ff.

18. Cornel Zwierlein, *Imperial Unknowns: The French and British in the Mediterranean, 1650–1750* (Cambridge: Cambridge University Press, 2016); Ghobrial, *Whispers of Cities.*

19. Isabelle Landry-Deron, "Les Mathématiciens envoyés en Chine par Louis XIV en 1685," *Archive for History of Exact Sciences* 55, no. 5 (April 1, 2001): 423–463.

20. Erika Monahan, "Locating Rhubarb," in *Early Modern Things: Objects and Their Histories, 1500–1800,* ed. Paula Findlen (London: Routledge, 2013), 227–251; Clifford Foust, *Rhubarb: The Wondrous Drug* (Princeton, NJ: Princeton University Press, 1992), 46ff; see also Rachel Koroloff, "Juniper: From Medicine to Poison and Back Again in 17th-Century Muscovy," *Kritika: Explorations in Russian and Eurasian History* 19, no. 4 (November 22, 2018): 697–716.

21. Ilya Toropitsyn, "Chto stoialo za kartoi Severo-Vostochnoi Azii N. Vitsena, prepodnesennoi v dar russkim tsariam v 1690 g?" *Acta Slavica Iaponica,* no. 33 (2012): 67–78; on information and commerce more generally, see Harold Cook, *Matters of Exchange: Commerce, Medicine, and Science in the Dutch Golden Age* (New Haven, CT: Yale University Press, 2007).

22. Andreev, *Ocherki po istochnikovedeniiu Sibiri: XVII vek,* 43–45.

23. Johan Gabriel Sparwenfeld, *J.G. Sparwenfeld's Diary of a Journey to Russia 1684–87* (Stockholm: KunglVitterhets Historie Och Antikvitets Akademien, 2002), 205; Bagrow, "Sparwenfeld's Map of Siberia," 65–70. The Spafarii manuscript is in BNF, Fonds Slave 35.

24. "Tsars" is plural because Peter and his half brother Ivan were corulers in this period. Foy de la Neuville, *A Curious and New Account of Muscovy in the Year 1689* (London: School of Slavonic and East European Studies, University of London, 1994), 65–71; BNF, NAF-5114, l. 57–59. On Neuville's role as agent for the French and Polish kings, see Isabel de Madariaga, "Who Was Foy de la Neuville?" *Cahiers du Monde russe et soviétique* 28, no. 1 (January 1, 1987): 21–30.

25. Mancall, *Russia and China*, 65–70.

26. Gottfried Wilhelm Leibniz, *Novissima Sinica Historiam Nostri Temporis Illustrata* (n.p., 1697); Franklin Perkins, *Leibniz and China: A Commerce of Light* (Cambridge: Cambridge University Press, 2004), 131ff; V. I Ger'e, *Otnosheniia Leibnitsa k Rossii i Petru Velikomu po neizdannym bumagam Leibnitsa v Gannoverskoi biblioteke* (St. Petersburg: Pechatnia V. Golovina, 1871).

27. For a more critical look at these statistics, see Vermote, "Travellers Lost and Redirected"; see also Frederik Vermote, "Passage Denied! Dangers and Limitations of Jesuit Travel throughout Eurasia during the Seventeenth and Eighteenth Centuries," *World History Connected* 10, no. 3 (October 2013), https://worldhistoryconnected .press.uillinois.edu/10.3/forum_vermote.html; Wu Huiyi, "'The Observations We Made in the Indies and in China': The Shaping of the Jesuits' Knowledge of China by Other Parts of the Non-Western World," *East Asian Science, Technology, and Medicine* 46 (2017): 47–88.

28. Sebes, *Diary of Thomas Pereira*, 88–134.

29. Henri Bosmans, "Le problème des relations de Verbiest avec la Cour de Russie," *Annales de la Société d'Émulation de Bruges*, no. 63 (1913): 193–223; no. 64 (1914): 98–101.

30. David's interest in China is reflected in passing in his 1690 account of the state of Muscovy, where he describes the Qing trade goods for sale at the local markets. The complete text is published in translation in A. S. Mylnikov, ed., "Svidetel'stvo inostrannogo nabliudatelia o zhizni russkogo gosudarstva kontsa XVII veka," *Voprosy istorii*, no. 1, 3, 4 (April 1968).

31. ARSI Jap-Sin 105-1, l. 97–100. See Anthony Florovsky, "Maps of the Siberian Route of the Belgian Jesuit, A. Thomas (1690)," *Imago Mundi*, no. 8 (1951): 103–108; Eugenio Lo Sardo, "Antoine Thomas's and George David's Maps of Asia," in *The History of the Relations between the Low Countries and China in the Qing Era (1644–1911)*, ed. W. F. Vande Walle (Leuven, Belgium: Leuven University Press, 2003), 75–84. Both writers appear to find it difficult to account for these similarities.

32. Liam Matthew Brockey, *Journey to the East: The Jesuit Mission to China, 1579–1724* (Cambridge, MA: Harvard University Press, 2007), 166ff.

33. Ronald S. Love, "'A Passage to China': A French Jesuit's Perceptions of Siberia in the 1680s," *French Colonial History* 3, no. 1 (2003): 85–100.

34. Sebes, *Diary of Thomas Pereira*, 96–100.

35. Philippe Avril, *Voyage en divers états d'Europe et d'Asie, entrepris pour découvrir un nouveau chemin à la Chine* (n.p.: J. Boudot, 1693).

36. Avril, *Voyage en divers états d'Europe et d'Asie*, 160–161.

37. Avril, 170ff; Spafarii, *Opisanie pervyia chasti vselennyia imenuemoi Azii*, 15–19.

38. "Soobrazheniia kasatel'no moskovskoi missii / Cogitationes circa missionem Moscoviticam," in M. O. Koialovich, ed., *Pis'ma i doneseniia iezuitov o Rossii:*

kontsa XVII i nachala XVIII veka (St. Petersburg: Senatskaia Tipografiia, 1904), 196–202, 370–374. For attribution, see Paul Pierling, *La Russie et le Saint-Siège* (Paris: Editions Plon, 1896–1907), 4:154n2.

39. See Johannes Keuning, "Nicolaas Witsen as a Cartographer," *Imago Mundi*, no. 11 (1954): 95–110.

40. Melchisédech Thévenot, *Recueil de voyages de Mr Thevenot* (Paris: Estienne Michallet, 1681), 69ff. For more on European editions of Baikov's *spisok*, see N. F. Demidova, "O variantakh stateinogo spiska posol'stva F. I. Baikova v Kitai," in *Voprosy sotsial'no-ekonomicheskoi istorii i istochnikovedeniia perioda feodalizma v Rossii: sbornik statei k 70-letiiu A. A. Novosel'skogo*, ed. N. V. Ustiugov (Moscow: Izd-vo Akademii nauk SSSR, 1961), 270–280.

41. Nicolaas Witsen, *Severnaia i vostochnaia Tartariia: vkliuchaiushchaia oblasti, raspolozhennye v severnoi i vostochnoi chastiakh Evropy i Azii*, trans. V. G. Trisman (Amsterdam: Pegasus, 2010), 3:35–139; see also A. N. Kirpichnikov, *Rossiia XVII veka v risunkakh i opisaniiakh gollandskogo puteshestvennika Nikolaasa Vitsena* (St. Petersburg: Slavia, 1995).

42. On the relationship between "Tartary" and "Manchuria," see Mark C. Elliott, "The Limits of Tartary: Manchuria in Imperial and National Geographies," *Journal of Asian Studies* 59, no. 3 (2000): 603–646. I have found no evidence to support a Russian origin for "Manchuria" as a place name; Russians typically referred to it as "Dauriia."

43. Witsen, *Severnaia i vostochnaia Tartariia*, 1:ix. Emphasis in original.

44. See also László Hajnal, "Witsen's 'Dagur' Material," *Acta Orientalia Academiae Scientiarum Hungaricae* 47, no. 3 (January 1, 1994): 279–326; W. J. L. van Noord and M. A. Weststeijn, "The Global Trajectory of Nicolaas Witsen's Chinese Mirror," *Rijksmuseum Bulletin* 63, no. 4 (2015): 325–361.

45. Witsen, *Severnaia i vostochnaia Tartariia*, 2:1085ff, 2:853.

46. Witsen, 2:815; 1:364.

47. Witsen, 1:113. It is hard to say whether Witsen claims originality here: though the passage marks the end of a report, it does not clearly mark its beginning.

48. Witsen, 1:71.

49. Witsen, 3:8–9. (This is a commentary by the Dutch historian Bruno Naarden.)

50. Philipp Johann von Strahlenberg, *An Historico-Geographical Description of the North and Eastern Parts of Europe and Asia* (London: printed for W. Innys and R. Manby, 1738), 4.

51. Nicolaas Witsen, *Noord en oost Tartaryen: behelzende eene beschryving van verscheidene Tartersche en nabuurige gewesten, in de noorder en oostelykste deelen van Aziën en Europa . . . ontworpen, beschreven, geteekent, en in 't licht gegeven* (n.p.: M. Schalekamp, 1785).

52. London Metropolitan Archives, Robert Hooke MSS, CLC / 495 / MS01757.

53. Andreas Müller, *Abdallae Beidavaei Historia Sinensis . . .* (Berlin: Bielkius, 1689), 64ff.

54. Schleswig-Holstein in the seventeenth century was still Danish territory, which explains why certain sources insist on referring to Ides as a Dane. Isbrant Ides and Adam Brand, *Zapiski o russkom posol'stve v Kitai, 1692–1695,* ed. M. I Kazanin (Moscow: Glav. red. vostochnoǐ lit-ry, 1967), 1–14; Mancall, *Russia and China,* 200ff.

55. Christian Mentzel, *Kurze Chinesische Chronologia* (n.p.: Rüdiger, 1696), 141ff.

56. Andreev, *Ocherki po istochnikovedeniiu Sibiri: XVII vek,* 82–85.

57. Ides and Brand, *Zapiski o russkom posol'stve,* 23–25.

58. The full spisok is in Ides and Brand, 323–347.

59. For example, Evert Ysbrants Ides, *Three Years Travels from Moscow Over-Land to China: Thro' Great Ustiga, Siriania, Permia, Sibiria, Daour, Great Tartary, &c. to Peking* (London: W. Freeman, 1706), 92.

60. T. K. Shafranovskaia, "Puteshestvie Lorentsa Langa," 188–205; T. K. Shafranovskaia, "O poezdkakh Lorentsa Langa," 155–159.

61. Friedrich Christian Weber, *Das Veränderte Rußland* (n.p.: Nicolaus Förster, 1721), 72–116; Laurent Lange, *Journal de la résidence de Laur. Lange, agent de sa Maj. Impér. de la Grande Russie à la cour de la Chine dans les ann. 1721 et 1722* (Leiden, Netherlands: Abraham Kallewier, 1726).

62. Lorenz Lange, *Reise nach China* (München: VCH, Acta humaniora, 1986), 86–90. This is the first full publication of the text; it includes a fragment from a manuscript Jesuit historical text called the *Acta Pekinensia,* compiled in Beijing by the German Jesuit Kilian Stumpf in 1705–1712.

63. OR RGB, f. 205, n. 19.

64. OR RNB, f. 777, n. 252.

65. John Bell, *Travels from St. Petersburg in Russia to Diverse Parts of Asia* (Glasgow: Foulis, 1763), 1:336.

66. George Macartney, *An Account of Russia* (London, 1768), 157. (The author, then recently returned from Russia, would eventually head the first British embassy to China.)

67. *Lloyd's Evening Post,* February 24–27, 1764.

68. William Coxe, *Account of the Russian Discoveries between Asia and America* (London: Nichols, 1780), 180–250.

69. Strahlenberg, *Historico-Geographical Description.*

70. SPbII, f. 36, op. 1, d. 153; OPI GIM, f. 450, n. 204; AV IVR, R. I, op. 1, d. 12; AV IVR, R. I, op. 1, d. 13. The text was published by Spasskii without a preface as Savva Vladislavich, "Sekretnaia informatsiia o sile i sostoianii Kitaiskago gosudarstva," *Russkii vestnik,* no. 2–3 (March 1842): 180–244, 281–337. This short-lived publication is now a bibliographical rarity.

71. Dr. Williams's Library, London, Samuel Say Papers 12.107, p. 252.

72. Linnaean Society, London, Richard Pulteney MS 163.

73. Daniel Defoe, *The Farther Adventures of Robinson Crusoe: Being the Second and Last Part of His Life, and of the Strange Surprizing Accounts of His Travels Round Three Parts of the Globe* (London: W. Taylor, 1719), 306. Emphasis in original.

74. Oliver Goldsmith, *The Citizen of the World; or Letters from a Chinese Philosopher, Residing in London, to His Friends in the East* (London: R. Whiston, 1785), 1:9–11.

75. C. A Bayly, *The Birth of the Modern World, 1780–1914: Global Connections and Comparisons* (Malden, MA: Blackwell, 2004), 44ff; Andre Gunder Frank, *Re-Orient: Global Economy in the Asian Age* (Berkeley: University of California Press, 1998); Miles Ogborn, *Global Lives: Britain and the World, 1550–1800* (Cambridge: Cambridge University Press, 2008), 295ff; for the "crisis," see Hazard, *La crise de la conscience européenne.*

3. Secret Missions, Troublesome Missionaries

1. Influential works that make this argument include James Cracraft, *The Petrine Revolution in Russian Culture* (Cambridge, MA: Belknap, 2004); Raeff, *Well-Ordered Police State;* other perspectives include Robert Collis, *The Petrine Instauration: Religion, Esotericism and Science at the Court of Peter the Great, 1689–1725* (Leiden, Netherlands: Brill, 2012); Ernest A. Zitser, *The Transfigured Kingdom: Sacred Parody and Charismatic Authority at the Court of Peter the Great* (Ithaca, NY: Cornell University Press, 2004).

2. Wakefield, *Disordered Police State.*

3. For a similar effort to unpack conflicting imperatives, see Sebastian Felten, "The History of Science and the History of Bureaucratic Knowledge: Saxon Mining, circa 1770," *History of Science* 56, no. 4 (December 1, 2018): 403–431.

4. The definitive account of Fick's role is Claes Peterson, *Peter the Great's Administrative and Judicial Reforms: Swedish Antecedents and the Process of Reception* (Stockholm: A-B Nordiska Bokhandeln, 1979).

5. Joukovskaïa, "Le service diplomatique russe," 26ff; S. L. Turilova, "Gosudarstvennaia kollegiia inostrannykh del (ot Petra I k Ekaterine II)," in *Rossiiskaia diplomatiia: istoriia i sovremennost': materialy Nauchno-prakticheskoi konferentsii,* ed. I. S. Ivanov (Moscow: ROSSPEN, 2001), 155–168.

6. Andreas Gestrich, *Absolutismus und Öffentlichkeit: politische Kommunikation in Deutschland zu Beginn des 18. Jahrhunderts* (Göttingenm Germany: Vandenhoeck & Ruprecht, 1994), esp. 78–90.

7. Mikhail Speranskii, ed., *Polnoe sobranie zakonov Rossiiskoi imperii,* series 1 (St. Petersburg: Tip. II otdeleniia Sobstvennoi EIV Kantseliarii, 1830), 6:158; see also Jan Plamper, "Archival Revolution or Illusion? Historicizing the Russian Archives

and Our Work in Them," *Jahrbücher Für Geschichte Osteuropas*, n.s., 51, no. 1 (January 1, 2003): 57–69.

8. Speranskii, *PSZ*, 7:445; Gary Marker, *Publishing, Printing, and the Origins of Intellectual Life in Russia, 1700–1800* (Princeton, NJ: Princeton University Press, 1985), 27–29, 48–50; Ingrid Maier and Stepan Shamin, "Obzory inostrannoi pressy v kollegii inostrannykh del v poslednie gody pravleniia Petra I," *Rossiiskaia istoriia*, 2011, 91–112; Ingrid Maier, "Zeventiende-eeuwse Nederlandse couranten vertaald voor de tsaar," *Tijdschrift voor Mediageschiedenis*, no. 12 (2009): 27–49.

9. V. E. Grabar', *The History of International Law in Russia, 1647–1917: A Bio-Bibliographical Study*, trans. William Elliott Butler (Oxford: Clarendon Press, 1990), 52. I am grateful to an anonymous reviewer for the reference.

10. Peterson, *Administrative and Judicial Reforms*, 383–393; Joukovskaïa, "Le service diplomatique russe," 63–68, 180ff.

11. N. A. Voskresenskii, *Petr Velikii kak zakonodatel': Issledovanie zakonodatel'nogo prottsessa v Rossii v epokhu reform pervoi chetverti XVIII veka*, ed. D. O. Serov (Moscow: Novoe literaturnoe obozrenie, 2017), 161–162. *PSZ*, 7:200, 7:204.

12. *PSZ*, 10:672, 11:730, 12:743. There is a clear parallel to be made here to the privileged communication systems that emerged in China during the Kangxi and Yongzheng periods—that is, contemporaneously with the developments in Russia. See Beatrice S. Bartlett, *Monarchs and Ministers: The Grand Council in Mid-Ch'ing China, 1723–1820* (Berkeley: University of California Press, 1991).

13. M. M. Shtrange, *Demokraticheskaia intelligentsiia Rossii v XVIII veke* (Moscow: Nauka, 1965).

14. Joukovskaïa, "Le service diplomatique russe," 180–181.

15. G. F. Kim, *Istoriia otechestvennogo vostokovedeniia*, 40–66.

16. See, for example, Sebouh David Aslanian, *From the Indian Ocean to the Mediterranean: The Global Trade Networks of Armenian Merchants from New Julfa* (Berkeley: University of California Press, 2011), 66–85.

17. The most authoritative recent history of the mission is V. G. Datsyshen, *Istoriia Rossiiskoi dukhovnoi missii v Kitae* (Hong Kong: Pravoslavnoe Bratstvo . . . Petra i Pavla, 2010); though older, Widmer, *Russian Ecclesiastical Mission* is insightful and witty in equal measure; see also A. S. Avtonomov, "Diplomaticheskaia deiatel'nost' Russkoi pravoslavnoi missii v Pekine v XVIII–XIX vv.," *Voprosy istorii*, no. 7 (2005): 100–111; S. L. Tikhvinskii, *Istoriia Rossiiskoi Dukhovnoi Missii v Kitae: sbornik statei* (Moscow: Izd-vo Sviato-Vladimirskogo Bratstva, 1997). This last volume in particular contains a reprint of Nikolai Adoratskii's classic work on the mission.

18. N. I Veselovskii, *Materialy dlia istorii rossiiskoi dukhovnoi missii v Pekine* (St. Petersburg: Tip. Glavnogo Upravleniia Udelov, 1905), 22. These reflections appear in a composite historical text and are either from the 1740s or the 1790s. On

drunkenness among the clergy, see, for example, Gregory L. Freeze, *The Russian Levites: Parish Clergy in the Eighteenth Century* (Cambridge, MA: Harvard University Press, 1977), 211–212.

19. See the composite list in P. E. Skachkov, *Ocherki istorii russkogo kitaevedeniia* (Moscow: Nauka, 1977), 358–360. For a sample list with ages, see RGIA, f. 796, op. 73, d. 327, l. 13–16.

20. On the Lifanyuan, see Dittmar Schorkowitz and Ning Chia, eds., *Managing Frontiers in Qing China: The Lifanyuan and Libu Revisited* (Leiden, Netherlands: Brill, 2017); Ning Chia, "The Lifanyuan and the Inner Asian Rituals in the Early Qing (1644–1795)," *Late Imperial China* 14, no. 1 (1993): 60–92.

21. Widmer, *Russian Ecclesiastical Mission*, 103–112. See also Meng Ssu-ming, "The E-Lo-Ssu Kuan (Russian Hostel) in Peking," *Harvard Journal of Asiatic Studies* 23 (January 1, 1960): 19–46.

22. RGADA, f. 199, p. 391, n. 3, l. 18.; OPI GIM, f. 450, n. 207, l. 187–199.

23. RGADA, f. 248, op. 39, kn. 2634, l. 574.

24. The principal scholarly discussions of Rossokhin, whose birthdate and birthplace have been much disputed, are V. P. Taranovich, "Ilarion Rossokhin," 225–241; M. I. Radovskii, "Russkii kitaeved I. K. Rossokhin," in *Iz istorii nauki i tekhniki v stranakh Vostoka* (Moscow: Izd-vo vostochnoĭ lit-ry, 1960), 88–99; P. E. Skachkov, "Znachenie rukopisnogo," 117–123; Skachkov, *Ocherki istorii russkogo kitaevedeniia,* 41–52. Gaston Cahen made a suggestion, which V. P. Taranovich appears to support, that Rossokhin was born in 1707, but this was not supported by evidence and is disconfirmed by numerous references to him as a child in the archival documents and by his entry into Platkovskii's Mongol school. Although later sources identify a variety of birthplaces, the only contemporary document identifies him as being from Khilok; see RGIA, f. 796, op. 11, d. 23, l. 359–360.

25. RGIA, f. 796, op. 19, d. 356, l. 20ff.

26. RGIA, f. 796, op. 11, d. 23, l. 164ff.

27. Veselovskii, *Materialy dlia istorii rossiiskoi,* 69.

28. The diary is included in a massive folio volume that (together with its second half) incorporates the entire voluminous archive of the Platkovskii mission. RGIA, f. 796, op. 11, d. 23, l. 137–155.

29. RGIA, f. 796, op. 11, d. 23, l. 158ff.

30. RGIA, f. 796, op. 11, d. 23, l. 644–645; RGIA, f. 796, op. 19, d. 356, l. 181ff.

31. RGIA, f. 796, op. 11, d. 23, l. 450.

32. Marianna Muravyeva has discussed the remarkably laissez-faire attitude of the early modern Russian Orthodox Church to homosexuality and even homosexual rape. See her "Personalizing Homosexuality and Masculinity in Early Modern Russia," in *Gender in Late Medieval and Early Modern Europe*, ed. Marianna Muravyeva and Raisa Maria Toivo (London: Routledge, 2012), 205–225.

33. RGIA, f. 796, op. 11, d. 23, l. 137–155.

34. RGIA, f. 796, op. 11, d. 23, l. 133–134, l. 359.

35. RGIA, f. 796, op. 24, d. 213, l. 7–8. The specific phrase is *imeli staranie o bliadiakh.*

36. OR BAN, 32.6.18; RGADA, f. 199, p. 359, ch. 2, n. 4.

37. RGADA, f. 199, p. 349, ch. 1, n. 5. The later missionary Feodosii Smorzhevskii, who certainly knew Latin, also referred to the Jesuits by their Chinese names.

38. SPb ARAN, f. 3, o. 1, d. 808a, l. 11ff; f. 3, op. 11, d. 15 / 3.

39. This was likely the 1721 edition. See Mosca, *From Frontier Policy,* 104–105.

40. Skachkov, *Ocherki istorii russkogo kitaevedeniia,* 56–61.

41. SPb ARAN, f. 3, op. 11, d. 15 / 2; f. 3, op. 1, d. 59, l. 201.

42. SPb ARAN, f. 3, op. 1, d. 465, l. 272.

43. AV IVR, f. 42, op. 1, d. 1, l. 286. (This comment in Kamenskii's hand is on a stack of notebooks written by a previous set of students.)

44. RGIA, f. 796, op. 19, d. 293; Skachkov, *Ocherki istorii russkogo kitaevedeniia,* 58–62.

45. See Veselovskii, *Materialy dlia istorii rossiiskoi;* Barbara Widenor Maggs, "'The Jesuits in China': Views of an Eighteenth-Century Russian Observer," *Eighteenth-Century Studies* 8, no. 2 (December 1, 1974): 137–152; Smorzhevskii, *Notes on the Jesuits.*

46. RGIA, f. 796, op. 27, d. 341, l. 15ff.

47. RGIA, f. 796, op. 27, d. 341, l. 73; RGIA, f. 796, op. 11, d. 23, l. 154–155.

48. Gaubil to [academy president] Razumovskii, April 28, 1755, in Antoine Gaubil, *Correspondance de Pekin, 1722–1759,* ed. Rene Simon (Geneva: Éditions Plon, 1971), 808–809.

49. RGADA, f. 248, op. 39, kn. 2634, l. 273ff.

50. RGADA, f. 248, op. 39, kn. 2634, l. 273–304.

51. It was likely Leont'ev who wrote the Chinese characters on the grave, because the date on the right is rendered in the Julian calendar, substituting only Qianlong reign years. (Other Russian graves at Zhalan omitted the Chinese characters entirely and used dates from the Creation, traditional among the clergy.)

52. ARAN, f. 3, op. 1, d. 225, l. 431–432.

53. RGADA, f. 1261, op. 1, d. 440. See also Yanagisawa Akira, "Some Remarks on the 'Addendum to the Treaty of Kiakhta' in 1768," *Memoirs of the Toyo Bunko,* no. 63 (2005): 65–88.

54. AVPRI, f. 62, op. 62 / 2, d. 5, l. 54. See also G. I. Sarkisova, "Nekotorye aspekty formirovaniia kadrovoi politiki Kollegii inostrannykh del na kitaiskom napravlenii vo vtoroi polovine XVIII v.," *Kitai v mire i regional'noi politike. Istoriia i sovremennost',* no. 19 (2014): 359–379.

55. RGADA, f. 17, d. 75; Veselovskii, *Materialy dlia istorii rossiiskoi,* 37.

56. AVPRI, f. 62, op. 62 / 2, d. 5, l. 102.

57. Bantysh-Kamenskii, *Diplomaticheskoe sobranie.*

58. RKO XVIII, 6:232, 6:386n1.

59. RGIA, f. 796, op. 42, d. 202, l. 33.

60. AVPRI f. 62, op. 62 / 2, d. 23, l. 55ff.

61. AVPRI f. 62, op. 62 / 2, d. 9, l. 283ff.

62. OR RGB, f. 273, k. 27, n. 2, l. 206–271.

63. OR RGB, f. 273, k. 27, n. 2, l. 225v–226v.

64. S. K. Smirnov, *Istoriia Troitskoi Lavrskoi seminarii* (Moscow: A. V. Tolokon-nikov, 1867), 522–23.

65. RGIA, f. 796, op. 59, d. 328, l. 13, 49–54, 110–113.

66. RGIA, f. 796, op. 76, d. 406.

67. RGADA, f. 24, n. 62, ch. 3, l68.

68. RGIA, f. 796, op. 99, d. 877, l. 147–148; RGIA, f. 796, op. 76, d. 406, l. 1.

69. OR RGB, f. 273, k. 27, n. 2, l. 272–281.

70. AV IVR, f. 42, op. 1, d. 2, l. 305.

71. RGIA, f. 796, op. 81, d. 195.

72. RKO XIX, 113.

4. Scholarship and Expertise at Home and Abroad

1. Gordin, "Importation of Being Earnest," 1–31; Werrett, "Odd Sort of Exhibition."

2. On Peter and absolutist prestige, see Richard Wortman, *Scenarios of Power: Myth and Ceremony in Russian Monarchy from Peter the Great to the Abdication of Nicholas II* (Princeton, NJ: Princeton University Press, 2006), 21–39.

3. Marker, *Publishing, Printing,* 44–50; J. L. Black, *G.-F. Müller and the Imperial Russian Academy* (Kingston, ON: McGill-Queen's University Press, 1986), 128–155.

4. Black, *G.-F. Müller,* 8–9.

5. See Rachel Koroloff, "The Beginnings of a Russian Natural History: The Life and Work of Stepan Petrovich Krasheninnikov (1711–1755)" (master's thesis, Oregon State University, 2007).

6. On the role of translators in eighteenth-century literary culture, see Oken-fuss, *Rise and Fall,* 138–197; Marker, *Publishing, Printing,* 50–57; Gesine Argent, Derek Offord, and Vladislav Rjeoutski, "The Functions and Value of Foreign Languages in Eighteenth-Century Russia," *Russian Review* 74, no. 1 (2015): 1–19.

7. Nikolai Novikov, "Opyt istoricheskogo sloviaria o rossiiskikh pisateliakh," in *Izbrannye proizvedeniia,* ed. G. P. Makogonenko (Moscow: Gos. izd-vo khu-dozh. lit., 1951), 277–370.

8. See Werrett, "Schumacher Affair," 104–126; another recent interpretation of this episode is Igor Fedyukin, "The 'German' Reign of Empress Anna: Russia's Dis-

ciplinary Moment?" *Kritika: Explorations in Russian and Eurasian History* 19, no. 2 (May 23, 2018): 363–384.

9. SPb ARAN, f. 3, op. 1, d. 59, l. 248ff.

10. SPb ARAN, f. 3, op. 1, d. 76, l25, l. 117–119. See, for example, OR RNB, f. 487, n. F-219.

11. SPb ARAN, f. 3, op. 1, d. 59, l. 218–242. The academy did eventually pay for Rossokhin to move to Vasilevskii Island, but he was forced to move out again a few months later, evidently due to lack of funds.

12. OR BAN, 32.6.17. Although it is missing a title, a trilingual version of this text, complete with original preface, is preserved in the library of the Academy of Sciences complete with the signatures of the students involved. Skachkov mistakenly attributes authorship of this text to Rossokhin himself.

13. Skachkov, *Ocherki istorii russkogo kitaevedeniia*, 46–47.

14. See, for example, RGADA, f. 199, p. 391, n. 3; f. 199, p. 349, ch. 1, n. 33. For salary information, see, for example, M. I Sukhomlinov, *Materialy dlia istorii Imperatorskoi akademii nauk* (St. Petersburg: Tip. Imp. akademii nauk, 1885), 7:453.

15. SPb ARAN, f. 21, op. 1, d. 101, l. 107.

16. For example, G. F. Miller, *Istoriia Sibiri* (Moscow: Izdatel'stvo Akademii nauk SSSR, 1937), 1:26, 529.

17. Johann Fischer, "Rassuzhdeniia o raznykh imenakh kitaiskogo gosudarstva i o khanskikh titulakh," *Ezhemesiachnye sochineniia,* October 1756, 321.

18. SPb ARAN, f. 3, op. 1, d. 225, l. 144; Taranovich, "Ilarion Rossokhin," 225–241.

19. Sukhomlinov, *Materialy dlia istorii,* 8:343–344, 359.

20. SPb ARAN, f. 3, op. 1, d. 836, l. 197–199.

21. SPb ARAN, f. 3, op. 1, d. 59, l. 200–208; SPb ARAN, f. 3, op. 1, d. 267, l. 50–53. For a complete description of Rossokhin's collection, see my "The Manchu Book in Eighteenth-Century St. Petersburg," *Saksaha: A Journal of Manchu Studies,* no. 14 (2016), http://dx.doi.org/10.3998/saksaha.13401746.0014.001.

22. For a translation and discussion of this text, see Mark C. Elliott, "The 'Eating Crabs' Youth Book," in *Under Confucian Eyes: Writings on Gender in Chinese History,* ed. Susan Mann and Yu-Yin Cheng (Berkeley: University of California Press, 2001), 263–281.

23. OR BAN, 16.2.9. Previous scholars have not connected this text to Rossokhin, but there is no question that it is a translation from the *Gu jin bu yuan leishu.* I am grateful to Wu Huiyi for pointing me to this text.

24. For a later catalog, see Julius Klaproth, *Katalog der chinesischen und mandjurischen Bücher der Bibliothek der Akademie der Wissenschaften in St. Petersburg,* ed. Hartmut Walravens (Berlin: C. Bell, 1988).

25. RGADA, f. 248, op. 113, d. 485a, l. 759ff.

26. RGADA, f. 248, op. 113, d. 485a, l. 767; Mikhail Vasil'evich Lomonosov, *Polnoe sobranie sochinenii* (Moscow: Nauka, 1950), 9:423–426; Skachkov, *Ocherki istorii*

russkogo kitaevedeniia, 67–69; Aleksei Leont'ev and Ilarion Rossokhin, *Obstoiatel'noe opisanie proiskhozhdeniia i sostoianiia Man'dzhurskago naroda i voiska, v osmi znamenakh sostoiashchago,* 17 vols. (St. Petersburg: izhdiveniem Imperatorskoi Akademii Nauk, 1784).

27. Radovskii, "Russkii kitaeved I. K. Rossokhin," 88–99.

28. Rossokhin, "Opisanie puteshestviia, koim ezdili kitaiskie poslanniki v Rossiiu," *Ezhemesiachnye sochineniia* (1764), 3ff.

29. Novikov, "Opyt istoricheskogo sloviaria."

30. See Hartmut Walravens, "Alexej Leont'ev und sein Werk," *Aetas Manjurica,* no. 3 (1992): 404–431. (Pace Walravens, Leont'ev never made a second trip to Beijing; the book *Kitaiskii mudrets,* a translation of Robert Dodsley's *The Oeconomy of Human Life,* is also incorrectly attributed to him here.)

31. For a recent summary of the debate, see Lim, *China and Japan,* 49–51.

32. See V. P. Semennikov, *Sobranie staraiushcheesia o perevode inostrannykh knig, uchrezhdennoe Ekaterinoi II 1768–1783 gg: Istoriko-literaturnoe izsledovanie* (St. Petersburg, 1900).

33. SPb ARAN, f. 3, op. 4, d. 53 / 2; f. 3, op. 4, d. 24 / 27; f. 3, op. 4, d. 31 / 17.

34. Marker, *Publishing, Printing,* 95ff.

35. SPb ARAN, f. 3, op. 4, d. 68 / 1.

36. SPb ARAN, f. 3, op. 4, d. 24 / 27; f. 3, op. 4, d. 28 / 22; f. 3, op. 4, d. 28 / 39; f. 3, op. 4, d. 31 / 17.

37. *Sanktpeterburgskii vestnik,* 1779, no. 4, 202–222; 1780, no. 6, 369–372; SPb ARAN, f. 3, op. 4, d. 53 / 2.

38. For example, Zhan-Baptist Diu Gal'd, *Geograficheskoe, istoricheskoe, khronologicheskoe, politicheskoe, i fizicheskoe opisanie Kitaiskiia imperii i Tatarii Kitaiskiia, tan,* trans. Ignatii De Teil's (St. Petersburg: Tip. Imp. Sukhoput. shliakhet. kad. korpusa, 1774).

39. *Chinesische Gedanken nach der von Alexjei Leont'ew aus der manshurischen Sprache verfertigten russischen Uebersetzung ins Deutsche übersetzt* (Weimar, Germany: Hoffmann, 1776).

40. Pierre-Charles Lévesque, *Pensées morales de divers auteurs chinois* (Paris: Didot aîné, 1782).

41. SPb ARAN, f. 1, op. 3, t. 61, l. 23–24.

42. *Monthly Review; or Literary Journal,* 21:338–339; *Philosophical Transactions,* 48:770; *Journal des Sçavans,* January 1759, 440–441.

43. Aleksei Agafonov also translated an abridged Chinese Catholic catechism by Giulio Aleni: OR BAN, 31.3.15.

44. The former was a book in Manchu published in 1731–1734, the *Dergi hese jakūn gusa de wasimbuhangge;* the Bibliothèque Nationale's copy is digitized at https://gallica.bnf.fr/ark:/12148/btv1b9003026g. The latter is a prominent early Qing anthology, the *Guwen yuanjian.* Rossokhin identifies the former simply as "jakūn gūsa," or "eight banners."

45. OPI GIM, f. 440, n. 1198 / a; OR RGB, f. 267, k. 21, n. 4.

46. OR RNB f. 550, FXVIII-24 / 3, l. 338.

47. RGADA, f. 24, n. 62, ch. 1, l. 284; Hartmut Walravens, *Aleksej Agafonov: ein unbekannter Ostasienwissenschaftler des 18. Jahrhunderts: eine Biobibliographie* (Hamburg: Bell, 1982).

48. SPbII, f. 175, op. 1, d. 40, l. 14–19.

49. OR RNB, f. 542, n. 727. I have been unable to identify the novel, and its supposed Chinese title is meaningless.

50. OR RNB, f. 885, n. 596.

51. AV IVR, R. I, op. 1, d. 38.

52. SPbII, f. 175, op. 1, d. 40, l. 14–19.

53. Elena Kuz'mina, "Pochemu kitaitsy takie . . ." *Otechestvennye zapiski* 61, no. 4 (2014), http://www.strana-oz.ru/2014/4/pochemu-kitaycy-takie.

54. Ivan Orlov, *Noveishee i podrobneishee istorichesko-geograficheskoe opisanie Kitaiskoi imperii* (Moscow: V Universitetskoi Tipografii, 1820), 1:3–9.

55. AVPRI, f. 62, op. 62 / 2, d. 9, l. 136.

56. For example, Orlov, *Opisanie Kitaiskoi imperii*, 1:176; Leont'ev and Rossokhin, *Obstoiatel'noe opisanie*, 17:219.

57. Aleksei Leont'ev, *Kratchaishee opisanie gorodam, dokhodam i protchemu Kitaiskago gosudarstva, a pri tom i vsem gosudarstvam, korolevstvam i kniazhestvam, koi Kitaitsam svedomy* (St. Petersburg: v Tipografii Akademii Nauk, 1778).

5. The Caravan as a Knowledge Bureaucracy

1. Ger'e, *Otnosheniia Leibnitsa*, 5. Quoted in Slezkine, "Naturalists versus Nations," 170–195.

2. John R. Harris, "Movements of Technology between Britain and Europe," in *International Technology Transfer: Europe, Japan, and the USA, 1700–1914*, ed. David J. Jeremy (Brookfield, VT: Edward Elgar, 1991), 9–30; John R. Harris, "Industrial Espionage in the Eighteenth Century," *Industrial Archaeology Review* 7, no. 2 (1985): 127–138; John R. Harris, *Industrial Espionage and Technology Transfer: Britain and France in the Eighteenth Century* (Brookfield, VT: Ashgate, 1998); see also Doron S. Ben-Atar, *Trade Secrets: Intellectual Piracy and the Origins of American Industrial Power* (New Haven, CT: Yale University Press, 2004).

3. See Bertucci, "Enlightened Secrets," 820–852; Ursula Klein and E. C. Spary, eds., *Materials and Expertise in Early Modern Europe: Between Market and Laboratory* (Chicago: University of Chicago Press, 2010); Elaine Leong and Alisha Rankin, eds., *Secrets and Knowledge in Medicine and Science, 1500–1800* (Burlington, VT: Ashgate, 2011); Long, *Openness, Secrecy, Authorship*; Karel Davids, "Craft Secrecy in Europe in the Early Modern Period: A Comparative View," *Early*

Science and Medicine 10, no. 3 (August 1, 2005): 341–348 (as well as the other articles in this issue).

4. Some of the earliest work includes Gaston Cahen, *Histoire des relations,* 93–114, 227–244; Cahen, *Le livre de comptes.* The definitive English-language study is Foust, *Muscovite and Mandarin,* 105–164.

5. See, for example, Luba Golburt, *The First Epoch: The Eighteenth Century and Russian Cultural Imagination* (Madison: University of Wisconsin Press, 2014), 205–238; see also Matthew P. Romaniello, *Enterprising Empires: Russia and Britain in Eighteenth-Century Eurasia* (Cambridge: Cambridge University Press, 2019); Matthew P. Romaniello and Tricia Starks, eds., *Tobacco in Russian History and Culture: From the Seventeenth Century to the Present* (London: Routledge, 2009). On tea, see Audra Yoder, "Tea Time in Romanov Russia: A Cultural History, 1616–1917" (PhD diss., University of North Carolina, 2017).

6. Jonathan Schlesinger, *A World Trimmed with Fur: Wild Things, Pristine Places, and the Natural Fringes of Qing* (Stanford, CA: Stanford University Press, 2017), 129–138.

7. Skachkov, *Ocherki istorii russkogo kitaevedeniia,* 30ff; Shafranovskaia, "O poezdkakh Lorentsa Langa," 155–159; Shafranovskaia, "Puteshestvie Lorentsa Langa," 188–205.

8. See, for example, Neil Kenny, *The Uses of Curiosity in Early Modern France and Germany* (Oxford: Oxford University Press, 2004); Justin Stagl, *History of Curiosity.*

9. RGADA, f. 248, op. 113, d. 1214, l. 22–27.

10. RGADA, f. 248, kn. 181, l. 25.

11. RGADA, f. 248, o. 113, d. 485a, l. 715ff.

12. RGADA, f. 214, op. 1, ch. 8, d. 5376, l. 10.

13. Hsia, *Sojourners,* 133–136.

14. For example, RGADA, f. 248, kn. 181, l. 246.

15. On the postal system, see John Randolph, "The Singing Coachman; or, The Road and Russia's Ethnographic Invention in Early Modern Times," *Journal of Early Modern History* 11, no. 1–2 (January 1, 2007): 33–61.

16. For example, RGADA, f. 248, op. 113, d. 485a, l. 109ff.

17. RGADA, f. 248, kn. 181, l. 58.

18. Denis J. B. Shaw, "Geographical Practice and Its Significance in Peter the Great's Russia," *Journal of Historical Geography* 22, no. 2 (April 1, 1996): 160–176; Willard Sunderland, "Imperial Space: Territorial Thought and Practice in the Eighteenth Century," in *Russian Empire: Space, People, Power, 1700–1930,* ed. Jane Burbank, Mark von Hagen, and Anatolyi Remnev (Bloomington: Indiana University Press, 2007), 33–66; L. A. Goldenberg and A. V. Postnikov, "Development of Mapping Methods in Russia in the Eighteenth Century," *Imago Mundi,* no. 37 (1985): 63–80.

19. OR RGB, f. 178, n. 1317, l. 99.

20. Both of these drawings are from OR RGB, f. 199, op. 1, p. 349, ch. 2 (one of G.-F. Müller's portfolios). The marginal annotations are by Larion Rossokhin.

21. RGADA, f. 248, op. 113, d. 485a, l. 109.

22. RGADA, f. 248, op. 113, d. 485a, l. 705v, 714.

23. RGADA, f. 248, op. 113, d. 485a, l. 685–688.

24. RGADA, f. 248, kn. 1102, l. 1564–1567.

25. Likely the 1721 edition. See Mosca, *From Frontier Policy,* 104–105. Although the later Yongzheng and Qianlong atlases were considerably larger, most of the new plates covered territories beyond the Qing borders that were long familiar to European cartographers.

26. SPb ARAN, f. 3, op. 1, d. 114, l. 45–52.

27. See Foust, *Rhubarb.*

28. Richard Burgess, "Thomas Garvine—Ayrshire Surgeon Active in Russia and China," *Medical History* 19, no. 1 (January 1975): 91–94.

29. RKO XVIII, 1:177.

30. RGADA, f. 248, kn. 181, l. 46–47. The old Muscovite Apothecary Bureau was replaced with the Medical Chancellery in 1721.

31. This was the German spelling, which he himself used. His name was Franc-Luka Jelačič in Croatian, Frants Luka Elachich in Russian.

32. SPb ARAN, f. 3, op. 1, d. 808, l. 15.

33. See, for example, Lindsey Hughes, *Russia in the Age of Peter the Great* (New Haven, CT: Yale University Press, 1998), 309–316.

34. Speranskii, *PSZ,* 8:351.

35. Robert Finlay, *The Pilgrim Art: Cultures of Porcelain in World History* (Berkeley: University of California Press, 2010), 48–77, 274ff; Martin Schönfeld, "Was There a Western Inventor of Porcelain?" *Technology and Culture* 39, no. 4 (October 1, 1998): 716–727.

36. Baron N. B. von Vol'f, ed., *Imperatorskii farforovyi zavod, 1744–1904* (St. Petersburg: Izdanie Upravleniia farforovymi zavodami, 1906), 1–6. This chapter in von Vol'f also contains a description of Miasnikov and the Kursins' experiments.

37. RGADA, f. 248, kn. 1102, l. 1403–1409, 1537–1538.

38. RGADA, f. 248, kn. 1102, l. 514–516.

39. RGADA, f. 214, op. 1, ch. 8, d. 5378, l. 10; f. 248, kn, 181, l. 171.

40. RGADA, f. 248, kn. 183, l. 206–221.

41. RGADA, f. 248, kn. 181, l. 361; f. 248, op. 113, d. 968, l. 17ff.

42. RGADA, f. 248, kn. 188, l. 62–88. See also Iurii Dushkov, "Kursiny v Irkutske," *Zemlia irkutskaia,* no. 5 (1995): 13–17.

43. RGADA, f. 248, kn. 1102, l. 1564–1568.

44. RGADA, f. 248, op. 40, kn. 2930, l. 530–535; f. 248, kn. 183, l. 255ff.

45. RGADA, f. 248, kn. 1102, l. 514–516.

46. RGADA, f. 248, op. 113, d. 1322.

6. The Commerce of Long-Distance Letters

1. Examples of the Jesuit network approach include Noël Golvers, "The Jesuit Mission in China (17th–18th Cent) as the Framework for the Circulation of Knowledge between Europe and China," *Lusitania Sacra,* no. 36 (July 2017): 179–199; Albrecht Classen, "A Global Epistolary Network: Eighteenth-Century Jesuit Missionaries Write Home," *Studia Neophilologica* 86, no. 1 (January 2, 2014): 79–94; Mordechai Feingold, *Jesuit Science and the Republic of Letters* (Cambridge, MA: MIT Press, 2003).

2. Goldgar, *Impolite Learning;* David N Livingstone, *Putting Science in Its Place: Geographies of Scientific Knowledge* (Chicago: University of Chicago Press, 2003).

3. The social and economic context of this exchange was a major feature of the first Russian-language work on this correspondence, written by V. P. Taranovich in the 1940s. It was unpublished until it was printed in Pan and Shatalov, *Arkhivnye materialy.* See also Stanislav Juznic, "Building a Bridge between the Observatories of Petersburg and Beijing: A Study on the Jesuit Avguštin Hallerstein from Present-Day Slovenia, Celebrating the 310th Anniversary of His Birth," *Monumenta Serica,* no. 60 (2012): 309–406; Noël Golvers, *Libraries of Western Learning for China: Circulation of Western Books between Europe and China in the Jesuit Mission (ca. 1650–ca. 1750),* vol. 1, *Logistics of Book Acquisition and Circulation* (Leuven, Belgium: Ferdinand Verbiest Institute, 2012). The Gaillard letters are held partially in the Henri Bosmans collection at the Jesuit archives in Vanves near Paris and in the Fonds Chine of the Belgian Jesuit archives at KADOC in Leuven.

4. Jan Joseph Santich, *Missio Moscovitica: The Role of the Jesuits in the Westernization of Russia, 1582–1689* (New York: P. Lang, 1995).

5. ARSI, Jap-Sin 138 (Acta Pekinensia), l. 848.

6. OR RGB, f. 299, n. 81; OR BAN, 17.8.34 and 25.2.1. I have conjectured the addressees of the letter based on dates and other circumstantial evidence.

7. SPb ARAN, f. 784, op. 1, d. 56.

8. Steven Shapin, *A Social History of Truth: Civility and Science in Seventeenth-Century England,* Science and Its Conceptual Foundations (Chicago: University of Chicago Press, 1994), 65–125.

9. Gaubil, *Correspondance de Pekin,* 635–638.

10. Dmitrii A Tolstoi, *Rimskii katolitsizm v Rossii: istoricheskoe izsliedovanie* (St. Petersburg: Izdanie i tip. V.F. Demakova, 1876), 1:134–135.

11. Gaubil, *Correspondance de Pekin,* 167, 254.

12. Gaubil, 313.

13. SPb ARAN, f. 784, op. 1, d. 29. N. I. Nevskaia, *Letopis' Rossiiskoi Akademii Nauk* (St. Petersburg: Nauka, 2000), 1:73, 143.

14. Lang to Korff, October 21, 1737, SPb ARAN, R. III, op.1, d. 187a, l. 89–90.

15. Gaubil, *Correspondance de Pekin,* 373.

16. Bayer to Parrenin, November 3, 1737, SPb ARAN, R. III, op. 1, d. 187a, l. 39–40.

17. SPb ARAN, R. III, op.1, d. 187a, l. 105–107.

18. Knud Lundbæk, *T. S. Bayer, 1694–1738: Pioneer Sinologist* (London: Curzon, 1986).

19. Bayer to Parrenin, November 15, 1733 (draft), SPb ARAN, R. III, op. 1, d. 187a, l. 22–24.

20. Parrenin to Bayer, December 29, 1736, SPb ARAN, R. III, op. 1, d. 82, l. 54–56.

21. Delisle to Gaubil, end of 1734, SPb ARAN, R. III, op. 1, d. 82, l. 45v.

22. De la Charme to Delisle, July 13, 1734, SPb ARAN, R. III, op. 1, d. 82, l. 32–35.

23. Delisle to Grammatici, June 11, 1729, AN, 2\JJ\61, n. 88.

24. Delisle to Gaubil, end of 1734, SPb ARAN, R. III, op. 1, d. 82, l. 47v.

25. Gaubil, *Correspondance de Pekin,* 374.

26. Gaubil, 560.

27. Delisle to Louis Léon Pajot d'Ons en Bray ("Donsenbray"), December 23, 1727, AN, 2\JJ\61, n. 45.

28. An extensive scholarly debate has raged about Delisle's loyalties, goals, and contributions to Russian science. The latest pro-Delisle intervention is Dmitrii Guzevich and Irina Guzevich, "Karta-zadanie Zh. N. Delilia dlia Vtoroi Kamchatksoi ekspeditsii: 'bessovestnyi obman' ili osnova dlia otkrytii?" in *Delili v Rossii: sbornik statei,* ed. Dmitrii Guzevich and Irina Guzevich (St. Petersburg: Mamatov, 2019), 60–92 (along with the other essays in that volume); see also Marie-Anne Chabin, "L'astronome français Joseph-Nicolas Delisle à la cour de Russie," in *L'influence française en Russie au XVIIIe siècle,* ed. Jean-Pierre Poussou, Anne Mézin, and Yves Perret-Gentil (Paris: Institut d'etudes slaves, 2004), 504–520. Anti-Delisle perspectives include A. V. Postnikov, "Novye dannye o rossiiskikh kartograficheskikh materialakh pervoi poloviny XVIII v., vyvezennykh Zh.-N. Delilem vo Frantsiiu," *Voprosy istorii estestvoznaniia i tekhniki,* no. 3 (2005): 17–38; Lydia T. Black, "The Question of Maps: Exploration of the Bering Sea in the Eighteenth Century," in *The Sea in Alaska's Past: First Conference Proceedings* (Anchorage: Office of History and Archaeology, Alaska Division of Parks, 1979), 6–50.

29. For example, Gaubil, *Correspondance de Pekin,* 647–648.

30. Pereyra to Korff, December 28, 1736, SPb ARAN, R. II, op. 1, d. 187, l. 8–9.

31. Aleksei Leont'ev, *Tian' shin' ko: to est' Angel'skaia beseda* (St. Petersburg: Imperatorskaia Akademiia Nauk, 1781); Aleksei Leont'ev, *Depei kitaets* (St. Petersburg: Imperatorskaia Akademiia Nauk, 1771). See also Aleksei Agafonov, *Van udzhin iuan* (1791), OR BAN 31.3.15.

32. Rachel Koroloff, "Seeds of Exchange: Collecting for Russia's Apothecary and Botanical Gardens in the Seventeenth and Eighteenth Centuries" (PhD diss., University of Illinois at Urbana-Champaign, 2015).

33. SPb ARAN, f. 3, op. 1, d. 14, l. 556; Amman to Parrenin (?), May 31, 1739, SPb ARAN, R. III, op. 1, d. 6, l. 62v–68v. My thanks to Rachel Koroloff for these documents.

34. Lang to Korff, March 17, 1735, SPb ARAN, f. 3, op. 1, d. 14, l. 523–524.

35. SPb ARAN, R. III, o. 1 d. 6.

36. RGADA, f. 248, kn. 181, l. 115ff.

37. Gaubil, *Correspondance de Pekin*, 565.

38. RGADA, f. 248, kn. 181, l. 194.

39. SPb ARAN, f. 3, o. 1, d. 808, l. 3.

40. SPb ARAN, f. 3, o. 1, d. 808, l. 10–12.

41. Pan and Shatalov, *Arkhivnye materialy*, 39–40; Wu, "'Observations We Made,'" 76–77.

42. SPb ARAN, f. 3, o. 1, d. 808, l. 13–14.

43. SPb ARAN, f. 3, o. 1, d. 808a.

44. SPb ARAN, f. 3, o. 1, d. 808a, l. 11ff. See [Etienne Fourmont], *Catalogus codicum manuscriptorium Bibliothecae Regiae* (Paris: E Typographia Regia, 1739).

45. SPb ARAN, f. 3, op. 1, d. 808, l. 200ff.

46. SPb ARAN, f. 3, op. 1, d. 464, l221ff, d. 808, l. 46ff.

47. SPb ARAN, R. III, op. 1, d. 187, l. 34–51.

48. SPb ARAN, f. 3, op. 1, d. 464, l. 244–250.

49. SPb ARAN, f. 3, op. 1, d. 808, l. 137–147; Klaproth, *Katalog der chinesischen*.

50. SPb ARAN, f. 3, op. 1, d. 808, l. 42v.

51. Desrobert to Razumovskii, May 9, 1755, SPb ARAN, R. II, op. 1, d. 187, l. 24–25.

52. See Pierre D'Incarville, "Catalogue alphabétique des plantes et autres objets d'histoire naturelle en usage en Chine," *Mémoires de la Société impériale des naturalistes de Moscou*, 1812, 3:103–128, 4:26–88.

53. Richmann to the Jesuits, n.d., SPb ARAN, R. III, op. 1, d. 187a, l. 109–112. On electricity in Qing Beijing, see Alexander Statman, "A Forgotten Friendship: How a French Missionary and a Manchu Prince Studied Electricity and Ballooning in Late Eighteenth Century Beijing," *East Asian Science, Technology, and Medicine*, no. 46 (2017): 89–118.

54. Rumovskii to D'Ollières, March 15, 1756, SPb ARAN, R.III, op. 1, d. 187a, l. 119–120.

55. RGADA, f. 248, op. 113, d. 485a, l. 821.

56. SPb ARAN, R. III, op. 1, d. 187a, l. 140–146.

57. SPb ARAN, f. 21, op. 3, d. 305 / 2, 305 / 4.

58. Copies of the 1763 letters are in Fonds Bosmans, Chine II, f. 97–119.

59. Pierre-Martial Cibot, "Fungus Sinensium Mo-Ku-Sin," *Novi Commentarii Academiae Scientiarum Imperialis Petropolitanae*, no. 19 (1774): 373–78. On the letter books, see I. I. Liubimenko, D. S. Rozhdestvenskii, and M. A. Borodina, eds., *Uche-*

naia korrespondentsiia Akademii nauk XVIII veka, 1766–1782: nauchnoe opisanie (Moscow: Izd-vo Akademii nauk SSSR, 1937).

60. Cibot to Euler, October 10, 1777, SPb ARAN, f. 1, op. 3, d. 61, l. 87–88.

61. Cibot to de Stehlin, September 21, 1773, KADOC, Fonds Bosmans III-224 (Chine Lettres II) f. 17.

62. RGIA, f. 796, o. 81, d. 195; RGIA, f. 1374, o. 2, d. 1617.

7. Frontier Intelligence and the Struggle for Inner Asia

1. Michael Warner, "Intelligence as Risk Shifting," in *Intelligence Theory: Key Questions and Debates,* ed. Peter Gill, Stephen Marrin, and Mark Phythian (London: Routledge, 2009), 16–32.

2. Examples of this approach include Alfred J. Rieber, "The Comparative Ecology of Complex Frontiers," in *Imperial Rule,* ed. Alfred J. Rieber and Alexei Miller (Budapest: Central European University Press, 2004), 177–208; Alfred J. Rieber, *The Struggle for the Eurasian Borderlands: From the Rise of Early Modern Empires to the End of the First World War* (Cambridge: Cambridge University Press, 2014); John LeDonne, *The Russian Empire and the World, 1700–1917: The Geopolitics of Expansion and Containment* (Oxford: Oxford University Press, 1997).

3. Foust, *Muscovite and Mandarin,* 203–329; John LeDonne, "Proconsular Ambitions on the Chinese Border," *Cahiers du Monde russe* 45, no. 1–2 (January 1, 2004): 31–60; Fred W. Bergholz, *The Partition of the Steppe: The Struggle of the Russians, Manchus, and the Zunghar Mongols for Empire in Central Asia, 1619–1758; A Study in Power Politics* (New York: Peter Lang, 1993), 351–404; Perdue, *China Marches West,* 256–292. Soviet perspectives include Besprozvannykh, *Priamur'e v sisteme russko-kitaiskikh otnoshenii;* B. P. Gurevich, *Mezhdunarodnye otnosheniia v Tsentral'noi Azii v XVII–pervoi polovine XIX v.* (Moscow: Nauka, 1983). V. S. Miasnikov's introduction to the sixth volume of *Russko-kitaiskie otnosheniia v XVIII v.* (2011) echoes the same Soviet-era narratives.

4. The most complete account in English is Perdue, *China Marches West;* see also I. Ia. Zlatkin, *Istoriia Dzhungarskogo khanstva, 1635–1758,* 2nd ed. (Moscow: Nauka, 1983), 279–302.

5. RGADA, f. 24, n. 40, l. 8–11. See below for the context of this quotation.

6. Mark Mancall, "China's First Missions to Russia, 1729–1731," *Harvard Papers on China,* no. 9 (1955): 88; Giovanni Stary, *Chinas erste Gesandte in Russland* (Wiesbaden, Germany: Harrassowitz, 1976).

7. This is a Russian translation with key Manchu phrases noted separately. The author is not identifiable; Manchu letters from the Lifanyuan are always signed simply "daicing gurun i tulergi golo be dasara jurgan." RGADA, f. 248, op. 113, d. 485, l. 7.

8. AV IVR, R. I, op. 1, d. 8, l. 29.

9. On the specificity of the Yongzheng era, see Zuo Fangzhou, "Yongzheng shiqi Zhong E guanxi zhong de jindai tezheng," *Xin yuanjian*, no. 9 (2008): 72–80; on the changing diplomatic tone in the Qianlong period, Chen Weixin, *Qingdai dui E waijiao liyi tizhi ji fanshu guishu jiaoshe: 1644–1861* (Harbin, China: Heilongjiang jiaoyu chubanshe, 2012), 153–160.

10. Alain Peyrefitte, *The Immobile Empire* (New York: Knopf, 1992); John Darwin, *After Tamerlane: The Rise and Fall of Global Empires, 1400–2000* (New York: Bloomsbury, 2008), 201; but for a revisionist view of the edict, see Henrietta Harrison, "The Qianlong Emperor's Letter to George III and the Early-Twentieth-Century Origins of Ideas about Traditional China's Foreign Relations," *American Historical Review* 122, no. 3 (June 1, 2017): 680–701.

11. RGADA, f. 10, op. 1, d. 94, l. 1–2.

12. RGADA, f. 248, op. 113, d. 485, l. 18–19.

13. AV IVR, R. I, op. 1, d. 8, l. 29.

14. RGADA, f. 248, op. 113, d. 256.

15. John Hobart, 2nd Earl of Buckinghamshire, *The Despatches and Correspondence of John, Second Earl of Buckinghamshire, Ambassador to the Court of Catherine II of Russia 1762–1765*, Camden third series (London: Longmans, Green, and Co, 1900), 2:161–168. These dispatches are discussed in Foust, *Muscovite and Mandarin*, 266–267.

16. A detailed discussion of this problem, dating from thirty years later, is in RGIA, f. 1147, op. 1, d. 103, l. 1–6.

17. RKO XVIII, 6:205.

18. Schlesinger, *World Trimmed with Fur*, 55–91.

19. RGADA, f. 248, op. 113, d. 485b, l. 59–61.

20. His memorandum is reproduced in Bantysh-Kamenskii, *Diplomaticheskoe sobranie*, 376–393.

21. RGADA, f. 248, op. 113, d. 864, l. 2–4.

22. Lo-shu Fu, *A Documentary Chronicle of Sino-Western Relations, 1644–1820* (Tucson: University of Arizona Press, 1966), 238–239. (Here and below, translations from this collection are his.)

23. RGADA, f. 214, op. 5, d. 2722.

24. RGADA, f. 248, op. 113, d. 491.

25. For Qing equipment, see, for example, RGADA, f, 248, op. 113, d. 1551, l. 1055–1058 (a report from a Buriat about Mongol soldiers' weaponry).

26. Fu's claim to the contrary in *Documentary Chronicle*, 551n232 is based on a misreading of a thirdhand account. For the military reform plan, see Ch. Ch. Valikhanov, *Sobranie sochinenii* (Almaty, Russia: Glav. red. Kazakhskoi Sov. Entsiklopedii, 1984), 4:215–223. See also LeDonne, "Proconsular Ambitions."

27. Michael Khodarkovsky, *Where Two Worlds Met: The Russian State and the Kalmyk Nomads, 1600–1771* (Ithaca, NY: Cornell University Press, 1992), 207–235;

on the exodus as "Return of the Jungars," see Benjamin Samuel Levey, "Jungar Refugees and the Making of Empire on Qing China's Kazakh Frontier, 1759–1773" (PhD diss., Harvard University, 2014), 209ff.

28. See Loretta Eumie Kim, "Marginal Constituencies: Qing Borderland Policies and Vernacular Histories of Five Tribes on the Sino-Russian Frontier" (PhD diss., Harvard University, 2009), 136–169.

29. See Perdue, *China Marches West,* 306–307.

30. AN, MAR\2JJ\77. (This is the copy of Unkovskii's report collected by Joseph-Nicolas Delisle during his residence in Russia.)

31. SPbII, koll. 115, op. 1, d. 1136, l. 130ff.

32. V. A. Moiseev, *Dzhungarskoe khanstvo i kazakhi: XVII–XVIII vv.* (Almaty, Russia: Gylym, 1991), 121ff.

33. RGADA, f. 248, op. 113, d. 108, l. 943–944.

34. SPbII, koll. 115, op. 1, d. 1136, l2, l. 116–120. This second report may have been by a relative of Bakhmuratov's; the name is garbled.

35. SPbII, koll. 115, op. 1, d. 1136, l2, l. 198.

36. RGADA, f. 248, op. 113, d. 1527, l. 111–122.

37. AV IVR, R. I, op. 1, d. 8, l. 1–3.

38. But see Charles R. Bawden, "The Mongol Rebellion of 1756–1757," *Journal of Asian History* 2, no. 1 (1968): 1–31.

39. Levey, "Jungar Refugees."

40. The most thorough treatment of the Amursana, Junghar, and Kazakh question is now Jin Noda, *The Kazakh Khanates between the Russian and Qing Empires: Central Eurasian International Relations during the Eighteenth and Nineteenth Centuries* (Leiden, Netherlands: Brill, 2016), 101–143.

41. OR RGB, f. 178, n. 1246.1, l. 42ff. This lengthy and revealing text, "Istoricheskaia spravka o zengorskom narode," appears to have been composed within the College of Foreign Affairs shortly after 1760, perhaps as a memorandum for higher officials.

42. OR RGB, f. 178, n. 1246. l. 54–55.

43. RGADA, f. 248, op. 113, d. 1223, l. 1–4.

44. OR RGB, f. 178, n. 1246.1. 53.

45. See Perdue, *China Marches West,* 288–289.

46. RGADA, f. 24, n. 40, l. 8–11; AVPRI, f. 62, op. 3, 1764, d. 4.

47. OR RGB, f. 178, n. 1246.1. 23–25.

48. SPbII, koll. 115, op. 1, d. 1136, l. 396; RGADA, f. 248, op. 113, d. 874, l3-4; AVPRI, f. 113, op. 113 / 1, d. 145, 1757; V. A. Moiseev, *Russko-dzhungarskie otnosheniia: konets XVII–60-e gg. XVIII vv.: dokumenty i izvlecheniia* (Barnaul, Russia: Azbuka, 2006), 224.

49. RGADA, f. 248, op. 113, d. 1551, l. 1–30ff.

50. See Noda, *Kazakh Khanates,* 101–143; Stary, *Chinas erste Gesandte.*

51. For the history of this arrangement, see O. V. Boronin, *Dvoedannichestvo v Sibiri XVII–60e gg. XIX v.* (Barnaul, Russia: Azbuka, 2004); V. B. Borodaev and A. V. Kontev, *Formirovanie rossiiskoi granitsy v Irtyshsko-Eniseiskom mezhdurech'e v 1620–1720 gg* (Barnaul, Russia: AltSPU, 2015).

52. For example, RGADA, f. 15, d. 150.

53. Fu, *Documentary Chronicle,* 237–238.

54. See my "Languages of Hegemony on the Eighteenth-Century Kazakh Steppe," *International History Review* 41, no. 5 (2019): 1020–1038.

55. For example, Michael Khodarkovsky, *Russia's Steppe Frontier: The Making of a Colonial Empire, 1500–1800* (Bloomington: Indiana University Press, 2002), 161ff.

56. Valikhanov, *Sobranie sochinenii,* 4:111–117.

57. Jin Noda and Takahiro Onuma, *A Collection of Documents from the Kazakh Sultans to the Qing Dynasty* (Tokyo: Department of Islamic Area Studies, University of Tokyo, 2010), 11–13 (translation theirs).

58. "Svedeniia o stepnykh kochuiushchikh narodakh," SPbII, f. 36, op. 1, d. 439, l. 40–46.

59. RGADA, f. 248, op. 113, d. 1551, l. 3ff.

60. OR RGB, f. 178, n. 1246, l. 69–70, 90.

61. OR RGB, f. 178, n. 1246, l. 70.

62. RGADA, f. 248, op. 113, d. 864, l. 14–19.

63. RGADA, f. 24, n. 40, l. 11ff.

64. I. P. Kamenetskii, "Sekretnaia missiia kuptsa A. Verkhoturova: k voprosu ob organizatsii russkoi razvedki v Dzhungarii v seredine XVIII v.," *Gumanitarnye nauki Sibiri,* no. 2 (2013): 24–28.

65. AVPRI, f. 130, op. 3, d. 1 (1763). A partial transcription is in Gurevich, Kim, and Tikhvinskii, *Mezhdunarodnye otnosheniia v Tsentral'noi Azii,* 2:176–178.

66. SPbII, f. 36, op. 1, d. 554, l. 556–559.

67. Perdue, *China Marches West,* 289–292.

68. OR RGB, f. 178, n. 1246, l. 106–113.

69. AVPRI, f. 113, op. 113 / 1, 1761, d. 1, l. 112–115.

70. Levey, "Jungar Refugees," 1381–1353.

71. Chen, *Qing dai dui E wai jiao,* 253–320; Gulnar T. Kendirbai, "The Politics of the Inner Asian Frontier and the 1771 Exodus of the Kalmyks," *Inner Asia* 20, no. 2 (October 23, 2018): 261–289; Khodarkovsky, *Where Two Worlds Met,* 207–35. See also Perdue, *China Marches West,* 292–299. For a contemporary Russian account, see Pëtr Rychkov, "Kratkoe izvestie o pobege torgoutskikh kalmyk," RGADA, f. 199, p. 150, ch. 9, n. 5.

72. See Jin Noda, "Russo-Chinese Trade through Central Asia: Regulations and Reality," in *Asiatic Russia: Imperial Power in Regional and International Contexts,* ed. Tomohiko Uyama (New York: Routledge, 2012), 153–173.

73. RGADA, f. 24, n. 64, part 2, l. 8–14. Gabun is almost certainly identical to the "Sa-mai-lin" mentioned in the Qing Shilu, although it is not clear where the difference in names comes from. See Fu, *Documentary Chronicle,* 309–316.

74. RGIA, f. 1264, op. 1, d. 314, l. 1–11.

75. See, e.g., RGIA, f. 13, op. 2, d. 781, l. 1–3.

76. RGIA, f. 13, op. 2, d. 1547. For more on trade in this region, see Noda, "Russo-Chinese Trade."

77. R. K. I. Quested, *The Expansion of Russia in East Asia, 1857–1860* (Kuala Lumpur: University of Malaya Press, 1968), 1–63.

78. RGADA, f. 24, n. 62, ch. 4, l. 91–94.

8. Spies and Subversion in Eastern Siberia

1. On the regional dimension of imperial politics, see, for example, Susan Smith-Peter, "Bringing the Provinces into Focus: Subnational Spaces in the Recent Historiography of Russia," *Kritika: Explorations in Russian and Eurasian History* 12, no. 4 (October 29, 2011): 835–848; Leonid Gorizontov, "Anatolii Remnev and the Regions of the Russian Empire," *Kritika: Explorations in Russian and Eurasian History* 16, no. 4 (October 29, 2015): 901–916.

2. See, for example, N. I. Pavlenko, *Ptentsy gnezda Petrova* (Moscow: Prospekt, 2016), 144ff.

3. SPbII, koll. 115, op. 1, d. 353, l. 28–41.

4. RGADA, f, 199, p. 349, ch. 1, n. 20.

5. OR BAN, 1.5.90, l. 15ff.

6. RGADA, f. 248, op. 113, d. 885, l. 1–6.

7. Songyun, *Emu tanggū orin sakda-i gisun sarkiyan,* 414–416.

8. OR IVR, C 33 Mss [Pang 89], l. 100. (This is a collection of eighteenth-century Manchu memorials, many relating to Russo-Qing relations, from Qiqihar in northern Manchuria.)

9. OR IVR, C 33 Mss, l. 102–104.

10. OR IVR, C 33 Mss, l. 142.

11. RGADA, f. 248, op. 113, d. 485a, l779–783; RKO XVIII, 6:136–137.

12. Bergholz, *Partition of the Steppe,* 387–394; Perdue, *China Marches West,* 276–80; Bawden, "Mongol Rebellion," 1–31.

13. RGADA, f. 248, op. 113, d. 1551, l. 1047–1048.

14. RGADA, f. 248, op. 113, d. 1551, l. 1050–1058.

15. RGADA, f. 248, op. 113, d. 1551, l. 1082–1088.

16. RGADA, f. 248, op. 113, d. 1527, l. 58.

17. RGADA, f. 248, op. 113, d. 1527, l. 1–4, 22–27.

18. RGADA, f. 248, op. 113, d. 1223, l. 24–32.

19. RGADA, f. 248, op. 113, d. 1527, l. 76–83.

20. For more critical views see LeDonne, "Proconsular Ambitions," 38–40; Bergholz, *Partition of the Steppe,* 390–391.

21. RGADA, f. 248, op. 113, d. 1527, l. 1–4.

22. RGADA, f. 248, op. 113, d. 1527, l. 1–75; OR RGB, f. 178, n. 1246, l. 14–15.

23. RGADA, f. 248, op. 113, d. 1551, l. 1123–1129.

24. RGADA, f. 248, op. 113, d. 865, l. 1–11, 26.

25. RGADA, f. 248, op. 113, d. 1214; RGADA, f. 248, op. 113, d. 464, l. 24–30.

26. See N. V. Tsyrempilov, "'Chuzhie' lamy. Rossiiskaia politika v otnoshenii zagranichnogo buddiiskogo dukhovenstva v XVIII–nachale XX v.," *Vestnik SPbGU* 13, no. 4 (2010): 9–18.

27. OR RNB (Russian National Library Manuscript Department), f. 487, n. F-219.

28. RGADA, f. 248, op. 113, d. 1551, l. 1098–1099; RGADA, f. 248, op. 113, d. 610, l. 2–3.

29. See, for example, H. S. Hundley, "Defending the Periphery: Tsarist Management of Buriat Buddhism," *Russian Review* 69, no. 2 (2010): 231–250.

30. RGADA, f. 248, op. 113, d. 1214, l. 53–56.

31. RGADA, f. 248, op. 113, d. 1212, l. 23–51. On the assistant Garma, see RGADA, f. 248, op. 113, d. 864, l. 2–7.

32. Fu, *Documentary Chronicle,* 242–243.

33. RGADA, f. 248, op. 113, d. 1551, l. 1100.

34. RGADA, f. 248, op. 113, d. 1212, l. 25ff.

35. RGIA, f. 1643, op. 1, d. 27, l. 1–3.

36. For example, RGADA, f. 15, n. 237.

37. Amiot to Bignon, April 29, 1772, Archives Jésuites—Vanves, Fonds Henri Bernard-Maitre 69, f. 40.

38. RGIA, f. 1643, op. 1, d. 27. This document is an extensive overview of the careers of three generations of Igumnovs.

39. Valikhanov, *Sobranie sochinenii,* 4:212–214.

40. RGADA, f. 248, op. 113, d. 885, l. 1–6.

41. RGADA, f. 248, op. 113, d. 610, l. 9–12; RGADA, f. 248, op. 113, d. 662, l. 10–14.

42. RGADA, f. 248, op. 113, d. 612, l. 2–5.

43. RGADA, f, 248, op. 113, d. 610, l. 1–4.

44. Fu, *Documentary Chronicle,* 231–242.

45. RGADA, f. 248, op. 113, d. 1215, l. 3.

46. RGADA, f. 248, op. 113, d. 488, l. 1–7. For more on Russo-Mongol frontier trade, see Devon Margaret Dear, "Marginal Revolutions: Economies and Economic Knowledge between Qing China, Russia, and Mongolia, 1860–1911" (PhD diss., Harvard University, 2014).

47. RGADA, f. 248, op. 113, d. 662.

48. RGADA, f. 248, op. 113, d. 612, l. 2–5.

49. See Yanagisawa, "Some Remarks," 65–88.

50. RKO XVIII, 6:235ff.

51. His instructions are in RGADA, f. 1261, op. 1, d. 440, l. 2ff.

52. IVR, R. I, op. 1, d. 12, l. 47–131.

53. Fu, *Documentary Chronicle*, 238.

54. IVR, R. I, op. 1, d. 12, l. 138–140.

55. RGADA, f. 248, op. 113, d. 1214, l. 111ff.

56. RGIA, f. 796, op. 59, d. 328, l. 110–113.

57. AVPRI, f. 62, op. 62 / 2, d. 9, l. 225–282; RGADA, f. 248, op. 113, d. 1214, l. 167ff.

58. On the significance of governor-generalships (namestnichestva), see John Le-Donne, "Russian Governors General, 1775–1825: Territorial or Functional Administration?" *Cahiers du Monde russe* 42, no. 1 (January 1, 2001): 5–30.

59. Foust, *Muscovite and Mandarin*, 307–309.

60. For example, OPI GIM, f. 450, d. 206, l. 37.

61. RGADA, f. 1261, op. 1, d. 1404–1406.

62. RGADA, f. 24, n. 62, part 1, l. 247–249, 295.

63. RGADA, f. 24, n. 62, part 1, l. 314–316v.

64. RGADA, f. 24, n. 62, part 1, l. 247–255.

65. RGADA, f. 24, n. 62, part 3, l. 1–17.

66. LeDonne, "Proconsular Ambitions."

67. RGADA, f. 24, n. 62, part 4, l. 164.

68. RGADA, f. 24, n. 62, part 4, l. 232–234.

69. RGADA, f. 24, n. 62, part 4, l. 322–329.

70. OPI GIM, f. 445, n. 16, l. 108ff; RGIA, f. 1263, op. 1, d. 69, l. 248–250, 550–553.

71. On a later attempt to manage Mongol loyalties, see Sören Urbansky, "Tokhtogo's Mission Impossible: Russia, China, and the Quasi-Independence of Hulunbeir," *Inner Asia* 16, no. 1 (2014): 64–94.

9. Imperial Encounters in the North Pacific

1. The literature on Russia's North Pacific is increasingly voluminous. See, for example, Jones, *Empire of Extinction*; Martina Winkler, *Das Imperium und die Seeotter: Die Expansion Russlands in den nordpazifischen Raum, 1700–1867,* Transnationale Geschichte (Göttingen, Germany: Vandenhoeck & Ruprecht, 2016); N. N. Bolkhovitinov, ed., *Istoriia Russkoi Ameriki, 1732–1867* (Moscow: Mezhdunarodnye otnosheniia, 1997); Glynn Barratt, *Russia in Pacific Waters, 1715–1825: A Survey of the Origins of Russia's Naval Presence in the North and South Pacific* (Vancouver: University of British Columbia Press, 1981).

2. Thierry Balzacq, Sarah Léonard, and Jan Ruzicka, "'Securitization' Revisited: Theory and Cases," *International Relations* 30, no. 4 (December 1, 2016): 494–531. My thanks to Sarah Rosenthal for this reference.

3. Hamish Scott, *The Birth of a Great Power System, 1740–1815* (London: Routledge, 2014).

4. Louis Dermigny, *La Chine et l'Occident: le commerce à Canton au XVIIIe siècle, 1719–1833* (Paris: S. E. V. P. E. N., 1964), 768ff.

5. James R. Gibson, *Otter Skins, Boston Ships, and China Goods: The Maritime Fur Trade of the Northwest Coast, 1785–1841* (Seattle: University of Washington Press, 1992); on the empire's gradual awareness of the extinction crisis, see Jones, *Empire of Extinction.*

6. Joyce Chaplin, "The Pacific before Empire, c. 1500–1800," in *Pacific Histories: Ocean, Land, People,* ed. David Armitage and Alison Bashford (Basingstoke: Palgrave Macmillan, 2014), 53–74.

7. David Igler, *The Great Ocean: Pacific Worlds from Captain Cook to the Gold Rush* (Oxford: Oxford University Press, 2013); Matt K. Matsuda, "The Pacific," *American Historical Review* 111, no. 3 (2006): 758–780.

8. José Torrubia, *The Muscovites in California, Or Rather, Demonstration of the Passage from North America: Discovered by the Russians and of the Ancient One of the Peoples Who Transmigrated There from Asia* (Fairfield, WA: Ye Galleon Press, 1996).

9. Lydia T. Black, "Question of Maps," 6–50; Guzevich and Guzevich, "Kartazadanie Zh. N. Delilia," 60–92.

10. Alexandre Stroev, "Les espions français en Russie durant la guerre entre la Russie et la Turquie (1768–1774)," in *L'influence française en Russie au XVIIIe siècle,* ed. Jean-Pierre Poussou, Anne Mézin, and Yves Perret-Gentil (Paris: Institut d'etudes slaves, 2004), 581–598; Marcus C. Levitt, "An Antidote to Nervous Juice: Catherine the Great's Debate with Chappe d'Auteroche over Russian Culture," *Eighteenth-Century Studies* 32, no. 1 (October 1, 1998): 49–63.

11. Miklós Molnár, "Héros ou imposteur? Un aventurier au XVIIIe siècle," *Revue européenne des sciences sociales* 27, no. 85 (January 1, 1989): 75–91. The name is spelled a number of different ways, including Maurice Benyowsky and Benjowski.

12. For Benyovszky's reception in Japan, see Robert Liss [Lissa Roberts], "Frontier Tales: Tokugawa Japan in Translation," in *The Brokered World: Go-Betweens and Global Intelligence, 1770–1820,* ed. Simon Schaffer (Sagamore Beach, MA: Science History, 2009), 1–47; A. S. Sgibnev, "Istoricheskii ocherk glavneishikh sobytii v Kamchatke, 1650–1855," *Morskoi sbornik,* no. 4–8 (1869).

13. BIF, MS 5404, f. 11.

14. D'Aigullon to Durand de Distroff, August 9, 1772, Correspondance Politique-Russie, t. 90, f. 150–151.

15. D'Aigullon to Durand de Distroff, August 9, 1772, AAE (Archives Diplomatiques du Ministère des Affaires Etrangères, Paris), Correspondance Politique-Russie, t. 90, f. 150, 191–195. For Durand's espionage activities, see Stroev, "Les espions français en Russie."

16. Durand to d'Aiguillon, March 12, 1773, AAE, CP-Russie, t. 91, f. 241–252.

17. Durand to d'Aiguillon, April 10, 1773, AAE, CP-Russie, t. 91, f. 348–353.

18. Durand to d'Aiguillon, April 10, 1773, AAE, CP-Russie, t. 91, f. 353–356.

19. Gerault (in the absence of Durand) to d'Aiguillon, March 14, 1773, AAE, CP-Russie, t. 91, f. 263–266.

20. For example, Pallas to Euler, December 5, 1772, f. 1, op. 3, t. 58, n. 64.

21. See Hosea Ballou Morse, *The Chronicles of the East India Company, Trading to China 1635–1834* (Oxford: Clarendon, 1926), 1:295ff.

22. Bertin to Ko and Yang, January 1, 1774, BIF, MS 1522, f. 3–39. In fact most of the letter was written by Bertin's secretary Parent. For more on this correspondence, see Gwynne Lewis, "Henri-Léonard Bertin and the Fate of the Bourbon Monarchy," in *Enlightenment and Revolution: Essays in Honour of Norman Hampson,* ed. Malcolm Crook, William Doyle, and Alan Forrest (Hampshire: Ashgate, 2004), 69–90.

23. Yang to Bertin, December 8, 1775, BIF, MS 1520, f. 228–229.

24. AAE, CP-Russie, t. 90, f. 191–195.

25. George Verne Blue, "A Rumor of an Anglo-Russian Raid on Japan, 1776," *Pacific Historical Review* 8, no. 4 (December 1, 1939): 453–463.

26. Maurice Auguste Benyowsky, *Memoirs and Travels of Mauritius Augustus Count de Benyowsky . . .* (London: G. G. J. and J. Robinson, 1790), 272.

27. "S. N. Sh," "Anglichane v Kamchatke v 1779 godu," *Istoricheskii vestnik* 19 (1885), 394–401.

28. SPbII, f. 36, op. 1, d. 553, l. 41.

29. Simon Werrett, "Russian Responses to the Voyages of Captain Cook," in *Captain Cook: Explorations and Reassessments,* ed. Glyndwr Williams (London: Boydell & Brewer, Boydell Press, 2004), 179–197.

30. RGADA, f. 24, n. 62, part 3, l. 20ff.

31. Romaniello, *Enterprising Empires,* 211–56.

32. Lydia T. Black, *Russians in Alaska, 1732–1867* (Fairbanks: University of Alaska Press, 2004), 92–95.

33. John Meares, *Voyages Made in the Years 1788 and 1789, from China to the North West Coast of America . . .* (London: Logographic, 1790), lxvii–xcv.

34. RGADA, f. 24, n. 62, part 2, l. 419–422. See Edward G. Gray, *The Making of John Ledyard: Empire and Ambition in the Life of an Early American Traveler* (New Haven, CT: Yale University Press, 2007); John Ledyard, *Journey through Russia and Siberia, 1787–1788: The Journal and Selected Letters,* ed. Stephen D. Watrous (Madison: University of Wisconsin Press, 1966).

35. See, for example, BL, IOR, R / 10 / 14-15.

36. Dermigny, *La Chine et l'Occident,* 1161–1198.

37. Martin Sauer, *An Account of a Geographical and Astronomical Expedition to the Northern Parts of Russia . . .* (London: T. Cadell, 1802), vii–x.

38. RGIA, f. 1147, op. 1, d. 103.

39. G. I Shelikhov, *General'naia karta: predstavliaiushchaia udobnye sposoby k umnozheniiu Rossiiskoi torgovli i moreplavaniia po Tikhomu i Iuzhnomu Okianu* (St. Petersburg, 1787); A. I. Alekseev, *Osvoenie russkimi liud'mi Dal'nego Vostoka i Russkoi Ameriki do kontsa XIX veka* (Moscow: Nauka, 1982), 102ff; Ilya Vinkovetsky, *Russian America: An Overseas Colony of a Continental Empire, 1804–1867* (Oxford: Oxford University Press, 2011), 29–35.

40. SPbII, f. 36, op. 1, d. 554, l. 535–540.

41. RGADA, f. 24, n. 64, part 2, l. 195–196; AVPRI, f. 130, op. 3, d. 11; Sauer, *Account*, 287–288.

42. A. A. Guber, *Politika evropeiskikh derzhav v Iugo-Vostochnoi Azii: 60-e gody XVIII–60-e gody XIX v.: dokumenty i materialy* (Moscow: Izd-vo vostochnoi lit-ry, 1962), 428–432.

43. SPbII, f. 36, op. 1, d. 553, l. 520–526. See also J. L. Cranmer-Byng, "Russian and British Interests in the Far East 1791–1793," *Canadian Slavonic Papers* 10, no. 3 (October 1, 1968): 357–375.

44. The major work on the embassy is James Louis Hevia, *Cherishing Men from Afar: Qing Guest Ritual and the Macartney Embassy of 1793* (Durham, NC: Duke University Press, 1995); but see Ulrike Hillemann, *Asian Empire and British Knowledge: China and the Networks of British Imperial Expansion* (Basingstoke: Palgrave Macmillan, 2009) for a more careful and intelligence-focused treatment.

45. Semën Vorontsov to Aleksandr Vorontsov, October 5, 1792, in P. I. Bartenev, ed., *Arkhiv kniazia Vorontsova* (Moscow: Tip. A.I. Mamontova, 1870), 9:261–264. For more on this, see my "Jesuit Conspirators," 56–76.

46. OPI GIM, f. 450, d. 206, l. 35ff.

47. See Marek Inglot, *How the Jesuits Survived Their Suppression: The Society of Jesus in the Russian Empire (1773–1814)*, trans. Daniel L. Schlafly (St. Louis: Saint Joseph's University Press, 2015); Marek Inglot, ed., *Rossiia i iezuity, 1772–1820* (Moscow: Nauka, 2006).

48. Cibot to Euler, October 10, 1777, ARAN, f. 1, op. 3, d. 61, l. 87–88.

49. RGADA, f. 1261, op. 1, d. 968, l. 13–24; AVPRI, f. 62, op. 62/3, 1792, d. 2, l. 1–28.

50. RGADA, f. 24, d. 64, l. 132–133.

51. RGADA, f. 24, d. 64, l. 182.

52. OPI GIM, f. 450, d. 206, l. 37v–38. RGIA, f. 1643, op. 1, d. 27; RKO XIX, 372.

53. Fu, *Documentary Chronicle*, 1:331.

54. British Library, IOR/G/12/90, f. 108–124; François Froger, *A Journal of the First French Embassy to China, 1698–1700* (n.p.: T. C. Newby, 1859), 209–226.

55. E. H. Pritchard, "The Instructions of the East India Company to Lord Macartney on His Embassy to China and His Reports to the Company, 1792–4. Part

I: Instructions from the Company," *Journal of the Royal Asiatic Society* 70, no. 02 (1938): 201–230.

  56. IOR / G / 12 / 92, f. 49ff; Mosca, *From Frontier Policy*, 127–162.

  57. BRB, Osborne MSS 181, box 1, f. 8, p. 7–8.

  58. BRB, Osborne MSS 181, box 2, f. 15, p. 1–6.

  59. BRB, Osborne MSS 181, box 2, f. 13; f. 15, p. 6–8; British Library, IOR / G / 12 / 91, l. 12–13.

  60. A similar point has been made by Hillemann, *Asian Empire*, 37–42.

  61. Johannes Nieuhof, *L'ambassade de la Compagnie orientale des Provinces Unies vers l'empereur de la Chine, ou grand cam de Tartarie, faite par les Srs. Pierre de Goyer, & Jacob de Keyser* (Leiden, Netherlands: Pour J. de Meurs, 1665).

  62. Sostegno Viani and Giovanni Ambrogio Mezzabarba, *Istoria delle cose operate nella China da Monsignor Gio. Ambrogio Mezzabarba . . . Vescovo di Lodi* (n.p.: Monsù Briasson, 1739).

  63. BL, IOR / G / 12 / 91, p. 5ff.

  64. Bell, *Travels from St. Petersburg*.

  65. BL, IOR / G / 12 / 91, p. 257–273.

  66. BL, IOR / G / 12 / 91, p. 181–182.

  67. BL, IOR / G / 12 / 91, p. 43, 57.

  68. BL, IOR / G / 12 / 92, p. 289.

  69. BL, IOR / G / 12 / 91, p. 5–7.

  70. BL, IOR / G / 12 / 92, p. 54ff.

  71. RGADA, f. 15, n. 237, l. 8ff.

  72. BL, IOR / G / 12 / 92, p. 72–90.

  73. RGADA, f. 15, d. 237, l. 2–17.

  74. RGADA, f. 15, d. 237, l. 18.

  75. RGIA, f. 1101, op. 1, d. 115, l. 36–38.

  76. The document is treated as authentic in Ye Baichuan and Yuan Jian, "The Sino-Russian Trade and the Role of the Lifanyuan, 17th–18th Centuries," in *Managing Frontiers in Qing China*, ed. Dittmar Schorkowitz and Chia Ning (Leiden, Netherlands: Brill, 2012), 254–289.

  77. *Arkhiv Gosudarstvennago Soveta* (St. Petersburg: Tip. Vtorago otd-niia Sobstvennoi E. I. V. kantseliarii, 1869), 3:733ff.

  78. RGIA, f. 1409, op. 1, d. 53.

  79. RGIA, f. 1147, op. 1, d. 682, l. 41ff; see also OR RGB, f. 344, n. 256, l. 133–136.

  80. RGIA, f. 1147, op. 1, d. 682, l. 1–43.

  81. RKO XIX, 114–115.

  82. RKO XIX, 5–10.

  83. Aleksandr Vorontsov to Arsen'ev, June 23, 1805, in Bartenev, *Arkhiv kniazia Vorontsova*, 36:84–90.

84. RKO XIX, 208–209; on the changing but not necessarily declining role of the Kiakhta trade, see Aleksandr Petrov and Aleksei Ermolaev, "Znachenie Kiakhty v istorii Dal'nego Vostoka i Russkoi Ameriki," *Rossiiskaia istoriia,* no. 2 (2018): 51–66.

85. RKO XIX, 126–131.

86. RGIA, f. 1643, op. 1, d. 25.

87. RGIA, f. 1643, op. 1, d. 33.

88. OV IVR, f. 7, op. 1, d. 38, l. 12–37. These are the same instructions mentioned in the opening of the introduction.

89. RKO XIX, 5–20.

90. OPI GIM, f. 24, op. 1, d. 26, l. 113–127 (emphasis in original).

91. RGIA, f. 1643, op. 1, d. 31.

92. RKO XIX, 812–813.

93. RGIA, f. 1643, op. 1, d. 23, l. 69–81.

94. RKO XIX, 586–588.

95. RKO XIX, 837–844.

96. BL, IOR / G / 12 / 150, p. 149–151; IOR / G / 12 / 152, p. 33–78. For an explanation of this attitude on the part of the Qing, see Mosca, "Qing State," 103–116.

97. AV IVR, f. 7, op. 1, l. 93ff.

98. BL, IOR / G / 12 / 197, p. 63–64. For the scientific significance of Amherst's embassy, see Gao Hao, "The Amherst Embassy and British Discoveries in China," *History* 99, no. 337 (October 1, 2014): 568–587.

99. Gao Hao, "Prelude to the Opium War? British Reactions to the 'Napier Fizzle' and Attitudes towards China in the Mid Eighteen-Thirties," *Historical Research* 87, no. 237 (August 1, 2014): 491–509.

100. RGIA, f. 994, op. 2, d. 353. (This is mistakenly attributed to Admiral N. S. Mordvinov.) See also Mark Bassin, *Imperial Visions: Nationalist Imagination and Geographical Expansion in the Russian Far East, 1840–1865* (Cambridge: Cambridge University Press, 1999).

101. Guber, *Politika evropeïskikh derzhav,* 428–436.

102. Michael Green, *By More Than Providence: Grand Strategy and American Power in the Asia Pacific since 1783* (New York: Columbia University Press, 2017), 27–30.

10. Making Russian Sinology in the Age of Napoleon

1. Louis Langlès, *De l'importance des langues orientales pour l'extension du commerce, les progrès des lettres et des sciences: adresse à l'Assemblée Nationale* (Paris, 1790), 13–14. I am grateful to Mårten Soderblom Saarela for pointing me to this source.

2. Kapil Raj, *Relocating Modern Science: Circulation and the Construction of Knowledge in South Asia and Europe, 1650–1900* (Basingstoke: Palgrave Macmillan, 2007), 139–158.

3. At the same time, Russian sinology's reception in the Qing orbit had unpredictable effects. See, for example, Lobsang Yongdan, "Tibet Charts the World: The Btsan Po No Mon Han's Detailed Description of the World, an Early Major Scientific Work in Tibet," in *Mapping the Modern in Tibet (PIATS 2006: Tibetan Studies: Proceedings of the Eleventh Seminar of the International Association for Tibetan Studies, Königswinter 2006)*, ed. Gray Tuttle (Andiast, International Institute for Tibetan and Buddhist Studies, 2011) 73–134.

4. See Chad Wellmon, *Organizing Enlightenment: Information Overload and the Invention of the Modern Research University* (Baltimore: Johns Hopkins University Press, 2015); Jan Golinski, *Making Natural Knowledge: Constructivism and the History of Science* (Chicago: University of Chicago Press, 2005), 66–78; Alex Csiszar, *The Scientific Journal: Authorship and the Politics of Knowledge in the Nineteenth Century* (Chicago: University of Chicago Press, 2018); Paul Forman, "On the Historical Forms of Knowledge Production and Curation: Modernity Entailed Disciplinarity, Postmodernity Entails Antidisciplinarity," *Osiris* 27, no. 1 (2012): 56–97.

5. Knud Lundbæk, "Notes on Abel Remusat and the Beginning of Academic Sinology in Europe," in *Echanges culturels et religieux entre la Chine et l'Occident: Actes du VIIe Colloque International de Sinologie de Chantilly*, ed. Edward Malatesta (San Francisco: Ricci Institute, 1992), 207–220; Mark C. Elliott, "Abel-Rémusat, la langue mandchoue et la sinologie," *Comptes-rendus des séances de l'année . . . (Académie des inscriptions et belles-lettres)*, no. 2 (2014): 973–993; see also Urs App, *The Birth of Orientalism* (Philadelphia: University of Pennsylvania Press, 2010); Marchand, *German Orientalism;* Cohn, *Colonialism and Its Forms*.

6. G. F. Kim, *Istoriia otechestvennogo vostokovedeniia*, 96–167.

7. Svetlana Ponomareva, "Grigorii Ivanovich Spasskii: issledovatel' Sibiri i prosvetitel'" (PhD diss., Sibirskii federal'nyi universitet, 2002).

8. See, for example, Peter J. Kitson, *Forging Romantic China* (Cambridge: Cambridge University Press, 2013), 13ff; Chi-ming Yang, *Performing China: Virtue, Commerce, and Orientalism in Eighteenth-Century England, 1660–1760* (Baltimore: Johns Hopkins University Press, 2011), 148ff; on changing Russian attitudes, Yan Guodong and Liang Zhongqi, "19 shiji shangbanqi Eguoren lai hua xing ji yu Eguoren Zhongguo guan de zhuanxiang," *Eluosi wenyi*, no. 1 (2017): 118–26; Lim, *China and Japan*, 59–75.

9. Michael Adas, *Machines as the Measure of Men: Science, Technology, and Ideologies of Western Dominance* (Ithaca, NY: Cornell University Press, 1989), 79–95; see also Millar, *Singular Case*.

10. Jean-Pierre Abel-Rémusat, *Mélanges asiatiques, ou choix de morceaux de critiques et de mémoires relatifs aux religions, aux sciences, aux coutumes, à l'histoire et à la géographie des nations orientales,* . . . (Paris: Dondey-Dupré, 1826), 2:2–32.

11. Robert Morrison, *Chinese Miscellany; Consisting of Original Extracts from Chinese Authors, in the Native Character* (London: London Missionary Society, 1825).

12. RGIA, f. 796, op. 86, d. 167, l. 402–406.

13. Skachkov, *Ocherki istorii russkogo kitaevedeniia,* 89–138; Huan Lilian, "O. Iakinf (N. Ia. Bichurin)—vydaiushchiisia russkii kitaeved (K 230-letiiu so dnia rozhdeniia)," *Problemy Dal'nego Vostoka,* no. 5 (2007): 124–136; P. V. Denisov, *Slovo o monakhe Iakinfe Bichurine* (Cheboksary, Russia: Chuvash. kn. izd-vo, 2007). See also David Schimmelpenninck van der Oye, "The Genesis of Russian Sinology," *Kritika: Explorations in Russian and Eurasian History* 1, no. 2 (2000): 355–364; O. V. Shatalov, "Arkhimandrit Petr (Kamenskii)—nachalnik 10-i Rossiiskoi dukhovnoi missii v Pekine," *Pravoslavie na Dal'nem Vostoke,* no. 3 (2001): 85–98.

14. For example, SPb ARAN, f. 1, op. 3, vol. 60, l. 21.

15. RKO XIX, 106–107.

16. Potocki was also the author of the legendary *Manuscript Found in Saragossa,* a bizarre novel composed of interlocking, nested frame narratives.

17. See Lundbæk, *T. S. Bayer.*

18. Hartmut Walravens, *Julius Klaproth (1783–1835): Leben und Werk* (Wiesbaden, Germany: Harrassowitz, 1999).

19. RKO XIX 775. See also T. Iu. Feklova, "Ekspeditsii Akademii nauk i izuchenie Kitaia v pervoi polovine XIX v.," in *Rossiia i Kitai: aspekty vzaimodeistviia i vzaimovliianiia,* ed. N. L. Glazacheva and O. V. Zalesskaia (Blagoveshchensk, Russia: Izdatel'stvo BGPU, 2011), 26–34.

20. Vasilii Golovin [Julius Klaproth], *Die russische Gesandschaft nach China im Jahr 1805: nebst einer Nachricht von der letzten Christen-Verfolgung in Peking* (St. Petersburg: Ziemsen, 1809); see Wladyslaw Kotwicz and Hartmut Walravens, *Die russische Gesandtschaftsreise nach China 1805: zu Leben und Werk des Grafen Jan Potocki* (Berlin: Bell, 1991).

21. RKO XIX, 732. See the biographical materials collected in Walravens, *Leben und Werk;* and the correspondence in Hartmut Walravens, ed., *Julius Klaproth (1783–1835): Briefe und Dokumente* (Wiesbaden, Germany: Harrassowitz, 1999); Hartmut Walravens, ed., *Julius Klaproth (1783–1835): Briefwechsel mit Gelehrten grossenteils aus dem Akademiearchiv in St. Petersburg* (Wiesbaden, Germany: Harrassowitz, 2002).

22. Klaproth to Friedländer, July 9, 1811, in Walravens, *Briefe und Dokumente,* 53–54.

23. Klaproth to Academy, June 25, 1812, RGIA, f. 733, op. 12, d. 18, l. 42–45. The reference to the globe suggests that Klaproth wanted to distinguish between se-

rious scholarship and the type of public-oriented demonstrative scientific practice the academy embraced in the eighteenth century.

24. RGIA, f. 733, op. 12, d. 18, l. 40.

25. RGIA, f. 733, op. 12, d. 18, l. 104ff.

26. Klaproth to Cotta, January 24, 1814, in Walravens, *Briefe und Dokumente*, 59–60.

27. See, for example, Louis Gabriel Michaud, ed., "Klaproth (Jules-Henri)," *Biographie universelle, ancienne et modern*, no. 68 (1841): 532–549.

28. "Literary Forgeries by Klaproth," *Notes and Queries on China and Japan*, no. 3 (December 1869): 111–112.

29. RKO XIX, 238.

30. The relevant documents are in AV IVR, f. 7, op. 1, d. 37–39.

31. RGIA, f. 796, op. 99, d. 877, l. 156–170. Evidence that salary funds had been withheld due to the Napoleonic Wars, a claim that often appears in secondary sources, is scanty. The citation for this claim is typically either to Nikolai Adoratskii, "Otets Iakinf Bichurin: biograficheskii etiud," *Pravoslavnyi sobesednik*, March 1886, 164–80; 245–78; or to N. S. Shchukin, "Iakinf Bichurin," *Zhurnal Ministerstva narodnago prosveshcheniia*, September 1857, 111–26. Adoratskii cites an unpublished term paper from 1870, and Shchukin cites no sources at all. Bichurin's letters appear not to mention it, and it seems unlikely that the students would invent a salary shipment if it did not actually arrive, since this could easily be verified by the reviewing authorities in Russia.

32. RGIA, f. 796, op. 99, d. 877, l. 171–172.

33. RGIA, f. 797, op. 2, d. 6352, l. 114–124.

34. Klaproth to Fuß, June 2, 1806, in Walravens, *Briefwechsel mit Gelehrten*, 145ff.

35. RGIA, f. 796, op. 86, d. 167, l. 207–212. Salary information can be found in, for example, OR RGB, f. 273, k. 27, n. 2, l. 160–163.

36. RGIA, f. 796, op. 86, d. 167, l. 401–410.

37. Recent reevaluations of Kamenskii include Shatalov, "Arkhimandrit Petr (Kamenskii)"; A. B. Chegodaev, "Mongol'sko-man'chzhursko-kitaisko-russko-latinskii piatiiazychnyi slovar' P. I. Kamenskogo: voprosy ego sozdaniia i izdaniia," *Vestnik Tomskogo gosudarstvennogo universiteta* 1, no. 13 (2011): 8–10; Datsyshen, *Istoriia Rossiiskoi dukhovnoi missii*, 117–170. The only book-length biography of Kamenskii is V. G. Datsyshen and A. B. Chegodaev, *Arkhimandrit Petr (Kamenskii)* (Hong Kong: Sts. Peter and Paul Orthodox Church, 2013); more generally on religious culture, see Wirtschafter, *Religion and Enlightenment*.

38. Datsyshen and Chegodaev, *Arkhimandrit Petr (Kamenskii)*, 1–37. Kamenskii's recommendation letters are in RGIA, f. 796, op. 73, d. 327, l. 4–10.

39. RGIA, f. 796, op. 73, d. 327, l. 136–152.

40. OR RNB, f. 550, FXVIII-24 / 1, l. 62.

41. RGIA, f. 1341, op. 10, d. 2086, l. 5; RGIA, f. 796, op. 99, d. 877, l. 52–55.

42. OR RNB, f. 550, FXVIII-24/3, l. 112ff; PD, Peretts coll., n. 568, 144–159, 208, and passim.

43. On the Free Economic Society as paradigmatic early civil society organization, see Joseph Bradley, *Voluntary Associations in Tsarist Russia: Science, Patriotism, and Civil Society* (Cambridge, MA: Harvard University Press, 2009), 38–58.

44. OR RNB, f. 542, n. 661, l. 3ff.

45. OR RNB, f. 542, n. 661, l. 1–3.

46. OR RNB, f. 550, FXVIII-24/1, l. 64ff.

47. OR RNB, f. 550, FXVIII-24/3, l. 392–395.

48. OR RNB, f. 542, n. 661, l. 1–3.

49. Christopher A. Daily, *Robert Morrison and the Protestant Plan for China* (Hong Kong: Hong Kong University Press, 2013), 37–82; Hillemann, *Asian Empire,* 68–70.

50. These ranks correspond to acolyte, deacon, priest, and bishop among the secular clergy.

51. RGIA, f. 797, op. 2, d. 6352, l. 1–26; RGIA, f. 796, op. 99, d. 877, l. 14–62.

52. RGIA, f. 796, op. 99, d. 877, l. 145–146.

53. RGIA, f. 796, op. 99, d. 877, l. 147–154.

54. RGIA, f. 796, op. 99, d. 877, l. 207ff. Russian-speaking historians have tended to downplay this entire episode as a witch-hunt, but this relies on a tendentious misrepresentation of the archival sources. For example, see Denisov, *Slovo o monakhe Iakinfe Bichurine,* 90–91.

55. RGIA, f. 796, op. 99, d. 877, l. 145–146.

56. RGIA, f. 797, op. 2, d. 7012, l. 1–2; RGIA, f. 796, op. 99, d. 877, l. 299ff.

57. Datsyshen and Chegodaev, *Arkhimandrit Petr (Kamenskii),* 279–317.

58. See OR RNB, f. 550, FXVIII-24/1-3 and PD, Peretts, n. 568.

59. See, for example, Joseph Dehergne, "Une grande collection: Mémoires concernant les Chinois (1776–1814)," *Bulletin de l'Ecole française d'Extrême-Orient* 72, no. 1 (1983): 267–298.

60. OR RNB, f. 550, FXVIII-24/3, l. 298ff; f. 550, FXVIII-24/1, l. 59.

61. RGIA, f. 797, op. 2, d. 6352, l. 126–140.

62. RGIA, f. 797, op. 2, d. 6352, l. 174ff.

63. SPb ARAN, f. 1, op. 1a, d. 29, l. 121.

64. SPb ARAN, f. 2, op. 1, 1819.1, l. 103–109.

65. SPb ARAN, f. 2, op. 1, 1819.1, l. 75–102.

66. For an analysis of this remarkably ill-conceived argument, see App, *Birth of Orientalism,* 188–253.

67. SPb ARAN, f. 2, op. 1, 1819.1, l. 29–48.

68. SPb ARAN, f. 2, op. 1, 1819.1, l. 49–66.

69. SPb ARAN, f. 1, op. 1a, d. 30, l. 98, 118. For the Bantysh-Kamenskii book, see Bantysh-Kamenskii, *Diplomaticheskoe sobranie.*

70. Veselovskii, *Materialy dlia istorii,* 47ff.

71. OR RNB, f. 775, n. 1098, l. 2–3.

72. RGIA, f. 796, op. 104, d. 714; RGIA, f. 733, op. 15, d. 116.

73. RGIA, f. 733, op. 232, d. 10.

74. Egor Timkovskii, *Puteshestvie v Kitai chrez Mongoliiu, v 1820 i 1821 godakh* (St. Petersburg: Tip. Meditsinskago departamenta, 1824); *Reise nach China Durch die Mongoley in den jahren 1820 und 1821* (Leipzig, Germany: Fleischer, 1825); *Voyage à Peking, à travers la Mongolie, en 1820 et 1821* (Paris: Dondey-Dupré père et fils, 1827); *Travels of the Russian Mission: Through Mongolia to China, and Residence in Peking, in the Years 1820–1821* (London: Longman, Rees, Orme, Brown, and Green, 1827).

75. *Asiatic Journal and Monthly Register,* January–June 1827, 23:822–824.

76. Heinrich Julius von Klaproth, *Rapport sur les ouvrages du P. H. Bitchourinski: relatifs à l'histoire des Mongols* ([Paris], 1830). See also David Brophy, "Tending to Unite? The Origins of Uyghur Nationalism" (PhD diss., Harvard University, 2011), 19–64.

77. P. G. von Möllendorf, "Ula Grass," *China Review* 15, no. 3 (1886), 180–181.

78. [Aleksandr Rikhter], "O sostoianii vostochnoi slovesnosti v Rossii," *Aziatskii vestnik,* no. 8 (August 1825): 81–154.

79. Lorraine Daston, "The Sciences of the Archive," *Osiris* 27, no. 1 (2012): 156–187.

80. Vitalii Rodionov, "Po puti k khramu," in N. I. Bichurin, *Radi vechnoi pamiati: poeziia, stat'i, ocherki, zametki, pis'ma* (Cheboksary, Russia: Chuvash. kn. izd-vo, 1991); V. G. Datsyshen, *Izuchenie istorii Kitaia v Rossiiskoi Imperii* (Moscow: Prospekt, 2015) draws attention to the way that praise for Bichurin has contributed to erasing the memory of his predecessors.

11. Conspiracy and Conquest on the Amur

1. Willard Sunderland, "The Ministry of Asiatic Russia: The Colonial Office That Never Was but Might Have Been," *Slavic Review* 69, no. 1 (2010): 120–150; Alexander Morrison, "Metropole, Colony, and Imperial Citizenship in the Russian Empire," *Kritika: Explorations in Russian and Eurasian History* 13, no. 2 (May 10, 2012): 327–364.

2. For example, Anders Åslund, *The Russia Balance Sheet* (Washington, DC: Peterson Institute for International Economics, 2009), 15.

3. Vladislavich, "Sekretnaia informatsiia," 180–244, 281–337.

4. OPI GIM, f. 445, n. 16, l. 108ff.

5. The best account of the conquest in a broader imperial perspective is A. V. Remnev, *Rossiia Dal'nego Vostoka: imperskaia geografiia vlasti XIX–nachala XX vekov* (Omsk, Russia: Izdanie OmGU, 2004), 122–198; other accounts have tended to be hagiographical or deterministic. See, for example, Lukin, *Bear Watches the Dragon*, 67–68; A. Iu. Plotnikov, *Russkaia dal'nevostochnaia granitsa v XVIII–pervoi polovine XIX v.* (Moscow: KomKniga, 2007), 10–45; Mikhail Kutuzov, *Chest' general-gubernatora: N. N. Murav'ev-Amurskii: dokumental'no-istoricheskii ocherk* (Vladivostok, Russia: Ob-vo izucheniia Amurskogo kraia, 1997); E. L. Besprozvannykh, *Priamur'e v sisteme.*

6. On Nessel'rode and his alleged passivity, see, for example, Patricia Kennedy Grimsted, *The Foreign Ministers of Alexander I: Political Attitudes and the Conduct of Russian Diplomacy, 1801–1825* (Berkeley: University of California Press, 1969), 269–286.

7. RKO XIX, 407–411.

8. On attempts to secure navigation, see, for example, LeDonne, "Proconsular Ambitions," 31–60.

9. RKO XIX, 126–132.

10. RGIA, f. 796, op. 448, d. 9, l. 1–7.

11. RGIA, f. 772, op. 1, d. 331.

12. RGIA, f. 777, op. 1, d. 1531.

13. The most extensive study of this is Bassin, *Imperial Visions.*

14. Aleksandr Middendorf, *Puteshestvie na sever i vostok Sibiri* (St. Petersburg, 1860), 1:166–167.

15. Bassin, *Imperial Visions*, 79–80, 130.

16. Middendorf, *Puteshestvie na sever*, 1:156.

17. Middendorf, 1:159.

18. Middendorf, 1:150.

19. Bassin, *Imperial Visions*, 69–78. For an early report on navigability, see RGAVMF, f. 14., op. 1, d. 162.

20. A. N. Ermolaev, *Rossiisko-amerikanskaia kompaniia v Sibiri i na Dal'nem Vostoke (1799–1871 gg)* (Kemerovo, Russia: INT, 2013), 481–485.

21. On the Russian-American Company, see Bolkhovitinov, *Istoriia Russkoi Ameriki*, vol. 2; Vinkovetsky, *Russian America*; Lydia T. Black, *Russians in Alaska.*

22. For example, RKO XIX, 619.

23. Ermolaev, *Rossiisko-amerikanskaia kompaniia*, 488–513.

24. OR RGB, f. 137, p. 201, d. 2. This version of Nevel'skoi's instructions has never been published. Nevel'skoi's version is in *Podvigi russkikh morskikh ofitserov na krainem vostoke Rossii* (Moscow: Drofa, 2009), 125; Barsukov's similar versions are in *Graf Nikolai Nikolaevich Murav'ev-Amurskii po ego pis'mam, offitsial'nym dokumentam, razskazam sovremennikov i pechatnym istochnikam* (Moscow:

Sinodal'naia tip., 1891), 2:36–42. Crucially, neither published version makes any reference to settlement or territorial claims, and Nevel'skoi's explicitly denies that the Russian flag should be raised.

25. OR RGB, f. 137, p. 201, d. 2, l. 4; OR RGB, f. 137, p. 201, d. 3.

26. OR RGB, f. 137, p. 201, d. 2; f. 137, p. 201, d. 4; f. 137, p. 201, d. 6, l. 3.

27. Kabanov, *Amurskii vopros*, 64–66. See also, for example, RGIA, f. 796, op. 448, d. 58.

28. Bassin, *Imperial Visions*, 123–127.

29. RGAVMF, f. 14, op. 1, d. 83.

30. Barsukov, *Graf Nikolai Nikolaevich*.

31. "I. Markelov" to "I. I. Markelov," July 2, 1860, GARF f. 109, op. 3a, d. 1309, l. 8–10.

32. "I. Markelov" to "I. I. Markelov," July 11, 1860, GARF f. 109, op. 3a, d. 1309, l. 12–13.

33. Examples of works that tell this story include Kabanov, *Amurskii vopros;* Alekseev, *Delo vsei zhizni;* A. I. Alekseev, *Amurskaia ekspeditsiia 1849–1855 gg.* (Moscow: Mysl', 1974); Alekseev, *Osvoenie russkimi;* John L. Evans, *Russian Expansion on the Amur, 1848–1860: The Push to the Pacific* (Lewiston, NY: Edwin Mellen, 1999).

34. Murav'ev to Rostovtsev, May 15, 1852, GARF, f. 1155, op. 1, d. 1400, l. 2–3.

35. Murav'ev to Konstantin Pavlovich, November 29, 1853, in Barsukov, *Graf Nikolai Nikolaevich*, 2:104–105.

36. Barsukov, 2:110–114.

37. Barsukov, 2:81–87.

38. Sharyl Corrado, "A Land Divided: Sakhalin and the Amur Expedition of G. I. Nevel'skoi, 1848–1855," *Journal of Historical Geography*, no. 45 (July 1, 2014): 70–81; Nevel'skoi, *Podvigi russkikh morskikh ofitserov*, 102ff.

39. Nevel'skoi to Orlov, November 1 [misdated from subsequent report in this file], 1850, RGAVMF, f. 1374, op. 1, d. 26, l. 1–3.

40. Barsukov, *Graf Nikolai Nikolaevich*, 2:67–79.

41. Barsukov, 2:114–115.

42. Zavoiko to Korsakov, May 29, 1850, OR RGB, f. 137, p. 90, d. 12, l. 9.

43. Nevel'skoi to Korsakov, May 24, 1850, OR RGB, f. 137, p. 113, d. 11, l. 1–6.

44. RGAVMF, f. 1374, op. 1, d. 26, l. 1v.

45. Nevel'skoi, *Podvigi russkikh morskikh ofitserov*, 172.

46. RGAVMF, f. 410, op. 2, d. 1052.

47. Nevel'skoi, *Podvigi russkikh morskikh ofitserov*, 54.

48. Nevel'skoi, 169–170.

49. Zavoiko to Korsakov, December 10, 1851, OR RGB, f. 137, p. 90, d. 12, l. 27–29.

50. Nevel'skoi to Korsakov, [August 1850], OR RGB, f. 137, p. 113, d. 11, l. 7ff.

51. Murav'ev to Rostovtsev, May 15, 1852, GARF, f. 1155, op. 1, d. 1400, l. 2–3.

52. OR RGB, f. 137, p. 204, d. 1.

53. Ernest George Ravenstein, *The Russians on the Amur: Its Discovery, Conquest, and Colonization, with a Description of the Country, Its Inhabitants, Productions, and Commercial Capabilities . . .* (London: Trübner, 1861), 110.

54. Ermolaev, *Rossiisko-amerikanskaia kompaniia,* 503–506; Nevel'skoi, *Podvigi russkikh morskikh ofitserov,* 174–178.

55. Kabanov, *Amurskii vopros,* 154–55.

56. "K istorii priobreteniia Amura," *Russkii arkhiv,* 1878, no. 11, 274.

57. Barsukov, *Graf Nikolai Nikolaevich,* 2:130.

58. Andrew C. Rath, *The Crimean War in Imperial Context, 1854–1856* (New York: Palgrave Macmillan, 2015), 111–164; John D. Grainger, *The First Pacific War: Britain and Russia, 1854–56* (Woodbridge: Boydell and Brewer, 2008), 27–49; John J. Stephan, "The Crimean War in the Far East," *Modern Asian Studies* 3, no. 3 (1969): 257–277.

59. R. K. I. Quested, *The Expansion of Russia in East Asia, 1857–1860* (Kuala Lumpur: University of Malaya Press, 1968), 50.

60. For the orders concerning this, see RGIA, f. 1265, op. 5, d. 130.

61. Ermolaev, *Rossiisko-amerikanskaia kompaniia,* 511; Vinkovetsky, *Russian America,* 181–188.

62. Qtd. in Rath, *Crimean War,* 162.

63. S. C. M. Paine, *Imperial Rivals: China, Russia, and Their Disputed Frontier* (Armonk, NY: M. E. Sharpe, 1996), 52.

64. The most important work on the Qing response is Quested, *Expansion of Russia;* see also R. K. I. Quested, "Further Light on the Expansion of Russia in East Asia: 1792–1860," *Journal of Asian Studies* 29, no. 2 (1970): 327–345.

65. V. Kryzhanovskii, ed., "Perepiska nachal'nika Pekinskoi missii arkhimandrita Palladiia s Generalom-Gubernatorom Vostochnoi Sibiri Gr. N. N. Murav'evym-Amurskim," *Russkii arkhiv,* no. 8 (1914): 492–515; no. 9 (1914): 5–32; no. 10 (1914), 155–206. For this, see no. 8, p. 503.

66. Bassin, *Imperial Visions,* 233–73; on the river in the postannexation era, see Victor Zatsepine, *Beyond the Amur* (Vancouver: University of British Columbia Press, 2017).

67. Kryzhanovskii, "Perepiska nachal'nika," no. 9, p. 22.

68. Archimandrite Palladii, "Dnevnik arkh. Palladiia za 1858 g.," *Izvestiia Ministerstva Inostrannykh Del,* no. 2 (1912): 257.

69. N. P. Ignat'ev, *Otchetnaia zapiska podannaia v Aziatskii Departament v ianvare 1861 goda* (St. Petersburg: Tip. V. V. Komarova, 1895), 1.

70. Ignat'ev, 139.

71. Quested, *Expansion of Russia,* 77, 229–230.

72. Paine, *Imperial Rivals,* 9–11.

73. Barsukov, *Graf Nikolai Nikolaevich,* 2:56.

74. OR RGB, f. 137, p. 209, d. 13.

75. OR RGB, f. 137, p. 209, d. 11.

76. GARF, f. 730, o. 1, d. 354.

77. I. M. Popov, *Rossiia i Kitai: 300 let na grani voiny* (Moscow: AST-Ermak-Astrel', 2004), 141–159; A. Buksgevden, *Russkii Kitai: ocherki diplomaticheskikh snoshenii Rossii s Kitaem* (Port Arthur, Russia: Izd-vo kniznogo sklada "Novyi Krai," 1902), 72ff.

78. GARF, f. 730, op. 1, d. 354.

79. GARF, f. 730, op. 1, d. 426. See Paine, *Imperial Rivals,* 90–91.

80. Archimandrite Gurii to Ignat'ev, December 1, 1860, and December 2, 1860, GARF, f. 730, op. 1, d. 398, l. 1–8.

81. GARF, f. 730, op. 1, d. 428.

82. RGAVMF, f. 315, op. 1–2, d. 1108, l. 21–25.

Conclusion

1. V. V. Bartol'd, *Sochineniia* (Moscow: Izd-vo vostochnoi lit-ry, 1963), 9:482.

2. Widmer, *Russian Ecclesiastical Mission,* 166–167.

3. M. A. Polievktov, *Ekonomicheskie i politicheskie razvedki Moskovskogo gosudarstva XVII v. na Kavkaze* (Tiflis, Georgia: NII Kavkazovedeniia AN SSSR, 1932), 54.

4. Eric H. Ash, *Power, Knowledge, and Expertise in Elizabethan England* (Baltimore: Johns Hopkins University Press, 2004); William J. Ashworth, "Quality and the Roots of Manufacturing 'Expertise' in Eighteenth-Century Britain," *Osiris* 25, no. 1 (2010): 231–254; Thomas Broman, "The Semblance of Transparency: Expertise as a Social Good and an Ideology in Enlightened Societies," *Osiris* 27, no. 1 (2012): 188–208; Klein and Spary, *Materials and Expertise.*

5. OR RGB, f. 344, n. 91; Bantysh-Kamenskii, *Diplomaticheskoe sobranie.*

6. Stepan Lipovtsov and Pavel Kamenskii, "Kratkoe nachertanie o predubezhdenii kitaitsev k samim sebe," *Vostok-zapad: istoriko-kulturnyi al'manakh,* 2003–2004, 221–245.

7. Nevel'skoi, *Podvigi russkikh morskikh ofitserov,* 33–82.

8. V. P. Vasil'ev, *Otkrytie Kitaia i dr. st. V. P. Vasil'eva* (St. Petersburg: Stolichnaia tip, 1900), 1–33, 63–101.

9. Pëtr Shumakher, "Nashi snosheniia s Kitaem," *Russkii arkhiv* 2, no. 10 (1879): 145–182.

10. I. Korostovets, "Russkaia dukhovnaia missiia v Pekine," *Russkii arkhiv* 2, no. 6 (1893): 57–86.

11. Badmaev, *Rossiia i Kitai,* 12–13.

12. On the "special relationship," see Paine, *Imperial Rivals.*

13. Bantysh-Kamenskii, *Diplomaticheskoe sobranie*, 536–540.

14. Kurts, *Russko-kitaiskie snosheniia*, 145–146, 156.

15. Kabanov, *Amurskii vopros*, 15.

16. Kabanov, 231–240.

17. Alekseev, *Delo vsei zhizni*, 8–9; other works in this tradition include Alekseev, *Amurskaia ekspeditsiia*; Alekseev, *Gennadii Ivanovich Nevel'skoi*; Besprozvannykh, *Priamur'e v sisteme*.

18. Alekseev, *Delo vsei zhizni*, 20, 24.

19. RKO XVII, 2:54.

20. RKO XVII, 2:5–55.

21. For example, V. S. Miasnikov, *The Ch'ing Empire and the Russian State in the 17th Century* (Moscow: Progress, 1985).

22. Plotnikov, *Russkaia dal'nevostochnaia granitsa*, 104.

Bibliography

Archives and Manuscript Collections

London

British Library (BL) India Office Records (IOR)
London Metropolitan Archives
National Archives (NA)

Paris

Archives jésuites, Vanves
Archives du Ministère des Affaires étrangères, La Courneuve (AAE)
Archives nationales (AN)
Bibliothéque de l'Institut de France (BIF)
Bibliothéque Nationale (BN)

Moscow

Archive of Foreign Affairs of the Russian Empire (AVPRI)
Russian State Archive of Ancient Acts (RGADA)
Russian State Library Manuscript Department (OR RGB)
State Archive of the Russian Federation (GARF)
State Historical Museum Department of Written Sources (OPI GIM)
State Historical Museum Manuscript Department (OR GIM)

St. Petersburg

Archive of the Russian Academy of Sciences, St. Petersburg Branch (SPb ARAN)
Institute of Oriental Manuscripts Archive of Orientalists (AV IVR)

Institute of Oriental Manuscripts Manuscript Department (OR IVR)
Library of the Academy of Sciences Manuscript Department (OR BAN)
Pushkin House (PD)
Russian National Library Manuscript Department (OR RNB)
Russian State Archive of the Navy (RGAVMF)
Russian State Historical Archive (RGIA)
St. Petersburg Institute of History (SPbII)

Other Collections

Archivum Romanum Societatis Iesu (ARSI), Rome
KU-Leuven Documentation and Research Centre on Religion, Culture and
    Society (KADOC), Leuven, Belgium
Yale Beinecke Rare Books Library (BRB), New Haven, CT

Published and Secondary Sources

Abel-Rémusat, Jean-Pierre. *Mélanges asiatiques, ou choix de morceaux de
    critiques et de mémoires relatifs aux religions, aux sciences, aux coutumes, à
    l'histoire et à la géographie des nations orientales, . . .* Paris: Dondey-Dupré,
    1826.
Adams, Robyn, and Rosanna Cox, eds. *Diplomacy and Early Modern Culture.*
    New York: Palgrave Macmillan, 2011.
Adas, Michael. *Machines as the Measure of Men: Science, Technology, and
    Ideologies of Western Dominance.* Ithaca, NY: Cornell University Press,
    1989.
Adoratskii, Nikolai. "Otets Iakinf Bichurin: biograficheskii etiud." *Pravoslavnyi
    sobesednik,* March 1886, 164–180, 245–278.
———. *Pravoslavnaia missiia v Kitaie za 200 let eia sushchestvovaniia: opyt
    tserkovno-istoricheskago izsledovaniia po arkhivnym dokumentam.* Kazan,
    Russia: Tip. Imperatorskago universiteta, 1887.
Afinogenov, Gregory. "Jesuit Conspirators and Russia's East Asian Fur Trade,
    1791–1807." *Journal of Jesuit Studies* 2, no. 1 (February 24, 2015): 56–76.
———. "Languages of Hegemony on the Eighteenth-Century Kazakh Steppe."
    International History Review 41, no. 5 (2019): 1020–1038.
———. "The Manchu Book in Eighteenth-Century St. Petersburg." *Saksaha: A
    Journal of Manchu Studies,* no. 14 (2016). http://dx.doi.org/10.3998/saksaha
    .13401746.0014.001.
Akkerman, Nadine. *Invisible Agents: Women and Espionage in Seventeenth-
    Century Britain.* Oxford: Oxford University Press, 2018.

Alekseev, A. I. *Delo vsei zhizni. Kniga o podvige adm. G. I. Nevel'skogo.* Khabarovsk, Russia: Knizd-vo, 1972.

——. *Amurskaia ekspeditsiia 1849–1855 gg.* Moscow: Mysl', 1974.

——. *Osvoenie russkimi liud'mi Dal'nego Vostoka i Russkoi Ameriki do kontsa XIX veka.* Moscow: Nauka, 1982.

——. *Gennadii Ivanovich Nevel'skoi (1813–1876).* Moscow: Nauka, 1984.

Andreev, A. I. *Ocherki po istochnikovedeniiu Sibiri: XVII vek.* Leningrad: Izd-vo Glavsevmorputi, 1939.

——. *Ocherki po istochnikovedeniiu Sibiri: XVIII vek. 2. izd., ispr. I dop.* Leningrad: Izd-vo Akademii nauk SSSR [Leningradskoe otd-nie], 1960.

App, Urs. *The Birth of Orientalism.* Philadelphia: University of Pennsylvania Press, 2010.

Argent, Gesine, Derek Offord, and Vladislav Rjeoutski. "The Functions and Value of Foreign Languages in Eighteenth-Century Russia." *Russian Review* 74, no. 1 (2015): 1–19.

Arkhiv Gosudarstvennago Soveta. St. Petersburg: Tip. Vtorago otd-niia Sobstvennoi E. I. V. kantseliarii, 1869.

Armitage, David. "The International Turn in Intellectual History." In *Rethinking Modern European Intellectual History,* edited by Darrin M. McMahon and Samuel Moyn, 232–252. Oxford: Oxford University Press, 2014.

Armstrong, T. "In Search of a Sea Route to Siberia, 1553–1619." *Arctic* 37, no. 4 (December 1, 1984): 429–440.

Ash, Eric H. *Power, Knowledge, and Expertise in Elizabethan England.* Baltimore: Johns Hopkins University Press, 2004.

Ashworth, William J. "Quality and the Roots of Manufacturing 'Expertise' in Eighteenth-Century Britain." *Osiris* 25, no. 1 (2010): 231–254.

Aslanian, Sebouh David. *From the Indian Ocean to the Mediterranean: The Global Trade Networks of Armenian Merchants from New Julfa.* Berkeley: University of California Press, 2011.

Åslund, Anders. *The Russia Balance Sheet.* Washington, DC: Peterson Institute for International Economics, 2009.

Avril, Philippe. *Travels into Divers Parts of Europe and Asia: Undertaken . . . to Discover a New Way by Land into China.* N.p.: Goodwin, 1693.

——. *Voyage en divers états d'Europe et d'Asie, entrepris pour découvrir un nouveau chemin à la Chine.* N.p.: J. Boudot, 1693.

Avtonomov, A. S. "Diplomaticheskaia deiatel'nost' Russkoi pravoslavnoi missii v Pekine v XVIII–XIX vv." *Voprosy istorii,* no. 7 (2005): 100–111.

Baddeley, John F. *Russia, Mongolia, China.* London: Macmillan, 1919.

Badmaev, P. A. *Rossiia i Kitai.* St. Petersburg: Izd. red. "Novago Zhurnala literatury, iskusstva i nauki," 1905.

Bagrow, Leo. "Sparwenfeld's Map of Siberia." *Imago Mundi,* no. 4 (1947): 65–70.

———. "The First Russian Maps of Siberia and Their Influence on the West-European Cartography of N. E. Asia." *Imago Mundi,* no. 9 (1952): 83–93.

———. "A Russian Communications Map, ca. 1685." *Imago Mundi,* no. 9 (1952): 99–101.

———. "A Few Remarks on Maps of the Amur, the Tartar Strait and Sakhalin." *Imago Mundi,* no. 12 (1955): 127–136.

Balabanlilar, Lisa. "Lords of the Auspicious Conjunction: Turco-Mongol Imperial Identity on the Subcontinent." *Journal of World History* 18, no. 1 (February 27, 2007): 1–39.

Balzacq, Thierry, Sarah Léonard, and Jan Ruzicka. "'Securitization' Revisited: Theory and Cases." *International Relations* 30, no. 4 (December 1, 2016): 494–531.

Bantysh-Kamenskii, N. N. *Diplomaticheskoe sobranie del mezhdu Rossiiskim i Kitaiskim gosudarstvami s 1619 po 1792-i g.* Edited by V. M. Florinskii. Kazan, Russia: Imperatorskii Universitet, 1882.

Barratt, Glynn. *Russia in Pacific Waters, 1715–1825: A Survey of the Origins of Russia's Naval Presence in the North and South Pacific.* Vancouver: University of British Columbia Press, 1981.

Barsukov, Ivan. *Graf Nikolai Nikolaevich Murav'ev-Amurskii po ego pis'mam, offitsial'nym dokumentam, razskazam sovremennikov i pechatnym istochnikam.* Moscow: Sinodal'naia tip., 1891.

Bartenev, P. I, ed. *Arkhiv kniazia Vorontsova.* Moscow: Tip. A. I. Mamontova, 1870.

Bartlett, Beatrice S. *Monarchs and Ministers: The Grand Council in Mid-Ch'ing China, 1723–1820.* Berkeley: University of California Press, 1991.

Bartol'd, V. V. *Sochineniia.* Moscow: Izd-vo vostochnoi lit-ry, 1963.

Bassin, Mark. *Imperial Visions: Nationalist Imagination and Geographical Expansion in the Russian Far East, 1840–1865.* Cambridge: Cambridge University Press, 1999.

Batchelor, Robert K. *London: The Selden Map and the Making of a Global City, 1549–1689.* Chicago: University of Chicago Press, 2014.

Bawden, Charles R. "The Mongol Rebellion of 1756–1757." *Journal of Asian History* 2, no. 1 (1968): 1–31.

Bayly, C. A. *Empire and Information: Intelligence Gathering and Social Communication in India, 1780–1870.* Cambridge: Cambridge University Press, 2000.

———. *The Birth of the Modern World, 1780–1914: Global Connections and Comparisons.* Malden, MA: Blackwell, 2004.

Bedford, R. D. "Jodocus Crull and Milton's *A Brief History of Moscovia.*" *Review of English Studies,* n.s., 47, no. 186 (May 1, 1996): 207–211.

Begheyn, Paul. "Dutch Publications on the Jesuit Mission in China in the Seventeenth and Eighteenth Centuries." *Quaerendo* 49, no. 1 (March 26, 2019): 49–65.

Begunov, Iu. K. "Rukopisnaia literatura XVIII veka i demokraticheskii chitatel' (Problemy i zadachi izucheniia)." *Russkaia literatura,* no. 1 (1977): 121–132.

Bell, John. *Travels from St. Petersburg in Russia to Diverse Parts of Asia.* Glasgow: Foulis, 1763.

Belobrova, O. A. "Ob avtografakh Nikolaia Spafariia." *Trudy otdela drevnerusskoi literatury,* no. 36 (1969): 259–265.

Bély, Lucien. *Espions et ambassadeurs au temps de Louis XIV.* Paris: Fayard, 1990.

Ben-Atar, Doron S. *Trade Secrets: Intellectual Piracy and the Origins of American Industrial Power.* New Haven, CT: Yale University Press, 2004.

Benyowsky, Maurice Auguste. *Memoirs and Travels of Mauritius Augustus Count de Benyowsky . . .* London: G. G. J. and J. Robinson, 1790.

Bergholz, Fred W. *The Partition of the Steppe: The Struggle of the Russians, Manchus, and the Zunghar Mongols for Empire in Central Asia, 1619–1758; A Study in Power Politics.* New York: Peter Lang, 1993.

Bertucci, Paola. "Enlightened Secrets: Silk, Intelligent Travel, and Industrial Espionage in Eighteenth-Century France." *Technology and Culture* 54, no. 4 (2013): 820–852.

Besprozvannykh, E. L. *Priamur'e v sisteme russko-kitaiskikh otnoshenii: XVII–seredina XIX v.* Khabarovsk, Russia: Khabarovskoe Knizhoe izd-vo, 1986.

Bevilacqua, Alexander. *The Republic of Arabic Letters: Islam and the European Enlightenment.* Cambridge, MA: Belknap, 2018.

Black, J. L. *G.-F. Müller and the Imperial Russian Academy.* Kingston, ON: McGill-Queen's University Press, 1986.

Black, Lydia T. "The Question of Maps: Exploration of the Bering Sea in the Eighteenth Century." In *The Sea in Alaska's Past: First Conference Proceedings,* 6–50. Anchorage: Office of History and Archaeology, Alaska Division of Parks, 1979.

———. *Russians in Alaska, 1732–1867.* Fairbanks: University of Alaska Press, 2004.

Blair, Ann. "Humanist Methods in Natural Philosophy: The Commonplace Book." *Journal of the History of Ideas* 53, no. 4 (October 1, 1992): 541–551.

———. *Too Much to Know: Managing Scholarly Information before the Modern Age.* New Haven, CT: Yale University Press, 2010.

Blair, Ann, and Devin Fitzgerald. "A Revolution in Information?" In *The Oxford Handbook of Early Modern European History, 1350–1750,* edited by H. M. Scott, 1:244–268. Oxford: Oxford University Press, 2015.

Blue, George Verne. "A Rumor of an Anglo-Russian Raid on Japan, 1776." *Pacific Historical Review* 8, no. 4 (December 1, 1939): 453–463.

Blum, Alain. "Circulation, Transfers, Isolation." *Kritika: Explorations in Russian and Eurasian History* 9, no. 1 (March 10, 2008): 231–242.

Bolkhovitinov, N. N., ed. *Istoriia Russkoi Ameriki, 1732–1867.* Moscow: Mezhdunarodnye otnosheniia, 1997.

Borodaev, V. B., and A. V. *Kontev. Formirovanie rossiiskoi granitsy v Irtyshsko-Eniseiskom mezhdurech'e v 1620–1720 gg.* Barnaul, Russia: AltSPU, 2015.

Boronin, O. V. *Dvoedannichestvo v Sibiri XVII–60e gg. XIX v.* Barnaul, Russia: Azbuka, 2004.

Bosmans, Henri. "Le problème des relations de Verbiest avec la Cour de Russie." *Annales de la Société d'Émulation de Bruges,* no. 63 (1913): 193–223; no. 64 (1914): 98–101.

Bradley, Joseph. *Voluntary Associations in Tsarist Russia: Science, Patriotism, and Civil Society.* Cambridge, MA: Harvard University Press, 2009.

Brockey, Liam Matthew. *Journey to the East: The Jesuit Mission to China, 1579–1724.* Cambridge, MA: Harvard University Press, 2007.

Brockliss, Lawrence. *Calvet's Web: Enlightenment and the Republic of Letters in Eighteenth-Century France.* Oxford: Oxford University Press, 2002.

Broman, Thomas. "The Semblance of Transparency: Expertise as a Social Good and an Ideology in Enlightened Societies." *Osiris* 27, no. 1 (2012): 188–208.

Brophy, David. "Tending to Unite? The Origins of Uyghur Nationalism." PhD diss., Harvard University, 2011.

Brown, Peter B. "How Muscovy Governed: Seventeenth-Century Russian Central Administration." *Russian History* 36, no. 4 (November 1, 2009): 459–529.

Buksgevden, A. *Russkii Kitai: ocherki diplomaticheskikh snoshenii Rossii s Kitaem.* Port Arthur, Russia: Izd-vo kliznogo sklada "Novyi Krai," 1902.

Burgess, Richard. "Thomas Garvine—Ayrshire Surgeon Active in Russia and China." *Medical History* 19, no. 1 (January 1975): 91–94.

Burton, Audrey. *The Bukharans: A Dynastic, Diplomatic, and Commercial History, 1550–1702.* New York: St. Martin's, 1997.

Cahen, Gaston. *Le livre de comptes de la caravane russe à Pékin en 1727–1728.* Paris: F. Alcan, 1911.

———. *Histoire des relations de la Russie avec la Chine sous Pierre le Grand (1689–1730).* Paris: F. Alcan, 1912.

Campbell, Ian W. *Knowledge and the Ends of Empire: Kazak Intermediaries and Russian Rule on the Steppe, 1731–1917.* Ithaca, NY: Cornell University Press, 2017.

Campbell, John L. "Institutional Analysis and the Role of Ideas in Political Economy." *Theory and Society* 27, no. 3 (1998): 377–409.

Campbell, John L., and Ove Kaj Pedersen. *The National Origins of Policy Ideas: Knowledge Regimes in the United States, France, Germany, and Denmark.* Princeton, NJ: Princeton University Press, 2014.

Cams, Mario. *Companions in Geography: East-West Collaboration in the Mapping of Qing China (c. 1685–1735).* Leiden, Netherlands: Brill, 2017.

Chabin, Marie-Anne. "L'astronome français Joseph-Nicolas Delisle à la cour de Russie." In *L'influence française en Russie au XVIIIe siècle,* edited by

Jean-Pierre Poussou, Anne Mézin, and Yves Perret-Gentil, 504–520. Paris: Institut d'etudes slaves, 2004.

Chakravarti, Ananya. *The Empire of Apostles: Religion, Accommodation, and the Imagination of Empire in Early Modern Brazil and India.* New Delhi: Oxford University Press, 2018.

Chaplin, Joyce. "The Pacific before Empire, c. 1500–1800." In *Pacific Histories: Ocean, Land, People,* edited by David Armitage and Alison Bashford, 53–74. Basingstoke: Palgrave Macmillan, 2014.

Chegodaev, A. B. "Mongol'sko-man'chzhursko-kitaisko-russko-latinskii piatiiazychnyi slovar' P. I. Kamenskogo: voprosy ego sozdaniia i izdaniia." *Vestnik Tomskogo gosudarstvennogo universiteta* 1, no. 13 (2011): 8–10.

Chen Weixin. *Qingdai dui E waijiao liyi tizhi ji fanshu guishu jiaoshe: 1644–1861.* Harbin, China: Heilongjiang jiaoyu chubanshe, 2012.

Chia, Ning. "The Lifanyuan and the Inner Asian Rituals in the Early Qing (1644–1795)." *Late Imperial China* 14, no. 1 (1993): 60–92.

Chinesische Gedanken nach der von Alexjei Leont'ew aus der manshurischen Sprache verfertigten russischen Uebersetzung ins Deutsche übersetzt. Weimar, Germany: Hoffmann, 1776.

Ching, Julia, and Willard Gurdon Oxtoby, eds. *Discovering China: European Interpretations in the Enlightenment.* Rochester, NY: University of Rochester Press, 1992.

Chrissidis, Nikolaos A. *An Academy at the Court of the Tsars: Greek Scholars and Jesuit Education in Early Modern Russia.* DeKalb: Northern Illinois University Press, 2016.

Cibot, Pierre-Martial. "Fungus Sinensium Mo-Ku-Sin." *Novi Commentarii Academiae Scientiarum Imperialis Petropolitanae,* no. 19 (1774): 373–378.

Classen, Albrecht. "A Global Epistolary Network: Eighteenth-Century Jesuit Missionaries Write Home." *Studia Neophilologica* 86, no. 1 (January 2, 2014): 79–94.

Cohn, Bernard S. *Colonialism and Its Forms of Knowledge: The British in India.* Princeton, NJ: Princeton University Press, 1996.

Collins, Samuel. *The Present State of Russia in a Letter to a Friend at London; Written by an Eminent Person Residing at the Great Czars.* Edited by Marshall Poe. London, 1671. http://ir.uiowa.edu/history_pubs/1.

Collis, Robert. *The Petrine Instauration: Religion, Esotericism and Science at the Court of Peter the Great, 1689–1725.* Leiden, Netherlands: Brill, 2012.

Cook, Harold. *Matters of Exchange: Commerce, Medicine, and Science in the Dutch Golden Age.* New Haven, CT: Yale University Press, 2007.

Corrado, Sharyl. "A Land Divided: Sakhalin and the Amur Expedition of G. I. Nevel'skoi, 1848–1855." *Journal of Historical Geography,* no. 45 (July 1, 2014): 70–81.

Coxe, William. *Account of the Russian Discoveries between Asia and America.* London: Nichols, 1780.

Cracraft, James. *The Petrine Revolution in Russian Culture.* Cambridge, MA: Belknap, 2004.

Cranmer-Byng, J. L. "Russian and British Interests in the Far East 1791–1793." *Canadian Slavonic Papers* 10, no. 3 (October 1, 1968): 357–375.

Crossley, Pamela Kyle. *A Translucent Mirror: History and Identity in Qing Imperial Ideology.* Berkeley: University of California Press, 2000.

Crull, Jodocus. *The Antient and Present State of Muscovy: Containing a Geographical, Historical and Political Account of All Those Nations and Territories under the Jurisdiction of the Present Czar [. . .].* N.p.: A. Roper and A. Bosvile, 1698.

———. *The Compleat History of the Affairs of Spain, from the First Treaty of Partition, to This Present Time . . .* London: Jos. Barns, 1707.

Csiszar, Alex. *The Scientific Journal: Authorship and the Politics of Knowledge in the Nineteenth Century.* Chicago: University of Chicago Press, 2018.

Daily, Christopher A. *Robert Morrison and the Protestant Plan for China.* Hong Kong: Hong Kong University Press, 2013.

Darwin, John. *After Tamerlane: The Global History of Empire since 1405.* New York: Bloomsbury, 2008.

———. *After Tamerlane: The Rise and Fall of Global Empires, 1400–2000.* New York: Bloomsbury, 2008.

Daston, Lorraine. "The Sciences of the Archive." *Osiris* 27, no. 1 (2012): 156–187.

———. "The History of Science and the History of Knowledge." *KNOW: A Journal on the Formation of Knowledge* 1, no. 1 (March 1, 2017): 131–154.

Datsyshen, V. G. *Istoriia Rossiiskoi dukhovnoi missii v Kitae.* Hong Kong: Pravoslavnoe Bratstvo . . . Petra i Pavla, 2010.

———. *Izuchenie istorii Kitaia v Rossiiskoi Imperii.* Moscow: Prospekt, 2015.

Datsyshen, V. G., and A. B. Chegodaev. *Arkhimandrit Petr (Kamenskii).* Hong Kong: Sts. Peter and Paul Orthodox Church, 2013.

Davids, Karel. "Craft Secrecy in Europe in the Early Modern Period: A Comparative View." *Early Science and Medicine* 10, no. 3 (August 1, 2005): 341–348.

Dear, Devon Margaret. "Marginal Revolutions: Economies and Economic Knowledge between Qing China, Russia, and Mongolia, 1860–1911." PhD diss., Harvard University, 2014.

Defoe, Daniel. *The Farther Adventures of Robinson Crusoe: Being the Second and Last Part of His Life, and of the Strange Surprizing Accounts of His Travels Round Three Parts of the Globe.* N.p.: W. Taylor, 1719.

Dehergne, Joseph. "Une grande collection: Mémoires concernant les Chinois (1776–1814)." *Bulletin de l'Ecole française d'Extrême-Orient* 72, no. 1 (1983): 267–298.

Demidova, N. F. "O variantakh stateinogo spiska posol'stva F. I. Baikova v Kitai."
   In *Voprosy sotsial'no-ekonomicheskoi istorii i istochnikovedeniia perioda*
   feodalizma v Rossii: sbornik statei k 70-letiiu A. A. Novosel'skogo, edited by
   N. V. Ustiugov, 270–280. Moscow: Izd-vo Akademii nauk SSSR, 1961.
Denisov, P. V. *Slovo o monakhe Iakinfe Bichurine.* Cheboksary, Russia: Chuvash.
   kn. izd-vo, 2007.
Dermigny, Louis. *La Chine et l'Occident: le commerce à Canton au XVIIIe siècle,*
   1719–1833. Paris: S. E. V. P. E. N., 1964.
Dewerpe, Alain. *Espion: une anthologie historique du secret d'état contemporain.*
   Paris: Gallimard, 1994.
D'Incarville, Pierre. "Catalogue alphabétique des plantes et autres objets
   d'histoire naturelle en usage en Chine." *Mémoires de la Société impériale des*
   naturalistes de Moscou, 1812, 3:103–128, 4:26–88.
Diu Gal'd, Zhan-Baptist. *Geograficheskoe, istoricheskoe, khronologicheskoe,*
   politicheskoe, i fizicheskoe opisanie Kitaiskiia imperii i Tatarii Kitaiskiia,
   tan. Translated by Ignatii De Teil's. St. Petersburg: Tip. Imp. Sukhoput.
   shliakhet. kad. korpusa, 1774.
Dodson, Michael. *Orientalism, Empire, and National Culture: India, 1770–1880.*
   Basingstoke: Palgrave Macmillan, 2007.
Dushkov, Iurii. "Kursiny v Irkutske." *Zemlia irkut*skaia, no. 5 (1995): 13–17.
Elliott, Mark C. "The Limits of Tartary: Manchuria in Imperial and National
   Geographies." *Journal of Asian Studies* 59, no. 3 (2000): 603–646.
———. "The 'Eating Crabs' Youth Book." In *Under Confucian Eyes: Writings on*
   Gender in Chinese History, edited by Susan Mann and Yu-Yin Cheng,
   263–281. Berkeley: University of California Press, 2001.
———. *The Manchu Way: The Eight Banners and Ethnic Identity in Late Imperial*
   China. Stanford, CA: Stanford University Press, 2001.
———. "Abel-Rémusat, la langue mandchoue et la sinologie." *Comptes-rendus des*
   séances de l'année . . . (Académie des inscriptions et belles-lettres), no. 2
   (2014): 973–993.
Elverskog, Johan. *Our Great Qing: The Mongols, Buddhism and the State in Late*
   Imperial China. Honolulu: University of Hawai'i Press, 2006.
Ermolaev, A. N. *Rossiisko-amerikanskaia kompaniia v Sibiri i na Dal'nem*
   Vostoke (1799–1871 gg). Kemerovo, Russia: INT, 2013.
Evans, John L. *Russian Expansion on the Amur, 1848–1860: The Push to the*
   Pacific. Lewiston, NY: Edwin Mellen, 1999.
Evtuhov, Catherine. *Portrait of a Russian Province: Economy, Society, and*
   Civilization in Nineteenth-Century Nizhnii Novgorod. Pittsburgh: Univer-
   sity of Pittsburgh Press, 2011.
Fediukin, Igor'. "Rol' administrativnogo predprinimatel'stva v petrovskikh
   reformakh: navigatskaia shkola i pozdnemoskovskie knizhniki." *Rossiiskaia*
   istoriia, no. 4 (2014): 80–101.

Fedyukin, Igor. "The 'German' Reign of Empress Anna: Russia's Disciplinary Moment?" *Kritika: Explorations in Russian and Eurasian History* 19, no. 2 (May 23, 2018): 363–384.

Feingold, Mordechai. *Jesuit Science and the Republic of Letters.* Cambridge, MA: MIT Press, 2003.

Feklova, T. Iu. "Ekspeditsii Akademii nauk i izuchenie Kitaia v pervoi polovine XIX v." In *Rossiia i Kitai: aspekty vzaimodeistviia i vzaimovliianiia,* edited by N. L. Glazacheva and O. V. Zalesskaia, 26–34. Blagoveshchensk, Russia: Izdatel'stvo BGPU, 2011.

Felten, Sebastian. "The History of Science and the History of Bureaucratic Knowledge: Saxon Mining, circa 1770." *History of Science* 56, no. 4 (December 1, 2018): 403–431.

Finlay, Robert. *The Pilgrim Art: Cultures of Porcelain in World History.* Berkeley: University of California Press, 2010.

Fischer, Johann. "Rassuzhdeniia o raznykh imenakh kitaiskogo gosudarstva i o khanskikh titulakh." *Ezhemesiachnye sochineniia,* no. 10 (1756), no. 5 (1757).

Florovsky, Anthony. "Maps of the Siberian Route of the Belgian Jesuit, A. Thomas (1690)." *Imago Mundi,* no. 8 (1951): 103–108.

Forman, Paul. "On the Historical Forms of Knowledge Production and Curation: Modernity Entailed Disciplinarity, Postmodernity Entails Antidisciplinarity." *Osiris* 27, no. 1 (2012): 56–97.

Forsyth, James. *A History of the Peoples of Siberia: Russia's North Asian Colony, 1581–1990.* Cambridge: Cambridge University Press, 1992.

[Fourmont, Etienne]. *Catalogus codicum manuscriptorium Bibliothecae Regiae.* Paris: E Typographia Regia, 1739.

Foust, Clifford. *Muscovite and Mandarin: Russia's Trade with China and Its Setting, 1727–1805.* Chapel Hill: University of North Carolina Press, 1969.

———. *Rhubarb: The Wondrous Drug.* Princeton, NJ: Princeton University Press, 1992.

Foy de la Neuville. *A Curious and New Account of Muscovy in the Year 1689.* London: School of Slavonic and East European Studies, University of London, 1994.

Frank, Andre Gunder. *ReOrient: Global Economy in the Asian Age.* Berkeley: University of California Press, 1998.

Freeze, Gregory L. *The Russian Levites: Parish Clergy in the Eighteenth Century.* Cambridge, MA: Harvard University Press, 1977.

Friedrich, Markus. "Archives as Networks: The Geography of Record-Keeping in the Society of Jesus (1540–1773)." *Archival Science* 10, no. 3 (October 2, 2010): 285–298.

Froger, François. *A Journal of the First French Embassy to China, 1698–1700.* N.p.: T. C. Newby, 1859.

Fu, Lo-shu. *A Documentary Chronicle of Sino-Western Relations, 1644–1820.*
Tucson: University of Arizona Press, 1966.

Gaubil, Antoine. *Correspondance de Pekin, 1722–1759.* Edited by Rene Simon.
Geneva: Éditions Plon, 1971.

Gerasimov, Il'ia, Marina Mogilner, and Sergey Glebov. "Glava 7. Dolgii XVIII
vek i stanovlenie modernizatsionnoi imperii." *Ab Imperio,* no. 1 (May 28,
2015): 387–447.

Ger'e, V. I. *Otnosheniia Leibnitsa k Rossii i Petru Velikomu po neizdannym
bumagam Leibnitsa v Gannoverskoi biblioteke.* St. Petersburg: Pechatnia V.
Golovina, 1871.

Gestrich, Andreas. *Absolutismus und Öffentlichkeit: politische Kommunikation
in Deutschland zu Beginn des 18. Jahrhunderts.* Göttingen, Germany:
Vandenhoeck & Ruprecht, 1994.

Ghobrial, John-Paul A. *The Whispers of Cities: Information Flows in Istanbul,
London, and Paris in the Age of William Trumbull.* Oxford: Oxford University Press, 2013.

Gibson, James R. *Otter Skins, Boston Ships, and China Goods: The Maritime Fur
Trade of the Northwest Coast, 1785–1841.* Seattle: University of Washington
Press, 1992.

Golburt, Luba. *The First Epoch: The Eighteenth Century and Russian Cultural
Imagination.* Madison: University of Wisconsin Press, 2014.

Goldenberg, L. A., and A. V. Postnikov. "Development of Mapping
Methods in Russia in the Eighteenth Century." *Imago Mundi,* no. 37
(1985): 63–80.

Goldgar, Anne. *Impolite Learning: Conduct and Community in the Republic of
Letters, 1680–1750.* New Haven, CT: Yale University Press, 1995.

Goldsmith, Oliver. *The Citizen of the World; or Letters from a Chinese Philosopher, Residing in London, to His Friends in the East.* London: R. Whiston,
1785.

Golinski, Jan. *Making Natural Knowledge: Constructivism and the History of
Science.* Chicago: University of Chicago Press, 2005.

Golovin, Vasilii [Julius von Klaproth]. *Die russische Gesandtschaft nach China
im Jahr 1805: nebst einer Nachricht von der letzten Christen-Verfolgung in
Peking.* St. Petersburg: Ziemsen, 1809.

Golvers, Noël. *Libraries of Western Learning for China: Circulation of Western
Books between Europe and China in the Jesuit Mission (ca. 1650–ca. 1750).*
Vol. 1, *Logistics of Book Acquisition and Circulation.* Leuven, Belgium:
Ferdinand Verbiest Institute, 2012.

———. "The Jesuit Mission in China (17th–18th Cent) as the Framework for the
Circulation of Knowledge between Europe and China." *Lusitania Sacra,*
no. 36 (July 2017): 179–199.

Golvers, Noël, and Efthymios Nicolaidis. *Ferdinand Verbiest and Jesuit Science in 17th Century China: An Annotated Edition and Translation of the Constantinople Manuscript (1676)*. Athens: Institute for Neohellenic Research, 2009.

Gordin, Michael D. "The Importation of Being Earnest: The Early St. Petersburg Academy of Sciences." *Isis* 91, no. 1 (March 1, 2000): 1–31.

Gorizontov, Leonid. "Anatolii Remnev and the Regions of the Russian Empire." *Kritika: Explorations in Russian and Eurasian History* 16, no. 4 (October 29, 2015): 901–916.

Grabar', V. E. *The History of International Law in Russia, 1647–1917: A Bio-Bibliographical Study*. Translated by William Elliott Butler. Oxford: Clarendon, 1990.

Grainger, John D. *The First Pacific War: Britain and Russia, 1854–56*. Woodbridge: Boydell and Brewer, 2008.

Grandjean, Katherine. *American Passage: The Communications Frontier in Early New England*. Cambridge, MA: Harvard University Press, 2015.

Gray, Edward G. *The Making of John Ledyard: Empire and Ambition in the Life of an Early American Traveler*. New Haven, CT: Yale University Press, 2007.

Green, Michael. *By More than Providence: Grand Strategy and American Power in the Asia Pacific since 1783*. New York: Columbia University Press, 2017.

Grimsted, Patricia Kennedy. *The Foreign Ministers of Alexander I: Political Attitudes and the Conduct of Russian Diplomacy, 1801–1825*. Berkeley: University of California Press, 1969.

Guber, A. A. *Politika evropeiskikh derzhav v Iugo-Vostochnoi Azii: 60-e gody XVIII–60-e gody XIX v.: dokumenty i materialy*. Moscow: Izd-vo vostochnoi lit-ry, 1962.

Gurevich, B. P. *Mezhdunarodnye otnosheniia v Tsentral'noi Azii v XVII–pervoi polovine XIX v*. Moscow: Nauka, 1983.

Gurevich, B. P., G. F. Kim, and S. L. Tikhvinskii, eds. *Mezhdunarodnye otnosheniia v Tsentral'noi Azii: XVII–XVIII vv.: dokumenty i materialy*. Moscow: Nauka, 1989.

Gürkan, Emrah Safa. "Espionage in the 16th Century Mediterranean: Secret Diplomacy, Mediterranean Go-Betweens and the Ottoman Habsburg Rivalry." PhD diss., Georgetown University, 2012.

———. "Mediating Boundaries: Mediterranean Go-Betweens and Cross-Confessional Diplomacy in Constantinople, 1560–1600." *Journal of Early Modern History* 19, no. 2–3 (April 21, 2015): 107–128.

Guzevich, Dmitrii, and Irina Guzevich. "Karta-zadanie Zh. N. Delilia dlia Vtoroi Kamchatksoi ekspeditsii: 'bessovestnyi obman' ili osnova dlia otkrytii?" In *Delili v Rossii: sbornik statei*, edited by Dmitrii Guzevich and Irina Guzevich, 60–92. St. Petersburg: Mamatov, 2019.

Hajnal, László. "Witsen's 'Dagur' Material." *Acta Orientalia Academiae Scientiarum Hungaricae* 47, no. 3 (January 1, 1994): 279–326.

Halperin, Charles J. *Russia and the Golden Horde: The Mongol Impact on Medieval Russian History*. Bloomington: Indiana University Press, 1987.

Hamburg, Gary. *Russia's Path toward Enlightenment: Faith, Politics, and Reason, 1500–1801*. New Haven, CT: Yale University Press, 2016.

Hao, Gao. "Prelude to the Opium War? British Reactions to the 'Napier Fizzle' and Attitudes towards China in the Mid Eighteen-Thirties." *Historical Research* 87, no. 237 (August 1, 2014): 491–509.

———. "The Amherst Embassy and British Discoveries in China." *History* 99, no. 337 (October 1, 2014): 568–587.

Harris, John R. "Industrial Espionage in the Eighteenth Century." *Industrial Archaeology Review* 7, no. 2 (1985): 127–138.

———. "Movements of Technology between Britain and Europe." In *International Technology Transfer: Europe, Japan, and the USA, 1700–1914*, edited by David J. Jeremy, 9–30. Brookfield, VT: Edward Elgar, 1991.

———. *Industrial Espionage and Technology Transfer: Britain and France in the Eighteenth Century*. Brookfield, VT: Ashgate, 1998.

Harris, Steven J. "Jesuit Scientific Activity in the Overseas Missions, 1540–1773." *Isis* 96, no. 1 (2005): 71–79.

Harrison, Henrietta. "The Qianlong Emperor's Letter to George III and the Early-Twentieth-Century Origins of Ideas about Traditional China's Foreign Relations." *American Historical Review* 122, no. 3 (June 1, 2017): 680–701.

Hazard, Paul. *La crise de la conscience européenne: 1680–1715*. Paris: Fayard, 1978.

Hennings, Jan. *Russia and Courtly Europe: Ritual and the Culture of Diplomacy, 1648–1725*. Cambridge: Cambridge University Press, 2016.

Hevia, James Louis. *Cherishing Men from Afar: Qing Guest Ritual and the Macartney Embassy of 1793*. Durham, NC: Duke University Press, 1995.

———. *English Lessons: The Pedagogy of Imperialism in Nineteenth-Century China*. Durham, NC: Duke University Press, 2003.

Hillemann, Ulrike. *Asian Empire and British Knowledge: China and the Networks of British Imperial Expansion*. Basingstoke: Palgrave Macmillan, 2009.

Hsia, Florence. *Sojourners in a Strange Land: Jesuits and Their Scientific Missions in Late Imperial China*. Chicago: University of Chicago Press, 2009.

Hughes, Lindsey. *Russia in the Age of Peter the Great*. New Haven, CT: Yale University Press, 1998.

Hundley, H. S. "Defending the Periphery: Tsarist Management of Buriat Buddhism." *Russian Review* 69, no. 2 (2010): 231–250.

Ides, Evert Ysbrants. *Three Years Travels from Moscow Over-Land to China: Thro' Great Ustiga, Siriania, Permia, Sibiria, Daour, Great Tartary, &c. to Peking.* London: W. Freeman, 1706.

Ides, Isbrant, and Adam Brand. *Zapiski o russkom posol'stve v Kitai, 1692–1695.* Edited by M. I. Kazanin. Moscow: Glav. red. vostochnoi lit-ry, 1967.

Igler, David. *The Great Ocean: Pacific Worlds from Captain Cook to the Gold Rush.* Oxford: Oxford University Press, 2013.

Ignat'ev, N. P. *Otchetnaia zapiska podannaia v Aziatskii Departament v ianvare 1861 goda.* St. Petersburg: Tip. V. V. Komarova, 1895.

Inglot, Marek, ed. *Rossiia i iezuity, 1772–1820.* Moscow: Nauka, 2006.

———. *How the Jesuits Survived Their Suppression: The Society of Jesus in the Russian Empire (1773–1814).* Translated by Daniel L. Schlafly. St. Louis: Saint Joseph's University Press, 2015.

Ivanov, Andrey V. "Conflicting Loyalties: Fugitives and Traitors in the Russo-Manchurian Frontier, 1651–1689." *Journal of Early Modern History* 13, no. 5 (2009): 333–358.

Jacobsen, Stefan Gaarsmand. "Chinese Influences or Images? Fluctuating Histories of How Enlightenment Europe Read China." *Journal of World History* 24, no. 3 (2013): 623–660.

Jersild, Austin. *Orientalism and Empire: North Caucasus Mountain Peoples and the Georgian Frontier, 1845–1917.* Montreal: McGill-Queen's University Press, 2002.

John Hobart, 2nd Earl of Buckinghamshire. *The Despatches and Correspondence of John, Second Earl of Buckinghamshire, Ambassador to the Court of Catherine II. of Russia 1762–1765.* Camden third series, vols. 2–3. London: Longmans, Green, and Co, 1900.

Jones, Ryan Tucker. *Empire of Extinction: Russians and the North Pacific's Strange Beasts of the Sea, 1741–1867.* Oxford: Oxford University Press, 2014.

Joukovskaïa, Anna. "Le service diplomatique russe au XVIIIe siècle: genèse et fonctionnement du collège des Affaires étrangères." PhD diss., EHESS, 2002.

———. "Unsalaried and Unfed: Town Clerks' Means of Survival in Southwest Russia under Peter I." Translated by Yelizaveta Raykhlina. *Kritika: Explorations in Russian and Eurasian History* 14, no. 4 (2013): 715–739.

Jütte, Daniel. *The Age of Secrecy: Jews, Christians, and the Economy of Secrets, 1400–1800.* Translated by Jeremiah Riemer. New Haven, CT: Yale University Press, 2015.

Juznic, Stanislav. "Building a Bridge between the Observatories of Petersburg and Beijing: A Study on the Jesuit Avguštin Hallerstein from Present-Day Slovenia, Celebrating the 310th Anniversary of His Birth." *Monumenta Serica,* no. 60 (2012): 309–406.

"K istorii priobreteniia Amura." *Russkii arkhiv,* no. 11 (1878): 274.

Kabanov, P. I. *Amurskii vopros.* Blagoveshchensk, Russia: Amurskoe knizhnoe izd-vo, 1959.

Kamenetskii, I. P. "Sekretnaia missiia kuptsa A. Verkhoturova: k voprosu ob organizatsii russkoi razvedki v Dzhungarii v seredine XVIII v." *Gumanitarnye nauki Sibiri,* no. 2 (2013): 24–28.

Kendirbai, Gulnar T. "The Politics of the Inner Asian Frontier and the 1771 Exodus of the Kalmyks." *Inner Asia* 20, no. 2 (October 23, 2018): 261–289.

Kenny, Neil. *The Uses of Curiosity in Early Modern France and Germany.* Oxford: Oxford University Press, 2004.

Keuning, Johannes. "Nicolaas Witsen as a Cartographer." *Imago Mundi,* no. 11 (1954): 95–110.

Khalid, Adeeb. "Russian History and the Debate over Orientalism." *Kritika: Explorations in Russian and Eurasian History* 1, no. 4 (2000): 691–699.

Khodarkovsky, Michael. *Where Two Worlds Met: The Russian State and the Kalmyk Nomads, 1600–1771.* Ithaca, NY: Cornell University Press, 1992.

———. *Russia's Steppe Frontier: The Making of a Colonial Empire, 1500–1800.* Bloomington: Indiana University Press, 2002.

Kim, G. F. *Istoriia otechestvennogo vostokovedeniia: do serediny XIX veka.* Moscow: Nauka, 1990.

Kim, Loretta Eumie. "Marginal Constituencies: Qing Borderland Policies and Vernacular Histories of Five Tribes on the Sino-Russian Frontier." PhD diss., Harvard University, 2009.

Kireev, F. N., ed. *Kazakhsko-russkie otnosheniia v XVI–XVIII vekakh: sbornik dokumentov i materialov.* Almaty, Kazakhstan: Izd. Akademii Nauk Kazakhskoi SSR, 1961.

Kirpichnikov, A. N. *Rossiia XVII veka v risunkakh i opisaniiakh gollandskogo puteshestvennika Nikolaasa Vitsena.* St. Petersburg: Slavia, 1995.

Kitson, Peter J. *Forging Romantic China.* Cambridge: Cambridge University Press, 2013.

Kivelson, Valerie A. *Cartographies of Tsardom: The Land and Its Meanings in Seventeenth-Century Russia.* Ithaca, NY: Cornell University Press, 2006.

Klaproth, Heinrich Julius von. *Rapport sur les ouvrages du P. H. Bitchourinski: relatifs à l'histoire des Mongols.* [Paris], 1830.

Klaproth, Julius von. *Katalog der chinesischen und mandjurischen Bücher der Bibliothek der Akademie der Wissenschaften in St. Petersburg.* Edited by Hartmut Walravens. Berlin: C. Bell, 1988.

Klein, Ursula, and E. C. Spary, eds. *Materials and Expertise in Early Modern Europe: Between Market and Laboratory.* Chicago: University of Chicago Press, 2010.

Knight, Nathaniel. "Grigor'ev in Orenburg, 1851–1862: Russian Orientalism in the Service of Empire?" *Slavic Review* 59, no. 1 (2000): 74–100.

Koialovich, M. O., ed. *Pis'ma i doneseniia iezuitov o Rossii: kontsa XVII i nachala XVIII veka.* St. Petersburg: Senatskaia Tipografiia, 1904.

Kollmann, Nancy S. *The Russian Empire 1450–1801.* Oxford: Oxford University Press, 2017.

Kopotilova, V. V. "Izdanie kitaiskikh proizvedenii predstaviteliami rossiiskoi obshchestvennosti (konets XVIII–pervaia polovina XIX vv.)." *Vestnik Omskogo universiteta,* no. 2 (1998): 60–64.

Koroloff, Rachel. "The Beginnings of a Russian Natural History: The Life and Work of Stepan Petrovich Krasheninnikov (1711–1755)." Master's thesis, Oregon State University, 2007.

———. "Seeds of Exchange: Collecting for Russia's Apothecary and Botanical Gardens in the Seventeenth and Eighteenth Centuries." PhD diss., University of Illinois at Urbana-Champaign, 2015.

———. "Juniper: From Medicine to Poison and Back Again in 17th-Century Muscovy." *Kritika: Explorations in Russian and Eurasian History* 19, no. 4 (November 22, 2018): 697–716.

Korostovets, I. "Russkaia dukhovnaia missiia v Pekine." *Russkii arkhiv,* no. 6 (1893): 57–86.

Kotilaine, Jarmo, and Marshall Poe, eds. *Modernizing Muscovy: Reform and Social Change in Seventeenth-Century Russia.* London: RoutledgeCurzon, 2004.

Kotoshikhin, Grigorii. *O Rossii v carstvovanie Alekseja Mixajloviča.* Oxford: Oxford University Press, 1980.

Kotwicz, Wladyslaw, and Hartmut Walravens. *Die russische Gesandtschaftsreise nach China 1805: zu Leben und Werk des Grafen Jan Potocki.* Berlin: Bell, 1991.

Kryzhanovskii, V, ed. "Perepiska nachal'nika Pekinskoi missii arkhimandrita Palladiia s Generalom-Gubernatorom Vostochnoi Sibiri Gr. N. N. Murav'evym-Amurskim." *Russkii arkhiv,* no. 8 (1914): 492–515; no. 9 (1914): 5–32; 10 (1914): 155–206.

Kurts, B. G. *Russko-kitaiskie snosheniia v XVI, XVII i XVIII stoletiiakh.* Dnepropetrovsk, Ukraine: Gosudarstvennoe izd-vo Ukrainy, 1929.

Kutuzov, Mikhail. *Chest' general-gubernatora: N. N. Murav'ev-Amurskii: dokumental'no-istoricheskii ocherk.* Vladivostok, Russia: Ob-vo izucheniia Amurskogo kraia, 1997.

Kuz'mina, Elena. "Pochemu kitaitsy takie . . ." *Otechestvennye zapiski* 61, no. 4 (2014). http://www.strana-oz.ru/2014/4/pochemu-kitaycy-takie.

Landry-Deron, Isabelle. "Les Mathématiciens envoyés en Chine par Louis XIV en 1685." *Archive for History of Exact Sciences* 55, no. 5 (April 1, 2001): 423–463.

———. *La preuve par la Chine: la "Description" de J.-B. Du Halde, Jésuite, 1735.* Paris: Editions de l'Ecole des hautes études en sciences sociales, 2002.

Lange, Laurent. *Journal de la résidence de Laur. Lange, agent de sa Maj. Impér. de la Grande Russie à la cour de la Chine dans les ann. 1721 et 1722.* Leiden, Netherlands: Abraham Kallewier, 1726.

Lange, Lorenz. *Reise nach China.* Munich: VCH, Acta humaniora, 1986.

Langer, Lawrence N. "Muscovite Taxation and the Problem of Mongol Rule in Rus'." *Russian History* 34, no. 1/4 (2007): 101–129.

Langlès, Louis. *De l'importance des langues orientales pour l'extension du commerce, les progrès des lettres et des sciences: adresse à l'Assemblée Nationale.* Paris, 1790.

Latour, Bruno. *Science in Action: How to Follow Scientists and Engineers through Society.* Cambridge, MA: Harvard University Press, 1987.

LeDonne, John. *Absolutism and Ruling Class: The Formation of the Russian Political Order, 1700–1825.* Oxford: Oxford University Press, 1991.

———. *The Russian Empire and the World, 1700–1917: The Geopolitics of Expansion and Containment.* Oxford: Oxford University Press, 1997.

———. "Russian Governors General, 1775–1825: Territorial or Functional Administration?" *Cahiers du Monde russe* 42, no. 1 (January 1, 2001): 5–30.

———. "Proconsular Ambitions on the Chinese Border." *Cahiers du Monde russe* 45, no. 1–2 (January 1, 2004): 31–60.

Ledyard, John. *Journey through Russia and Siberia, 1787–1788: The Journal and Selected Letters.* Edited by Stephen D. Watrous. Madison: University of Wisconsin Press, 1966.

Leibniz, Gottfried Wilhelm. *Novissima Sinica Historiam Nostri Temporis Illustrata.* N.p., 1697.

Leong, Elaine, and Alisha Rankin, eds. *Secrets and Knowledge in Medicine and Science, 1500–1800.* Burlington, VT: Ashgate, 2011.

Leont'ev, Aleksei. *Depei kitaets.* St. Petersburg: Imperatorskaia Akademiia Nauk, 1771.

———. *Kratchaishee opisanie gorodam, dokhodam i protchemu Kitaiskago gosudarstva, a pri tom i vsem gosudarstvam, korolevstvam i kniazhestvam, koi Kitaitsam svedomy.* St. Petersburg: v Tipografii Akademii Nauk, 1778.

———. *Tian' shin' ko: to est' Angel'skaia beseda.* St. Petersburg: Imperatorskaia Akademiia Nauk, 1781.

Leont'ev, Aleksei, and Ilarion Rossokhin. *Obstoiatel'noe opisanie proiskhozhdeniia i sostoianiia Man'dzhurskago naroda i voiska, v osmi znamenakh sostoiashchago.* 17 vols. St. Petersburg: izhdiveniem Imperatorskoi Akademii Nauk, 1784.

Lévesque, Pierre-Charles. *Pensées morales de divers auteurs chinois.* Paris: Didot aîné, 1782.

Levey, Benjamin Samuel. "Jungar Refugees and the Making of Empire on Qing China's Kazakh Frontier, 1759–1773." PhD diss., Harvard University, 2014.

Levitt, Marcus C. "An Antidote to Nervous Juice: Catherine the Great's Debate with Chappe d'Auteroche over Russian Culture." *Eighteenth-Century Studies* 32, no. 1 (October 1, 1998): 49–63.

Lewis, Gwynne. "Henri-Léonard Bertin and the Fate of the Bourbon Monarchy." In *Enlightenment and Revolution: Essays in Honour of Norman Hampson,* edited by Malcolm Crook, William Doyle, and Alan Forrest, 69–90. Hampshire: Ashgate, 2004.

Lilian, Huan. "O. Iakinf (N. Ia. Bichurin)—vydaiushchiisia russkii kitaeved (K 230-letiiu so dnia rozhdeniia)." *Problemy Dal'nego Vostoka,* no. 5 (2007): 124–136.

Lim, Susanna Soojung. *China and Japan in the Russian Imagination, 1685–1922: To the Ends of the Orient.* New York: Routledge, 2013.

Lipovtsov, Stepan, and Pavel Kamenskii. "Kratkoe nachertanie o predubezhdenii kitaitsev k samim sebe." *Vostok-zapad: istoriko-kulturnyi al'manakh,* 2003–2004, 221–245.

"Literary Forgeries by Klaproth." *Notes and Queries on China and Japan,* no. 3 (December 1869): 111–112.

Liubimenko, I. I., D. S. Rozhdestvenskii, and M. A. Borodina, eds. *Uchenaia korrespondentsiia Akademii nauk XVIII veka, 1766–1782: nauchnoe opisanie.* Moscow: Izd-vo Akademii nauk SSSR, 1937.

Livingstone, David N. *Putting Science in Its Place: Geographies of Scientific Knowledge.* Chicago: University of Chicago Press, 2003.

Lo Sardo, Eugenio. "Antoine Thomas's and George David's Maps of Asia." In *The History of the Relations between the Low Countries and China in the Qing Era (1644–1911),* edited by W. F. Vande Walle, 75–84. Leuven, Belgium: Leuven University Press, 2003.

Lomonosov, Mikhail Vasil'evich. *Polnoe sobranie sochinenii.* Moscow: Nauka, 1950.

Long, Pamela O. *Openness, Secrecy, Authorship: Technical Arts and the Culture of Knowledge from Antiquity to the Renaissance.* Baltimore: Johns Hopkins University Press, 2001.

Love, Ronald S. "'A Passage to China': A French Jesuit's Perceptions of Siberia in the 1680s." *French Colonial History* 3, no. 1 (2003): 85–100.

Lukin, Alexander. *The Bear Watches the Dragon: Russia's Perceptions of China and the Evolution of Russian-Chinese Relations since the Eighteenth Century.* Armonk, NY: M. E. Sharpe, 2003.

Lundbæk, Knud. *T. S. Bayer, 1694–1738: Pioneer Sinologist.* London: Curzon, 1986.

———. "Notes on Abel Remusat and the Beginning of Academic Sinology in Europe." In *Actes du VIIe Colloque International de Sinologie de Chantilly,* edited by Edward Malatesta, 207–220. San Francisco: Ricci Institute, 1992.

Lux, David, and Harold Cook. "Closed Circles or Open Networks? Communicating at a Distance during the Scientific Revolution." *History of Science* 36, no. 112 (1998): 179–211.

Macartney, George. *An Account of Russia.* London, 1768.

Madariaga, Isabel de. "Who Was Foy de la Neuville?" *Cahiers du Monde russe et soviétique* 28, no. 1 (January 1, 1987): 21–30.

Maggs, Barbara. *Russia and "Le Rêve Chinois": China in Eighteenth-Century Russian Literature.* Oxford: Voltaire Foundation, 1984.

Maggs, Barbara Widenor. "'The Jesuits in China': Views of an Eighteenth-Century Russian Observer." *Eighteenth-Century Studies* 8, no. 2 (December 1, 1974): 137–152.

Maiakovskii, I. L. *Ocherki istorii arkhivnogo dela v SSSR.* Moscow: Glavnoe arkhivnoe upravlenie NKVD, 1941.

Maier, Ingrid. "Zeventiende-eeuwse Nederlandse couranten vertaald voor de tsaar." *Tijdschrift voor Mediageschiedenis*, no. 12 (2009): 27–49.

Maier, Ingrid, and Stepan Shamin. "Obzory inostrannoi pressy v kollegii inostrannykh del v poslednie gody pravleniia Petra I." *Rossiiskaia istoriia*, 2011, 91–112.

Maier, Ingrid, and Daniel C. Waugh. "How Well Was Muscovy Connected with the World?" In *Imperienvergleich. Beispiele und Ansätze aus osteuropäischer Perspektive. Festschrift für Andreas Kappeler*, edited by Guido Haussmann and Angela Rustemeyer, 17–38. Wiesbaden, Germany: Harrassowitz, 2009.

Mancall, Mark. "China's First Missions to Russia, 1729–1731." *Harvard Papers on China* 9 (1955): 88.

———. *Russia and China: Their Diplomatic Relations to 1728.* Cambridge, MA: Harvard University Press, 1971.

Manz, Beatrice Forbes. *Power, Politics and Religion in Timurid Iran.* Leiden, Netherlands: Cambridge University Press, 2007.

Marchand, Suzanne. *German Orientalism in the Age of Empire: Religion, Race, and Scholarship.* New York: Cambridge University Press, 2009.

Marker, Gary. *Publishing, Printing, and the Origins of Intellectual Life in Russia, 1700–1800.* Princeton, NJ: Princeton University Press, 1985.

Matsuda, Matt K. "The Pacific." *American Historical Review* 111, no. 3 (2006): 758–780.

Mattingly, Garrett. *Renaissance Diplomacy.* London: Cape, 1955.

Meares, John. *Voyages Made in the Years 1788 and 1789, from China to the North West Coast of America . . .* London: Logographic, 1790.

Mentzel, Christian. *Kurze Chinesische Chronologia.* N.p.: Rüdiger, 1696.

Miasnikov, V. S. *Dogovornymi stat' iami utverdili: diplomaticheskaia istoriia russko-kitaiskoi granitsy XVII–XX vv.* Khabarovsk, Russia: Priamurskoe geograficheskoe obshchestvo, 1997.

——. *The Ch'ing Empire and the Russian State in the 17th Century.* Moscow: Progress, 1985.

Michaud, Louis Gabriel, ed. "Klaproth (Jules-Henri)." *Biographie universelle, ancienne et modern,* no. 68 (1841): 532–549.

Middendorf, Aleksandr. *Puteshestvie na sever i vostok Sibiri.* St. Petersburg, 1860.

Millar, Ashley Eva. *A Singular Case: Debating China's Political Economy in the European Enlightenment.* Montreal: McGill-Queen's University Press, 2017.

Miller, G. F. *Istoriia Sibiri.* Moscow: Izdatel'stvo Akademii nauk SSSR, 1937.

Millward, James A. *Eurasian Crossroads: A History of Xinjiang.* New York: Columbia University Press, 2007.

Miyawaki, Junko. "The Chinggisid Principle in Russia." *Russian History* 19, no. 1 (January 1, 1992): 261–77.

Moiseev, V. A. *Dzhungarskoe khanstvo i kazakhi: XVII–XVIII vv.* Almaty, Kazakhstan: Gylym, 1991.

——. *Russko-dzhungarskie otnosheniia: konets XVII–60-e gg. XVIII vv.: dokumenty i izvlecheniia.* Barnaul, Russia: Azbuka, 2006.

Möllendorf, P. G. von. "Ula Grass." *China Review* 15, no. 3 (1886): 180–181.

Molnár, Miklós. "Héros ou imposteur? Un aventurier au XVIIIe siècle." *Revue européenne des sciences sociales* 27, no. 85 (January 1, 1989): 75–91.

Monahan, Erika. "Locating Rhubarb." In *Early Modern Things: Objects and Their Histories, 1500–1800,* edited by Paula Findlen, 227–251. Routledge, 2013.

——. *The Merchants of Siberia: Trade in Early Modern Eurasia.* Ithaca, NY: Cornell University Press, 2016.

Moon, David. "The Russian Academy of Sciences Expeditions to the Steppes in the Late Eighteenth Century." *Slavonic and East European Review* 88, no. 1 / 2 (January 1, 2010): 204–236.

Morrison, Alexander. "Metropole, Colony, and Imperial Citizenship in the Russian Empire." *Kritika: Explorations in Russian and Eurasian History* 13, no. 2 (May 10, 2012): 327–364.

Morrison, Robert. *Chinese Miscellany; Consisting of Original Extracts from Chinese Authors, in the Native Character.* London: London Missionary Society, 1825.

Morse, Hosea Ballou. *The Chronicles of the East India Company, Trading to China 1635–1834.* Oxford: Clarendon, 1926.

Mosca, Matthew W. "Empire and the Circulation of Frontier Intelligence: Qing Conceptions of the Ottomans." *Harvard Journal of Asiatic Studies* 70, no. 1 (2010): 147–207.

——. *From Frontier Policy to Foreign Policy: The Question of India and the Transformation of Geopolitics in Qing China.* Stanford, CA: Stanford University Press, 2013.

————. "The Qing State and Its Awareness of Eurasian Interconnections, 1789–1806." *Eighteenth-Century Studies* 47, no. 2 (2014): 103–116.

Mufti, Aamir R. "Orientalism and the Institution of World Literatures." *Critical Inquiry* 36, no. 3 (2010): 458–493.

Müller, Andreas. *Abdallae Beidavaei Historia Sinensis . . .* Berlin: Bielkius, 1689.

Mungello, David. *Curious Land: Jesuit Accommodation and the Origins of Sinology.* Honolulu: University of Hawaii Press, 1989.

————. *The Great Encounter of China and the West, 1500–1800.* Lanham, MD: Rowman & Littlefield, 2009.

Muravyeva, Marianna. "Personalizing Homosexuality and Masculinity in Early Modern Russia." In *Gender in Late Medieval and Early Modern Europe,* edited by Marianna Muravyeva and Raisa Maria Toivo, 205–225. London: Routledge, 2012.

Mylnikov, A. S., ed. "Svidetel'stvo inostrannogo nabliudatelia o zhizni russkogo gosudarstva kontsa XVII veka." *Voprosy istorii,* no. 1, 3, 4 (April 1968).

Nevel'skoi, G. I. *Podvigi russkikh morskikh ofitserov na krainem vostoke Rossii.* Moscow: Drofa, 2009.

Nevskaia, N. I. *Letopis' Rossiiskoi Akademii Nauk.* St. Petersburg: Nauka, 2000.

Nieuhof, Johannes. *L'ambassade de la Compagnie orientale des Provinces Unies vers l'empereur de la Chine, ou grand cam de Tartarie, faite par les Srs. Pierre de Goyer, & Jacob de Keyser.* Leiden, Netherlands: Pour J. de Meurs, 1665.

Noda, Jin. "Russo-Chinese Trade through Central Asia: Regulations and Reality." In *Asiatic Russia: Imperial Power in Regional and International Contexts,* edited by Tomohiko Uyama, 153–173. New York: Routledge, 2012.

————. *The Kazakh Khanates between the Russian and Qing Empires: Central Eurasian International Relations during the Eighteenth and Nineteenth Centuries.* Leiden, Netherlands: Brill, 2016.

Noda, Jin, and Takahiro Onuma. *A Collection of Documents from the Kazakh Sultans to the Qing Dynasty.* Tokyo: Department of Islamic Area Studies, University of Tokyo, 2010.

Noord, W. J. L. van, and M. A. Weststeijn. "The Global Trajectory of Nicolaas Witsen's Chinese Mirror." *Rijksmuseum Bulletin* 63, no. 4 (2015): 325–361.

Norris, Stephen M., and Willard Sunderland, eds. *Russia's People of Empire: Life Stories from Eurasia, 1500 to the Present.* Bloomington: Indiana University Press, 2012.

Novikov, Nikolai. "Opyt istoricheskogo sloviaria o rossiiskikh pisateliakh." In *Izbrannye proizvedeniia,* edited by G. P. Makogonenko, 277–370. Moscow: Gos. izd-vo khudozh. lit., 1951.

Ogborn, Miles. *Global Lives: Britain and the World, 1550–1800.* Cambridge: Cambridge University Press, 2008.

Okenfuss, Max. *The Rise and Fall of Latin Humanism in Early-Modern Russia: Pagan Authors, Ukrainians, and the Resiliency of Muscovy.* Leiden, Netherlands: Brill, 1995.

Orlov, Ivan. *Noveishee i podrobneishee istorichesko-geograficheskoe opisanie Kitaiskoi imperii.* Moscow: V Universitetskoi Tipografii, 1820.

Ostrowski, Donald G. *Muscovy and the Mongols: Cross-Cultural Influences on the Steppe Frontier, 1304–1589.* Cambridge: Cambridge University Press, 1998.

Paine, S. C. M. *Imperial Rivals: China, Russia, and Their Disputed Frontier.* Armonk, NY: M. E. Sharpe, 1996.

Palladii, Archimandrite. "Dnevnik arkh. Palladiia za 1858 g." *Izvestiia Ministerstva Inostrannykh Del,* no. 2 (1912): 228–282.

Pan, T. A., and O. V. Shatalov. *Arkhivnye materialy po istorii zapadnoevropeiskogo i rossiiskogo kitaevedeniia.* St. Petersburg: Sankt-Peterburgskii filial Instituta vostokovedeniia, 2004.

Pavlenko, N. I. *Ptentsy gnezda Petrova.* Moscow: Prospekt, 2016.

Pavlovsky, Michel N. *Chinese-Russian Relations.* New York: Philosophical Library, 1949.

Penrose, G. L. "Inner Asian Influences on the Earliest Russo-Chinese Trade and Diplomatic Contacts." *Russian History* 19, no. 1 (January 1, 1992): 361–392.

Perdue, Peter. *China Marches West: The Qing Conquest of Central Eurasia.* Cambridge, MA: Belknap, 2005.

———. "Boundaries and Trade in the Early Modern World: Negotiations at Nerchinsk and Beijing." *Eighteenth-Century Studies* 43, no. 3 (2010): 341–356.

Perkins, Franklin. *Leibniz and China: A Commerce of Light.* Cambridge: Cambridge University Press, 2004.

Peterson, Claes. *Peter the Great's Administrative and Judicial Reforms: Swedish Antecedents and the Process of Reception.* Stockholm: A-B Nordiska Bokhandeln, 1979.

Petrov, Aleksandr, and Aleksei Ermolaev. "Znachenie Kiakhty v istorii Dal'nego Vostoka i Russkoi Ameriki." *Rossiiskaia istoriia,* no. 2 (2018): 51–66.

Peyrefitte, Alain. *The Immobile Empire.* New York: Knopf, 1992.

Pierling, Paul. *La Russie et le Saint-Siège.* Paris: Editions Plon, 1896–1907.

Plamper, Jan. "Archival Revolution or Illusion? Historicizing the Russian Archives and Our Work in Them." *Jahrbücher Für Geschichte Osteuropas,* n.s., 51, no. 1 (January 1, 2003): 57–69.

Plavsic, Borivoj. "Seventeenth-Century Chanceries and Their Staffs." In *Russian Officialdom: The Bureaucratization of Russian Society from the Seventeenth to the Twentieth Century,* edited by Walter McKenzie Pintner and Don Karl Rowney, 19–45. Chapel Hill: University of North Carolina Press, 1980.

Plotnikov, A. Iu. *Russkaia dal'nevostochnaia granitsa v XVIII–pervoi polovine XIX v.* Moscow: KomKniga, 2007.

Poe, Marshall. *A People Born to Slavery: Russia in Early Modern European Ethnography, 1476–1748.* Ithaca, NY: Cornell University Press, 2000.

Poliakova, E. O. "Otechestvennaia istoriografiia russko-kitaiskikh otnoshenii XVII v." *Dokument. Arkhiv. Istoriia. Sovremennost'*, no. 11 (2010): 11–26.

Polievktov, M. A. *Ekonomicheskie i politicheskie razvedki Moskovskogo gosudarstva XVII v. na Kavkaze.* Tiflis, Georgia: NII Kavkazovedeniia AN SSSR, 1932.

Ponomareva, Svetlana. "Grigorii Ivanovich Spasskii: issledovatel' Sibiri i prosvetitel'." PhD diss., Sibirskii federal'nyi universitet, 2002.

Poovey, Mary. *A History of the Modern Fact: Problems of Knowledge in the Sciences of Wealth and Society.* Chicago: University of Chicago Press, 1998.

Popov, I. M. *Rossiia i Kitai: 300 let na grani voiny.* Moscow: AST-Ermak-Astrel', 2004.

Postnikov, A. V. "Novye dannye o rossiiskikh kartograficheskikh materialakh pervoi poloviny XVIII v., vyvezennykh Zh.-N. Delilem vo Frantsiiu." *Voprosy istorii estestvoznaniia i tekhniki*, no. 3 (2005): 17–38.

Postnikov, V. V. "Knizhnyi pamiatnik istorio-geograficheskikh znanii v Rossii XVII v." *Oikumena. Regionovedcheskie issledovaniia*, no. 1 (2012): 133–137.

Pritchard, E. H. "The Instructions of the East India Company to Lord Macartney on His Embassy to China and His Reports to the Company, 1792–4. Part I: Instructions from the Company." *Journal of the Royal Asiatic Society* 70, no. 2 (1938): 201–230.

Purchas, Samuel. *Hakluytus Posthumus: Or Purchas His Pilgrimes: Contayning a History of the World in Sea Voyages and Lande Travells by Englishmen and Others*, 20 vols. Glasgow: J. MacLehose and Sons, 1905.

Puteshestviia russkikh poslov XVI–XVII vv.: stateinye spiski. Moscow: Izd-vo Akademii nauk SSSR, 1954.

Quested, R. K. I. *The Expansion of Russia in East Asia, 1857–1860.* Kuala Lumpur: University of Malaya Press, 1968.

———. "Further Light on the Expansion of Russia in East Asia: 1792–1860." *Journal of Asian Studies* 29, no. 2 (1970): 327–345.

Radovskii, M. I. "Russkii kitaeved I. K. Rossokhin." In *Iz istorii nauki i tekhniki v stranakh Vostoka*, edited by A. T. Grigor'ian, 88–99. Moscow: Izd-vo vostochnoi lit-ry, 1960.

Raeff, Marc. *The Well-Ordered Police State: Social and Institutional Change through Law in the Germanies and Russia, 1600–1800.* New Haven, CT: Yale University Press, 1983.

Raj, Kapil. *Relocating Modern Science: Circulation and the Construction of Knowledge in South Asia and Europe, 1650–1900.* Basingstoke: Palgrave Macmillan, 2007.

Randolph, John. "The Singing Coachman; or, The Road and Russia's Ethno-graphic Invention in Early Modern Times." *Journal of Early Modern History* 11, no. 1–2 (January 1, 2007): 33–61.

Rappaport, Rhoda. *When Geologists Were Historians, 1665–1750*. Ithaca, NY: Cornell University Press, 1997.

Rath, Andrew C. *The Crimean War in Imperial Context, 1854–1856*. New York: Palgrave Macmillan, 2015.

Ravenstein, Ernest George. *The Russians on the Amur: Its Discovery, Conquest, and Colonization, with a Description of the Country, Its Inhabitants, Productions, and Commercial Capabilities . . .* London: Trübner, 1861.

Remnev, A. V. *Rossiia Dal'nego Vostoka: imperskaia geografiia vlasti XIX–nachala XX vekov*. Omsk, Russia: Izdanie OmGU, 2004.

Rieber, Alfred J. "The Comparative Ecology of Complex Frontiers." In *Imperial Rule,* edited by Alfred J. Rieber and Alexei Miller, 177–208. Budapest: Central European University Press, 2004.

———. *The Struggle for the Eurasian Borderlands: From the Rise of Early Modern Empires to the End of the First World War*. Cambridge: Cambridge University Press, 2014.

[Rikhter, Aleksandr]. "O sostoianii vostochnoi slovesnosti v Rossii." *Aziatskii vestnik,* no. 8 (August 1825): 81–154.

Robert Liss [Lissa Roberts]. "Frontier Tales: Tokugawa Japan in Translation." In *The Brokered World: Go-Betweens and Global Intelligence, 1770–1820,* edited by Simon Schaffer, 1–47. Sagamore Beach, MA: Science History, 2009.

Rodionov, Vitalii. "Po puti k khramu." In N. I. Bichurin, *Radi vechnoi pamiati: poeziia, stat'i, ocherki, zametki, pis'ma*. Cheboksary, Russia: Chuvash. kn. izd-vo, 1991.

Romaniello, Matthew P. *The Elusive Empire: Kazan and the Creation of Russia, 1552–1671*. Madison: University of Wisconsin Press, 2012.

———. *Enterprising Empires: Russia and Britain in Eighteenth-Century Eurasia*. Cambridge: Cambridge University Press, 2019.

Romaniello, Matthew P., and Tricia Starks, eds. *Tobacco in Russian History and Culture: From the Seventeenth Century to the Present*. London: Routledge, 2009.

Rossabi, Morris. "The 'Decline' of the Central Asian Caravan Trade." In *The Rise of Merchant Empires: Long-Distance Trade in the Early Modern World, 1350–1750,* edited by James D. Tracy, 351–370. Cambridge: Cambridge University Press, 2010.

Rossokhin, Larion. "Opisanie puteshestviia, koim ezdili kitaiskie poslanniki v Rossiiu." *Ezhemesiachnye sochineniia,* no. 6 (1764): 3–48.

Rowe, William. *China's Last Empire: The Great Qing*. Cambridge, MA: Belknap, 2009.

Rubiés, Joan-Pau. *Travellers and Cosmographers: Studies in the History of Early Modern Travel and Ethnology.* Aldershot: Ashgate, 2007.

Rubiés, Joan-Pau, and Manel Ollé. "The Comparative History of a Genre: The Production and Circulation of Books on Travel and Ethnographies in Early Modern Europe and China." *Modern Asian Studies* 50, no. 1 (January 2016): 259–309.

Rustemeyer, Angela. "Systems and Senses: New Research on Muscovy and the Historiography on Early Modern Europe." *Kritika: Explorations in Russian and Eurasian History* 11, no. 3 (2010): 563–579.

"S. N. Sh." "Anglichane v Kamchatke v 1779 godu." *Istoricheskii vestnik* 19 (1885), 394–401.

Santich, Jan Joseph. *Missio Moscovitica: The Role of the Jesuits in the Westernization of Russia, 1582–1689.* New York: P. Lang, 1995.

Sarkisova, G. I. "Nekotorye aspekty formirovaniia kadrovoi politiki Kollegii inostrannykh del na kitaiskom napravlenii vo vtoroi polovine XVIII v." *Kitai v mire i regional'noi politike. Istoriia i sovremennost',* no. 19 (2014): 359–379.

Satia, Priya. *Spies in Arabia: The Great War and the Cultural Foundations of Britain's Covert Empire in the Middle East.* Oxford: Oxford University Press, 2008.

Sauer, Martin. *An Account of a Geographical and Astronomical Expedition to the Northern Parts of Russia . . .* London: T. Cadell, 1802.

Schaffer, Simon, Lissa Roberts, Kapil Raj, and James Delbourgo, eds. *The Brokered World: Go-Betweens and Global Intelligence, 1770–1820.* Sagamore Beach, MA: Science History, 2009.

Schimmelpenninck van der Oye, David. "The Genesis of Russian Sinology." *Kritika: Explorations in Russian and Eurasian History* 1, no. 2 (2000): 355–364.

———. *Russian Orientalism: Asia in the Russian Mind from Peter the Great to the Emigration.* New Haven, CT: Yale University Press, 2010.

Schlesinger, Jonathan. *A World Trimmed with Fur: Wild Things, Pristine Places, and the Natural Fringes of Qing.* Stanford, CA: Stanford University Press, 2017.

Schönfeld, Martin. "Was There a Western Inventor of Porcelain?" *Technology and Culture* 39, no. 4 (October 1, 1998): 716–727.

Schorkowitz, Dittmar, and Ning Chia, eds. *Managing Frontiers in Qing China: The Lifanyuan and Libu Revisited.* Leiden, Netherlands: Brill, 2017.

Schurink, Fred. "Manuscript Commonplace Books, Literature, and Reading in Early Modern England." *Huntington Library Quarterly* 73, no. 3 (September 1, 2010): 453–469.

Scott, Hamish. *The Birth of a Great Power System, 1740–1815.* London: Routledge, 2014.

Scott, James C. *Seeing like a State: How Certain Schemes to Improve the Human Condition Have Failed*. New Haven, CT: Yale University Press, 1998.

Sebes, Joseph, ed. *The Jesuits and the Sino-Russian Treaty of Nerchinsk (1689): The Diary of Thomas Pereira*. Rome: Institutum Historicum S. I., 1962.

Secord, James A. "Knowledge in Transit." *Isis* 95, no. 4 (December 2004): 654–672.

Seegel, Steven. *Mapping Europe's Borderlands: Russian Cartography in the Age of Empire*. Chicago: University of Chicago Press, 2012.

Semennikov, V. P. *Sobranie staraiushcheesia o perevode inostrannykh knig, uchrezhdennoe Ekaterinoi II 1768–1783 gg: Istoriko-literaturnoe izsledovanie*. St. Petersburg, 1900.

Sgibnev, A. S. "Istoricheskii ocherk glavneishikh sobytii v Kamchatke, 1650–1855." *Morskoi sbornik*, no. 4–8 (1869).

Shafranovskaia, T. K. "O poezdkakh Lorentsa Langa v Pekin." *Sovetskoe kitaevedenie*, no. 4 (1958): 155–159.

———. "Puteshestvie Lorentsa Langa v 1715–1716 gg. v Pekin i ego dnevnik." *Strany i narody vostoka*, no. 2 (1961): 188–205.

Shapin, Steven. *A Social History of Truth: Civility and Science in Seventeenth-Century England*. Science and Its Conceptual Foundations. Chicago: University of Chicago Press, 1994.

Sharpe, Kevin. *Reading Revolutions: The Politics of Reading in Early Modern England*. New Haven, CT: Yale University Press, 2000.

Shatalov, O. V. "Arkhimandrit Petr (Kamenskii)—nachalnik 10-i Rossiiskoi dukhovnoi missii v Pekine." *Pravoslavie na Dal'nem Vostoke* 3 (2001): 85–98.

Shaw, Denis J. B. "Geographical Practice and Its Significance in Peter the Great's Russia." *Journal of Historical Geography* 22, no. 2 (April 1, 1996): 160–176.

———. "Mapmaking, Science and State Building in Russia before Peter the Great." *Journal of Historical Geography* 31, no. 3 (July 2005): 409–429.

Shchukin, N. S. "Iakinf Bichurin." *Zhurnal Ministerstva narodnago prosveshcheniia*, September 1857, 111–126.

Shelikhov, G. I. *General'naia karta: predstavliaiushchaia udobnye sposoby k umnozheniiu Rossiiskoi torgovli i moreplavaniia po Tikhomu i Iuzhnomu Okianu*. St. Petersburg, 1787.

Sher, Richard B. *The Enlightenment and the Book: Scottish Authors and Their Publishers in Eighteenth-Century Britain, Ireland, and America*. Chicago: University of Chicago Press, 2006.

Sherman, William H. *Used Books: Marking Readers in Renaissance England*. Philadelphia: University of Pennsylvania Press, 2009.

Shtrange, M. M. *Demokraticheskaia intelligentsiia Rossii v XVIII veke*. Moscow: Nauka, 1965.

Shumakher, Pëtr. "Nashi snosheniia s Kitaem." *Russkii arkhiv II*, no. 10 (1879): 145–182.

Sibirskiia letopisi. St. Petersburg: Tip. I. N. Skorokhodova, 1907.

Skachkov, P. E. "Znachenie rukopisnogo naslediia russkikh kitaevedov." *Voprosy istorii*, no. 1 (1960): 117–123.

———. "Vedomost' o Kitaiskoi zemle." *Strany i narody vostoka*, no. 2 (1961): 206–213.

———. *Ocherki istorii russkogo kitaevedeniia.* Moscow: Nauka, 1977.

Slezkine, Yuri. *Arctic Mirrors: Russia and the Small Peoples of the North.* Ithaca, NY: Cornell University Press, 1994.

———. "Naturalists versus Nations: Eighteenth-Century Russian Scholars Confront Ethnic Diversity." *Representations*, no. 47 (July 1, 1994): 170–195.

Smirnov, S. K. *Istoriia Troitskoi Lavrskoi seminarii.* Moscow: A.V. Tolokonnikov, 1867.

Smith, Alison K. *For the Common Good and Their Own Well-Being: Social Estates in Imperial Russia.* Oxford: Oxford University Press, 2014.

Smith-Peter, Susan. "Bringing the Provinces into Focus: Subnational Spaces in the Recent Historiography of Russia." *Kritika: Explorations in Russian and Eurasian History* 12, no. 4 (October 29, 2011): 835–848.

Smorzhevskii, Ieromonakh Feodosii. *Notes on the Jesuits in China [Ob Ezuitakh v Kitae].* Translated by Gregory Afinogenov. Chestnut Hill, MA: Institute of Jesuit Sources, 2016.

Soll, Jacob. *The Information Master: Jean-Baptiste Colbert's Secret State Intelligence System.* Ann Arbor: University of Michigan Press, 2009.

Songyun. *Emu tanggū orin sakda-i gisun sarkiyan.* Edited by Giovanni Stary. Wiesbaden, Germany: Otto Harrassowitz, 1983.

Soucek, Svat. *A History of Inner Asia.* Cambridge: Cambridge University Press, 2000.

Spafarii, Nikolai. *Opisanie pervyia chasti vselennyia imenuemoi Azii, v nei zhe sostoit Kitaiskoe gosudarstvo s prochimi ego gorody i provintsii.* Kazan, Russia: Imperatorskii Universitet, 1910.

Sparwenfeld, Johan Gabriel. *J. G. Sparwenfeld's Diary of a Journey to Russia 1684–87.* Stockholm: Kungl Vitterhets Historie Och Antikvitets Akademien, 2002.

Speranskii, Mikhail, ed. *Polnoe sobranie zakonov Rossiiskoi imperii,* series 1. St. Petersburg: Tip. II otdeleniia Sobstvennoi EIV Kantseliarii, 1830.

Ssu-ming, Meng. "The E-Lo-Ssu Kuan (Russian Hostel) in Peking." *Harvard Journal of Asiatic Studies* 23 (January 1, 1960): 19–46.

Stagl, Justin. *A History of Curiosity: The Theory of Travel, 1550–1800.* Langhorne, PA: Harwood Academic, 1995.

Stary, Giovanni. *Chinas erste Gesandte in Russland*. Wiesbaden, Germany: Harrassowitz, 1976.

Statman, Alexander. "A Forgotten Friendship: How a French Missionary and a Manchu Prince Studied Electricity and Ballooning in Late Eighteenth Century Beijing." *East Asian Science, Technology, and Medicine*, no. 46 (2017): 89–118.

Stephan, John J. "The Crimean War in the Far East." *Modern Asian Studies* 3, no. 3 (1969): 257–277.

Sterne, Laurence. *The Life and Opinions of Tristram Shandy, Gentleman*. N.p.: R. and J. Dodsley, 1761.

Strahlenberg, Philipp Johann von. *An Historico-Geographical Description of the North and Eastern Parts of Europe and Asia*. London: printed for W. Innys and R. Manby, 1738.

Stroev, Alexandre. "Les espions français en Russie durant la guerre entre la Russie et la Turquie (1768–1774)." In *L'influence française en Russie au XVIIIe siècle*, edited by Jean-Pierre Poussou, Anne Mézin, and Yves Perret-Gentil, 581–598. Paris: Institut d'etudes slaves, 2004.

Sukhomlinov, M. I. *Materialy dlia istorii Imperatorskoi akademii nauk*. St. Petersburg: Tip. Imp. akademii nauk, 1885.

Sunderland, Willard. "Imperial Space: Territorial Thought and Practice in the Eighteenth Century." In *Russian Empire: Space, People, Power, 1700–1930*, edited by Jane Burbank, Mark von Hagen, and Anatolyi Remnev, 33–66. Bloomington: Indiana University Press, 2007.

———. "The Ministry of Asiatic Russia: The Colonial Office That Never Was but Might Have Been." *Slavic Review* 69, no. 1 (2010): 120–150.

Sychevskii, E. I. *Istoricheskaia zapiska o kitaiskoi granitse, sostavlennaia sovetnikom troitsko-savskago pogranichnago pravleniia Sychevskim v 1846 godu*. Edited by V. N. Basnin. Moscow: V Universitetskoi Tipografii, 1875.

Taranovich, V. P. "Ilarion Rossokhin i ego trudy po kitaevedeniiu." *Sovetskoe vostokovedenie*, no. 3 (1945): 225–241.

Thévenot, Melchisédech. *Recueil de voyages de Mr Thevenot*. Paris: Estienne Michallet, 1681.

Tikhvinskii, S. L, ed. *Russko-kitaiskie otnosheniia v XVII veke. Materialy i dokumenty*. 2 vols. Moscow: Nauka, 1969.

———, ed. *Russko-kitaiskie otnosheniia v XVIII veke. Materialy i dokumenty*. 6 vols. Moscow: Nauka, 1978.

———, ed. *Russko-kitaiskie otnosheniia v XIX veke: materialy i dokumenty*. Moscow: Pamiatniki istoricheskoi mysli, 1995.

———. *Istoriia Rossiiskoi Dukhovnoi Missii v Kitae: sbornik statei*. Moscow: Izd-vo Sviato-Vladimirskogo Bratstva, 1997.

Timkovskii, Egor. *Puteshestvie v Kitai chrez Mongoliiu, v 1820 i 1821 godakh.* St. Petersburg: Tip. Meditsinskago departamenta, 1824.

———. *Reise nach China Durch die Mongoley in den jahren 1820 und 1821.* Leipzig, Germany: Fleischer, 1825.

———. *Travels of the Russian Mission: Through Mongolia to China, and Residence in Peking, in the Years 1820–1821.* London: Longman, Rees, Orme, Brown, and Green, 1827.

———. *Voyage à Peking, à travers la Mongolie, en 1820 et 1821.* Paris: Dondey-Dupré père et fils, 1827.

Titov, A. A. *Sibir' v XVII veke: sbornik starinnykh russkikh statei o Sibiri i prilezhashchikh k nei zemliakh.* Moscow: G. Iudin, 1890.

Tolstoi, Dmitrii A. *Rimskii katolitsizm v Rossii: istoricheskoe izsliedovanie.* St. Petersburg: Izdanie i tip. V. F. Demakova, 1876.

Tolz, Vera. *Russia's Own Orient: The Politics of Identity and Oriental Studies in the Late Imperial and Early Soviet Periods.* Oxford: Oxford University Press, 2011.

Toropitsyn, Ilya. "Chto stoialo za kartoi Severo-Vostochnoi Azii N. Vitsena, prepodnesennoi v dar russkim tsariam v 1690 g?" *Acta Slavica Iaponica,* no. 33 (2012): 67–78.

Torrubia, José. *The Muscovites in California; or rather, Demonstration of the Passage from North America: Discovered by the Russians and of the Ancient One of the Peoples Who Transmigrated There from Asia.* Fairfield, WA: Ye Galleon, 1996.

Trusevich, Kh. *Posol'skiia i torgovyia snosheniia Rossii s Kitaem.* Moscow: Malinskii, 1882.

Tsyrempilov, N. V. "'Chuzhie' lamy. Rossiiskaia politika v otnoshenii zagranich-nogo buddiiskogo dukhovenstva v XVIII–nachale XX v." *Vestnik SPbGU* 13, no. 4 (2010): 9–18.

Turilova, S. L. "Gosudarstvennaia kollegiia inostrannykh del (ot Petra I k Ekaterine II)." In *Rossiiskaia diplomatiia: istoriia i sovremennost': materialy Nauchno-prakticheskoi konferentsii,* edited by I. S. Ivanov, 155–168. Moscow: ROSSPEN, 2001.

Urbansky, Sören. "Tokhtogo's Mission Impossible: Russia, China, and the Quasi-Independence of Hulunbeir." *Inner Asia* 16, no. 1 (2014): 64–94.

Valikhanov, Ch. Ch. *Sobranie sochinenii.* Almaty, Kazakhstan: Glav. red. Kazakhskoi Sov. Entsiklopedii, 1984.

Vasil'ev, V. P. *Otkrytie Kitaia i dr. st. V. P. Vasil'eva.* St. Petersburg: Stolichnaia tip, 1900.

Vermote, Frederik. "Passage Denied! Dangers and Limitations of Jesuit Travel throughout Eurasia during the Seventeenth and Eighteenth Centuries." *World History Connected* 10, no. 3 (October 2013). https://worldhistoryconnected.press.uillinois.edu/10.3/forum_vermote.html.

————. "Travellers Lost and Redirected: Jesuit Networks and the Limits of European Exploration in Asia." *Itinerario* 41, no. 3 (December 2017): 484–506.

Veselovskii, N. I. *Materialy dlia istorii rossiiskoi dukhovnoi missii v Pekine.* St. Petersburg: Tip. Glavnogo Upravleniia Udelov, 1905.

Viani, Sostegno, and Giovanni Ambrogio Mezzabarba. *Istoria delle cose operate nella China da Monsignor Gio. Ambrogio Mezzabarba . . . Vescovo di Lodi.* N.p.: Monsù Briasson, 1739.

Vinkovetsky, Ilya. *Russian America: An Overseas Colony of a Continental Empire, 1804–1867.* Oxford: Oxford University Press, 2011.

Vivo, Filippo de. *Information and Communication in Venice: Rethinking Early Modern Politics.* Oxford: Oxford University Press, 2007.

Vladislavich, Savva. "Sekretnaia informatsiia o sile i sostoianii Kitaiskago gosudarstva." *Russkii vestnik,* no. 2–3 (March 1842): 180–244, 281–337.

Vol'f, Baron N. B. von, ed. *Imperatorskii farforovyi zavod, 1744–1904.* St. Petersburg: Izdanie Upravleniia farforovymi zavodami, 1906.

Volkov, Denis. *Russia's Turn to Persia: Orientalism in Diplomacy and Intelligence.* Cambridge: Cambridge University Press, 2018.

Voskresenskii, N. A. *Petr Velikii kak zakonodatel': Issledovanie zakonodatel'nogo prottsessa v Rossii v epokhu reform pervoi chetverti XVIII veka.* Edited by D. O. Serov. Moscow: Novoe literaturnoe obozrenie, 2017.

Wakefield, Andre. *The Disordered Police State: German Cameralism as Science and Practice.* Chicago: University of Chicago Press, 2009.

Walravens, Hartmut. *Aleksej Agafonov: ein unbekannter Ostasienwissenschaftler des 18. Jahrhunderts: eine Biobibliographie.* Hamburg: Bell, 1982.

————. "Alexej Leont'ev und sein Werk." *Aetas Manjurica,* no. 3 (1992): 404–431.

————, ed. *Julius Klaproth (1783–1835): Briefe und Dokumente.* Wiesbaden, Germany: Harrassowitz, 1999.

————. *Julius Klaproth (1783–1835): Leben und Werk.* Wiesbaden, Germany: Harrassowitz, 1999.

————, ed. *Julius Klaproth (1783–1835): Briefwechsel mit Gelehrten grossenteils aus dem Akademiearchiv in St. Petersburg.* Wiesbaden, Germany: Harrassowitz, 2002.

Warner, Michael. "Intelligence as Risk Shifting." In *Intelligence Theory: Key Questions and Debates,* edited by Peter Gill, Stephen Marrin, and Mark Phythian, 16–32. London: Routledge, 2009.

Waugh, Daniel C. "The View from the North: Muscovite Cartography of Inner Asia." *Journal of Asian History* 49, no. 1–2 (2015): 69–95.

Weber, Friedrich Christian. *Das Veränderte Rußland.* N.p.: Nicolaus Förster, 1721.

Weber, Max. *Economy and Society: An Outline of Interpretive Sociology.* Berkeley: University of California Press, 1978.

Wehling, Peter. "Wissensregime." In *Handbuch Wissenssoziologie und Wissensforschung,* edited by Rainer Schützeichel, 704–713. Cologne, Germany: Herbert von Halem Verlag, 2018.

Wellmon, Chad. *Organizing Enlightenment: Information Overload and the Invention of the Modern Research University.* Baltimore: Johns Hopkins University Press, 2015.

Werrett, Simon. "An Odd Sort of Exhibition: The St. Petersburg Academy of Sciences in Enlightened Russia." DPhil diss., University of Cambridge, 2000.

———. "Russian Responses to the Voyages of Captain Cook." In *Captain Cook: Explorations and Reassessments,* edited by Glyndwr Williams, 179–197. London: Boydell & Brewer, Boydell Press, 2004.

———. "The Schumacher Affair: Reconfiguring Academic Expertise across Dynasties in Eighteenth-Century Russia." *Osiris* 25, no. 1 (January 2010): 104–126.

Whittaker, Cynthia. *Russian Monarchy: Eighteenth-Century Rulers and Writers in Political Dialogue.* DeKalb: Northern Illinois University Press, 2003.

Widmer, Eric. *The Russian Ecclesiastical Mission in Peking during the Eighteenth Century.* Cambridge, MA: Harvard University Press, 1976.

Winkler, Martina. *Das Imperium und die Seeotter: Die Expansion Russlands in den nordpazifischen Raum, 1700–1867.* Transnationale Geschichte. Gottingen, Germany: Vandenhoeck & Ruprecht, 2016.

Wirtschafter, Elise. *Religion and Enlightenment in Catherinian Russia: The Teachings of Metropolitan Platon.* DeKalb: Northern Illinois University Press, 2011.

Wirtschafter, Elise Kimerling. *Structures of Society.* DeKalb: Northern Illinois University Press, 1994.

Witsen, Nicolaas. *Noord en oost Tartaryen: behelzende eene beschryving van verscheidene Tartersche en nabuurige gewesten, in de noorder en oostelykste deelen van Aziën en Europa . . . ontworpen, beschreven, geteekent, en in 't licht gegeven.* N.p.: M. Schalekamp, 1785.

———. *Severnaia i vostochnaia Tartariia: vkliuchaiushchaia oblasti, raspolozhennye v severnoi i vostochnoi chastiakh Evropy i Azii.* Translated by V. G. Trisman. Amsterdam: Pegasus, 2010.

Wolff, Larry. *Inventing Eastern Europe: The Map of Civilization on the Mind of the Enlightenment.* Stanford, CA: Stanford University Press, 1994.

Wortman, Richard. *Scenarios of Power: Myth and Ceremony in Russian Monarchy from Peter the Great to the Abdication of Nicholas II.* Princeton, NJ: Princeton University Press, 2006.

Wu Huiyi. "'The Observations We Made in the Indies and in China': The Shaping of the Jesuits' Knowledge of China by Other Parts of the Non-Western World." *East Asian Science, Technology, and Medicine,* no. 46 (2017): 47–88.

———. *Traduire la Chine au XVIIIe siècle. jésuites traducteurs de textes chinois et le renouvellement des connaissances européennes sur la Chine (1687–ca. 1740).* Paris: Honore Champion Editions, 2017.

Wu Huiyi, Alexander Statman, and Mario Cams. "Displacing Jesuit Science in Qing China." *East Asian Science, Technology, and Medicine,* no. 46 (2017): 15–23.

Yan Guodong. "18 shiji Eguo hanxue jia de Zhongguo lishi wenhua guan." *Jinan xuebao (Zhexue shehui kexue ban)* 36, no. 7 (2014): 122–129.

Yan Guodong, and Liang Zhongqi. "19 shiji shangbanqi Eguoren lai hua xing ji yu Eguoren Zhongguo guan de zhuanxiang." *Eluosi wenyi,* no. 1 (2017): 118–126.

Yanagisawa Akira. "Some Remarks on the 'Addendum to the Treaty of Kiakhta' in 1768." *Memoirs of the Toyo Bunko,* no. 63 (2005): 65–88.

Yang, Chi-ming. *Performing China: Virtue, Commerce, and Orientalism in Eighteenth-Century England, 1660–1760.* Baltimore: Johns Hopkins University Press, 2011.

Ye Baichuan. "17–18 shiji Eguo lai hua shi chen yanzhong de Beijing cheng." *Lishi dang'an,* no. 4 (2014): 81–88.

Ye Baichuan, and Yuan Jian. "The Sino-Russian Trade and the Role of the Lifanyuan, 17th–18th Centuries." In *Managing Frontiers in Qing China,* edited by Dittmar Schorkowitz and Chia Ning, 254–289. Leiden, Netherlands: Brill, 2012.

Yoder, Audra. "Tea Time in Romanov Russia: A Cultural History, 1616–1917." PhD diss., University of North Carolina, 2017.

Yongdan, Lobsang. "Tibet Charts the World: The Btsan Po No Mon Han's Detailed Description of the World, an Early Major Scientific Work in Tibet." In *Mapping the Modern in Tibet (PIATS 2006: Tibetan Studies: Proceedings of the Eleventh Seminar of the International Association for Tibetan Studies, Königswinter 2006),* edited by Gray Tuttle, 73–134. Andiast, Switzerland: International Institute for Tibetan and Buddhist Studies, 2011.

Zatsepine, Victor. *Beyond the Amur.* Vancouver: University of British Columbia Press, 2017.

Zitser, Ernest A. *The Transfigured Kingdom: Sacred Parody and Charismatic Authority at the Court of Peter the Great.* Ithaca, NY: Cornell University Press, 2004.

Zlatkin, I. Ia. *Istoriia Dzhungarskogo khanstva, 1635–1758.* 2nd ed. Moscow: Nauka, 1983.

Zlatkin, I. Ia., and N. V. Ustiugov, eds. *Russko-mongol'skie otnosheniia, 1607–1636: sbornik dokumentov.* Moscow: Izd-vo vostochnoi lit-ry, 1959.

Zuo Fangzhou. "Yongzheng shiqi Zhong E guanxi zhong de jindai tezheng." *Xin yuanjian,* no. 9 (2008): 72–80.

Zwierlein, Cornel. *Imperial Unknowns: The French and British in the Mediterranean, 1650–1750.* Cambridge: Cambridge University Press, 2016.

Acknowledgments

This book owes so much to so many people that I fear I will never be able to properly represent the depth of their contributions. My greatest debt is to David Armitage, who saw the project's potential early and encouraged me to develop it in new directions. Without Kelly O'Neill, Mark Elliott, John Randolph, Ann Blair, and John LeDonne, the book would never have taken shape as it did. Likewise, it could never have been finished without the contributions of friends and colleagues like Josh Specht, Kathryn Schwartz, Philippa Hetherington, Tom Hooker, Nick Crawford, Mircea Raianu, Heidi Tworek, Michael Tworek, Polina Ivanova, Ania Aizman, David Brophy, Eric Schluessel, Devin Fitzgerald, Sofia Grachova, and many others. The memory of Stephen Walsh lives on in our hearts. My research was funded by grants from the American Councils for International Education and the Social Science Research Council, as well as short-term grants from the Weatherhead Center for International Affairs and the Davis Center for Russian and Eurasian Studies.

My colleagues at Georgetown and elsewhere in the DC area have made incalculable contributions to this book's development. My thanks go especially to John McNeill, Michael David-Fox, Christine Worobec, Ananya Chakravarti, Katie Benton-Cohen, Jo Ann Moran Cruz, Elizabeth Cross, Carol Benedict, Kathy Olesko, Amy Leonard, Toshi Higuchi, Dagomar Degroot, Jim Millward, and Sarah Cameron. Carole Sargent's expert and patient advice helped get the manuscript through the final stages. The graduate students with whom I've had the privilege of working, especially Yuan Gao, Maria Telegina, Andrey Gornostaev, Sarah Rosenthal, and Stanislav Tarasov, have shaped my thinking in a variety of ways. Amy Chidester, Jan Liverance, and Carolina Madinaveitia make our departmental community possible.

This book has also drawn on other connections near and far. Matthew Mosca, Mario Cams, Wu Huiyi, Nicolas Standaert, Erika Monahan, and Julia Leikin have shaped the work at different stages of the process. I am grateful to have had the chance to discuss draft chapters at the Russian History and Culture Workshop at the University of Pennsylvania, at the Russia's Global Legal Trajectories conference at the University College London School of Slavonic and East European Studies, and at the Enlightenment Reading Group at the Göttingen Lichtenberg-Kolleg. At Harvard University Press, Kathleen McDermott's untiring support and confidence proved indispensable, and the incisive reviews by Willard Sunderland and Michael Gordin helped me reimagine the manuscript. I am grateful for Amanda Peery's deft editing, for Evangeline McGlynn's cartographic expertise, and for David Prout's indexing skills. Among the many dedicated archivists and library staff who made the research for this book possible, I particularly want to acknowledge Mark Mir at the Ricci Institute of the University of San Francisco, Gudrun Bucher at the Staats- und Universitätsbibliothek Göttingen, and Alla Viktorovna Abrambekova at the Arkhiv vneshnei politiki Rossiiskoi Imperii in Moscow.

This project has also taken shape in a broader web of ties, not all of which are primarily intellectual. My Twitter community was an essential source of advice and support throughout the process. My comrades in Stomp Out Slumlords and Metro DC DSA never cease to astound me with their dedication and skill in working for the material change we so desperately need. Sophie has been my closest ally in the writing process. Naturally, this book would never have appeared without my mother and father's advice, support, and intellectual companionship; it was my father who first gave me the Russian translation of *The Three Kingdoms* that many years later started me down the road to this topic. But more than anyone, my gratitude goes to Rachel Koroloff. No amount of thanks would suffice to do justice to her.

Index

Note: Italicized page numbers indicate illustrations.

Abel-Rémusat, Jean-Pierre, 211, 227
Ablai Khan, 149, 153–154
Ablin, Seitkul, 29, 30, 37, 67
Abulmamet Khan, 148, 153
Academy of Sciences (Russia), 5, 221, 261; caravans and, 108–109; censorship and, 239; College of Foreign Affairs and, 19, 91; establishment of, 90; Golovkin and, 214; Jesuits and, 123, 133; Klaproth at, 214–216; newspaper of, 69, 130; priorities of, 11; Rossokhin at, 79, 82, 91–96, 220, 258; sinology at, 225–233
ad-Din, Khoja Burhan, 154
Adoratskii, Nikolai, 315n31
Agafonov, Aleksei, 85–86, 100, 102, 220, 233
Aian, 236, 245
Aiguillon, duc d', 190–193
Aigun, 163, 164, 247, 251–253; maps of, 161, 236
Akhte, Nikolai, 239
Alaska, 22, 144, 196, 197, 241
Albazin, 31, 72
Albazinians, 74, 94, 218; Russian Orthodox, 72, 85, 218, 222
Alekseev, A. I., 264
Aleni, Giulio, 127, 222, 294n43
Alexander I, 157, 186, 204, 208–209
Alexander II, 234, 249
Almeida, José Bernardo de, 202
Altai territory, 158, 181
Altan Khan, 27, 29, 32
Amherst, William, 208
Amiot, Joseph, 99–101, 170, 226

Amman, Johann, 124, 127–128
Amursana, 149–150, 165, 303n40
Amur valley, 34–35, 112, 174; Anglo-French threat to, 246, 249; exploration of, 144–145, 197; maps of, 31, 161, 181, 188, 236; navigation rights for, 133, 204–205, 237, 240–241, 243, 246; Russian annexation of, 234–235, 239–240, 243–253, 263–265; Russian retreat from, 236–242; Shulgin on, 163; Sinclair on, 200; Spafarii on, 41, 42. See also Manchuria
Andreev, A. I., 280n36
Anna Ioannovna, Russian empress, 92
Anson, George, 187
"anti-imperial imperialism," 252–254
Arshinskii, Danila, 35
Astrakhan, 28, 29, 86, 109
Austrian Succession, War of (1740–1748), 79
authorship, 43–45, 96–103; academic, 22, 212, 214, 233, 261; hybrid texts and, 25, 35–39, 41–43, 46–47, 55; plagiarism and, 41–42, 47, 55, 57. See also book market
Avril, Philippe, 47, 52–53

Baddeley, John, 41
Badmaev, Pëtr, 262–263
Baikov, Fëdor, 30–35, 56, 57
Baikov, Lev, 206
Baksheev, Fëdor, 85–86, 100
Bantysh-Kamenskii, N. N., 84, 205, 229, 262, 263
Bar Confederation, 189
Bartold'd, V. V., 257

Bayer, Theophilus Siegfried, 123–127, 214
Beijing treaty (1860), 235, 251–254
Belei, Batur, 165–166
Bell, John, 60, 200–201
Beneveni, Florio, 71
Benyovszky, Móric, 189–193, 259
Bering, Vitus, 144
Bertin, Henri-Léonard, 100, 192, 198, 309n22
Bichurin, Nikita "Iakinf," 1–2, 13, 213–214;
    complaints against, 217–218, 223–224;
    Klaproth on, 232; legacy of, 233, 317n80;
    punishment of, 224, 231; reform proposal
    of, 219
Billings, Joseph, 196
Blumentrost, Lavrentii, 90
book market, 10, 14, 25, 48–49, 60, 260–261.
    See also Republic of Letters
Böttger, Johann Friedrick, 115
Bougainville, Louis-Antoine de, 187
Brancati, Francesco, 99
Brand, Adam, 57–59
Bratishchev, Vasilii, 15, 133, 145
British East India Company, 194, 195, 199, 207
Buckinghamshire, Earl of, 144, 252
Buddhism, 26, 27, 220, 229, 263; Khalkha, 165;
    Tibetan, 37
Bukharans, 11, 26, 29, 155, 216; diplomacy by,
    139, 185; trade networks of, 31
Bukholts, Ivan, 160–162
Bukhtarma trading post, 204, 205
bureaucracy, 104–113, 120–123; cameralism
    and, 10–11, 68–69, 79, 90; Table of Ranks
    in, 12, 79, 82, 170; Weber on, 15, 68
Buriats, 16, 145, 147; intelligence network of,
    159–162; Mongol ties of, 12, 159–160, 168;
    territory of, 161

Cahen, Gaston, 290n24
California, 188, 241
cameralism, 10–11, 68–69, 79, 90
Campbell, John L., 7–8
caravans, 78, 107–109; as knowledge
    bureaucracy, 104–113, 120–123
cartography, 35–39, 37, 41–43, 78, 112;
    Rossokhin on, 94–95
Cathcart, Lord, 199, 200
Catherine I, 69, 162
Catherine II the Great, 98, 143–145, 259,
    265; French spies and, 189; Iakobii and,
    170–171, 177–180; Jesuits and, 10, 197–198;

Junghars and, 144; Kazakhs and, 154;
    naval expeditions of, 3, 186–187; Polish-
    Lithuanian territories of, 10, 186, 189, 197;
    Torghuts and, 156–157
Chekanov, Nikita, 80, 122
Chinese language, 211; dictionaries of, 124–125,
    223, 233; training in, 71–73, 80, 84, 220–221
Chinese literature, 211–213, 229
Chinggis Khan, 27, 28, 38, 165, 229
Chingünjav, Mongol prince, 165–166, 174
chinoiserie style, 16, 17, 97
Chugan (Ciwang), 167–168, 171
Cibot, Pierre Martial, 134, 198
Clement XIV, pope, 10, 197
Clerke, Charles, 194
Cobb, James, 201
Colbert, Jean-Baptiste, 16
Collas, Jean-Paul-Louis, 134
College of Foreign Affairs (Russia), 11, 13,
    68–70, 141, 261; Academy of Sciences and,
    19, 91; Amursana and, 150; caravans and,
    107–109; Kamenskii at, 220; Rossokhin
    and, 77–79
Collins, Samuel, 33
Columbia River (US), 187
Concert of Europe, 236
Confucianism, 15, 93, 104, 143, 204
conspiracy theories, 186, 189–193
Cook, James, 187, 193, 196
Cossacks, 25, 28, 34, 159, 185
Cotta, Friedrich von, 216
Couplet, Philippe, 51
Coxe, William, 61, 196
Crampton, John, 252
Crimean War (1853–1856), 234, 237, 244, 246,
    248
Crull, Jodocus, 46–47, 53

Datsyshen, V. G., 317n80
Dauria, 34. See also Manchuria
David, Jerzy, 51–52, 285n30
de Bruyn, Cornelius, 58
Defoe, Daniel, 62, 63
Delisle, Joseph-Nicolas, 90, 91, 125–126, 188,
    299n28
Depei, Manchu prince, 99, 127
Desrobert, Louis, 132
Divov, Pavel, 262
Dobell, Peter, 208
Dolon Nor, 27, 31

Dorji, Sanzai, 149, 169, 172
Dositheos II, Patriarch of Jerusalem, 40
Du Halde, Jean-Baptiste, 41, 43, 49, 61, 98, 131
Dunyn-Szpot, T. I., 52
Durand de Distroff, François-Michel, 189–193
Dutch East India Company, 200
dvoedantsy, 152, 179

Eggebrecht, Peter, 115
Eight Trigrams Rebellion (1813), 180
Elizabeth, Russian empress, 92, 98, 149, 160, 186
Engels, Friedrich, 264
Enlightenment philosophy, 14–15, 43, 90; academic disciplines and, 211, 225; Orientalia and, 63, 99, 120, 228; translators and, 97. *See also* Republic of Letters
Entrecolles, François d', 115
Euler, Johann, 98
Euler, Leonhard, 90, 134
Evenki (Tungus) hunters, 12, 27, 145, *161*, 240
Evseev, Ivan, 154–155

Fëdorovich, Mikhail, 30
Fick, Heinrich, 68
Filaret (Drozdov), archbishop of Tver', 226, 227
Firsov, Erofei, 116, 128
Fischer, Johann, 94
Fitzhugh, Thomas, 201
Flint, James, 192
Florinskii, V. M., 263
Foucault, Michel, 3–4, 8
Fourmont, Etienne, 131
Foy de la Neuville, 50, 53, 284n24
Franklin, Benjamin, 133
Free Economic Society, 220, 221, 316n43
Freemasons, 99, 204
Fren (Frähn), Christoph, 227–230
Frolov, Sava, 165
frontier texts. *See* hybrid texts
fur trade, 29, 139, 144, 195, 197

Gagarin, Matvei, 113
Gaillard, François-Marie, 121, 298n3
Galdan Tsereng, 148, 152, 160
Gamel', I. Kh., 100, 101
Gannibal, Abram, 161
Gantimur, Evenki prince, 169
Gantimurov, Pavel, 162, 169, 171
Garvine, Thomas, 113, 122
Gaubil, Antoine, 81, 122–126, 128–130, 227

Gavrilov, A. M., 241
General Regulation (of colleges), 69
Gerbillon, Jean-François, 34–35
Glazenap, Grigorii, 157
Gmelin, Samuel Gottlieb, 131, 132
go-betweens, 12, 16–19, 169–170, 169
Godunov, Pëtr, 35–39; maps of, 35–36, *37*, 50; sources of, 42
Golden Horde (Qipchaq Khanate), 26, 28
Goldsmith, Oliver, 62–63
Golitsyn, A. N., 218, 223
Golitsyn, Vasilii, 38, 52
Golovin, Fëdor, 88; Nerchinsk treaty and, 34–35; sources of, 43; Witsen and, 54, 55
Golovkin, Iurii, 157, 180, 204–205, 217; on Amur navigation rights, 237, 240; Bichurin and, 214, 217; failure of, 21, 206–208, 215
Gordeev, Filat, 153
Governing Senate (Russia), 70, 107–108
Grassi, Giovanni, 205
Great Wall, 11, 26, *31*, 46, *181*; gate cities of, 36, 38, 110
Grebenshchikov, Ivan, 115
Gribovskii, Sofronii, 87–88, 134–135, 219
Gruber, Gabriel, 198, 204
Guarient, Christoph Ignaz von, 53
Guibert, Jacques de, 192
Guignes, Joseph de, 229

Hakluyt, Richard, 48
Hallerstein, Augustin, 134, 298n3
Hebenstreit, Johann, 132, 133
Hevia, James Louis, 310n44
Hillemann, Ulrike, 310n44
Hoffmann, Karl Ludolf, 98
Hohhot, *31*, 38
Holy Governing Synod, 11, 18, 72–75. *See also* Russian Orthodox Church
Holy Roman Empire, 59, 122
homosexuality, 76, 218, 224, 290n32
Hong Taiji, 27
Hooke, Robert, 56
Hudson's Bay Company, 191
hybrid texts, 25, 35–39, 41–43, 46–47, 55. *See also* authorship

Iakobii, Ivan, 100, 158, 177, 194–195, 235, 243
Iakobii, Varfolomei, 145–147, 152, 159, 235; Catherine II and, 170–171, 174, 177–180; on governing borderlands, 243–245, 250

Ides, Isbrandt, 56–59
Ignat'ev, Nikolai, 251, 253–255
Igumnov, Aleksandr, 206
Igumnov, Vasilii, 166, 168, 170, 199, 202, 206
Imperial Benevolent Society, 220
Incarville, Pierre d', 132
India, 26, 199, 204; British rule of, 4, 5, 16, 198; Kashmir and, 217
intelligence, 6–14, 203–209, 261, 265; conspiracy theories and, 186, 189–193; industrial espionage and, 3, 9, 20, 105–106, 113–118, 135; knowledge versus, 6–7, 15, 203, 209, 259; Russian terms for, 7; Siberian Bureau and, 7, 113–116
Irkutsk, 100, 132, 146, 176–177; Iakobii's governorship of, 177, 179, 194, 195; Klichka's governorship of, 194; Kornilov's governorship of, 182, 235; Lang's governorship of, 59, 75, 106, 128–129; maps of, 31, 161, 181, 188; military importance of, 235; North Pacific expansion and, 185; Voznesenskii Monastery in, 74, 217
Irtysh River, 146–150, 156–159; maps of, 31, 142, 181
Iumatov, Amvrosii, 85
Ivan IV the Terrible, 28
Izmailov, Lev, 57, 60, 201

Jan III Sobieski, Polish king, 52
Jebtsundamba Khutukhtu, 165–166, 169
Jellatschitsch, Franz Lukas, 114, 122, 130–132, 214
Jesuits, 13, 25, 81, 211, 238; Academy of Sciences and, 123, 133; Catherine II and, 10, 197–198; dissolution of, 10, 197; early Chinese missions of, 43–46, 73; Enlightenment and, 99; expulsion from Muscovy of, 52; French ties with, 49, 192; in Holy Roman Empire, 59, 122; Kamenskii on, 221–222, 226; in Poland, 123; Qing converts of, 2, 39; Russian overland route for, 51–53; sea route to China of, 40, 51; Shtorkh on, 228; Smorzhevskii and, 80. See also Roman Catholicism
Jiaqing emperor, 208
Jungharia, 26, 54, 150, 163–165, 204; gold exploration in, 148, 160; Russian refugees from, 147, 152–158
Junghars, 21, 26–27, 31, 142, 144, 158, 258; Qing Conquest of, 85, 140–142, 147–151; Russian alliance with, 202; Torghuts and, 151–152
Jurchens, 27–28

Kabanov, Pëtr, 263–264
Kafarov, Palladii, 252, 254
Kalmyks. See Torghuts
Kamchatka, 91, 112, 144, 188–189
Kamenskii, Pavel (Pëtr), 80, 219–227, 230–231, 262
Kangxi Atlas, 79, 112
Kangxi emperor, 52, 57, 113, 122, 142
Kaniaev, Andrei, 80, 81, 82, 83, 291n51
kaolin, 114, 116–117
Karpov, Gurii, 254–255
Kazakhs, 16, 27, 152–154; Junghars and, 151; Juz, 147, 148; territory of, 31, 142; Veimarn on, 155
Kazan University, 212, 217–218
Kehr, Georg-Jacob, 71
Khabarov, Ivan, 34
Khabun (or Gabun), 156, 305n73
Khalkha Mongols, 27, 112, 146–147, 163–165, 205
Kharkov University, 212
Khoqand khanate, 254
Kiakhta, 1, 61, 175, 177–178; British trade at, 202; language school in, 231; maps of, 161, 181, 188; Russian trade at, 205, 207, 237, 242
Kiakhta treaty (1727–1728), 72, 82–83, 85, 139; addendums to, 172; border posts of, 159–162; caravans after, 107; provisions of, 141, 152, 166
Klaproth, Julius, 204, 214–218, 227, 228, 230; Abel-Rémusat and, 211; Bichurin and, 232; manuscript catalogue of, 131–132
knowledge, 2, 31–35, 250–255; archives of, 14–20, 74–75, 144; as commodity, 130–132; conspiracy theories and, 186, 189–193; intelligence versus, 6–7, 15, 203, 209, 259; network approach to, 272n13
knowledge regimes, 6–14, 56, 260–261; bureaucracy and, 68, 104–113, 120–123, 261; changes in, 9; characteristics of, 7–8; Golovkin and, 208; imperial, 210–211; manipulation of, 235–236, 255, 259
Kögler, Ignatius, 124, 125
Konstantin, Grand Duke, 242
Korea, 42, 55, 110, 112, 246
Korff, Baron, 124, 126–127, 129
Korkin, Iakov, 84, 85
Kornilov, Aleksei, 182, 235
Koroloff, Rachel, 300n33
Korsak, Norbert, 205
Korsakov, Mikhail, 246

Kotoshikhin, Grigorii, 33
Kovalevskii, Egor, 252
Krasheninnikov, Stepan, 91, 132
Kropotov, Ivan, 82, 172–174, 191
Krug, Philipp, 229
Kruzenshtern, Ivan, 196, 205, 207, 243
Kurakin, Ivan, 32
Kursin, Andrei, 116–118
Kurts, B. G., 17, 263, 264

Ladyzhenskii (Kiakhta commissioner), 178, 179
Laksman, Adam, 196–197
Laksman, Erik, 196–197
Lambert, Iakov, 205–207, 213
Langlès, Louis-Mathieu, 210, 227
Lang, Lorents, 59–60, 106, 112, 115–116, 122–124; Amman and, 127; Bayer and, 127; Bell's journal and, 200–201; as Irkutsk vice-governor, 128, 129; Rossokhin and, 75–77
Lebratovskii, Gerasim, 116–117
LeDonne, John, 276n38
Ledyard, John, 195
Leibniz, Gottfried Wilhelm, 51, 58, 63, 104, 120
Leont'ev, Aleksei, 79–85, 87, 96–100, 172, 227; Da Qing yitongzhi, 102; Kaniaev and, 291n51; Kitaiskiia mysli, 99; Rikhter on, 233; Rossokhin and, 84, 96, 98, 230
Lifanyuan (Bureau of Foreign Tributaries), 73–74, 142–144; Amursana and, 150; on Kazakhs, 153; on Kiakhta, 203–204; Kropotov and, 172; Nessel'rode and, 248; Rossokhin at, 77; translators of, 238; on Uladzai affair, 200
Lintsevskii, Gervasii, 80–82
Lipovtsov, Stepan, 220, 227, 262
literacy, 7, 49; book market and, 10, 14, 25, 48–49, 60, 260–261. See also Republic of Letters
Lithuanian territory, 52, 121, 140; Catherine II and, 10, 186, 197
Liven (Lieven), Karl, 238–239
Li Zicheng, 30
Lomonosov, Mikhailo Vasil'evich, 91, 92, 97, 99
Louis XIV, 15–16, 49
Louis XV, 189, 193
Luvan (Mongol lama), 162, 171

Macao, 46, 51, 63, 188, 208
Macartney, Lord, 18, 143, 170, 197, 199–203; failed mission of, 21, 202, 242
Manchu language, 162, 211, 220–221, 230; dictionaries of, 100, 101, 232; grammars of, 100–101, 215, 232; training in, 71–74, 80–81, 84
Manchuria, 147, 265; border of, 161; early name of, 34; Tartary and, 54, 286n42. See also Amur valley
Manchu Russian School, 81, 87
Manzhou shilu, 38
Markelov, I., 243
Martini, Martino, 40–42, 47, 55, 67
Marx, Karl, 264
Masons, 99, 204
Matveev, Artamon, 40, 54
Meares, John, 195
Medical Chancellery (Russia), 113–114, 130
Medico-Surgical Academy (Russia), 221
Meissen porcelain, 115
Men'shikov, Dmitrii, 244
Mentzel, Christian, 58
Merrick, John, 48
Mezzabarba, Giovanni Ambrogio, 200
Miasnikov, Osip, 106–107, 115–118
Miasnikov, V. S., 264–265
Miatlev, Vasilii, 150
Middendorf, Aleksandr, 239, 247
Milescu, Nicolae. See Spafarii, Nikolai
Milton, John, 47
Ming Dynasty, 26, 27, 47–48
Missions Étrangères de Paris, 248
Moldavia, 40
Möllendorf, Paul von, 232
Mongols, 26–28, 31, 142, 161, 207; Buriat ties with, 12, 159–160, 168; language of, 37, 71, 219; Russian defectors from, 165–166; subversion of, 163–174
Monroe Doctrine, 209
Montesquieu, 63, 258
Morachevich, Veniamin, 238
Morrison, Robert, 212–213, 223, 227
Moscow Ecclesiastical Academy, 226–227
Moscow Slavic-Latin-Greek Academy, 80
Mughal Empire, 26, 198
Müller, Andreas, 57
Müller, Gerhard Friedrich, 90, 94–96, 134, 145–146
Mulovskii, Grigorii, 196

Murav'ev, Nikolai, 160, 235, 243–255, 259, 264
Muravyeva, Marianna, 290n32
Murr, Christoph Gottlieb von, 98, 99
Muscovy Company, 48

Nanjing treaty (1842), 242
Napoleonic wars, 1, 262
Nepliuev, Ivan, 149
Nerchinsk, 31, 72, 159, 161, 162
Nerchinsk treaty (1689), 9, 43, 107, 139, 263–265; Amur annexation and, 237, 248; provisions of, 31, 34–35
Nessel'rode, Karl, 223, 226, 231, 241; Amur annexation and, 235–237, 245–246; détente policy of, 237–239, 242; dismissal of, 250
Nevel'skoi, Gennadii, 241, 244–250, 262
Nicholas I, 231, 241–242, 248
Nieuhof, Johannes, 200
Nikolaevsk, 236, 245–246, 248–250
Nivkh (Giliaks), 241, 245–247
Northeast Passage, 47–48, 191, 193
Northwest Passage, 188, 193
Novikov, Nikolai, 92, 96, 97
Nurali Khan, 153
Nurga (Mongol zaisang), 150
Nurhaci emperor, 27

Oirats, 26–27, 147, 149. See also Torghuts: Junghars
Okhotsk, 145, 187, 249; founding of, 34; maps of, 181, 188, 236
Okladnikov, A. P., 264
Old Believers, 158
Ol'denburg, Sergei, 257
Opium War, First (1839–42), 208, 242–243
Opium War, Second (1856–60), 234, 243, 251, 253, 263, 264
Orientalism, 16–17, 22, 43; Enlightenment philosophy and, 63, 99, 120; European views of, 210–213, 234; Said on, 4, 271n6. See also sinology
Orlov, Dmitrii, 245, 246
Orlov, Ivan, 87, 101–102
Osterman, Andrei, 68–69, 124–125, 129
Ostrovskikh, Luka, 170
Ottoman Empire, 5, 189; historians of, 9–10; Iakobii and, 162; Russian wars with, 140, 179, 186, 191, 192; Spafarii and, 40; Timur and, 26

Pallas, Peter Simon, 191, 200, 214
Palmqvist, Erik, 50
Panshi zonglun, 94
Parrenin, Dominique, 121, 123–127
Paryshev, Aleksei, 85–86, 100
Paul I, 97, 204
Pedersen, Ove Kaj, 7–8
Pereira, Caetano Pires, 238
Pereira, Tomás, 34–35
Pereyra, Andrea, 124
Perry, Matthew C., 248
Peter II, 162
Peter III, 170, 186
Peter I the Great, 5, 9; archives of, 19; cameralism of, 10–11, 68–69, 79, 90; death of, 45, 67, 162; European tour of, 47; Ides and, 57; Leibniz on, 51; Table of Ranks of, 12, 79, 82, 170; Weber on, 59
Petlin, Ivashko, 30, 32–34, 48–49, 56, 279n21
Petropavlovsk, 188, 194, 236, 249–250
Pil', Ivan, 156, 180
Pitt, William, the Younger, 195
plagiarism, 41–42, 47, 55. See also authorship
Platkovskii, Antonii, 74–77, 80, 81, 224
Plotnikov, A. Iu., 265
Poiarkov, Vasilii, 34
Polievktov, M. A., 260
Polish territory, 52, 121, 140; Catherine II conflicts with, 10, 186, 189, 197; Jesuits in, 123
Polo, Marco, 45, 48
Ponomarev, Mikhailo, 76–77
Popov, Dmitrii, 117–118
porcelain manufacture, 20, 115–116
Potemkin, Grigory Aleksandrovich, 177, 178
Potocki, Jan, 214–215, 314n16
Prévost, Abbé, 101
Prokopovich, Feofan, 93
Protestant missionaries, 51, 222–223, 226
Pulteney, Richard, 62
Purchas, Samuel, 48
Pushkin, Aleksandr, 1, 161
Putiatin, Evgenii, 251–254
Puységur, Maréchal de, 192

Qianlong emperor, 141, 145–146, 150; Ablai Sultan and, 153; Amursana and, 149; Macarthy embassy to, 199–203; Torghuts and, 155–156
Qing Eight Banner system, 72, 95, 99j

Qingwen qimeng, 93, 96
Qipchaq Khanate (Golden Horde), 26, 28

Rabdan, Tsewang, 148
Raynal, Abbé, 201
Razumovskii, Kirill, 132
Remezov, Semën, 35, 38–39
Remnev, A. V., 318n5
Renat, J. G., 148
Republic of Letters, 14, 89, 135; Asian trade and, 48; caravans' role in, 120, 135; Russian diplomats and, 57–63; universalism of, 126. *See also* book market
rhubarb trade, 49–50, 113, 132, 206
Ricci, Matteo, 77, 222
Richmann, G. V., 133
Rikhter, Aleksandr, 232–233
Rinhuber, Lorenz, 50–51
Rites Controversy, 121–122
Roman Catholicism, 221–222, 226, 238. *See also* Jesuits
Roman Empire, 28
Rossokhin, Ilarion Kalinovich, 19, 74–82, 112, 130, 290n24; at Academy of Sciences, 79, 82, 91–96, 220, 258; family of, 96; as language teacher, 93; legacy of, 233; Leont'ev and, 84, 96, 98, 230; library of, 95, 99
Rostovtsev, Iakov, 244
Royal Asiatic Society, 211
Rumiantsev, Nikolai, 157, 207
Rumovskii, Stepan, 133
Russian-American Company, 196, 235, 241; financial decline of, 250; Ministry of Foreign Affairs, 244–246; Nevel'skoi and, 248
Russian Bible Society, 220
Russian Ecclesiastical Mission, 7, 20, 68, 139, 186, 258; Beijing treaty and, 252, 262; British view of, 201; language instruction at, 71–73, 213; after Opium Wars, 234; reforms of, 213–225, 238, 254–255; supply caravans to, 107–109. *See also* Bichurin, Nikita "Iakinf"
Russian Orthodox Church, 262–263; Holy Governing Synod of, 11, 18, 72–75; Old Believers and, 158

Said, Edward, 4, 271n6
Sakhnovskii, Egor, 81, 84
San Nicola, Sigismondo di, 145
Say, Samuel, 62

Schumacher, Johann, 90, 92, 95
Scott, James C., 8
Secret du Roi (royal correspondents), 189
Seitov, Ezhbab, 30
Selenginsk, 141, 145, 147, *161*
Semipalatinsk, *142*, 149–150
Seniavin, L. G., 238
Šereng (Junghar *zaisang*), 151–152
Seven Years' War (1756–1763), 167, 186, 187, 189
Sharin, Grigorii, 176–177
Sharin, Vasilii, 166, 167–168, 177
Shchegorin, Fëdor, 203–204
Shelikhov, Grigorii, 196
Shiskhovskii, Ioakim, 86–87, 101, 176
Shpringer, Ivan, 151, 152, 154
Shtorkh, Genrikh fon (Heinrich von Storch), 228
Shukhov, Alim, 153, 154
Shulgin, Mikhail, 163
Siberian Bureau, 7, 11, 108–109, 113–116
Siberian Line, 147–148, 153–154, 157, 171
Sinclair, John, 200
sinology, 17, 22, 43, 225–233; censorship and, 239; *kitaevedenie* and, 17; origins of, 210–225. *See also* Orientalism
Sino-Soviet split, 17–18, 263
Skachkov, P. E., 17
Skokowski, Manswet, 198
Slavicek, Carel, 124
smallpox, 150, 165, 166, 194
Smith, Adam, 228
Smith, Thomas, 29
Smorzhevskii, Feodosii, 80–81
Société Asiatique, 211, 233
Society for the Translation of Foreign Books, 97
Sofiia, Muscovite princess, 38, 52
Soimonov, Fëdor, 144–146, 163
Songgotu (Qing amban), 34
Soviet Union, 257, 260; Mao's split with, 17–18, 263; Russo-Qing studies of, 17, 18, 97, 263–264; on tsarist imperialism, 17–18, 140, 263–265; Tuvan Republic of, 152
Spafarii, Nikolai, 40–42, 67; Avril and, 53; Crull and, 47; Neuville and, 50; Rossokhin and, 77, 79; Witsen and, 55, 57
Sparwenfeld, J. G., 50
Spasskii, Grigorii, 212
Steller, Georg, 91
Sterne, Laurence, 47

Strahlenberg, Philipp von, 55, 61
Struve, P. N., 207
Stumpf, Kilian, 121, 287n62
Stürmer, Jan, 205
Surgutskii, Semën, 166
Sweden, 5, 68, 189, 195

Table of Ranks, 12, 79, 82, 170. *See also*
    bureaucracy
Taiping Rebellion (1850–64), 2, 251, 254
Taiwan, 190
Taranovich, V. P., 290n24
Tarbagatai treaty (1864), 254
Tartars, 25, 54, 144, 286n42; Bell on, 60;
    Catherine II on, 144; Crull on, 46; Gaubil
    on, 125; language of, 81; Martini on, 40–41;
    Witsen on, 53–56, 61, 258
Tashkent, 31, 181
Tatars, 28; Godunov on, 36–37; language of,
    212, 219
Tatishchev, Vasilii, 115
tea trade, 105, 132, 199
Thévenot, Melchisédech, 53, 57
Thomas, Antoine, 52
Tianjin treaty (1858), 251, 262
Tibet, 140, 192, 204; Buddhism of, 37;
    language of, 220
Timkovskii, Egor, 231–232
Timofeevich, Ermak, 28
Timur (Tamerlane), 26
Tipu Sultan, 199
Titsingh, Isaac, 203
Tobolsk, 28–30, 31, 181
Torckler, Pierre, 196
Tordesillas treaty (1494), 51
Torghuts, 17, 77; Junghars and, 151–152; Volga,
    26–27, 147, 150–151, 155–157, 165; of Xinjiang,
    84–87, 259
Torrubia, José, 188, 190
Toši (Qing ambassador), 152
trade secrets, 113–119
Transbaikalia, 158, 160–162, 207
Trans-Siberian Railroad, 237
Trediakovskii, Vasilii, 91, 97
Tretiakov, Aleksei, 160
Trinity Sergius Monastery, 85, 86
Tschirnhaus, Ehrenfried von, 115
Tsvet, Nikolai, 85, 86
Tulišen (Qing diplomat), 96, 113, 114

Tungus. *See* Evenki (Tungus) hunters
Turkish language, 71
turquerie style, 16
Tüsiyetü-Khan, 165, 173
Tuvan Republic, 152

Uladzai (Buriat bandit), 156, 177–178, 200,
    201
Unkovskii, Ivan, 148
Urga, 206, 207, 215; Amur annexation and,
    253; maps of, 161, 181, 188
Uriangkhai, 147, 152
Urvantsov, Sergei, 157
Uvarov, Sergei, 216
Uzbekistan, 21

Vanifat'ev, Pëtr, 180, 207
Vasil'ev, V. P., 239, 262
Veniukov, Nikifor, 39, 42, 51
Verbiest, Ferdinand, 40, 51–52
Vigel', F. F., 207
Vinius, A. A., 38, 54
Vishnevskii, Vikentii, 227
Vladislavich, Savva, 61, 72, 109, 123, 125;
    intelligence network of, 160; on Russo-
    Qing confrontation, 234–235, 242; staff of,
    204
Vladykin, Aleksei, 74, 106, 112, 117
Vladykin, Anton, 17, 86–88, 100–101, 206,
    215
Vladykin, Eremei, 106, 110–112
Vlasov, Semën, 171, 174, 176–180; death of, 174;
    intelligence network of, 162–163, 165–167,
    180
Voeikov, Luka, 75, 80
Volga Torghuts. *See* Torghuts
Volkov, Pëtr, 173
Voltaire, 15, 43, 228, 258
Vorontsov, Aleksandr, 197–200, 202, 205
Vorontsov, Semën, 197–200
Voz'milov, Mikhail, 154

Warner, Michael, 140
Weber, Friedrich, 59
Weber, Max, 15, 68
Whitworth, Charles, 200
Witsen, Nicolaas, 43, 53–56, 58, 61, 258
Wodehouse, Lord, 252
Wolff, Larry, 272n12

Wu Huiyi, 293n23
Wu Sangui, 30

Xavier, Francis, Saint, 46
Xinjiang, 26, 147, 252, 254; intelligence
    gathering on, 147–158, 186; Qing conquest
    of, 143, 147; Tarim Basin of, 154; Torghuts
    of, 84–87, 259
Xuanfu, 110, *111*

Yongzheng emperor, 141–143, 202, 230
Yuan Dynasty, 26, 229
Yundondorji, Urga amban, 206, 208

Zaisan, Lake, 151
Zakharov, Ivan, 232, 252
Zavoiko, Vasilii, 246, 247
Zhangjiakou, 36, 110
Zhou Ge, 79, 80